St Mary the Virgin Primrose Hill

St Mary the Virgin Primrose Hill

A Church and its People, 1872-2022

Christopher Kitching

Copyright © 2022 Christopher Kitching

The moral right of the author has been asserted.

Apart from any fair dealing for the purposes of research or private study, or criticism or review, as permitted under the Copyright, Designs and Patents Act 1988, this publication may only be reproduced, stored or transmitted, in any form or by any means, with the prior permission in writing of the publishers, or in the case of reprographic reproduction in accordance with the terms of licences issued by the Copyright Licensing Agency. Enquiries concerning reproduction outside those terms should be sent to the publishers.

Matador
Unit E2 Airfield Business Park,
Harrison Road, Market Harborough,
Leicestershire. LE16 7WB
Tel: 0116 2792299
Email: books@troubador.co.uk
Web: www.troubador.co.uk/matador
Twitter: @matadorbooks

ISBN 978 1803130 224

British Library Cataloguing in Publication Data.
A catalogue record for this book is available from the British Library.

Printed and bound in the UK by TJ Books Ltd, Padstow, Cornwall
Typeset in 11pt Adobe Garamond Pro by Troubador Publishing Ltd, Leicester, UK

Matador is an imprint of Troubador Publishing Ltd

I walked into the church once, and spoke to a stranger who was there.

She said, 'I came here with some idea of making up a story of my troubles, but what I did was just sit and glory in the place. The poor sinner in me "stopped a-tremblin'". I suddenly realised that I did not know that I held so much goodness.'

'Perhaps the sun came out,' I suggested.

'Perhaps it did,' she replied. And we both laughed.

Geoffrey Dearmer, Parish Magazine, February 1987

Contents

Abbreviations		ix
Illustrations		xi
Preface and Acknowledgements		xiii

Part One (1867-1951)

Chapter 1:	Beginnings	1
Chapter 2:	Revd Charles James Fuller	15
Chapter 3:	Revd Albert Spencer	47
Chapter 4:	Revd Percy Dearmer	81
Chapter 5:	Revd Arthur Duncan-Jones	131
Chapter 6:	Revd Hubert Harcourt	166
Chapter 7:	Revd Anthony Hardcastle	178

Part Two (1952-2022)

Chapter 8:	Introduction to Part Two	221
Chapter 9:	Clergy	224
Chapter 10:	Women in the Church	241
Chapter 11:	Sacred and secular spaces	248
Chapter 12:	The beauty of holiness	262
Chapter 13:	Training for lifelong discipleship and mission	272
Chapter 14:	Maintaining and developing the St Mary's tradition:	
	1. Liturgy	286

Chapter 15:	Maintaining and developing the St Mary's tradition: 2. Music	299
Chapter 16:	Empowering the laity	311
Chapter 17:	Serving the community	333
Envoi		352

Appendix: Episcopal oversight of the parish　　353

Bibliography　　355

Index 1: St Mary's church and parish　　362
Index 2: Persons　　365
Index 3: Artists and craftworkers　　371
Index 4: General index　　373

Abbreviations

AKC	Associate of King's College [London]
APCM	Annual Parochial Church Meeting
Archives	Parish archives of St Mary the Virgin, Primrose Hill
BL	British Library
CERC	Church of England Record Centre. These records have recently been moved to the new Lambeth Palace Library.
CLWS	Church League for Women's Suffrage
CT	*Church Times*
D-J	Arthur Duncan-Jones
ECU	English Church Union
GFS	Girls' Friendly Society
H&H	*Hampstead and Highgate Express*
ICBS	Incorporated Church Building Society
LMA	London Metropolitan Archives
LPL	Lambeth Palace Library
PCC	Parochial Church Council
PM	[Parish Magazine]. St Mary's Parish Magazine (reference set held in the vicarage). The title of this publication has changed repeatedly.
RIBA	Royal Institute of British Architects
SMCCT	St Mary's Centre Community Trust
SMVPH	St Mary the Virgin, Primrose Hill
SSM	Self-supporting minister
TNA	The National Archives.

Illustrations

Black and white illustrations in the text.
Unless otherwise indicated all the illustrations are from the parish archives. Photographers, indicated by their initials, are as follows:

VB Violet Blaiklock
GF Geoffrey Franglen
CJK Christopher Kitching
DN Dan Nathanson
SR Steve Reynolds
JS John Salmon
TF Tony Firschman

Schoolroom at the Boys' Home. *Illustrated London News* supplement, 2 April 1870, p.349 (*Author's copy*).	2
The iron church, c.1867. Photograph once owned by Miss Alice Jones, one of the first parishioners.	6
What might have been: MP Manning's prospectus, c.1870, for a church with tower. (The tower was never built).	8
Revd Charles James Fuller. Portrait photograph (artist unknown).	16
Interior, 1872.	19
Figure 1: Sketch plan showing the approximate line of the railway tunnel.	34
Revd Albert Spencer. Portrait photograph (artist unknown).	48
Figure 2: Approximate floor plans, 1872, 1892.	53
Interior, 1893.	62
Revd Percy Dearmer (VB).	82
Exterior from north east. Edwardian postcard.	92

English altar at St Mary's. Drawing by Harold Stabler, in Percy Dearmer, 'The altar and its furniture', in *Essays on Ceremonial by various authors* (1904).	95
Temple Moore's proposed choir screen (never executed).	99
The reredos (a) by Cyril Ellis c.1911, courtesy of Lambeth Palace Library (CARE 23/329). (b) 1951 from a Warham Guild leaflet by Dearmer.	102
Percy Dearmer and the choir.	
The Duncan-Jones family (VB).	114
Scene from *The Mystery of the Nativity* as performed in 1924.	132
Jubilee 1920. Group photograph outside the Church Room. D-J front row, centre, behind the choristers.	145
Revd Colin Dunlop. Portrait photograph (artist unknown).	148
Jubilee 1930. Group photograph outside the Church Room. Hubert Harcourt front row, centre behind the choristers.	175
Jubilee 1930. Street procession.	176
Visit by Russian Orthodox choir, 1938.	183
Beginning of the Easter *Exultet* from the 16th-cent. Sarum *Manuale*.	188
One of Bodley's angels originally at the top of the High Altar reredos (The Courtauld).	223
Revds Richard Buck (centre), Michael Johnson (right) and Francis Stephens (left) with the choir, c.1980. (TF).	231
Revd Sally Webster (CJK).	245
St Paul's Avenue Road.	250
Sanctuary lamp by Frank Knight (Frank Knight).	264
Preaching: Revd George Timms (left), and Revd John Ovenden (right) (GF).	274
David Gedge at the organ.	301
Licensed Lay Ministers (Lay Reader): Roberta Berke (left), St Mary's first Lay Reader, and Clement Hutton-Mills (right), Licensed Lay Minister and a lay canon of St Paul's cathedral.	316
Revd Robert Atwell (CJK).	340

For a key to the colour plates preceding Part Two see p. 217

Front cover: view from the south east (CJK).

Preface and Acknowledgements

This book has been written to celebrate 150 years in the life of the church of St Mary the Virgin Primrose Hill, London, where the first services were held on 2 July 1872.

At that date the building was much smaller than the one we see today. It comprised only the chancel, nave, north aisle, transept, organ loft and a small bell turret, which was all that the congregation of the time could afford. In a way, that was providential, because less than five years from the date of its opening the building started to subside as a result of excavations by the London and North Western Railway for a second Primrose Hill tunnel that passed within a few feet of the church's north-west corner. As a direct result, in 1883 the entire north aisle had to be rebuilt and the chancel and crypt stabilised. The restored building was finally consecrated on 2 May 1885, and later that year the priest in charge, Revd Charles James Fuller, officially became the first vicar of the new parish of St Mary the Virgin Primrose Hill, by far the smallest of the parishes carved out of the ancient Parish of Hampstead.

It was only with the arrival of Revd Albert Spencer (second vicar, 1889-1901) that it became realistic to push ahead with completing the original plans of the architect, MP Manning – albeit without his proposed tower which was presumably thought too risky in view of the recent subsidence. By 1892 the Chapel of the Holy Spirit had been completed on the south side, together with a south aisle and sacristy, with a choir vestry on the north side and an ambulatory around the east end to link the two sides.

To complete the picture, in modern times extensions have been added at both the west and east ends of the building, and at the time of writing new works are under discussion as the church seeks to equip itself for the next 150 years.

* * *

Charles Fuller put St Mary's firmly on the map, but for controversial reasons, as a centre of Ritualism, an ailment that so much beset the Victorian church. After Fuller, Albert Spencer was a much needed calming influence as well as a great church builder. But St Mary's is perhaps best known throughout the Anglican Communion as the place where Percy Dearmer (third vicar, 1901-1915) developed and put into practice the ideas contained in his famous *Parson's Handbook*. In his time too, St Mary's was the birthplace of the *English Hymnal* (1906). Dearmer's successors faithfully continued his traditions, and his legacy of fine liturgy and music is in evidence to this day.

But it is for different reasons that St Mary's is currently admired: its strong support of women's ministry; its community outreach, especially its youthwork programme; its participation in the Cold Weather Shelter during the winter months; its crowd-pulling events such as the Designer Fairs and the Primrose Hill Lectures; and most recently the St Mary's Brewery. And it faces the future with confidence.

The very words 'Primrose Hill' conjure up images of comfortable living and a certain style. And yet, poverty and hardship have always co-existed with the area's general prosperity. St Mary's is justly proud of its origins in a home for destitute boys, although, as these pages show, that phase of its story was sadly short-lived. When he came to appeal for funds to complete the church in the 1890s, Albert Spencer had to remind even the church authorities that his parish was not as well-heeled as its location might suggest. A decade later, Dearmer would raise the hackles of some middle-class parents by insisting on teaching the Catechism to their children alongside those of the poor. Special afternoon services were held at that time for the large number of domestic servants, many far from well-off, whose duties did not allow them to attend church at the usual hours of worship. Every vicar from Dearmer to Hollis (1965-

76) remarked on the way in which the grand houses of the parish were being sub-divided into flats or tenancies, which lowered the overall social status of the parish, at the same time reducing its expectations of income. A deeper neediness would rear its head again during and after the Second World War, when parts of the parish were devastated by bombing; and everyone was subject to rationing. The rebuilding programme after that took the best part of three decades, bringing in its wake both hardship and insecurity. The 1970s saw the arrival of high-rise tower blocks for Council tenants, alongside new, expensive homes for the better off, and more recent surveys have confirmed that there is still significant poverty in parts of the parish. So the poor have always coexisted with the rich in Primrose Hill. This is certainly not a chronicle of luxury, and today the parish, with much of London, is having to face up to new problems: of disadvantaged young people, knife crime and gang violence.

Nor is this merely a chronicle of the famous: the clergy, musician, artists and craftsmen who, down the ages, have contributed so much to the life of St Mary's. The history of any church owes just as much to the countless (even if now nameless) people who have called it their spiritual home or been touched by its ministry. And the 'Angel' of St Mary's discussed in Part Two, has been at work through all of them.

* * *

This book is approached as a kind of twin 'biography': first of the building itself and the successive transformations it has undergone to reach its present state; and secondly of its changing congregation, both clerical and lay, who have brought the building alive and given it a sense of purpose, for the worship of God and the service of the community.

The book falls into two rather different parts.

Part One is the story of the founders and consolidators of the church from the beginnings through to 1951, when a whole era came to an end with the restoration of the church after the Second World War. It is told chronologically, drawing on the parish archives and other primary records, many previously unexplored, and on newspaper reports, harvested largely thanks to the British Newspaper Archive.

Part Two (1952 to the present) falls within the living memory of members of today's congregation. I began my own association with St Mary's in about 1975 and can therefore personally vouch for much of what is recorded, but I have also been privileged to draw extensively on reflections submitted by many past and present members of the clergy and congregation to make this more of a collective memoir and a guide to the direction in which St Mary's has been travelling. Since many of the principal actors in this part of the drama are still alive I have tried to avoid anything like 'living obituaries', and have proceeded thematically rather than strictly chronologically. I hope this will help today's congregation understand their roots, take pride in the achievements of their forebears as much as themselves, and face the future with both boldness and courage.

* * *

One particular limitation of this book which should be confessed at the outset is that it is first and foremost a parish history, told from archival sources that generally say little of the wider contemporary background to the buildings, people and events they describe. The reader is therefore asked to bear in mind the many changes throughout the period covered by this book: in social, economic and educational opportunities; in social attitudes and lifestyle; in the law, especially with regard to human rights, discrimination, and inter-personal relationships… and so on. Sheep no longer graze on the Hill; pony and trap are no longer the preferred means of travel into town. The internal combustion engine, the telephone, radio, television, the Internet and social media, and, yes, the National Health Service and vaccines which we all now take for granted, were all unknown when this story begins, but have all appeared in the years it covers. So, *Caveat lector!* Times move on. You may need to look elsewhere for more background. At a local level there is no better starting place than Martin Sheppard's *Primrose Hill, a History* (2013).

***

The book has been long in the making, and it took the approach of this Jubilee to move it on from the germ of an idea into a reality. Some of my primary research was undertaken more than a decade ago as I tried, as honorary archivist, to understand the parish's archives. Fortunately, I had completed most of the essential research on primary sources in libraries and record offices before they closed down as a result of the coronavirus epidemic of 2020-21.

All history-writing is necessarily selective, and no doubt others would have told this tale from a different perspective. I can only claim that what is presented here is my own selection of facts and stories, drawn from a very large field of source material.

Acknowledgements

Others had reached at least the base-camp of a parish history before me, particularly Kathleen Beck, Charles Plouviez and John Hawes. I gratefully acknowledge the inspiration of their trail-blazing efforts, and indeed their essays and notes, many of which are to be found in the parish magazine and in the archives.

It is a pleasure to record also my best thanks to the respective custodians of the many archives studied, and to their unfailingly helpful staff; in particular those of: the British Library (including the Humanities I Reading Room, the British Newspaper Archive and the Music Library); Camden Local Studies and Archives Centre, Holborn Library; the Church of England Record Centre (which was in Bermondsey when I consulted the records, but has recently been rehoused as part of Lambeth Palace Library); Islington Local History Library; Lambeth Palace Library itself; London Metropolitan Archives (the diocesan record office and custodian of the bulk of St Mary's parish archives); and the RIBA Architecture Archive (first consulted in situ at the RIBA but now held at the Victoria & Albert Museum). At an early stage of this research, Isobel Montgomery-Campbell generously allowed me to see Shaw family papers, many of which now form the Martin Shaw Archive in the British Library (Music Library). The Dearmer family and Revd Canon Donald Gray were generous with their time and help a decade ago when I was first researching Percy Dearmer.

Drafts of this work have been much improved by the friendly and learned critique, of many individuals, some of whom cannot remain anonymous. My wife and fellow parishioner, Ruth Kitching, kindly read and commented on the entire draft, as did Revd Preb. Marjorie Brown, vicar of St Mary's, John Hawes, a former head server, and Ven David Meara FSA. I am grateful, too, for the comments made on Part Two by Roberta Berke and Revd John Ovenden; and on relevant sections by Rt Revd Robert Atwell and Robert Wills (Liturgy), Roger Carter (Laity and Community chapters), Janet Cowen (Drama), Michael Willford and Tony Henwood (Music), and Revd Sally Webster (Women in the church). My best thanks also go to the many members of the congregation who kindly submitted recollections and reflections of their time at St Mary's. Many of their names are acknowledged in the text or footnotes, but where that is not the case they can at least be reassured that their input has helped to determine the content (or that their anonymity has been protected!). I hope nobody will feel left out if they have not specifically been named: in a tale such as this, of a church and its whole congregation over time, one name mentioned might well stand for a score who have contributed equally, or perhaps more, to the story. My thanks, too to the ever-helpful team at Matador for seeing the book into print, and to Christine Ayre for the cover design.

I hope that this book will at least lay the foundations of the church's history to date, so that it can be looked back on as an inspiration to future generations of worshippers and friends of this very special House of God, which has been my spiritual home for almost half a century.

Christopher Kitching
October 2021

Part One
(1867-1951)

Chapter 1

Beginnings

Late in 1865 an extraordinary procession arrived in Regent's Park Road. Fifty or so young boys, with their adult supervisors, carrying their own bedding and scant belongings, arrived to take up residence in three adjacent buildings at the junction with King Henry's Road. They were from the 'Boys' Home and Industrial School for Destitute Boys not Convicted of Crime', forced to move at short notice from its original site at 44 Euston Road which had been acquired for the construction of a railway goods shed for the new St Pancras Station.[1] In a manner of speaking they were refugees.

The Home had been opened seven years earlier by two philanthropic businessmen who, though namesakes, were unrelated: George Bell, the publisher (who soon disappears from the record) and George William Bell who is central to our story. It was part of a wider initiative to keep the destitute poor off the streets, inspired by a similar scheme in Cambridge run by George Bell's friend Dr Harvey Goodwin. It was an Anglican foundation, run on Christian Socialist principles, with the Bishop of London as its President, four of its 16-strong steering committee also being Anglican clergy, among them the great voice of Christian Socialism, Revd FD Maurice himself. The 'Master', until his death in 1871, was Sergeant Ebenezer Rayment, whose wife was known as 'Matron'. She continued in that role when their son George succeeded his father as Master. There was one other paid teacher who was helped, particularly for the Sunday School, by a number of volunteers.

The school-room at the Boys' Home, 1870

The Home's aims were to save orphaned or abandoned boys from a life of vagrancy; provide them with food, shelter and a basic education; and instruct and encourage them in cleanliness and self-sufficiency.[2] In return they had to learn such practical trades and manufacturing as could be carried out on the premises, and to earn their keep through their own labours, which included sawing and chopping firewood; carpentry, box- and cabinet-making; tailoring; printing; and the manufacture of brushes, shoes, and hammocks, the latter mostly used to provide a separate bed for children of the poor who would otherwise have had to sleep with their parents. The site initially accommodated the fifty boys who made the trek, but as extensions were built this soon rose to a hundred. The Home was always heavily oversubscribed, although there was a small turnover of places as boys found employment. Sadly, a few decided that the regime was not for them and left, or were dismissed for refusal to accept the Home's discipline.

The site (nos 115-117 Regent's Park Road) incorporated Bow Cottage, one of the three houses in Regent's Park Road that pre-dated the railway. Its garden would become the Home's yard, and the Cottage itself the Infirmary. Essex Villa nearby (1854) became the superintendent's house in 1870, and all the buildings would soon be adapted, and added to, to make a more effective campus with schoolroom, sleeping and dining quarters, workshops, and eventually a chapel.[3] The site actually lay within the parish of St Mark's Regent's Park, but right at the point where it met the parish of St Saviour's Eton Road, and everything suggests that, for whatever reason, the Home's managers looked to St Saviour's as their parish church. However that may be, the Home's arrival was to have a profound effect on the church-going habits of the whole neighbourhood.

St Saviour's was a new church, opened in 1856 to serve the south-eastern part of the ancient parish of Hampstead that reached as far as Primrose Hill. Much of St Saviour's lay within the Chalcots estate given as an endowment by King Henry VI to Eton College.[4] From the early decades of the 19th century that estate's fields had been gradually disappearing as the College issued building-leases to meet the demands of a growing population, but there was still undeveloped land in the area. As new housing spread, those residents who lived furthest away from Hampstead parish church found it tiresome to walk up the hill to services, and in the 1840s the largely middle-class inhabitants around Provost Road, Eton Villas and Eton Road – the street-names tell their own story – campaigned to have their own place of worship. With the vicar of Hampstead's approval they obtained from Eton College a site for a new church in Eton Road.[5] While funds were being raised for that they erected a temporary iron church nearby, but by 1856 the new church of 'St Saviour's South Hampstead' was up and running, serving what was at first a 'district chapelry' within Hampstead parish, but soon made the transition to full parochial status. Its tower and spire were added in 1864 but the vicarage would not be completed until 1870, so St Saviour's was very much a parish in development when the Boys' Home arrived.

The railway lines between London and the north west cut this new parish in two, and from the start people living south of the lines felt themselves to be a separate community. There were an estimated 1700 of them, the majority 'professional men with large families and limited incomes', but a surprisingly large total of 300 were said to be living in poverty. This population was confidently predicted to rise further as streets and houses were built on the undeveloped land to the west. If they were Anglicans, and if they went to a local church at all, we must suppose it was to St Saviour's, or St Mark's (1853) which took in Regent's Park Road and streets to the east and south. By 1865 when this story begins, house-building was under way on Ainger Road, Oppidans Road, Primrose Hill Road and King Henry's Road, but although these streets were already outlined on the maps of the day, they were not yet fully developed and occupied. Slightly further afield, housing was extending along Adelaide Road, whilst Elsworthy Road and the planned minor roads off it were barely beginning to take shape. The Hill itself had only recently been saved from similar housing development in a deal between Eton College and the Crown.[6]

* * *

At first there was no chapel at the Boys' Home, although the Revd Edward Walford was appointed to be its chaplain. On Sundays he read Morning Prayer in the schoolroom and preached a sermon. For Evensong, at least initially, he tried taking the boys and staff to either St Saviour's or 'St Stephen's',[7] but neither had sufficient space to accommodate the boys as well as their regular congregations. Meanwhile, no doubt in the hope of attracting benefactors, Sunday morning services, held in the schoolroom, were opened up to members of the public, who were also encouraged to come back to watch the boys at work, as was often the practice in other Victorian philanthropic institutions. Public interest grew, to the extent that the schoolroom could no longer contain all who wished to attend services, so the managers and their chaplain began to investigate setting up a separate chapel somewhere nearby, to serve primarily the Home but also its Sunday 'congregation'.

Charles James Fuller

After a very short period in office, Walford resigned the chaplaincy on health grounds, recommending in his stead an Oxford graduate, the Revd Charles James Fuller, a single man then aged about 40, who came with strong testimonials. With the blessing of the parish priest of St Saviour's, he was duly appointed chaplain. Remarkably little is known about him, beyond the bare outline in *Crockford's* which states that he graduated from Christ Church, Oxford in 1848 (MA 1851); was ordained deacon the following year and priest in 1850, and served a curacy at Leek Wootton, Warwickshire, before becoming chaplain of the Boys' Home. Nothing is known of his circle of friends and mentors at university or elsewhere; of how he found his vocation as a priest or came to be influenced – as we must suppose he did – by Christian Socialism. It was surely at Oxford that he was first drawn to high-church ceremonial; but through whose influence we do not know. No personal archive of his letters, diaries or sermons has been found, and for much of his subsequent ministry at St Mary's there are no surviving parish magazines to give us a steer.[8]

The Iron Church (1867-72)

Throughout the country the religious needs of a growing population were commonly being met, as at St Saviour's and St Mark's before that, by the use of temporary corrugated iron churches. Manufacturers advertised these 'tin tabernacles' for hire or sale in the church- and national press, sometimes second-hand, as they were dismantled and sold on once they had served their purpose. Some have survived to this day, although not necessarily in their original location or for their original purpose. George William Bell, as Treasurer of the Boys' Home, and Fuller as its chaplain (with the blessing of the vicar of St Saviour's) resolved to erect such a church as close as possible to the Home. They approached Eton College, as owner of the land to the north and west of their site (in St Saviour's parish), and were offered a three-year lease of

The iron church, 1867.

a plot off Ainger Road,[9] just a few minutes' walk from the Home. Bell generously loaned the money to buy an iron church for erection there. On Sunday 28 April 1867 it was opened for worship. A photograph originally owned by one of its worshippers, Miss Alice Jones, survives in the parish archives.[10]

The church (or 'chapel') was known from day one as 'St Mary's, Primrose Hill', or, in diocesan parlance, 'St Mary's, South Hampstead'. The vicar of St Saviour's agreed – inexplicably without any of the necessary paperwork – that all that part of his parish south of the railway lines should become a 'mission district' or chapelry served by the new church, so it had already taken on the character of a parish-in-the-making as opposed to being merely the Home's chapel. Two churchwardens were appointed: Bell himself (then of St John's Terrace) and John Moxon Clabon (of St George's Terrace).[11]

A contemporary press report described the church as:

very commodious, and really better than the ordinary class of iron churches. There are good-sized ventilators in the roof, besides ten windows made to open, so that there will be no lack of ventilation during the summer months, which is such a great desideratum in a small church.[12]

Cox and Son of Southampton Street supplied a reading desk, lectern and pulpit. A silver communion service and large alms dish were given anonymously. Mrs Bell presented an altar cloth embroidered with 'IHS', and Miss Walford and Miss Fuller (presumably the sisters respectively of the former and present chaplains) gave book-marks with white crosses.

This was no small hut! It was large enough to accommodate 400 worshippers in addition to the staff and Boys of the Home. The steering committee agreed that its seating should be 'free' – that is to say not allocated in exchange for pew rents as was the case in many churches, but open to all in return simply for their free-will offerings. According to Bell the 'little body of worshippers assembled every Sunday increased rapidly, and a harmonious and happy congregation was established.' Looking back over these early years, Percy Dearmer would report in 1911 that total attendances for the three months from October to December 1868 were 7,250, compared with only 2,464 in the corresponding period of 1867, whilst the number of Communions increased from 253 to 407, and Collections from £35 to £88.[13] Sunday services were: 11 a.m. Morning Prayer, Sermon, and Holy Communion and 3.30 p.m. Litany and Sermon. The choir initially comprised boys from the Home, under the direction of their schoolmaster.

As the number of worshippers rose, and with them the church's income, Fuller was soon in a position to pay back Bell's loan, and even to employ occasional assistant clergy. A fund-raising committee with three trustees, Fuller, Bell and George Pennell, confidently began to lay plans for a permanent church. Eton was again approached, and this time offered a green-field site (the site of today's St Mary's) at the junction of King Henry's Road and Primrose Hill Road. An architect member of the congregation, MP Manning, seized the opportunity of a lifetime[14] to design a church in what Francis Stephens would describe as 'French Gothic' style, and a public appeal was launched for a church on much the scale we see today but with a bell tower on the north side. It was hoped that a parsonage house, schools and a library could be added later. An illustrated prospectus was printed and circulated, and a formal appeal launched in the press.

In preparation, a mission was led in 1869 by Revd JW Chadwick, and although the very idea of a mission was frowned on by Bell (presumably as being rather high-church), it would later bear unexpected fruit. Eton very properly offered the site only provisionally to the Ecclesiastical Commissioners, aiming to make an outright gift of it once both the College and the Commissioners were satisfied that the new church was ready for consecration, which it was hoped might be within five years. But that did not simply mean completing the building: its viability would also depend on its debts being paid off or at least guaranteed, and on legally-binding arrangements being put in place for the appointment of future incumbents.

Sad to say, the appeal for funds was not an immediate success, and although the campaign continued to focus on raising the £8,400 needed to complete Manning's full scheme, which aimed to seat 600 people, the early rejection of a number of applications to grant-

MP Manning's original proposal for a church with a tower.

awarding bodies (including at first the diocese) served as a warning to the committee that it might have to settle for something less ambitious.

The rift between Fuller and the Boys' Home

There was an unpleasantly dark sub-plot to all this. By the end of 1869 relations between Bell and Fuller had seriously broken down. Fuller was turning progressively into a Ritualist, introducing high-church ceremonies and teaching of a kind that did not accord with Bell's churchmanship. But once Bell's initial loan for the iron church was fully repaid, Fuller felt free to drive forward his own liturgical agenda, and Bell admitted sadly that he had every right to do so. This led, slowly but surely, to a parting of the ways.

The two men (who on account of their respective offices must have rubbed shoulders regularly in the normal course of business) instead of meeting to thrash things out exchanged what would now be called 'frank' letters, after which Bell set out a defence of his views in a printed pamphlet lamenting his having to part company with 'the little Church which I founded, for which I worked diligently, and in which we had all earnestly hoped and expected to worship for many a year, as happily as we did until the apple of discord, in the shape of surplices and adorations, was thrown among us.' 'Fashionable Ritualism' had set in, he said, and he and his fellow churchwarden had protested. He added that the congregation had felt increasingly excluded: prayers were now sung, not said; and the people were given unwelcome instructions on how and where to bow during the service. The tone of preaching 'seemed to substitute Church for Christ'. To add insult to injury, the Collect for the Boys' Home had been dropped from its customary place before the sermon, in favour of an invocation; and the Lord's Prayer was no longer said by all. Fuller insisted that if the boys from the Home were going to continue singing in the choir they must wear surplices, and when on Bell's insistence they refused, Fuller corralled them instead into congregational seats and imported his own singers. More music was introduced, under the direction first of a Miss Francis and later of Bradbury Turner, a music graduate who had been organist at Harrow

School. But any singing was now restricted to the clergy and the new choir, not the boys and congregation. 'Adoration and genuflection,' as Bell put it, crept into the communion service, and the teaching took a distinctly more Catholic turn: 'I remember one Catechizing especially – on the Seven Deadly Sins – which made me tremble for the result,' said Bell. His fellow churchwarden resigned disheartened, but Bell stayed on a while longer, hoping all this would prove to be a bad dream that would pass. He observed that certain women in the congregation had rather taken a shine to crossings, bowings, kneelings and adorations 'that made several of the sober-minded in the congregation uncomfortable'. 'The externalisms of religion,' he wrote in a withering passage, 'have a wonderful attraction for small minds'.

On a purely personal level Bell still admired Fuller and praised his work among the poor of the district (which incidentally confirms that he was developing a ministry well beyond the Home), but he could no longer stomach the way Fuller conducted services. Fuller, however, simply took the line that since quite a lot of people rather enjoyed his ritual those who felt otherwise could worship somewhere else. Bell and a proportion of the senior men of the congregation decided to do just that, and in March 1870, having complained of the 'rapid progress towards Romanism and the Sacrifice of the Mass, Priestly Mediation and Auricular Confession, which have now made St Mary's so obnoxious in this neighbourhood where, but two years ago, all were warm and earnest friends,'[15] he ceased to present the Home's boys for confirmation classes with Fuller. Fuller countered by asking him to remove the boys from the church altogether. It therefore seems unlikely that they ever again worshipped in either the iron church or the permanent St Mary's church that followed it. And so the direct association between the Boys' Home and St Mary's Primrose Hill came to an end after only a few years, a fact that needs to be carefully weighed against successive (and truthful) statements made in the past that St Mary's origins lay in Christian Socialism and rescuing boys from a life of destitution and crime.

By some accounts a chapel (as distinct from the schoolroom) was built at the Home as early as 1872. And ironically, in the late 1880s, it was there that a number of members of the St Mary's congregation who had lost patience with Fuller would return. Bell continued to be a leading light in the Home's management, and after his death (which was not until 1910) a plaque to his memory was installed in its chapel. That came to St Mary's, together with another one dedicated to the Rayments, when the chapel was eventually demolished after the Home closed in 1920; they survive among the parish's archives. The site of the Boys' Home, after various subsequent incarnations, was converted into flats in 1982,[16] and only the small section facing on to King Henry's Road retains its original character.

Towards a new church

Having lost the support of Bell and his fellow warden, Fuller recruited two other men as churchwardens and set up a new Building Committee. After further negotiations with Eton and the Vicar of Hampstead a trust deed for the church's future Patronage arrangements was executed on 8 June 1870. Under its terms, *from the date of the church's eventual consecration*, presentation to the living would be vested in seven Trustees, of whom the Provost of Eton and the Vicar of Hampstead *ex officio* would be two. The other five were initially to be Fuller himself plus four named individuals from his close circle: George Pennell, Thomas Hill, Arthur George Lovell and Thomas A. Ridpath. Any vacancy thereafter was to be filled by the decision of the whole body of Trustees. The Trust has continued to operate on broadly these lines to the present day.[17]

Emily André, founder and benefactor

And so to the fruit of that 1869 mission. When fund-raising began to flag, Mary Emily André, a wealthy unmarried lady who had been much moved by Chadwick's call to mission and by Fuller's leadership, stepped in to save the day. She was the daughter of a prominent banker and director of the French (Huguenot) Hospital,[18] James Peter André, and had lived with her parents in St Mark's Square, Regent's Park. On her father's death in 1868 she had inherited a substantial fortune, at just the time St Mary's appeal was being launched. And Fuller (who would become her husband in 1874) seems rather quickly to have taken her into his confidence, for she clearly knew all about the future Patronage arrangements when in July 1870 she wrote a confidential letter promising a total of £3,000 to be paid in three instalments: in July and October that year, and then when the church was opened for worship. She imposed a number of conditions, all probably suggested by Fuller himself: that he should be the first priest in charge; that his successors should be appointed by Trustees (exactly as stated in the Patronage deed); that there should be a daily celebration of the eucharist, with an extra, early-morning celebration on Sundays and feast days; and that all the seating should continue to be free and unappropriated. So some kind of building was now guaranteed, even if it was not to be the full project as originally planned. Manning went back to the drawing board to develop slimmed-down plans for a church comprising only nave, chancel, north aisle, north transept and organ loft (ie with no tower, south aisle, chapel, or vestries).

The new church takes shape, 1870-1872

Dove Brothers of Islington, described by Sir John Summerson as 'one of the ablest and most productive church-building concerns in mid-Victorian England', were contracted to build the new church.[19] The first brick was laid on 8 December 1870, the feast of the Nativity of Our Lady, which therefore became one of the dates commemorated in subsequent jubilee celebrations, although the ceremony at which Lord Eliot laid the foundation stone was not held until 25 November 1871. Apart from two of Manning's original drawings, and Dove Bros' ledger entry verifying that St Mary's was built between 1870 and 1872 at a total building cost of £6,719 plus fees and expenses, there is no further surviving documentation.[20] But even from these figures we can at least see that Emily André's £3,000 amounted to almost half the basic cost. She therefore has every right to be considered the church's founder: without her donation St Mary's would never have been built.

The building was described at the time as in the 'Early pointed style, built on stiff clay, with no crypt,[21] a trussed rafter roof in yellow fir with plates, rafters, collars, braces, king posts and tie beams.' Eton College gave £200, and among individual benefactors were Fuller (£50), Bell (£25 in spite of all) and Manning himself (£10).[22] A substantial debt remained to be cleared in future years, by personal donations and subscriptions from within the congregation. Fund-raising efforts, large and small, ranged from a major local appeal to the sale of carte-de-visite sized photographs of the iron church. Most disappointingly, apart from one stray issue, no copies of the monthly parish magazine survive for the critical period between August 1872 (just a month after the church's opening) and 1876, nor is any picture of the exterior at that time known to survive.

Endnotes

1. For an outline of the early history see *www.childrenshomes.org.uk/EustonBoysIS/?LMCL=ceHrB9*. *Daily Telegraph and Courier*, 16 Nov. 1869 [British Newspaper Archive].
2. For more detail on the Home and its history see Beck, Gladys, 'A service bright and brief: the story of the Boys' Home, Regent's Park Road', in *Camden History Review*, 2, pp.4-6 (1974), and Gear, Gillian, 'The Boys' Home Industrial School…' in *Ibid.*, 18 (1994), pp.1-5.
3. Archives: Charles Plouviez notes p. 21, citing Anthony Cooper.
4. See Amsden, John, 'Eton College and the manor of Chalcots', in PM, Aug-Sep, 2008, pp.18-20 and Dec-Jan 2008-9, pp.5-7.
5. For more details of the creation and history of St Saviour's see 'Our friends and neighbours: the story of St Saviour's Church' in PM, Oct-Nov 2013 and Dec 2013-Jan 2014.
6. For further details see Sheppard, Martin, *Primrose Hill, a History* (2013), esp. chs 8 and 9.
7. Probably St Stephen the Martyr, Avenue Road, just across the Hill, rather than St Stephen's Rosslyn Hill.
8. After the August 1872 issue, with the single exception of January 1875 there are no surviving magazines until 1876, although the numbering makes clear that they did once exist. They almost certainly fell victim to Hardcastle's salvage drive in the Second World War. Complete sets survive for the three years 1876-78, but 1879 is represented only by two issues, and for the whole of the rest of Fuller's ministry 1880-89 no magazines were printed.
9. It is listed under Ainger Mews in the 1869 street Directory, but the exact location has not been traced. See Camden History Society, *Streets of Belsize* (2009), p.34.

10 See Beck, G, 'Looking Back', 3.
11 LMA: P81/MRV 7: a single page from the service register on the opening day.
12 Archives.
13 PM, Dec 1911.
14 He did not specialise in churches, although he had already designed St Olave's, Ramsey, IOM (1862) and Twickenham Congregational Chapel and Schools (1867).
15 10 Mar.1870: George W Bell's pamphlet of March 1870.
16 Camden History Society, *Streets of Belsize* (2009), p.33.
17 The deed was not formally recorded in the Diocesan Registry until after the consecration of the building and the institution of Fuller as vicar, in November 1885. Since 1931 the Trustees' role has been to recommend a candidate for approval by the churchwardens and the Bishop, see Browne's article in PM, Jul-Aug 1976.
18 On the French hospital see Tessa Murdoch and Randolph Vigne, *The French Hospital in England: its Huguenot history and collections* (Cambridge, 2009).
19 Braithwaite, David, *Building in the Blood: the story of Dove Brothers of Islington 1781-1981* (1981), *p.7*. [Scott family blog] https://gilbertscott.org/dove-brothers/; *VCH Middlesex* VIII, pp.69-76; Twelve firms submitted tenders, of which Dove Brothers' was easily the lowest (Islington Local History Library GD1032 S/DOV, Tender Books 1869-77).
20 When Dove Bros finally closed, in 1970 its archives, which were already in a parlous state, were mostly lost, except for a few select survivals, now divided between the Islington Local Studies Library (see citation above) and the RIBA archive, now at the V&A, which include Manning's 1870 drawings, PA 2000/2/1-2; and papers on the remedial work 1883, DB 36/1/1-2.
21 i.e. no crypt in the conventional sense. There was an arched undercroft below the chancel, not usable as a place of worship. It was always referred to as the 'crypt'.
22 PM, Sep 1890.

Chapter 2

Revd Charles James Fuller

Priest in charge, 1872-1885; first Vicar, 1885-1889

The new church opens for worship, 1872

In 1872, Fuller received the Bishop's licence to open St Mary's church, 'the consecration of which we have deemed it proper to defer for the present',[1] and on 2 July, which at that time was commemorated as the Feast of the Visitation, the opening services were held.[2] A second date had thereby been circled in the church calendar for future annual celebrations. Morning Prayer at 10.30 a.m. was followed at a little after noon by a procession with cross and banners, leading into a 'high' celebration of the Sung Eucharist. One reporter particularly enthused over the Banner of Our Lady made by one of the congregation, 'so perfect in design, material, colour and execution as to merit its being ranked as an excellent example of what a sacred banner ought to be.' The three ministers wore surplices and embroidered stoles. In keeping with tradition there was only one communicant other than the celebrant: a member of the choir. The altar had a handsome white frontal, cross and candlesticks. The music, still under the direction of Bradbury Turner, comprised Merbecke's Creed and Gloria, and the *De Angelis* plainsong setting of the Benedictus and Agnus Dei. *O Salutaris* was sung. The sermon was given by the 1869 missioner, Revd JW Chadwick of St Michael's Wakefield, who complimented the parish on segregating the seating for the two sexes (the men on the south side and the women on the north, including the north aisle), because, in

Revd Charles James Fuller.

his view, 'attractive services do not always bring devout worshippers', and 'personal domestic family feelings are out of place in the House of God'.

Afterwards, 114 invitees attended lunch at the Pavilion on Primrose Hill.[3] It was certainly a day of triumph for Fuller, but after his long delay in obtaining any financial help from the diocese he announced in his speech that although he had invited the bishop to preach he 'did not weep very bitterly when he learned that his many engagements would prevent him from doing so'. For his part, Chadwick justifiably claimed that the 1869 mission had been a major turning point, resulting in the establishment of the Building Committee whose members had made themselves ultimately liable for any debts.[4] The *Church Herald* commented that 'poverty, persecution and Protestantism have all been encountered by the noble-hearted Priest-in-Charge and by his faithful followers.'

Parish life

Two aspects of Fuller's time in office which happen to be disproportionately well documented are further explored below, namely the controversy with the bishop over ritualism and the dispute with the London and North Western Railway over the church's serious subsidence in the 1870s. But more deserving of emphasis at the outset are his pastoral achievements, even though these are much less well documented. They were applauded at the time, even by those like Bell who opposed him on other grounds.

For much of the first three years in the new church Fuller and his churchwardens were left in peace to build up the congregation and arrange services and activities, on a scale that would have daunted a lesser man. Fund-raising continued for fitting out the church and reducing its debts. But above all there was strong and compassionate outreach to the poor and to the large, but sometimes overlooked, class of domestic servants employed by the middle-class households of the district.

Fuller's own livelihood depended squarely on the church's financial success because he had agreed with the churchwardens that his stipend would consist of half the church's offertory takings, the other half being devoted to the building's running costs. That can hardly have given him a comfortable income, but if he was at all worried financially in his first two years, his marriage then to Emily André changed everything.[5] No clergy house had yet been provided. According to the censuses, Fuller while still a bachelor lived at 9 Ainger Terrace, very close to both the Boys' Home and the iron church. After their marriage he and Emily lived at 98 King Henry's Road.

Parish institutions
Notwithstanding the breach with the Boys' Home, Fuller's ministry was still strongly rooted in Christian Socialist principles. With the help of volunteers and modestly-paid helpers from his congregation, plus a great deal of *ad hoc* fund-raising for specific projects, he set up:

- A day school for children, at 4 Ainger Road, run initially by Miss Mary Ann Holeyman at a charge of 2d per child per week paid in advance. It became so popular that there soon had to be a subsidiary school at premises in St George's Road, serving as a feeder to the main school as vacancies arose.
- Two separate night schools: (a) for boys over 10 and men; and (b) for girls over 12 and women. By 1876 all these schools had migrated to premises at 77 Regent's Park Road, apparently owned or leased by Fuller personally.

- To assist the poor: a Provident Fund, a Maternity Society for the loan of baby clothes, and a Boot and Shoe Club for children attending the parish schools who could not afford them.

To encourage both bonding and fund-raising within the congregation, a number of 'guilds' sustained by members' subscriptions were established over the coming years. The Guild of St Mary the Virgin brought together those who in some capacity worked for the church. Its rather grand constitution[6] provided for a provost, chaplains and wardens, one of whom was initially the churchwarden Thomas Hill,[7] and a treasurer (Harry Snow). The Guild of St Joseph, for young women and children, was convened by Emily André/Fuller herself, and soon ran a lending library for its members. The Guild of the Guardian Angel, for boys aged 7 to 17, was created in 1877. A branch of the Confraternity of the Blessed Sacrament is also recorded, as well as a Primrose Hill branch of the Church of England Working Men's Society (also founded in 1877), whose name hid its real purpose, which was to secure 'freedom of worship and the preservation of [the Church of England's] rights and liberties on the basis of the Book of Common Prayer and the usages of the Primitive Church.'[8]

Liturgy

The first surviving parish magazine (1872) lists the services offered by Fuller and various assistant clergy. On Sundays, the early communion service at 8 a.m. was the one almost all communicants were encouraged, if not *required*, to attend in order that they should fast before receiving the sacrament. (As we shall see, this practice, which was common in high-church parishes, was upheld by Fuller's successor, Albert Spencer, but not insisted on by either Percy Dearmer or Arthur Duncan-Jones who followed). The segregation of the sexes so praised by Chadwick was not maintained for very long, because of objections from the two churchwardens and two of the sidesmen, whose support Fuller could not afford to lose. As a compromise, married couples were allowed to sit together, but when it came to receiving communion, single men went up first, then single women, and only finally the married couples.

Interior, 1872.

Matins and sermon followed at 10.30 leading into the Sung Eucharist (mass) at 11.45. Even those who had been at the early service were encouraged to attend, but not to receive communion which, at that time of day, remained restricted to the celebrant and a server. In the afternoon there followed public Catechising at 3, concluding with the Litany at 3.30, and that in turn led into a 'class' at 4 for domestic servants, whose household duties did not permit them to attend church at other times. The day concluded with Evensong and Sermon at 7 p.m.

Fitting out the church
Fitting out the church proceeded in stages. The sacred vessels and other necessities were funded from donations and subscriptions, the font

from penny-collections made by the children, and the Litany desk from similar offerings by the domestic servants. A thematic 'programme' was drawn up for prospective stained glass windows at the east end behind the altar, but only one or possibly two sets of such windows (out of the five two-window lights available) were actually endowed: by Emily André (as she then still was) in memory of her late father. The glass in all the remaining windows at the east end, as well as those in the north aisle, transept and clerestory, remained plain, thus allowing much needed natural light into the building, for it has to be remembered that the south wall, pending any future extension, was still of solid brick up to clerestory level. The lack of stained glass, in the north aisle in particular, proved to be a blessing in disguise when the building later began to subside (see next section).

Organ and music

The church was extremely fortunate in having among its founder churchwardens and Trustees the organ builder Thomas Hill, who had recently taken charge of the family firm after the death in 1870 of his father William, its founder. When the new St Mary's opened, Thomas, on behalf of his firm, supplied an interim organ at a cost of £800, agreeing to accept payment in instalments as and when the parish could raise the money.[9] This was not yet an instrument on the scale he wanted to see for a building so dear to his heart, but it was a start, and he had every intention of adding to it in future. The ultimate sanction, the removal of the instrument if the debt was not cleared, was actively threatened several times, but Thomas's patience and generosity always trumped the usual norms of business, and even before the debt was fully paid off he was proposing to augment the instrument, at his own risk.

Bradbury Turner, the organist, remained a loyal supporter of St Mary's into the 1880s. Several press accounts of services singled him out for praise, although the little we know of the choir's repertoire does not suggest that it was very wide-ranging. *Hymns Ancient and Modern* was used, and every Sunday not only were plainsong introits and propers sung by the choir (additional to the Book of Common Prayer text), but the words were printed in the parish magazines so that the congregation might follow. This marked out St Mary's as a pioneer in the singing of plainsong, and thereby established a tradition that is continued, although on a much smaller scale, to this day. An enthusiastic review, in the magazine for January 1876 by GW Bloxham (the local secretary of the Confraternity of the Blessed Sacrament), of Hayes's *The Anthem Book, an Antiphonal adapted to the Book of Common Prayer*, might suggest that that was also in use.

Turner evidently left the parish in 1881, for unrecorded reasons, although Arthur Hill's later suggestion that he left when Fuller's ceremonial became more eccentric, seems entirely plausible. Hill noted also that the music then went sharply downhill. Turner was followed, in rapid succession, by Mr H Johnson (1881-82) and Mr Northcutt (1882-83), the latter quite possibly standing down when the organ was decommissioned for the rebuilding of the church. From 1883 to 1888 the organist is listed as a Mr A Capel.

Drama

From time to time, members of the various parish Guilds, including the children, put on dramatic entertainments in the parish schoolroom. There is no record at this early date of an amateur dramatic society for adults, but something of the kind must have existed, even if on a rather inchoate basis, because there is mention of annual or twice-yearly dramatic evenings held in aid of the St Mary's schools. At least three such events were mounted off-site to take advantage of larger auditoria than were available in the parish. Harry Snow (now one of the churchwardens), as well as Mrs Hill (Thomas's wife) and Emily Fuller were among those who proved willing to tread the boards in a worthy cause. Charles Dance's *A Wonderful Woman,* a comic drama in two acts, and J Stirling Coyne and HC Coape's farce *Samuel in search of himself* were performed at the King's Cross Theatre on 23-24 January 1877. The reviewer[10] thought the audience frankly deserved better than the latter 'somewhat vapid production', but praised the standard of acting. Mr Heath Mills and his 'excellent little band' added to the entertainment. Thomas Hill's son Arthur, still a boy, had been learning the part of Rodolphe, a young painter, in the first play, but when illness at the last minute prevented his appearance Mr Skilbeck took his place. On 3-4 February 1879 Langham Hall in Great Portland Street hosted two further benefit performances for the parish schools, a three-act comedy by Henry J Byron entitled *Partners for Life* and a one-act farce by Thomas J Williams, *Ici on parle français*.[11] This time the amateur orchestra was conducted by CH Dickinson. The *Hampstead and Highgate Express* of 12 February 1881 reported another two similar evenings of amateur drama at 'the commodious theatre of the Kilburn Town Hall'. Both were well supported and the takings reduced the schools' debt from £60 to a more manageable £20 which it was hoped friends of the church would be able to clear. They began with a 'serio-comic drama in two acts' by FC Burnand, *The Deal Boatman*, with an 'ingenious and pathetic' plot. Emily Fuller again starred, this time as 'the good-hearted sister-in-law who took good care to let all know that she had been in "some of the *fust* of families", which 'provoked much amusement and ... gained hearty and well-deserved applause'. On a rather more serious note, fund-raising talks, concerts and lectures that might appeal to a wider audience were put on, among them a 'Popular Lecture on Birds' by Mr Bowdler Sharpe, FLS, FGS, held at the Assembly Rooms, Eyre Arms[12] in 1876 in aid of the organ fund.

Amid all the hard grind of fund-raising we should not forget the more relaxed occasions. In December 1876 – but probably in other years too – a party was held at the Pavilion on Holy Innocents' Day, at which 143 children from the St Mary's Schools sat down to tea and were given presents from a large Christmas tree, thanks to the generous sponsorship of Mr JF Hirsch of the Manor Hall, St John's Wood Park.[13]

Ritualism

Background
Tensions between the Evangelical wing of the Church of England and those of a more high-church persuasion came to a head in the 1860s.

Any clergyman who by then committed himself to practices outside the norms of the Church of England laid down in the Book of Common Prayer surely knew that he was courting controversy. At the very least he risked being disciplined by his bishop, and after the Public Worship Regulation Act of 1875 he could even be tried in a secular court and imprisoned if found guilty.

In 1867-8, as the iron church was in its first year, the case of Fr Mackonochie of St Alban's, Holborn was prominent in the headlines. He had been taken to court by a solicitor member of the Church Association, charged with five offences: the elevation of the host during the consecration; excessive kneeling at that time; the use of incense; using a 'mixed chalice' of wine and water; and placing lighted candles on the altar. The Dean of Arches ruled these activities illegal save for the kneeling and the lighted candles, but on appeal to the Judicial Committee of the Privy Council all were held to be illegal.[14] There was an increasingly unsavoury atmosphere in which those opposed to ritualism deliberately attended services conducted by clergy of a ritualist persuasion in order to note down exactly what happened and report it to the diocesan bishop in the hope of triggering disciplinary action and the enforcement of strictly Prayer-Book practice as they interpreted it. This kind of spying, which had become institutionalised with the foundation of the Church Association in 1865, would continue for half a century, and indeed Percy Dearmer would encounter precisely the same phenomenon in the 1900s. Bishops' daily postbags were filled with complaints and, whatever position they might wish to take on the matter as individuals, as diocesans they had to be seen to be exercising a degree of clerical discipline. Yet they were not eager to alienate their brother clergy or bring the full force of the law down on them if they could achieve compliance by persuasion and reminders of canonical obedience. This seems to have been exactly the position adopted by the Bishop of London, John Jackson.

The Church Association's members briefed themselves thoroughly on the likely doctrinal and symbolic implications of every kind of vestment, ornament and gesture of the ritualists, and sensitised themselves to the slightest whiff of Romanism or superstition. They infiltrated services and canvassed support for their views among the general population, church-goers or not. And between 1867 and 1870 – just as funds were being raised to build St Mary's – a Royal Commission on Ritual was sitting, which published four reports identifying the problems but without reaching agreed conclusions on exactly how discipline should be enforced. Fuller was by no means alone in feeling that it was worth risking the penalties in order to assert the legality of their alternative interpretation of the Prayer Book.

Fuller and ritualism

Bell's breach with Fuller over ritual in the iron church was the first sign of the trouble brewing at St Mary's, and it ignited a touch-paper. His pamphlet advertised Fuller's ritualist practices to a wider world, although his allegation that few of the congregation really understood Fuller's innovations was probably correct. Once the iron church was open, Fuller had little if any accountability to the vicar of St Saviour's as the parish priest; indeed, the vicar had personally agreed to this new district or chapelry being set up and had surrendered to Fuller any fees that might fall due for services he held within the district, and to that extent Fuller saw himself as largely free to proceed in any way he chose. He certainly *was* answerable, however, to the Bishop of London, by whose licence he exercised his ministry. The bishop, based as he was in Fulham Palace, might have been physically remote but, as his lawyers would later advise him, he could withdraw Fuller's licence to officiate at any time up to the consecration of St Mary's, for which no date had yet been set.[15]

Fuller was not without his strong supporters, and enthusiasts from further afield including St Mary's, Kilburn came to Primrose Hill to enjoy a particular kind of liturgy. On the other hand local opposition was also growing. One particular disaffected member of the iron church's congregation, Thomas Morse, a barrister living in King Henry's Road, would turn out to be Fuller's chief scourge. Just days after the opening services at the new church in 1872 he began a campaign of letters to the bishop. His main charge was that Fuller was, with impunity, flouting the law as interpreted by the Privy Council and the bishops. Enclosing Bell's pamphlet and taking particular offence at the segregation of men and women in the congregation he reported that: 'the church with its Cross and Candlesticks and the dresses of the Ministers[16] and or Priests, singing men or boys is more like a Romish place of worship than like a church belonging to the Establishment.'[17]

Turning his fire next on Charlton Lane, the Vicar of Hampstead, he asked if, as a prospective Trustee of St Mary's, Lane knew what was really going on: 'I think that the parishioners have a right to know whether the Church of England was intended for them, or for the teaching therein of Romish doctrine and practices !!!'.[18] Lane was sufficiently worried to suspend his Trusteeship for a time. To the Incorporated Church Building Society, from which Fuller was still trying to secure a grant, Morse wrote, 'I believe I am quite right in stating that the ceremonies and practices at the new church are as Romish as they can be.'[19] There is nothing in Bishop Jackson's correspondence to suggest that he took any immediate action, although the absence of a parish magazine or any other parish records for these years might give a false sense that all was well.

The complaints resume

It would be wrong to convey the impression that opposition to Fuller's ritualism was anything like continuous. There was an isolated complaint in February 1875 when Revd Charles Stuart, the chaplain of Kensal Green Cemetery, wrote to the bishop reporting that Fuller had recently come there to officiate at a child's burial, 'arrayed in what is generally understood to be the Ritualistic style', and had interpolated prayers not authorised by the Prayer Book.[20] The child's desolate father protested that all the interpolations were from Scripture, and were at his own special request,[21] but to be on the safe side Fuller, who seems genuinely not to have wished to antagonise his bishop, admitted his error, promised not to use unauthorised words in future, and signed off his letter of apology: 'Yours obediently'.[22] If the bishop was satisfied by that, he might nevertheless have been given pause for thought when the next day's post brought another complaint about Fuller ... Except that this time it came from a much less reliable source: a man describing himself as a 'mere lunatic patient', the Revd James Cardon. Lunatic or not, in many details his report seems entirely plausible: that Fuller used incense (including censing the people) with an abundance of candles and lights, and that caps were worn at his services by clergy and acolytes. He thought Fuller personally a good man, though in need of disciplining: 'a cunning, fanatic, ridiculously inflated, most obstinate, blind yet amiable person'. Cardon gave the impression that the liturgy at St Mary's was seductive, with 'beauty of manners from beginning to end', although that was probably not intended as a compliment.[23]

The rest of 1875 seems to have passed without serious incident, but during the following year the Church Association's agents were closing in on St Mary's, taking particular note of high-church ceremonies such as the blessing of candles at Candlemas[24] and the service and ceremonies of Tenebrae in Holy Week. FV Andrews, describing himself as a 'high churchman of the old school', gave the bishop a sensationalised account of Tenebrae at St Mary's, reporting that at the end of the ceremony the clergy and choristers 'crept into a hole in the back of the altar and chanted there the *Miserere* and said two prayers. Except a candle for the organist, total darkness reigned in the church while this was going on, and until the service terminated at 10.55 p.m.' Perhaps anxious not to be thought to have been worshipping there himself, he explained that he had only gone to the church 'to find my wife, and I have forbidden her going there again as unfit for any respectable woman'.[25]

The Church Association searched in vain for any public evidence either of Fuller's licence to officiate or of the formal promulgation of a Mission District for St Mary's Primrose Hill, and questioned the church's very right to exist. (As to the licence their conclusions were wrong; as to the district, probably right, as we shall see later.) In self-defence, Fuller urged members of his congregation to join the English Church Union, which had been founded in 1860 in part to defend ritualists from the attacks of extreme Protestants. But he also noted that: 'notwithstanding the prophecies to the contrary the reformed ritual introduced into the Church during the past two years has, so far from diminishing the congregation and injuring the offertory, had exactly the opposite effect.' In what now seem fairly provocative acts, in the summer of 1876 he advertised a booklet giving the full text of the Tenebrae service, and on 15 August he celebrated the unauthorised feast of the Assumption of the Blessed Virgin Mary.

Suspension of ritualist practices

1877 proved to be the *annus horribilis* for St Mary's that Fuller's opponents had been anticipating with relish. This was quite possibly the time referred to in a later memoir by Thomas Hill's son Walter, when Fuller, 'after a few years in the new building, launched out one Easter Day, much to the astonishment of the congregation, into vestments and full choral ceremonial communion after Matins' (at which Walter acted as one of the acolytes).[26]

The St Mary's patronal festival in July was cited in the national press as an example of how the law was being openly flouted and ritual tacitly allowed to continue unchecked by the bishops. The London correspondent of the *Manchester Guardian* reminded his readers that St Mary's was still an unconsecrated church, operating solely under episcopal licence, and had as yet no district assigned to it. He went on: 'The ritual as far as minutiae of elaboration is concerned defies description and has, I am told, astonished not a few of the ultra-Ritualists'.[27] The *Pall Mall Gazette* went further and described exactly what went on at the Festival:

> The procession of the celebrant and his assistants included the cross-bearer, with acolytes carrying immense candles on either side, the thurifer and the cantors. The acolytes, cross-bearer, and thurifer wore crimson cassocks with girdles, albs and crimson skull-caps, and, in one case, crimson shoes. The cantors wore black capes. The celebrant, Mr Newton Smith,[28] wore a gorgeous yellow cope, which on reaching the altar, he exchanged for a chasuble. Incense was used ceremonially before the celebrations commenced, again before the Gospel and

before the consecration of the elements, and while the celebrant was consecrating, the thurifer swung the incense incessantly behind him. Before the consecration the elements were brought in by the youth who had acted as crucifer, and who now wore a sort of scarf across his shoulder with long ends, which covered the elements. The vessels of wine and water were brought by little boys to the priest, who mixed the chalice before the people. At the consecration of each element bells were rung, and the celebrant elevated both the paten and the chalice high above his head, the people kneeling and in some cases touching the ground with their foreheads. There were no communicants besides the celebrant, who, while the choir were singing what seemed to be the *Agnus Dei*, turned quickly round and raised the paten, but immediately went on with the service, so that there was no pause for intending communicants to approach the altar. The Prayer of Consecration was almost inaudible, and while it was said the acolytes and candle bearers were grouped behind the celebrant. On the altar ledges, in addition to the two lights and the six lights, all of which were burning, there was a large number of smaller lighted candles. It is impossible to describe the frequent movements and gestures of the celebrant and his assistants. In the procession the first banner carried was that of the Virgin under whose figure were the words 'Ave Maria,' and the processional hymn was 'Ave Maria, blessed Maid'. Instead of the Collect, Epistle and Gospel for the day those for the Annunciation of the Virgin were used, and special Psalms were sung. In the procession a man wearing a black cape over his surplice (who subsequently read the Lessons) played the melody of the hymn tune on a cornet.[29]

Spies also attended services on the two Sundays following the Dedication Festival, to note down every deviation. By 1 August they had mobilised all but one of the magistrates of the ancient parish of Hampstead, plus other 'gentlemen of high standing', to sign a memorial or petition to the bishop, on the 'illegal proceedings and practices at the unconsecrated church of St Mary the Virgin in this parish'.[30] Having received representations from such distinguished signatories Bishop Jackson could no longer turn a blind eye, and on 17 August he wrote to Fuller formally requiring him to 'desist from all the illegal practices complained of ... [of which he supplied a list] and to remove the crucifix which is stated to be against the wall over the pulpit'.[31] The churchwardens and sidesmen fired back a detailed defence of the good work being done in the parish, in the course of which they pointed out that none of the petitioners had ever contributed a penny to the running of the church, which was maintained exclusively by voluntary donations, and that with one exception none of them even lived near the church, so they could not have been the least bit inconvenienced, and could, after all, worship elsewhere if they chose.

Something like a refined game of ping-pong ensued:

Bishop to Fuller: The law must be obeyed, and as I have just found out that you are directly answerable to me rather than to the local vicar I must ask you to obey me, otherwise I shall have to withdraw your licence. The law is the law. *Fuller*: Are you suggesting, my Lord, that you would go so far as to suspend my licence? *Bishop*: My aim is chiefly that you should obey the law and desist from illegal rituals. *Fuller*: But that would amount to the same thing because it would remove the very reason why people come to St Mary's, and its voluntary offerings would then dry up. In any case, what precisely are these illegalities and where is it stated that they are illegal? *Bishop*: I have given you a full list already, and with further research I can no doubt spell out for you why they are illegal. *Fuller, 31 October*: Very well, now I know from you which practices are not acceptable in church law I will desist from them at the Sunday midday celebration, and will also remove the crucifix. *Bishop*: But I would be just as opposed to those rituals taking place even at an early celebration. *Fuller, 12 November*: Nobody has ever complained about the early celebration! 'I conscientiously maintain that the vestments and catholic practices used at St Mary's Primrose Hill are the rightful inheritance of the Church of England and are in accordance with the Ornaments Rubric as it stands in the Book of Common Prayer, notwithstanding the judgment of a majority only of a lay tribunal'. May I appeal to the Archbishop of Canterbury? *Bishop*: I have no objection to such an appeal if he is willing to consider it.

While all this was in progress, the press featured St Mary's in further sensationalised reports. For example, the *Hampstead and Highgate Express* of 29 September 1877 picked up a report in *The Rock* from an anonymous writer signing himself 'An Indignant Churchman'*:*

> At home I attend a service which I can enter into and enjoy; but had I not seen I could not have believed that our solemn and beautiful Communion Service could have been so prostituted (I cannot use a milder phrase). … The 'Mass in Masquerade' … lasted from a quarter to twelve until one o'clock. It would take up too much of your space to enter fully into detail… I left the church with mingled feelings of deep sorrow and unmitigated disgust that such performances should be permitted in our Protestant Church…

And on 27 October the same journal carried a further report, this time on the elaborate ceremonial at the Harvest Festival, described rather in the manner of an entertainment:

> The background above the altar was graced with corn and wheat, whilst on the latter were placed vases of flowers, the dwarf stone screen dividing the chancel from the nave[32] being adorned with beautiful flowers, and tall bundles of pampas. The arrangements of the corn, wheat, ferns, flowers, fruit and fine specimens of cereals being in charming taste, and expressive of great beauty.
>
> At Matins there was not a large congregation, it being the practice here to go to church, not so much to hear the sermon which is preached at this service as to witness the elaborate performance at 'high celebration'. The clergy at Matins wore Ritualistic hoods above their white surplices and the chorister boys were attired in cassocks of mazarine blue, with short white surplices.
>
> Matins being over, the choir and clergy left the church, the bell tolled, and preparations began for what was termed 'High Choral Celebration of the Blessed Sacrament'. About fifty candles having

been lighted, the choir and clergy marched through the church to a processional hymn, preceded by the crucifix, and banner of the Virgin Mary and of the Saviour, the thurifer swinging his censer and filling the church with a fragrant cloud. The rear was brought up by the Rev. C.J. Fuller, MA, priest in charge, the celebrant. The playing of a cornet by Mr Ellerton, choir master, during the processional and other hymns, was a striking feature in the arrangements. The musical effects on the organ by Mr Bradbury Turner, and the singing of the choir were fairly efficient, the entire ritual being very ornate and elaborate, whilst incense was scattered about profusely…

Fuller did indeed try to appeal to the Archbishop of Canterbury, who took the line that there were no grounds for him to intervene unless the bishop were to revoke Fuller's licence. So, after four full months of struggle, and with a very heavy heart, Fuller wrote to Bishop Jackson on 29 November saying that he had no choice but to obey him, and that he would accordingly explain the woeful situation to his congregation. The press reported that he then met twelve of his principal supporters and agreed that, in obedience to the bishop's command, there would henceforth be no vestments, no mixed chalice, and no midday service at all but only an 8 a.m. service which he would conduct wearing a surplice. But he added that, as he still had liberty of the pulpit, those who stayed with him 'would have the Holy Catholic doctrine preached to them stronger than ever'.

Looking back on this period in 1920, a contributor to the Golden Jubilee booklet recalled that on Advent Sunday 1877,

after Evensong came the terrible stripping of the church, even to removing the crucifix over the pulpit; and then began the sorrowful time of no vestments and lights, and, for a time, no Sung Mass. It was agony to us all, and Mr Fuller from that time was a broken man, and had to face the grief that all his congregation were not at one with him. He was urged by some members of the congregation to open a Guild Chapel, and carry on the services as usual. Others wanted the Sung

Mass to be restored, without any ritual. He was censured by some for giving way to the Bishop, and he bore it all calmly and uncomplainingly.

Actually the last statement was not correct, as he printed and framed a list of those 'gentlemen of Hampstead' who had complained against him, and, as he reported in the parish magazine, placed a copy on the church wall, with the Scriptural text: 'Pray for them that despitefully use you and persecute you'.[33]

Support for Fuller, and for the ritualist cause at large, was not negligible. When the first anniversary meeting of the Church of England Working Men's Society was held in November in the Pavilion[34] a full house of over 200 people heard how a 'Monster Petition' for the repeal of the Public Worship Regulation Act, with 47,000 signatures, had been presented to Parliament: 'Is the Church of England to become a mere State Machine, or is she to strive and recover that freedom of Worship, which was guaranteed to her by Magna Carta?'

Nevertheless, it must have been with some satisfaction that the Church Association at its meeting in December 1877 recorded the bishop's disciplining of Fuller, adding that its agents had learnt from the bishop himself that he had even fixed a date on which Fuller's licence would have been revoked if he had failed to obey. They felt it would be advisable, however, for a shorthand writer to continue attending St Mary's to do spot-checks on Fuller's sermons.[35]

Scuffle and brawl

After one such visit in April 1878 the Association received a report that all was proceeding in accordance with the ban. But by July some of the illegal practices had returned. In some sections of the congregation something like a persecution complex was developing. A press reporter named CJ Banks (who stated that he was not himself an anti-ritualist), having made notes while attending a service, was assumed to be a member of the Church Association and was followed out of the building by a man he described as a 'gentleman', who accosted him and demanded his notes, saying, 'You are a spy; I will pull your nose and you will be served as we have served others'. He grabbed Banks's coat by the tails, tore it and snatched the notes from his pocket, while others whom Banks assumed to be 'vergers' stood by. Banks complained to Fuller who in due course replied that the man in question was a 'working man', and that no 'vergers' were involved. Was this a white lie to shield a real 'gentleman', such as a churchwarden or sidesman?

No matter: Fuller, as we have seen, was adept at ping-pong:

Fuller to Banks: Your notes have been recovered and you may have them back. *Banks*: Tell me his name at once. *Fuller*: He wants an assurance that there will be no further proceedings if he returns the notes and pays for the coat. *Banks*: I don't want any money now I have the notes back, but I do want an apology, to be printed in six newspapers of my choice. *Fuller*: 'I certainly do not consider it the part of either a clergyman or a gentleman to act as a detective of an informer'. If you call on me tomorrow between 10 a.m. and 1 p.m. or at 9 p.m. I will draw up the apology… By the way, you might not be aware of it but by acting in the way you did you have yourself been in breach of an 18th century Canon. 'It is really a matter of little consequence to me personally whether the matter which relates to an offence outside my jurisdiction[36] passes into other hands or not'. So do, please, let me mediate to bring this matter to a close. *Banks*: I didn't ask you to mediate, and I certainly won't be told to wait on you. I never offended anyone, except perhaps by not kneeling at a sentence of the Creed, 'a course I conscientiously objected to'.

Banks then put the matter into the hands of his solicitors. But, as they too failed to extract from Fuller the name of the offender, Banks (rather like Bell before him) printed a pamphlet to give his own account of the whole affair. Bishop Jackson was informed, and in August he again demanded Fuller's obedience, this time with the definite threat that without it his licence would be withdrawn. There were persistent reports throughout the autumn that both Fuller and his assistant clergy were still flouting the requirements, even if not as seriously as before. But, unless the silence is only for want of surviving evidence, this particular round of controversy died a natural death. What surprises is that the congregation remained overwhelmingly loyal to Fuller. Communicant figures for the year 1877/78 remained well up, and the number of early communions on Easter Day 1878, was 163, which was higher than for any previous year.[37] In 1879 it had fallen back to 151, but the annual meeting heard that 'considering the many unpalatable changes that had of late been forced upon them in the performance of Divine Service, the General Offertory might have been expected to have been even less satisfactory than it was.'

Quite apart from the question of ritualism, life was not at all easy for Fuller and his congregation for the best part of another decade for a quite different reason: the church had started to fall down.

Subsidence and rebuilding, 1876-1883

In the 1870s the London and North Western Railway built its second Primrose Hill Tunnel which, as it cut diagonally under King Henry's Road, came very close to the north-west corner of the newly built St Mary's church.

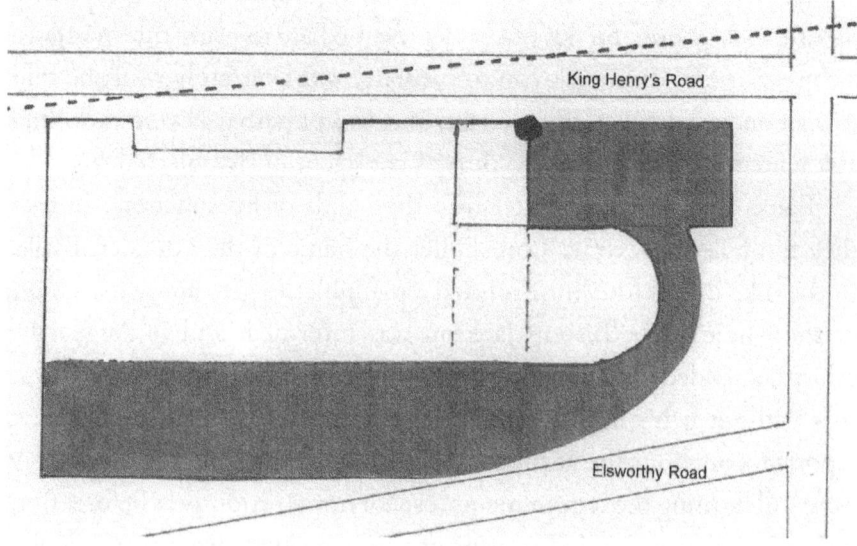

Sketch plan showing the approximate line of the railway tunnel.
The unshaded outline indicates the building's footprint in 1872,
the shaded area the additions of 1892.

For a time all seemed well, but in September 1876 – only four years after the church had opened its doors – Fuller began to notice ominous cracks in the fabric. He was worried enough to keep a diary, which is one of the few things from this period to survive in the parish archives.[38] The first entry, dated 19 September 1876, reads: 'Observed cracks in floor of church, in the concrete roof of crypt, in the step leading to furnace chamber, and in cross wall of foundation in crypt.'

The architect, churchwardens and Building Committee looked on nervously as the cracks became worse by the day, affecting the north aisle, the sanctuary and the crypt (under the sanctuary). Within ten days, contractors had been called in to shore up the crypt's vaulted ceiling. By late October the damage was spreading across the chancel floor and sanctuary, and by December the wall at the west end of the north aisle was also cracking and there were worrying new cracks even in the nave floor. When a number of gas fittings were 'partly drawn asunder' by the movement of the wall the danger was all the more serious, and these had to be repaired repeatedly over the coming months. Surveyors, builders and lawyers including those of Eton College (which still owned the freehold of the unconsecrated site) and the Ecclesiastical Commissioners (who would become its owners after consecration) anxiously took stock. By the spring of 1877 the wall of the north aisle was cracking, and throughout that year matters got slowly, though not dramatically, worse. In October a representative of the railway company came to observe the damage, probably merely to satisfy himself that it would still be safe to run the first trains through the tunnel as planned, starting at 2.50 p.m. on the afternoon of Low Sunday 1878.

The subsidence fortunately slowed down, and the vicar's diary is fairly sparse from 1879 to 1881, apart from occasional setbacks such as bits of roof mortar falling on the floor near the lectern. Until legal liability had been established and funds raised to cover the cost, and as long as there was the risk of further subsidence, it was too early to begin rebuilding. In 1882, in preparation for litigation, counsel were instructed by both the parish and the railway company.[39] But after much deliberation the matter was kept out of the courts in order to avoid the high legal fees, and was referred instead to arbitration by the Institute of Surveyors – whose records sadly do not survive. We learn merely that the Company initially offered a derisory £800. We do not know the final (reportedly 'substantial') figure determined by the arbitrator. The railway company argued that the subsidence had little or nothing to do with their tunnelling but was the fault of incompetent work by the church's architect and builders in the first place. That was certainly not the view of the parish, nor of Ewan Christian, architect/surveyor for the Ecclesiastical Commissioners, who in February 1883 noted approvingly that the church had been well built but now required major remedial work.[40]

The rebuilding of 1883 was on a far greater scale than has previously been appreciated. It required the compete demolition and rebuilding of the north aisle, from its west wall right up to the transept; the strengthening of the floor and vaulted ceiling of the crypt below the Chancel; the relaying of the Chancel/sanctuary floor; and the restoration of the Chancel arch itself. The work was done remarkably quickly, between April and August 1883, in accordance with a detailed specification by WL Spiers, architect for the contractors, Dove Brothers, the original builders.[41] The care and devotion put into this work under Spiers's guidance is striking. His aim – very successfully achieved – was to leave as little outward trace as possible of his radical intervention, by blending in the new work with the old and reusing original materials wherever possible. Any new material employed was to be of the best quality, scrupulously designed to match the originals. There were in fact some notable differences between the original building and the restored one, including new buttresses to strengthen the north wall, and a new north porch with internal doors and wainscot panelling. The total of builder's and contractors' costs for the work came to in excess of £1200 before legal fees and expenses.[42]

To allow services to continue during the work, two enormous hoardings were erected, one in front of the Chancel arch, extending all the way from the church floor to the roof and thus cutting off the Chancel/sanctuary completely from the nave; and the other running the full length of the inner north aisle as far as the transept, which was itself unaffected. The organ was decommissioned during the works, and protected by special coverings. A temporary altar was set up in front of the Chancel hoarding, and the chairs removed from the north aisle were stacked under a covering inside the west wall. The space remaining for worship was thus dramatically reduced on three of its four sides, and the interior must have been dark with the north side completely boarded up, although daylight was still admitted through the plain glass of the clerestory windows.

However, some benefits, other than a straight rebuild, arose in the course of the building work. The heating, particularly of the north aisle, was improved, and the opportunity was taken to have the corbels of the chancel carved with the four evangelists, and the capitals of the nave (on the north side) elaborated, all by Thomas Earp, a renowned and sought-after ecclesiastical sculptor and member of the Ecclesiological Society *[Plate 2a]*.[43] Most importantly for the longer term, the active involvement of the Ecclesiastical Commissioners brought them on board to declare the church finally to be viable and, on structural grounds at least, ready for consecration. But spare a thought for the beleaguered congregation, already reeling from the liturgical changes insisted upon by Bishop Jackson. They had to endure months of worshipping in a building site far less attractive than the iron church from which they had come a decade earlier.

Consecration (1885) and early years

It has often been said that Bishop Jackson refused to consecrate St Mary's because of his opposition to Fuller's ritualism. That may be a part of the equation, although he had in fact achieved most of the obedience he sought from Fuller, and it is perhaps more likely that his real concern about St Mary's was that its congregation would prove unable to raise enough regular income to maintain a parish church. That too might have been resolved soon enough had it not then been for the long period of uncertainty over the compensation claim against the railway. But as soon as the Ecclesiastical Commissioners were satisfied that the church was fit and ready for consecration, Eton College formally transferred to them the freehold of the site, on 18 December 1884, and the impasse was overcome.[44]

Just when it seemed there was no further impediment, Bishop Jackson died suddenly, on 5 January 1885. And yet somehow negotiations continued during the short episcopal vacancy that followed, and on 10 March the Secretary of the Ecclesiastical Commissioners was able to write to Fuller confirming that the deeds transferring the site had been duly registered and details forwarded to the Diocesan Registry, and asking him, finally, to confirm the patronage arrangements.[45] For the first time Fuller formally asked that a district be officially assigned to St Mary's. In all probability this should have been done way back in 1867 when the iron church was opened, or in 1872 when the permanent church first opened its doors, but for some reason this step had been omitted, as the Church Association had correctly suspected all along.

Jackson's successor, whose appointment was confirmed on 24 March 1885, was Frederick Temple, Bishop of Exeter (who had himself been consecrated by Jackson). On 27 April he received the Commissioners' report on St Mary's,[46] and on 2 May, on the petition[47] of the vicar of St Saviour's and the principal parishioners of the chapelry, Temple consecrated the Church of St Mary the Virgin, Primrose Hill. So a third date had been added to the parish's calendar of jubilee celebrations!

It is only right that the details of the ceremonial connected with this important milestone in St Mary's history should be fully recorded. The Bishop was met at the church by his Registrar (Harry Wilmot Lee), the Vicar of St Saviour's (Gerard A Herklots), the churchwardens of St Saviour's, the Revd Charles Fuller ('the intended minister of the new church') and others. They went first to the vestry and the Bishop then proceeded in his episcopal robes to the 'Communion Table', attended by these same people. The petition for the (retrospective) creation of the new district was formally presented by the Vicar of St Saviour's, read out by the Registrar, and accepted by the Bishop. There was then a procession to the West end and back to the Communion Table, the Bishop and clergy reciting alternate verses of Psalm 24. The Bishop sat to the north of the Communion Table while Herklots presented him with the deed of conveyance of the land, which the Bishop duly laid on the Communion Table. Prayers were said, after which the Registrar read out the formal Sentence of Consecration which was signed and recorded in the muniments of the diocese. Fuller then read Morning Prayer, with Psalms 84, 122 and 132. The Lessons were taken from 1 Kings 8, vv 22-62 and Hebrews 10, vv 19-25. After a hymn there followed Ante-Communion, where the Epistle (2 Corinthians 6, vv 13-end) was read by Fuller, and the Gospel (John 2, vv 14-18) by the Bishop's Chaplain. The Creed was said; notice was given of the services to be held the following Sunday; and the proceedings closed with a sermon by the Bishop and the Prayer for the Church.

Bounds of the new District[48]

The bounds of the district assigned to St Mary's were set out in an Order in Council of 12 August 1885, published in the *London Gazette* of 28 August.[49] But was St Mary's yet a parish? Technically not. All the official documentation up to this point still refers to the 'district'. The direction and intent of travel towards parochial status was not in doubt, but to complete the process one further stage was necessary, and a further ceremony was held in November 1885, at which Bishop Temple formally instituted Fuller to the vicarage of the new parish. This has left no trace at all in the parish archives but it was reported in the national and international press.[50] In terms of population the new parish was the smallest carved out of the ancient parish of Hampstead, although its area was greater than the population figure alone might suggest, because about half the geographical parish comprised a large, unpopulated section of the Hill itself.[51]

Fuller's failing health

The lack of parish magazines between 1879 and 1889 deprives us of a vital window into the church's history in the years up to and immediately following its consecration. However, a set of the annual Vestry Minutes, beginning immediately after the consecration (and from its opening words clearly implying that the consecration had in effect created a new parish)[52] helps fill that gap.

Charles Fuller had certainly had an unusually stressful ministry by the time he became first Vicar of the newly consecrated church in 1885, and perhaps this was a factor in his rapidly failing health thereafter. During the next four years, which should have been a time of joyful consolidation and advance, he became progressively more ill with some form of cancer, and eventually suffered a breakdown, both physical and mental.[53]

At first, parish life continued to be unaffected. At the 1887 Vestry, 140 children were reported to be on the Sunday school roll, with an average attendance of 95. The Provident Fund also continued to give out substantial grants to the poor. Fuller remained personally popular. True, the St Mary's schools at 77 Regent's Park Road closed in May 1885, but that was not due to any failing on Fuller's part but to the opening of a new Board School in Princess Road which syphoned off most of the pupils.[54]

It was during 1888 that things started to go seriously downhill. Fuller appears to have sought solace in ever more elaborate church rituals, but as Arthur Hill would write in 1890 after Fuller's resignation:

> the revival of the old ritual was viewed with dissatisfaction by the chief supporters of St Mary's, insomuch as it grew in elaboration to an extent which was regarded even by those acquainted with the literature of the subject as meaningless and distracting. ... St Mary's gradually lost the sympathy and support of its chief friends, and for the last few years struggled on under very adverse circumstances.

The music continued its downward path, and that, combined with objections to the ritual, led to a falling off in the congregation, some of them returning to worship in the Boys' Home chapel nearby. In November Francis Cancellor, the vicar's warden, took the unusual step of writing to Bishop Temple behind the vicar's back to express his concern. Fuller, he said, had appointed a Mr Bloxam as 'Ceremonarius' and Choir Master, 'a person ingrate to nearly all the other workers in the church'.[55] With the congregation's steep decline, the parish's 50% share of collections was no longer sufficient to pay the vicar a reasonable stipend; and he predicted that the congregation, and thus the income, would fall even further. He invited the bishop to send someone to a service to see for himself, and enclosed a note that Fuller was still comfortably off, living in a house costing him £120 a year, with a wife who was 'a rich woman with at least £40,000'.[56] As the Annual Parish Meeting set for April 1889 approached without any episcopal visit being forthcoming, Cancellor wrote again to the bishop saying that he now ideally wanted to resign as churchwarden but was unsure whether he could legally do so since nobody else was prepared to stand. Temple added a minute to his secretary: 'Ask Mr Fuller to call on me at 2 p.m. on Friday the 12th April. Tell Mr Cancellor that the only advice I can give is that he should retire from office as early as possible.'[57]

At what must have been a tense Annual Meeting, Cancellor stood down as churchwarden. The Vicar declined for the time being to nominate another warden, but invited nominations for a people's warden. Nobody came forward. A few weeks later another parish meeting was convened at which the vicar nominated as his warden a Mr AJ Corbett who, however, was said to be 'away in the country'. Once again the people proposed no warden. This impasse could not continue. Temple referred Fuller's case to Sir James Paget, one of the foremost medical specialists of the day and Surgeon to Queen Victoria, who having examined him ordered 'absolute rest and retirement from all work and worry'. Temple noted that 'the parish wants working up. Everything has fallen away under mismanagement, for Mr Fuller has long been unfit for work of this sort.'

The story of what happened in those sad last months of Charles James Fuller's ministry is tinged with mystery. After his resignation on medical grounds in 1889, he and Emily moved to 26 Primrose Hill Road where he died in May 1891, aged about 65. Although there is a report of a public meeting to raise subscriptions for a memorial to him, and of some initial success in doing so, nothing tangible seems to have come of it. Most likely, the donations were later added to the fund to build the reredos under Spencer, but even that is not certain. The Guild of St Joseph, led by Emily Fuller, commissioned and engraved an altar cross in his memory, but there is no record of its ever having been given to St Mary's: it has had a curiously undocumented history, but is now in the church of St Francis of Assisi, Isleworth.

And what of Emily Fuller herself? Although she lived on until 1900, she disappears from the history of St Mary's and has no memorial there. She moved to Kent Terrace, Regent's Park, and may have transferred her allegiance to St John's Wood chapel, to which she later left a small legacy, but she was eventually received into the Roman Catholic church. In her will she made no further mention of St Mary's, the church she had helped to found, as if she had erased that chapter of her life just as the parish seems to have erased its memory of her. It was not a happy ending.

An anonymous contributor to the golden jubilee booklet of 1920 recalled that Fuller 'was not a good preacher or reader, but his devotion at the altar made you feel our Lord's Presence there. He was a priest of high ideals, uncompromising and not always tactful, but ready with sympathy quite unexpectedly. As a confessor he was very strict; on the point of fasting Communion, rigid.' He had been a pioneer in ministry among the poor, and a worthy founder of St Mary's Primrose Hill. In 1903, Percy Dearmer acquired a portrait photograph of Fuller and had it framed to hang in the sacristy. It survives in the archives.

Appendix to Chapter 2

The bounds of St Mary's as described in the Order in Council of 1885

'All that part of the new parish (sometime district chapelry) of Saint Saviour South Hampstead… which is bounded upon the north by an imaginary line commencing at the point at the middle of the eastern side of the bridge which carries Regent's Park Road over the line of the London and North Western Railway where the boundary which divides the said new parish of Saint Saviour South Hampstead from the parish of the Holy Trinity Haverstock Hill … joins the boundary dividing the last named cure from the parish of Saint Mark Saint Pancras… and extending thence westward along the said line of railway for a distance of twenty four chains or thereabouts thereby following the middle of the local traffic line of the said railway to the eastern of the old or northern Primrose Hill Tunnel on the same line of railway and continuing thence still westward and in a direct line for a distance of one and a half chains or thereabouts to a point in the middle of Primrose Hill Road and extending thence northward along the middle of the last named road for a distance of four chains or thereabouts to it junction with Adelaide Road, and extending thence westward along the middle of the last named road for a distance of thirteen and a half chains or thereabouts to the boundary at the junction of the last named road with Merton Road, which boundary divides the said new parish of Saint Saviour…from the new parish of Saint Paul Hampstead … [and with boundaries of other parishes as follows: St Paul Hampstead, St Stephen Portland Town and St Mark St Pancras…]'

Endnotes

1. LPL: Jackson Papers.
2. Described in PM, IV no. 8, pp. xi-xv. and in the *Church Times* of 5 Jul 1872 and the *Church Herald* [BL Newspaper Library], also briefly mentioned in the *Illustrated London News* of 6 July 1872 p.11.
3. A modest kiosk, which had originally been part of the Great Exhibition of 1851, was transferred to near Barrow Hill Reservoir when the Crystal Palace moved to Sydenham in 1852. This was upgraded to tea rooms known as the Queen's Pavilion, built in 1859. They in turn were pulled down in 1905 and replaced by new ones a few years later. See Sheppard, *Primrose Hill, a History* (2013), p.140.
4. A strike in the building trade delayed completion of the work, and the Iron Church remained in use for a little while for some of the services after the consecration of the new building (PM, IV/8 p.iv). It was advertised for sale in PM, Aug 1872.
5. On 9 June 1874, to the church's principal benefactress Emily André, at Archbishop Tenison's chapel at St Thomas's, Regent Street, another centre of ritualism.
6. PM, Jan 1875.
7. His fellow warden being George Elgood, according to Walter Hill's 1920 letter (Archives).
8. PM, Apr 1876 and 1877. An undated tract describing the Society's activities up to about 1880 is bound in with PM, 1875-1879.
9. This would take much longer than he hoped. In February 1879 it was stated that £25 was still owed, and an estimated £250 needed to complete the instrument.
10. PM, Feb 1877.
11. Advertised with cast lists in PM, Feb 1879.
12. St John's Wood, at the junction of Grove End Road and Wellington Road. See www.stjohnswoodmemories.org.uk
13. Report in PM, Jan 1877.
14. Fr Mackonochie refused to obey the judgement and after a further action was suspended for 3 months; the rituals were gradually reintroduced. He suffered further trials throughout his ministry in the 1870s and was compelled to resign in 1882. See, for example, Yates, Nigel, *Anglican Ritualism in Victorian Britain* (Oxford, 1999).
15. As Jackson was advised by lawyers, 11 July 1872. LPL: Jackson Papers 19, fo. 236.
16. His emphasis.
17. 4 July 1872. LPL: Jackson Papers 19, fo. 214.
18. TF Morse to Charlton Lane, vicar of Hampstead, 4 July 1872. LPL: Jackson Papers 19, fo. 234, [enclosed in fo. 232].
19. 24 July 1872. LPL: ICBS file 7143.
20. 6 Feb 1875. LPL: Jackson Papers 19, fo. 240.
21. 11 Feb 1875. LPL: Jackson Papers 19, fo. 244.
22. 15 Feb 1875. LPL: Jackson Papers 19, fo. 246.
23. LPL: Jackson Papers 19, fo. 242.
24. LPL: CS 3 p.371; CS 4 p.4.
25. FV Andrews to Bishop, 13 April, LPL: Jackson Papers
26. Archives.
27. *Halifax Courier* [British Newspaper Archive].
28. Joseph Newton Smith, an assistant priest 1875-1882, was a renowned preacher.
29. This was presumably Mr Ellerton, the choir master (see the account of the 1877 harvest festival below). Archives, section B: History. John Hawes suggests that for the kind of

ceremonial here described Fuller might well have been following the second edition of John Purchas's *Directorium Anglicanum*.
30 LPL: Jackson Papers 19, fo. 250.
31 LPL: Jackson Papers.
32 Evidently later replaced by a metalwork screen which was eventually disposed of under Spencer.
33 *Edinburgh Evening News,* 15 Dec.1877 [British Newspaper Archive]. PM, Dec 1877.
34 Reported at length in PM, Dec 1877.
35 LPL: Church Association Minute Book CS4 p.249.
36 i.e. by being outdoors.
37 PM, May 1878.
38 LMA: P81/MRV/79/3.
39 LMA: P81/MRV/ 67-86: Correspondence and papers concerning compensation for damage to the church by the creation of the [second] railway tunnel at Primrose Hill.
40 CERC: Ecclesiastical Commissioners File EC/7/1/46277 part 1.
41 All this documentation survives in the very fragmentary Dove Bros archives now held by the RIBA/V&A: DB 36/1/1-2.
42 LMA: P81/MRV/43.
43 Earp would return a decade later to complete work on the capitals of the south side and the chapel. He is most famous for sculpting the Eleanor Cross at Charing Cross, and it may be no coincidence that he had just completed a screen in the chapel at Eton College in 1882. He also designed the pulpit and reredos at St Saviour's. website *http://www.victorianweb.org/sculpture/earp/index.html*
44 LMA: London Diocesan Registry, SMVPH file: DL/A/C/MS19224/449.
45 LMA: P81/MRV/14/2.
46 The only further reservation concerned the base on which the new communion table rested, which was not wide enough to permit a south-end celebration of the Holy Communion if this should be desired. Fuller, the writer said, had been very 'nice' about this, and had agreed to have the base extended after consecration. LPL: Fulham Papers, Temple 16, fo. 352.
47 LMA: DL/A/C/MS19224/449.
48 LMA: P81/MRV/14/3: See Appendix.
49 LMA: DL/A/C/MS19224/449, London Diocesan Registry, SMVPH file; CERC NB23/359.
50 *Christchurch Times,* 21 November 1885 [British Newspaper Archive]: The Bishop of London has instituted the Rev Charles J Fuller to the new vicarage of St Mary the Virgin PH'.
51 For the relative population figures of the Hampstead parishes, see *London Parish Map: A Map of the Ecclesiastical Divisions within the County of London 1903* (London Topographical Society, 1999).
52 LMA: P81/MRV/090.
53 An article on the history of St Mary's in the *Illustrated Church News* of 25 February 1898 records that after the church's consecration by Bp Temple in 1885 'Mr Fuller, though suffering from internal cancer, bravely struggled on, often single-handed, for four years, but at length in 1889 he broke down and had to resign. The delays and his illness had by this time almost wrecked the Church life in the parish' (Archives: History).
54 LMA P81/MRV/090, vicar's report to Vestry 1886.
55 This might have been the GW Bloxham, local secretary of the Confraternity of the Blessed Sacrament in 1876. A connection may be supposed with John Francis Bloxam,

the notably extreme later vicar of St Saviour's Hoxton. I owe this latter suggestion to John Hawes.
56 LPL: Fulham Papers Temple 16, fos 354-5, 27 Nov1888.
57 LPL Fulham Papers Temple 16 fo.360, 4 Apr 1889.

Chapter 3

Revd Albert Spencer

Vicar, 1889-1900

Appointment

In a pre-emptive strike in October, just a few days before the Trustees were due to meet to determine a successor to Fuller, two local residents sent the Bishop of London a petition with 126 local signatories requesting the appointment of the Revd John Street, chaplain of the Boys' Home who had 'zealously ministered to their spiritual wants'. Although they claimed to have the support of the majority of the parish, the prime movers were undoubtedly those who had transferred their allegiance to the Home's chapel when they lost patience with Fuller. Bishop Temple passed their letter over to his secretary with the diplomatic minute: 'Say that it would not be proper for me to recommend any one to the Patrons for presentation to St Mary's, but that I will duly institute Mr Street if presented.'[1]

What he knew, but did not say, was that he already had another candidate in mind, the Revd Albert Spencer, whose exemplary work in revivifying St Sidwell's, Exeter, he knew well from his time there as bishop. Spencer had resigned from that parish 'on health grounds', supposedly after suffering a breakdown caused by pressure of work. He had given his last sermon there in November 1886 and been presented with a testimonial gift of £200 from a grateful parish where, he said, he had 'hoped to spend the rest of his days.' Ever a most charitable man, he gave the whole of this sum back to the parish to pay off its debts.[2]

Revd Albert Spencer

Spencer had had a previous breakdown, caused by unmanageable pressure of work when he was diocesan inspector of schools.[3] Even so, something does not quite add up here: his 'health crisis' did not stop him postponing his departure from the parish until Christmas, and by then, even before finally leaving St Sidwell's, he had secured appointment as vicar of All Saints, St John's Wood, London, from Revd HS Eyre, the patron there.[4] This had been approved by Bishop Temple and the archdeacon, and within months the Spencers had moved to London. So his 'breakdown', if such there had ever been, was remarkably soon over, and Albert had again thrown himself vigorously into building up another parish. In the light of later events it seems almost certain that the real reason for his resignation and move from Exeter was not his own but rather his wife Ellen's state of health. Sensitivity and embarrassment surrounded that, and few, least of all Spencer, were prepared to speak openly about it, because she was suffering from a recurring mental illness, and had to seek periodic – but, alas, not very effective – health cures abroad. If they thought the move to London would help her they were soon disabused. In April 1889 after only two years at All Saints, Spencer abruptly resigned again, for reasons which neither the parish nor the bishop could fathom. The only thing anyone could point to was some alleged unpleasantness on the part of certain women in the congregation, but nobody believed that to be sufficient grounds for resignation. The parish pleaded with Temple to dissuade him from resigning: he was universally loved, even by those who did not share his 'Catholic' views – 'a light shining in a dark place', they said; and, as at

Exeter, he had done tremendous work in a short time. Whatever they thought of him, he had been negotiating a further local move, this time to All Souls' (Loudoun Road), but that turned out to have been based on a misunderstanding with the patron of that living. Temple handed the matter over to his suffragan, another former Exeter colleague, Alfred Earle, the Bishop of Marlborough, who had come to assist in London and who, after interviewing Spencer in May, reported:

> He was very sad and reserved and simply spoke of his decision [to resign] as being necessary and inevitable. You know that he has been and is heavily handicapped by his wife's peculiar condition of health: she suffers from hysteria – and I gathered that this was really at the bottom of the matter, but he was very reticent, very sad, shrugged his shoulders and said, 'My dear Bishop, I must go,' and that is all that I could get from him.

And so the Spencers set off on their travels once more to seek a cure for Ellen, this time in Montreux, Switzerland. Their return coincided with the vacancy at St Mary's, and presumably therefore it was either Temple or Earle behind the scenes who recommended Spencer to the Trustees of St Mary's. One wonders how much was said about Ellen's underlying health problems.

This was the first appointment since the church's consecration, and therefore the first time the Trustees had been called on to act, under their Patronage deed of 1870. Thomas Hill, now one of their number and quite possibly their Chairman, offered Spencer the preferment, being quite open with him about the run-down state of the parish and its need of revitalisation.[5] But that was nothing new to Spencer, and St Mary's was a very small parish compared with St Sidwell's, so he accepted the offer and was instituted as the second Vicar of St Mary's Primrose Hill on 8 November 1889. He and Ellen moved to a house in Primrose Hill Road, not far from the Fullers,[6] and so began ten years of rebirth and renewal for both the building and the congregation.

Albert Spencer was a man of moderately high-church traditions, but not a ritualist in the mould of Fuller. There will be a place below to consider such matters as liturgy and music, which of course underpinned everything else, but it was not so much for these that he was appointed as to rebuild the congregation, and above all to press ahead with completing Manning's original plans for a full-scale church. His inspired leadership would enable an ever-growing and more self-confident congregation to embark on schemes that must at times have seemed well beyond their reach.

Completing and fitting out the church

> St Mary's was never dull. I have frequently heard people speak of the sheer pleasure of sitting in the building. Manning, the architect, had never built a church before. But there was nothing stereotyped about him. He lived up to the great compliment of being invited to build a church. He was no copyist of a dead tradition once so gloriously alive…
> *Geoffrey Dearmer, PM Feb 1987*

1. Enhancing the existing church building

Nothing but the best
After organising a general clean-up Spencer appealed for donations to improve the church's furnishings and fittings, many of which were both temporary and tired. 'We shall hope to see them replaced eventually by others more worthy of God's house,' he said, 'but we would rather wait than have anything but the best.'[7] He proved particularly good at cultivating friends and donors and twisting arms to secure financial support, and as he was himself a man of some private means, he and Ellen were able to set a strong example as generous donors: their names appear in many of the subscription lists in the parish magazine, and indeed one suspects that even some of the passing references to donations 'by a friend' conceal further acts of generosity on their part.

Within two months a new altar book, choir books and an altar carpet had been donated; and it did not take long to raise the money to repair and varnish the chairs and for the ladies in the congregation to provide new cassocks and surplices for the choir. A new spirit was breathing in the place.

Stained glass
The interior of Fuller's diminutive building was quite plain, with very little stained glass: just the two André memorial windows behind the high altar and, most recently, the first window of the north aisle depicting St Anne and Our Lady. Spencer's first priority for the building as he found it was to have a third window installed on the south east side of the sanctuary, and by March 1890 there was enough money in hand to ask Clayton and Bell to make it, with scenes of the Annunciation, the Visitation and the Nativity. It was completed remarkably quickly, and dedicated at the Patronal Festival in July that same year.

Spencer next began – very successfully – to seek donations, and maybe even to call in a few favours, to get the north aisle windows fitted with stained glass, again from Clayton and Bell,[8] and at Pentecost 1891 all were installed and ready for dedication. First came a set depicting the 'three Maries' (the Blessed Virgin Mary, St Mary Magdalene and St Mary of Bethany), given by 'a friend'; next three lights depicting respectively St Helena, 'given by a friend in memory of one who loved St Mary's church, and was a regular worshipper at the services therein'; St Sidwell or Sativola, given by Spencer's former parishioners in Exeter; and St Monica, mother of St Augustine of Hippo, 'given by a friend of the Vicar's in memory of a beloved mother'. The two remaining lights, at the west end of the aisle, depicting Ruth and Naomi, were given by members of the Guild of St Joseph in memory of its deceased members, and were dedicated at the children's service that same afternoon.

Furniture: the lectern, Bishop's chair and credence
In April 1890 Elizabeth Bradford (anonymously) offered the entire cost of a brass eagle lectern and the Bible to sit on it. A copy in brass of

the early 16th-century eagle lectern of Newstead Abbey was ordered.[9] Spencer persuaded an old friend from St Sidwell's, the celebrated wood carver and sculptor Harry Hems, to design a Bishop's chair for the Sanctuary, which he said was inspired by the choir stalls in Salisbury cathedral. The cost was covered by 'another friend, who has in many ways helped us.'[10] In July 1892 a large credence table for the high altar was purchased from church funds.

2. Completing Manning's building

The overall plan
Revitalising the old building in this way was just the start. Within two months of his institution Spencer began discussing with senior laity the enlargement and completion of St Mary's, and in January 1890 they commissioned the original architect, MP Manning, to revise his original plans as necessary, so that they could seek tenders for the work.

Fund-raising
Clearly, this was going to require serious fund-raising, and they realised from the start that some aspects of the project might have to be delayed if cash-flow lagged behind aspirations. But as a result of his previous work at St Sidwell's Spencer had become an experienced project manager and knew not only how to prepare the way for fund-raising, but also how to deal (often in person) with builders and contractors. To avoid panic and discouragement at the large overall sum to be raised, and thus to make it easier for more donors to find something they could support, he broke it down into sub-projects, each with its own dedicated fund. With the Spencers once again leading by example, and contributors to each fund being named in the parish magazine to encourage others, donations came in steadily, and on top of this all manner of fund-raising methods were deployed: some offertory collections were ring-fenced for a particular project; there were jumble sales and sales of work, benefit concerts and

dramatic productions; the sale of photographs of the church; and so on. JL Child gave the proceeds from his readings of Dickens's *A Christmas Carol* at the Hampstead Conservatoire at Christmas 1890 (although, somewhat ironically, attendance was disappointing because of heavy snow). In addition to all this local effort notably successful approaches were made to grant-awarding bodies, including the Incorporated Church Building Society (£75), the Diocesan Church Building Society (£33), and most generously Eton College (£200).[11]

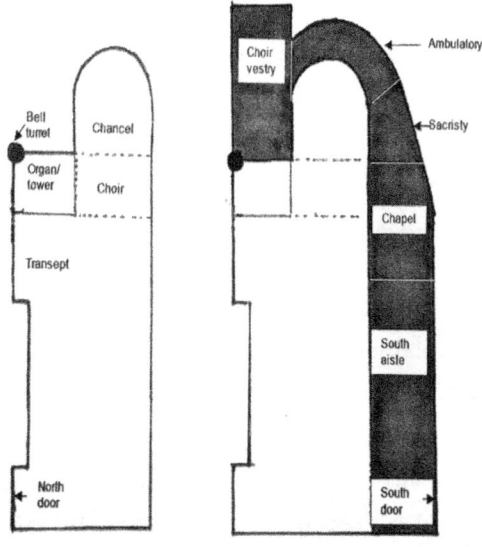

Approximate floor plans in 1872 (left) and 1892.

Phase 1: Choir Vestry

An unsightly hut that had stood outside the church, adjacent to the transept on the north, was removed, and already by early October 1890 a vestry had been built there, for use as a practice-room by the choir, and as a temporary clergy vestry pending the building of a dedicated sacristy. The new space also doubled as a store, enabling the transept to be cleared of furniture and other material that had accumulated there. The vestry was dedicated on the eve of the Harvest Festival, together with a newly donated processional cross.[12]

Phase 2: Chapel and south aisle, sacristy and ambulatory

When it came to the main building project, caution was Spencer's watchword, to ensure that the debts incurred did not become unserviceable, and in May 1891 he advised that work should not even begin until guarantees had been received for at least half the estimated cost. He ensured that this would be the case by acting as overall guarantor himself, at no small risk, but this encouraged others to make loans as well as benefactions. In the hope that local residents who were not members of the congregation might wish to support these efforts, Spencer wrote to Bishop Temple in January 1891 to seek his endorsement for a wider appeal. He rightly suspected that the popular perception of Primrose Hill as a well-heeled area would lead many to suppose that a congregation in such a locale should not need to seek outside help in fund-raising. But he explained that many of those who did attend the church were poorer, middle-class folk who came precisely because they could not afford the pew rents demanded by other churches, and conversely that many of the wealthier residents of the geographical parish had no affiliation at all with St Mary's, or even with the Church of England. 'Many of our best houses are inhabited by Jews; and the few rich tradesmen we have are, I believe without exception, either nonconformists or seat-holders in other churches.' Temple responded by saying to his secretary, 'Say that if he sends me the Appeal he proposes to issue … I will add some words to it.'[13] With this important symbolic backing, the Committee called a public Vestry meeting in February 1891, at which strong local support was expressed for an appeal. And as before, the money started to come in; so much so that by July it was possible to accept a tender of £1944 from Goddard and Sons of Farnham to build the chapel, aisle, sacristy and ambulatory.

Building work began in August 1891, but it was not far advanced before a nearby resident lodged a complaint with the recently-established London County Council that the proposed aisle would stick out beyond the line of house frontages on Elsworthy Road. (The boot was actually on the other foot, as it was the recent expansion eastwards of Elsworthy Road and its encroachment right up to the boundary of the church's plot of land that deprived St Mary's for ever of symmetry at the east end and made for the awkward site that exists to this day).[14] Manning soon convinced the LCC that he had complied with all planning requirements, and by today's standards everything then proceeded at an astonishing pace. On the Eve of All Saints, 31 October, Hampstead's MP, Edward Brodie Hoare, laid the chapel's foundation stone. Exactly as Spencer had predicted, the *Hampstead and Highgate Express*'s very first observation was that the church stood at the centre of a wealthy district. On the other hand, it noted that the church had no endowments but relied on donations and grants, and in support it quoted the parish's own estimates that the chapel and aisle would increase capacity from about 500 to 750 worshippers, at a cost of some £2000 of which £1150 had already been raised. [15]

> The ceremony commenced with a short service in which the Rev A Spencer, the vicar, the Rev WM Magrath and the Rev EJ Walker officiated, with Mr John C Ward at the organ; and then Mr E Brodie Hoare, assisted by the architect, laid the memorial stone which will form the base of one of the columns. The thanks of the congregation were awarded to Mr Hoare on the motion of Mr Avarne, a churchwarden, who said that the completion of the church was, until very lately, so far removed from the range of probabilities that few, if any, entertained any hope of seeing it carried out; but thanks to their estimable vicar they were now within measurable distance of its being an accomplished fact. Mr Hoare briefly replied and said that it had been a great pleasure to be present because he felt that the future of the English people rested mainly with the Church of England…

Samuel Fry, a sculptor and long-standing member of the choir[16] who lived nearby, was simultaneously creating a handsome sculpted tympanum of the Annunciation for the north door *[Plate 2b]*. (He would later carve a second one, depicting the Agony in the Garden, for the tower door).[17]

Services continued as usual while much of the south aisle, chapel and sacristy took shape outside, the works being unseen from within the building. The second phase, however, required the brick infill between the original nave and the new aisle to be knocked through. A few weekday services were cancelled while high wooden boarding was fitted along the original south wall to minimise dirt and damage. Prolonged frost and snow at the end of 1891 and beginning of 1892 held things up for a time, but eventually first the aisle and then the chapel and sacristy were roofed over. An ambitious date of 30 April 1892 was set with the Bishop for the consecration, but the Archdeacon then fired a broadside by insisting on a Faculty for setting up an altar in the chapel. This arrived only the day before the consecration!

3. Consecration

The consecration of the Chapel, on the Eve of Pentecost (a Saturday), was given extensive coverage in the *Church Times* of 6 May 1892. Matins was followed by Holy Communion celebrated by the Bishop of London, at which Spencer read the Epistle and the bishop's chaplain the Gospel. The choir sang a blend of R Tours in F and the Sanctus, Benedictus and Agnus Dei from AJ Eyre's Mass in E flat. In all, the proceedings took 2½ hours! Afterwards a luncheon was held at the Hampstead Conservatoire. There were apologies for absence from several prominent invitees including the Bishop of Marlborough, Brodie Hoare MP, Dr Hornby the Provost of Eton, and Thomas Hill. The vicar praised all who had contributed to the project's completion within just 2½ years of his appointment, and recalled Fuller's heroism in the face of 'difficulties', but the Bishop of London nicely turned the tables on him by saying that 'when a man had good reason to be grateful to everybody it was generally his own fault'. Appropriately for a Chapel dedicated to the Holy Spirit, the eucharist was first celebrated at its altar the next day, Pentecost.

4. Fitting out

It was always envisaged that the windows of the chapel and south aisle would be filled with stained glass as soon as donors could be found, and Spencer as usual broke down the costs, suggesting that a single window in the chapel might be endowed for £20, or one in the aisle for around £15.

Chapel windows

Almost certainly it was Spencer himself who determined the overall programme for the chapel windows, which were again commissioned from Clayton and Bell. All the glass was made in 1891, but unfortunately not in time for consecration day, as the firm had full order books. So for a short time after the chapel's inauguration the windows still contained only plain glass, and both clergy and people (who, we should remember, had been used to having a solid wall on the south side of the old nave, admitting no light) complained of being uncomfortably dazzled by the midday sun from the south.

Naturally, in view of the Chapel's dedication, the theme of its windows was the Gifts of the Spirit. Spencer himself endowed the first one (at the East end) in memory of his mother, Katherine (d.1870). It introduces the series, depicting the Descent of the Spirit, prefigured by the descent of Moses from the holy mountain. Next come two windows given anonymously in memory of 'PBR', a child who had recently died at the age of 3 months. These show respectively the Baptism of Our Lord, with Baptism in church; and Jesus commissioning the disciples, with Confirmation. The fourth window, donated anonymously in memory of the late Revd Andrew C Ramsay, vicar of St Botolph's, Lincoln, shows the call of St Matthias, with Ordination.

The retable and other gifts for the Chapel and Sacristy

Scarcely an issue of the parish magazine went by without gratitude being expressed for one or more gifts towards the chapel's furnishing. Chief among them, of course, were the altar itself, accompanied by a tall wooden retable or 'reredos' (no longer in existence), whose wooden frame and background were designed by GF Bodley, with figures painted by an artist member of the congregation, Miss Ethel Martyn. Some idea of what it looked like can be obtained from grainy old photographs (not shown here), and from a sketch by CM Ellwood in E Hermitage Day's *Some London Churches* (1911). Its iconography is described in the parish magazine for March 1894:

4 lower panels: Isaiah with the living coal from the altar; Jeremiah; Ezekiel with the roll; and Daniel. 4 upper panels: Hosea; Jonah; Zechariah and King David. Centre: the nine orders of angels, conveying the sense of perpetual adoration: Seraphim with red wings; Cherubim with blue wings; two Thrones; Dominions, Virtues and Powers, holding sceptres, spears and bundles of rods (their 'wands of office'); Principalities with lilies; and Angels with staves; and, at the bottom, the three archangels Michael, with Gabriel to the right and Raphael to the left, with a child 'as the guardian child'.

South aisle and west windows *[Plate 1]*

Stained glass for the south aisle followed a quite different programme. First in place, in 1893, was the small Comper window above the font, funded by a donation from 'a small child'. Then, following the sad death in 1893 of Thomas Hill, churchwarden and Trustee, his family endowed a total of six windows in his memory, commissioned from the local artist H Victor Milner whose studio was in Haverstock Hill. The first three to be installed were given by Hill's widow and depict Saints Nicholas, Cecilia and Thomas, all saints associated with music and craftsmanship. The second set of three, given by his sons, depict Saints Stephen, Margaret of Antioch (with a fine red dragon) and Alban. The final window of the south aisle to be filled, the one next to the south porch, depicts St Christopher who, in time-honoured fashion, faces the principal door (in this case, the north door), to greet and protect those entering the church. It too is Milner's work, and was funded from offertories at children's services.

The West window *[Plate 1]*

The overall glazing programme came to a triumphant conclusion three years later, with one of the greatest glories of St Mary's, the three-light west window by Kempe, depicting Our Lady and two glorious angels swinging censers. It was given in memory of the Revd EJ Tompson by his widow Emma, and dedicated in July 1896.

5. Re-fitting the main body of the church

Pulpit
In parallel with these developments the re-fitting of the body of the church continued, beginning with a new pulpit commissioned from Bodley. There was lengthy discussion about where it should be sited because the acoustics of the building were, and still are, notoriously difficult for speakers and listeners alike.[18] The parish tweaked Bodley's original design, for purely practical purposes, so that the steps descend towards the transept. The heraldic shields, added in the time of Percy Dearmer, are separately described below.

Taking stock
Spencer and his energetic Committee still had a large programme of desirable improvements in mind, which included a reredos behind the high altar; choir stalls; the embellishment of the blank capitals to the nave pillars; the extension of the chancel platform a little westward towards the nave; a screen of some kind on this new platform to separate the chancel more effectively from the nave; and finally a new heating system. With funds always tight, the screen was, for the time being, taken off the list, but seems to have been reinstated by at least 1893 when an ornate metalwork screen appears in an archive photograph. By contrast, the two bitter winters of 1891 and 1892 ensured that the overhaul of the old hot-water heating system moved higher up the priority list, and during 1893 a larger boiler was installed.[19] A more dangerous threat than down-draughts was lurking. On 9 February 1893 a fierce gale brought down the gable cross above the east end of the nave, which fell through the roof over the groining of the chapel, fortunately without injuring anyone below.

High altar reredos
GF Bodley, the head of Messrs Bodley and Garner, one of the most celebrated firms of church designers and fitters at the time, who had already designed both the retable for the chapel altar and the pulpit,

was the natural choice to design a much larger reredos for the high altar, and a set of choir stalls. Spencer paid several visits to Bodley's offices in Gray's Inn to discuss the project in person. Bodley advised that it would be best to start with the reredos, since work on that could be done in stages if funding was scarce, the main frame being made first and the decoration added later as finances permitted. The documentation that must once have existed for this work is now lost, but Michael Hall's magisterial study of Bodley shows how such a project would have been managed and run. Initial designs were approved by November 1894.

Artists and craftsmen
Bodley contracted Thomas Martin of Kennington to construct the basic wooden triptych, which was made of a special wood imported from Korea.[20] Painting and gilding was overseen by WO Powell of Lincoln. The main, central portion was the work of Robert Bridgeman of Lichfield, whom again Spencer visited in person. A talented sculptor who had trained with Messrs Rattee and Kett of Cambridge, Bridgeman was a fairly recent addition to Bodley's firmament.[21] He carved in full relief the principal figures of Our Lady, the prophet Isaiah, St John the Baptist and the two flanking angels. On the lowest portion (dismantled in 1915) were the Annunciation, comprising the Angel Gabriel kneeling before Our Lady with attendant angels kneeling one on either side of the main figures and each holding a crowned 'M' (for Mary, Queen of Heaven). Below everything was a gradine (shelf) for six candles, and a 'tabernacle' (which, though a standard design, was never used, as the Blessed Sacrament was not reserved at this time).[22] At the very top of the entire structure stood two magnificent gilded angels. The two hinged side panels were at first left blank, but in 1896 CFM Cleverly, a former pupil of Bodley's, offered to paint six two-dimensional angels to complete the design. To enable the reredos to be fitted into place and its embellishment to continue *in situ*, the high altar was temporarily brought down to below the chancel steps.

As with almost everything else in the church, the cost of the reredos was covered by subscriptions. Friends of the late Fr Fuller had hoped to underwrite the full estimated cost of £300 as a memorial to him, but were unable to raise the entire sum, so they drew back and the cost, or at least the balance of it, became a charge on parish funds.

In the archives is a photograph of the reredos completed to Bodley's original design, which shows how much bigger and bulkier it was than the reredos we see today. The difference is due to Percy Dearmer's intervention in 1915, described in the next chapter. The original background colour was a dark pink typical of Bodley's work. (In the late 1970s, as we shall see, it was changed to the present ivory colour, not without controversy, by Francis Stephens). There is no surviving account of what, if anything, was originally painted on the rear of the folding side panels (which were visible only when the reredos was closed during Lent), but a sketch made by Peter Anson in 1908 shows that by that date the reverse bore the prayer *Bone Pastor, Rex Aeterne, Miserere Miserissimis*: Good Shepherd, King Eternal, Have Mercy on your Most Miserable People.

Choir stalls and re-ordering in the Chancel

In July 1895 an estimate of £200 from Messrs Rattee and Kett of Cambridge (on behalf of Bodley) for making the choir stalls was approved.[23] It was a larger sum than expected but in view of the firm's high reputation it was thought worthwhile. A tender of £134 was also accepted from Thomas Martin (he of the reredos) to bring the stone flooring of the chancel a few feet forward. The entrance to the choir was flanked by wooden 'return stalls' for the clergy, so that for most of the time they sat facing the altar, with their backs to the people. This was not universally liked by the congregation, and had to be defended by the vicar in a long explanatory essay in the parish magazine in September 1895. Worse was to follow when it was objected that the return stalls as originally designed were so high that they obstructed the view of the altar for those seated at the front of the nave and so had to be adjusted. This was not the end of Spencer's ambition for the glorification of the choir and chancel. He suggested in January 1896 that there ought to be a full choir screen and rood. Nothing came of either suggestion at that time, but these ideas would come back into play under the next vicar, Percy Dearmer.

Interior, 1893

The reredos and choir stalls were dedicated by the Bishop of Marlborough at choral Evensong on 7 November 1895. The dossal and hangings of the old altar were disposed of in 1898 to 'a poor parish in the Potteries', and the iron screen and gates that had marked the entrance to the chancel in Fuller's day went at the same time to the church of St Mary's, Charterhouse (Golden Lane).

Organ

All these years of building work left the organ in need of a major clean. While it was out of action a small temporary organ known as a Vocalion was loaned by its inventor, J Baillie-Hamilton, who had been among those present at Thomas Hill's funeral in 1893 recorded below. As his publicity had it: 'The tones are very sweet, and remind one of some of the old organs'.[24]

Carved capitals

The capitals of the pillars on the south side, between the nave and the south aisle, were carved into their present form in 1893 by Messrs Earp & Hobbs who had undertaken the similar work in the chancel and north aisle ten years previously and had also sculpted those in the chapel.

Meeting the needs of the people

Rich and poor

Shortly after Spencer's arrival, the 1891 census would calculate that there were 328 houses and 2327 people in the parish. Whilst it would be true to say that most of the parish residents were middle class, as also were most of those who attended the church, only a few of them were truly well-heeled, and not all those who attended supported the church in proportion to their wealth. In the parish magazine for February 1891, Spencer was prompted to write, 'We have, we are thankful to say, a large number of young men at St Mary's who are earning incomes in the City ... A subscription of five shillings each would bring in a considerable sum'.

The Booth survey of poverty,[25] which in 1889 produced maps colour-coded according to the estimated wealth or poverty of the inhabitants, was reviewed and substantially corroborated in the late 1890s after an interview with the vicar. Only parts of Primrose Hill Road, Elsworthy Road and Harley Road were coded yellow (upper-middle and upper class, rich). Almost all the rest of the parish appeared in pink (fairly well off), purple (mixed), or red (middle-class), but there were patches of light blue (poor) mainly in Erskine Mews,[26] with nothing at all in the lowest categories of dark blue and black. But, as Spencer would soon argue, the position on the ground was a good deal more complex than the survey suggested, since many of the large, mostly semi-detached, houses were subdivided or had rooms let out. The parish well knew that there were (and had been since the District was created) some seriously indigent folk, mostly living in a few pockets of poverty in Oppidans Mews, Erskine Road and Mews, and Ainger Road. 'It may seem,' said Spencer in January 1891 'that there are very few houses in which our poor live, and such is the case, but there are sometimes six or eight families in a house'. They were on the radar of both clergy and laity. Donations were regularly sought from the congregation towards blankets, coal and food for the very poorest, whilst a number of ladies led by Mrs Spencer were appointed as poor-visitors, each responsible for visiting several houses.[27] Additional efforts were made, for example by sponsoring tickets for the soup kitchen in Weedington Road (Kentish Town) when the weather became particularly severe in the winters of 1890/91 and 1891/92.

Domestic servants cannot all be regarded as poor, although most were hardly well-off either. It was estimated that there might be between five and six hundred of them in the parish, and to bring them together a local branch of the Girls' Friendly Society was established, although it took a while to gain a following and required rather careful presentation to the congregation because in some quarters the Society had gained a reputation for (as the vicar put it) 'interfering between the employers and the employed', which might have offended the better-off.

It was partly with the needs of the poor and vulnerable in mind that some of the parish's clubs and societies were set up. The Needlework Society, for example, aimed in part to give poor women useful employment. Its embroidery classes contributed to a significant increase in the number of vestments and hangings donated during Spencer's time as vicar. They included a set of 'festal' vestments, a red set,[28] a red cope and a new superfrontal for the high altar. (This may explain why Spencer found it necessary to write an article[29] stressing that vestments were lawful, as they had been permitted by the rubrics of the first Prayer Book of Edward VI.) A branch of the Band of Hope was established, aiming to dissuade boys from taking to strong drink.[30] Money was also raised for a number of external charities, including the Children's Holiday Fund,[31] and a Working Men's Provident Club was set up by one of Spencer's assistant curates, the Revd Harry Cockson.[32] When he resigned from the parish in 1899 after seven years, to return to his home parish of St Agnes, Liverpool, the grateful Club, as well as the parish, made him a presentation. At about the same time the parish was reported as having given generously to the Lord Mayor's (Boer War) relief fund.[33]

Music, drama and liturgy

> We have no fancy ritual. It is a good, plain, solid English ritual, and we like things done decently and in order. St Mary's is the only church in the district where there is plainsong music at the services.
> *Albert Spencer (interview bound into the parish magazines, 1890-94)*

The church's music, which had suffered a blow with the departure of Bradbury Turner, began to revive under Spencer's first organist, a Mr Marsh about whom little other than his name is known. The magazine for May 1890 reported that on Easter Day the services had been 'hearty and jubilant, and considering the absence of many of the men [of the choir] the music reflected credit on the pains that Mr Marsh has taken with the choir.' Marsh, however, stayed only a few months, and the real revival must be credited to his successor, John Ward (of the Retreat, Haverstock Hill). He was an altogether more experienced organist and choir master, having previously conducted the Henry Leslie choir,[34] and therefore commanded a somewhat higher stipend. He established a dedicated support fund for the choir, and tried out the idea of having men and boys singing alternate verses of psalms and hymns, with the lower and higher voices of the congregation respectively joining them. Choir morale was maintained by outings and concerts, including what became an annual outing to sing carols at the Hampstead workhouse. A separate 'St Cecilia Choir' of ladies, with eventually up to 30 members, was established to sing for services for which the men and boys were not rostered.

In 1890-92 several musical and dramatic events were staged in aid of the church building fund, although little is known about the leading lights other than their names. A Miss Shaw organised the first, in St Peter's Lecture Hall by permission of the Revd Dr Tremlett, with 150 in the audience. Constance Erica organised another at West Hampstead

Town Hall. A year later the church's own John Ward and his daughter Clementine joined the massed voices that sang in a benefit performance by 'well-known artistes, assisted by the Choir of the Albert Hall and others from the neighbourhood' at the Hampstead Conservatoire, where the main work was William Carter's sacred cantata *Placida, the Christian Martyr*. Ward also gave regular organ recitals. At the end of 1891 Kilburn Town Hall was the venue for amateur performances (by members of the congregation) of WS Gilbert's farce *Engaged* preceded by WR Walkes's *A Pair of Lunatics*, which had only recently made its first appearances at the Drury Lane and Avenue theatres in 1889. The large room at the Blind School in Eton Avenue hosted several musical evenings, the first of which featured the choristers of All Saints' Margaret Street. In autumn 1892 Ward established a St Mary's choral society, which met fortnightly at the vicar's house in Primrose Hill Road. This too gave periodic concerts at the Blind School, with additional contributions by other solo artists to make up an evening's entertainment. It seems to have performed mostly lesser-known works, such as J B van Bree's cantata *St Cecilia's Day*.[35]

January 1893 saw the introduction of monthly music lists in the parish magazine – a sign perhaps of the music department's growing self-confidence. But by today's standards the fare on offer was mainly an unambitious diet of Stainer and plainsong.

Ward retired in 1897 after seven years, and was presented with a clock by the gentlemen of the choir.[36] His successor, Arthur E Godfrey, was another experienced choir master and composer, and is reported to have brought some of his existing choir with him to boost numbers. He mounted occasional musical entertainments in the Church Room and maintained Ward's tradition of organ recitals. In 1898, through the good offices of Arthur Hill, Thomas's son and like him a stalwart member of the congregation, two further stops were added to the organ, funded by the proceeds from a choir concert.

Thomas Hill's funeral

One of the most remarkable musical events St Mary's has ever seen was the funeral of the church's great benefactor, Thomas Hill. A founder member of the church and supplier of its organ, an early and revered churchwarden (until 1886) and Trustee (until his death), Hill died aged 71 on 22 October 1893. Without the new chapel and aisle it would have been impossible to accommodate all who attended his funeral, one of the saddest but also most glorious events ever held at St Mary's. The service was attended not only by many from the regular congregation and about a hundred staff from Hill's organ works but also by the cream of England's organists: Dr Alan Gray (Trinity College Cambridge), Dr Bridge (Westminster Abbey), Dr Monk (lately of York Minster), Dr Stegall, Dr Creser (Chapel Royal, St James's), Mr Hoyte (All Saints', Margaret Street), J Baillie Hamilton and many others. Afterwards, almost all of them followed the coffin on foot to Hampstead Cemetery (Fortune Green). To underline the esteem in which Hill was held nationally, the March 'In Saul' was played in his honour at Westminster Abbey on the afternoon of his funeral, and special music was also performed in Trinity College Chapel, Cambridge.[37]

Ritual still a minefield

Disputes over ritual in the Anglican church (although not this time at St Mary's) continued throughout Spencer's time as vicar. Most famously, Archbishop Benson's Judgement in a case against the Bishop of Lincoln, Edmund King, in 1890, went further than the earlier position of the Privy Council by allowing: (1) the mixing of water and wine in the chalice, provided it were done before the communion service and not as part of the ceremonial; (2) eastward-facing celebration of the eucharist, but only if the people could see the priest's gestures; (3) the singing of the Agnus Dei; and (4) the use of lighted candles on the altar provided their lighting itself was not done during the service. However, the use of the sign of the cross at the Absolution and for the Blessing were held to be illegal.[38]

As soon as Mandell Creighton succeeded Frederick Temple as Bishop of London in 1897, John Kensit and the low-church party began to lobby him against Romeward-leaning clergy. Creighton lamented that, as in an earlier generation, his episcopal postbag was brimming with accusations and spies' reports. He frequently stated his opposition to prosecutions and persecutions. Indeed, he rather welcomed a degree of diversity of expression and, like Temple before him, wished to proceed only by persuasion and example. But he came to feel that Temple's non-interventionist policy (which had so benefited St Mary's under Fuller) had encouraged a parish-by-parish individuality that was confusing to the lay person. This applied not only to ritual and ceremony, but to the more fundamental question of the use, non-use or only partial use of the Prayer Book and its rubrics.

Bishop Temple, though he later regretted the decision, had allowed additional collects and forms of prayer to be used on Black Letter days in the calendar (those for which no provision was made in the Prayer Book). Creighton withdrew this dispensation on the grounds that it was not fitting for an individual bishop to authorise deviations from the approved Book. He felt strongly that, without going so far as to impose complete uniformity of ceremonial, he should ensure that services throughout his diocese, as throughout the Church of England as the national church, should be recognisable and comprehensible to everyone. On that basis, the policy he progressively laid down for his clergy, through deanery and diocesan conferences, was that (a) the Prayer Book *in its entirety*, without selection, omission or addition, was to be the accepted norm; (b) Holy Communion (not to be termed 'mass') was to be celebrated strictly in accordance with the Prayer Book; (c) whenever possible Morning and Evening Prayer were to be said daily in church by the clergy; (d) Confession was not a requirement in the Prayer Book, and therefore must not be promoted by the clergy or be seen as a necessary prerequisite to Confirmation.

Those like Spencer who were accustomed to a rich liturgy, albeit firmly within the scope of the Prayer Book and without leaning towards Rome, were disappointed that Creighton appeared to be adopting an essentially low-church view on many issues, and in anticipation of wider attacks Spencer wrote a number of defensive articles in the parish magazine in the autumn of 1898, for example on the use of communion wafers instead of everyday bread and the use of the mixed chalice (with water added to the wine) in accordance with ancient practice. He feared, correctly, that other practices such as the reservation of the Sacrament for the sick would soon come under attack, and his sense of foreboding was heightened when, in order to standardise practice across the diocese, Creighton ordered the Ten Commandments to be read at every eucharist.

On the eve of his departure for a year's leave of absence in 1899 (see below), Spencer issued, through the parish magazine, a rallying cry to his congregation to be ready to defend the historic practices of the church in a practical way by supporting the efforts of the English Church Union.[39] Not long afterwards, as further testimony to the way the wind was blowing, the Archbishops in 1899 issued new requirements for the ordering of churches and their liturgy. Incense could be used, but only if burnt in a static container to sweeten the air before a service, not swung in procession or used to cense objects or people. (They were not to be sprinkled with water either.) Pictures and images were acceptable, but candles must not be lit in front of them. The reservation of consecrated elements, principally for the communion of the sick, was wholly disallowed. Six months into his leave Spencer wrote that this 'does not touch our practice at St Mary's', but he remained on the watch.

Creighton's diary was impossibly full, and the diocese of London was so large that there was no question of his attending every parish at all regularly. He let it be known that he would not accept routine requests to attend or preach at patronal festivals, harvest festivals and the like. Whilst he insisted that he alone had the authority and responsibility for the diocese, and that this was not delegated to his suffragans,[40] in practice episcopal oversight for St Mary's, and more regular attendance at its festivals, was still delegated to the Bishop of Marlborough.

Trends in church attendance

After its sharp decline in Fuller's last years, congregational attendance at St Mary's grew appreciably during Spencer's time as vicar. It was reported to the Archdeacon's Visitation in 1890 (before the Chapel of the Holy Spirit was built) that over Passiontide and Easter 'the church has been quite full, and the powers of our energetic churchwardens and sidesmen have been taxed to the utmost to provide accommodation for the worshippers'. The total of annual communions in Fr Fuller's final years is not recorded. In better days, back in 1887, it had reached 3941 but then, according to several reports, tailed off. Under Spencer numbers rose dramatically, reaching a peak of 6942 in 1896.

Table of annual communicant figures 1874-1900

Year	Communions
1873	--
1874	3995
1875	3481
1876	3725
1877	3502
1878	3721
1879	3294
1880	2969
1881	3045
1882	--
1883	--
1884	3162
1885	3573
1886	3579
1887	3941
1888	3418
1889	--
1890	--
1891	4732
1892	5653
1893	5748
1894	6447
1895	6453
1896	6942
1897	6851
1898	6626
1899	6920
1900	6519

Some of this increase is accounted for simply by a recovery from the doldrums, some no doubt by people's desire to try out the newly extended church, but much was due to the sheer hard work of Spencer, his assistant clergy and leading lay members of the congregation in making St Mary's a more welcoming place. By the mid 1890s it was developing a reputation as a child-friendly church,[41] and there were other useful innovations. For example, when the new vestry was completed those who cared to cycle to church were invited to bring their machines to the vestry door, for the verger to take them in and care for them during the service.[42]

Much emphasis was placed on the children, and in February 1896 Spencer was ahead of the game when he introduced Catechism according to the newly published system in use at St Sulpice in Paris. A Communicants' Guild was also established, to encourage attendance and devotion among its young members and halt the teenage drift away from church, which was already common. This Guild, rather like the GFS, seems to have been slow to catch on.[43] In winter, general attendance at church (and therefore income) was critically dependent on the weather. Ice, snow and fog could seriously reduce attendance, and in the two consecutive severe winters of 1891 and 1892 numbers were correspondingly down, whereas in the mild winter of 1894 they were buoyant.

What the above figures do not show is that during the later 1890s St Mary's, in common with most of the diocese, began to experience a gradual decline in total attendance. A six-day working week was not at all uncommon for men, and as Sunday was the only day off it was also the only opportunity they had for recreation and spending time with their families. Of course, that had been true from the beginnings of St Mary's, but now the opportunities to do something about it were growing. More people were taking up cycling; and quite widely in London the better-off joined the fashionable weekend exodus from the city. Strategies were considered for attracting more people to church, including making the services shorter, earlier or less formal, even having more of a 'concert' air about them, but none of these met with the congregation's approval. By the late 1890s, even though the number of communicants was still healthy, Spencer had begun to wonder publicly whether 'the unrest in religious matters, the differences and disputes, not only about ritual and outward things but about the very essentials of our faith have unsettled the minds of some?'[44]

There were always many more communicants at the early celebration on a Sunday, because few were minded to fast until late morning in order to communicate at the Sung Eucharist. Spencer's views on this were neither consistent nor clear. On the one hand he berated those, especially the young and fit, who came only to the later service: 'We cannot deprecate too strongly the habit that some young people have, who appear to be healthy and strong, of receiving at the later celebration.' On the other hand, as the Prayer Book required there to be at least three communicants before the Communion could be offered,[45] he also regretted that there were few communicants at this later, solemn celebration. In an endeavour to encourage more, he moved the sermon from its slot between Matins and the Sung Eucharist into the eucharist proper.[46] The congregation, however, did as they pleased, and there was a lot of coming and going, with some attending Matins only, some staying up to the Sermon in the Sung Eucharist, and others staying the whole course.[47]

On other points of order Spencer was prone to issue stern reminders, for example that in accordance with traditional practice the men should come up to receive communion first and the women only after that. He also expressed his disappointment on two other counts: that there were often only two or three regulars in attendance for the daily celebrations on weekdays, and that many of those who had communicated at the early morning service on a Sunday and who then came back for Matins, did not stay on for the Sung Eucharist that followed. For a short time he tried starting the daily celebration half an hour later on Wednesdays, but this was not a success and the regular pattern was restored. Another experiment was an occasional evening celebration with a period of instruction for those unable to get to the normal morning services.[48]

A major drive for spiritual revival was made in 1895 through a parish mission, carefully prepared in advance and led by the Revd T R Willacy of Thorganby, Yorkshire.[49] The vicar lamented in the magazine that the better-off members of the congregation tended to stay away from such events! But the life of St Mary's was not all strait-laced. There was an annual party on Boxing Day night and regular summer outings for the choir, the youth and the mothers.

The Church Room

The plot of land between King Henry's Road and Elsworthy Road on which St Mary's church was built was never large enough to accommodate a church hall, nor were any other premises available for the meetings and secular activities that any congregation and its wider community require. In order to house the Sunday schools and other meetings, Fr Fuller, at his own charge, had rented premises at 77 Regent's Park Road. But after his retirement he declined a request from the parish to continue using the premises. At the very start of his ministry, therefore, Spencer had to make repeated ad hoc arrangements for every kind of meeting, or else (as in the case of the Choral Society) host them in his own house. As he had plans to expand the Sunday school and clubs, this was distinctly frustrating. So, soon after his arrival, he set about looking for at least a temporary solution. An architect member of the congregation, Mr F Eiloart, was deputed to ask the London and North Western Railway if it would rent to the parish a house it occupied just across the road from the church door in King Henry's Road. How convenient that would have been! But, perhaps still smarting from its earlier dispute over subsidence, the Company would not oblige. Fortunately Spencer, who had quickly mastered the geography of his new parish, had become aware of a vacant four-roomed house at 9 Oppidans Mews, in a part of the parish already identified as having pockets of poverty, and over which Mrs Spencer and Mrs Cancellor were the designated poor-visitors. Although the house was small it offered a speedy and sensible temporary solution for the church's needs, and by early 1890 the parish began to rent it. For larger gatherings such as Christmas parties the private schoolroom of the Revd & Mrs Cherill, at 123 Adelaide Road was used.

Of course what was really needed was a church hall. But in the first half of the 1890s the main focus of the congregation's fund-raising effort had to be the completion and fitting-out of the church itself. At the Easter Vestry of 1895 alarm was expressed that, with 120 children now on the Sunday school's roll, the church was running out of accommodation, and that meetings were being held in strange if not unsavoury places, including a coach house and even a stable.

At the back of a large garden off Oppidans Mews were two plots of land owned by Eton College and let to separate tenants, both of whom proved willing to surrender their leases to the church. The site was large enough to hold a new purpose-built 'Church Room' – it was not normally referred to as the 'parish hall' until much later. There were also two cottages on the site, capable of adaptation to house the church's verger in return for his taking on additional responsibility as caretaker of the Room. Eton College agreed, and in 1896 the ever bountiful Spencer offered to lend the parish, at a reasonable rate of interest, the entire sum of £700 required to buy the lease and meet the legal costs. There were 68 years to run on the lease, and the reasonable assumption at that time was that when it expired in 1964 there would be no difficulty in renewing. The scheme eventually adopted was for a main building comprising one large Room (55 x 30 ft) with a sliding partition to divide it in two as necessary, two smaller meeting rooms and a kitchen. With the refurbishment of the two cottages, the total cost was around £3,000.

Spencer invited the Archdeacon to encourage further generous donations at a special public meeting. A dedicated Fund was set up and trustees for the Room were appointed – initially the Vicar and the two churchwardens – to oversee first the building project and then the running of the new facility. Building proceeded rapidly, and the St Mary's Church Room was officially opened by the Bishop of Marlborough on 19 December 1896.

No time was lost in putting it to good use: for Sunday Schools, concerts, dramatic presentations, clubs, indoor sports, parties and meetings of all kinds. And as expected the Room's very existence opened the way for new activities, including a St Mary's branch of the Church Lads' Brigade. Some of the events staged there, such as concerts by the St

Mary's Choral Society, were themselves fund-raising efforts. The Room was supported by occasional offertory collections from the church, but principally by the donations of individuals. It took a full ten years, until 1906, to pay off the debt on the building. The regular running costs for cleaning, re-painting and heating the premises were borne by the parish.

Mrs Spencer's illness and Spencer's retirement

For the first five or six years of Spencer's ministry at St Mary's his wife's health passes unmentioned, and as we have seen she was fit enough to engage actively in parish work, entertaining and keeping open house and heading up the parish's ministry to the poor and deprived. But in August 1897 an ominous note in the parish magazine thanked everyone for their flowers and expressions of concern during the Spencers' 'late anxiety'. This, alas, proved to be the resurgence of Ellen's mental illness, and from early in 1898 Spencer had to take a ten-week break from parish duties in order to accompany her first to Menton on the French Riviera and then to San Remo (Italy) and Locarno (Switzerland). Any benefit to her health was unfortunately transitory, and he seriously considered resigning. But Ellen herself persuaded him to discuss the whole matter with Bishop Creighton, and as a result he was granted a year's leave of absence from Easter 1899, during which he again took her to a succession of spas and health resorts, first in Britain and then abroad. As if arranging all that was not stressful enough, he was dealt a double blow when not one but both of his curates for the past seven years, Harry Cockson and JH Giles, announced that they were to move on. Cockson in particular was well liked, having done sterling work with the men of the parish. On the eve of his departure he was accorded the honour of preaching at St Paul's cathedral, and used the occasion to urge everyone, in view of the current disciplinary turmoil within the Church, to be charitable to those with opposing views. He went on to be senior curate of St Agnes, Liverpool. Giles's move was more local. But this meant that neither of the men with direct experience of St Mary's was available to serve as priest-in-charge during Spencer's absence. The Vicar therefore had to turn to old friends to help him out. He invited the Revd R M Fulford from the Exeter diocese to be 'Curate in Charge'. An architect who had become a lay reader before eventually being ordained later in life, Fulford had served in Crediton, as well as in Australia and then as rector of St Andrew's, Grenada (West Indies), from where he had been repatriated after contracting a fever. To assist Fulford, Spencer engaged a young ordained Keble graduate, WR Milns. Further complications arose in the autumn of 1899 when the elderly incumbent of Crediton asked Fulford to return urgently to help him, a request he felt unable to refuse. Spencer had little choice but to let him go, and so for the remaining months of his leave enlisted the help of the Revd S Hosking.

The Spencers returned to St Mary's as planned at Easter 1900, but all was very far from well. The vicar ceased to contribute his usual letter to the parish magazine throughout the summer, and in September he formally announced his intention of resigning at the end of the year. In his farewell letter he said about the services in church: 'I have always tried to make them dignified and reverent, in accordance with what I have believed to be the best traditions of the English Church, in strict loyalty to the spirit of our Prayer Book, without any following of modern Roman custom.'

One measure of the extent to which his efforts were supported is the level of congregational giving. It has been calculated that during his time as Vicar the parish raised a total of £22,000, half of it through collections and the remainder through donations, sales of work and other ad hoc initiatives, and that over £3,000 of this was given to external causes, especially to the mission field for which a Missionary Association was established. The annual total from collections which stood at £300 in 1889 had by 1899 risen to £1,000.

The cab rank

Soon into his ministry at St Mary's, in the early 1890s, Albert Spencer organised funding for a Primrose Hill shelter, just beside the church, for the local cabmen who parked their two-wheeled 'growlers', and often the odd, classier, 2-wheeled hansom there. Geoffrey Dearmer (a boy at the time), remembered this being 'one of the highlights of the parish.'[50] It remained in place until the 1950s. 'The roads were so dirty that, but for the crossing sweeper who ploughed a furrow through the mud from the cab rank to the north door, our boots would have been filthy all through the year... Attached to the shelter was 'the only public convenience within miles.' There was a stone trough to water the horses, with a cup for people. Mrs Dampier, an elderly resident of Elsworthy Road, used to organise a yearly Christmas dinner for the drivers, at which a bunch of carrots was provided for each horse and a muffler for each driver. Violet and Elsie Blaiklock from the congregation would assist as waitresses, while their father played the piano.

On hearing of Spencer's retirement from the parish the cabmen paid him a touching tribute, subscribing to present him with a handsome silver inkstand.

Appreciations

The Spencers, for a while at least, retained their house in Primrose Hill Road, and Spencer offered his services as an occasional assistant to his successor at St Mary's. They eventually retired to Exeter where, to mark their earlier ministry in the city, they named their house St Sidwell's. Albert Spencer died in 1913 and, as we shall see, St Mary's then refurbished and extended the Church Room in memory of this beloved priest. Percy Dearmer wrote the following tribute to his predecessor, Albert Spencer:

> He belonged to the best type of English priest, that type which other nations recognise as being the peculiar strength of our Church. He was in touch with all classes and all the varied interests of human life, devoted to his priestly work, a thorough organiser, a most successful manager of finance, a strenuous Catholic, sympathetic and tolerant to others, loyal to the Prayer Book and to the English Church, a simple

and humble-minded Christian. He won from all who knew him an instinctive affection and trust…

He was the second founder of St Mary's. Much as we owe to the early work of Mr Fuller, St Mary's as we know it is mainly Mr Spencer's creation. He came to be the Vicar at a most difficult time, when few men could have succeeded as he did in turning a dismal failure into a splendid success. The congregation had largely disappeared, the church was nearly empty; there was nothing definite about it but the unfinished walls and a heavy debt. Mr. Spencer cheerfully accepted the burden, drew helper after helper to his side, filled the church with an enthusiastic and devout congregation, and between 1889 and 1901 had raised £22,000; he built the south aisle and chapel, the vestries, reredos, Church Room and Verger's house, and established the whole parochial organisation with an efficiency that his successors can only aspire to maintain. What he did privately for countless individual souls can never be recorded.[51]

In 1934 the then vicar of St Mary's, the Revd Anthony Hardcastle, visited St Sidwell's church in Exeter where he found 'a conspicuous wall brass, depicting Mr Spencer in eucharistic vestments, … kneeling with hands raised, in an attitude somewhat reminiscent of the old pictures of St Gregory having his vision at Mass.' It is especially good to have that testimony because St Sidwell's was destroyed by bombing in 1942.

* * *

Other lives

Revd WM McGrath (Magrath) (curate 1890-92), having been from the age of 20, before theological training, one of the lay brothers ('Brother Dunstan') at Llanthony and a close associate of Fr Ignatius (Joseph Leycester Lyne), kept returning there, even during and after his curacy at St Mary's, 1890-92. He preached *ex tempore* and with evangelical zeal. He was one of the two people to see the controversial apparition of the Blessed Sacrament at Llanthony, and was the priest who officiated at Fr Ignatius's funeral.

Endnotes

1. LPL: Fulham Papers, Temple 16, fo. 362.
2. *Totnes Weekly Times*, 6 Nov 1886. *Exeter and Plymouth Gazette*, 8 Nov. [British Newspaper Library]
3. Press interview bound into PM, 1890-94.
4. LPL: Fulham Papers, Temple 30, fos 293 ff.
5. See *CT* report of consecration, 1892.
6. His address in *Crockfords 1892* was 30 Primrose Hill Road.
7. PM, Apr 90.
8. See Saunders, Matthew, 'Appreciating Victorian Arts and Crafts stained glass. A battle half won', in *Ecclesiology Today* 40 (July 2008), pp. 83-91. Alfred Bell lived in Hampstead and the firm's HQ was in Regent Street: Larkworthy, Peter, *Clayton and Bell, stained glass artists and decorators* (1984).
9. The supplier of the one at SMVPH is not recorded. The Newstead original, manufactured in the Netherlands, had been lost at the Reformation but after being rediscovered and given to Southwell Minster in the early 19th century it was already proving a popular model for reproductions. Other benefactors provided new cassocks and surplices for the choir and promised a white silk chasuble, alms bags, book markers, a maniple, veil and burse.
10. PM, Jan 1892.
11. PM, Mar 1892.
12. *H&H*, 18 October 1890 judged the vestry 'a handsome addition to the church'.
13. LPL: Fulham Papers, Temple 16 fo.366.
14. LMA: GLC/AR/BR/22/BA/003084.
15. More precise figures were given in December when Fr Spencer applied to the London Diocesan Fund for a grant. The estimated population of the parish was only 2390. The original building seated 489 and the extension would increase that by 166. The estimated cost was £2600 of which £960 had been raised in the parish and £380 from outside including £75 from the Incorporated Church Building Society and £33 from the Diocesan Church Building Society. The shortfall was then £1260. (LMA: DL/A/C/MS19244/449). These figures proved remarkably accurate. The final cost was £2451-17-7 plus architects £144-19-7 (LMA: P81/MRV/139). By December 1892 the total costs of aisle, chapel and sacristy were £2,668 compared with an estimate of £2,199. Partly because the chapel and vestry were larger than estimated 'owing to a mistake made in the drawings by the architect PM Dec 1892. The overall cost of the building work was £3260 (PM, Jan 1897).
16. PM, Jan 1892.
17. On 9 November the Committee gave the green light to building the priest's vestry [sacristy] and ambulatory as part of the same overall project while the builders were on site. LMA: P81/MRV/139.
18. There was already some kind of pulpit in the church, but it is nowhere described or depicted in a photograph. See the terrier of 1889-90 in LMA: P81/MRV/21.
19. As has been borne out by experience, cold down-draughts were unlikely ever to be prevented in a lofty building like St Mary's with so many windows.
20. *H&H*, 9 Nov 1895, cost: £415. He was later also commissioned to extend the stone chancel platform.
21. See Hall, Michael, *George Frederick Bodley and the later Gothic Revival in Britain and America* (2014).

22   I am grateful to John Hawes for this point.
23   Progress was slower than hoped when Bodley became ill: PM, Mar 95.
24   PM, Sep 1895.
25   Records held at the London School of Economics. Maps and notes available online.
26   According to Camden History Society, *Streets of Belsize* (2009) p. 36, the housing in Elsworthy Rise and Lower Merton Rise was designed principally for tradesmen, shopkeepers and stable men.
27   Mrs Spencer and Mrs F Cancellor (Oppidans Mews); Mrs Avarne (Erskine Road and Mews); Mrs Cherril (Ainger Road 1-4); Miss Batterbury (Ainger Road 5-7); and Mrs Snow for the parish's Caretakers.
28   John Hawes points out that the red High Mass set were for ordinary use, as at the time the parish followed the Sarum practice of wearing red for virtually all Sundays outside Eastertide.
29   PM, May 1894.
30   The temperance movement was a cause particularly close to Bishop Temple's heart. See Aitken, W F, *Frederick Temple, Archbishop of Canterbury* (1901), p.94.
31   PM, Jun 1891.
32   PM, 1895.
33   Sheppard, Martin, *Primrose Hill: A History* (Lancaster 2013), p.188.
34   Information from a press interview by Spencer bound into the parish magazines 1890-94. Henry David Leslie was a renowned musical pioneer of the day.
35   PM, Jun 1893.
36   *H&H*, 23 Oct 1897.
37   *H&H*, 4 Nov 1893.
38   See, for example, Carpenter, Edward, *Cantuar: the Archbishops in their office* (1971).
39   PM, Feb 1899.
40   Hinchliff, Peter, *Frederick Temple, Archbishop of Canterbury: a life* (Oxford 1998).
41   PM, Jan 1895.
42   PM, Jul 1896.
43   PM, Sep 1894; Jan 1896.
44   PM, Jan 1899.
45   PM, Mar 1896.
46   PM, Jan 1895.
47   PM, Jan 1899.
48   PM, Feb 1892.
49   Full description, PM, Jan 1896.
50   PM, Oct 1970, Mar 1980, Feb 1987.
51   PM, Jan 1914.

Chapter 4

Revd Percy Dearmer

Vicar, 1901-1915

Appointment and background

In succession to Fr Spencer the Trustees presented to the bishop the Revd Percy Dearmer, who had previously achieved some notice as author of the *Parson's Handbook* (1899). This was an imaginative, if risky appointment. He had not yet had overall charge of a parish. Nor would it have been to everyone's liking that he had firm socialist, or at least *Christian* Socialist, credentials as a leading member of the Christian Social Union (CSU) and secretary of its London Branch. He was still a young man (33), of markedly aesthetic tastes, and was an established journalist and writer as well as a priest. After reading history at Christ Church, Oxford, he had served an attachment at the college's Mission in Poplar during the London dock strike of 1889, an experience that strengthened his awareness of the need for social action among people of all classes and circumstances. After completing his theological training at Oxford he was ordained deacon in 1891, and soon afterwards, despite opposition from the parents on both sides, he married Mabel White, who had been training as an artist at Sir Hubert Herkomer's art school in Bushey. The rest of the '90s were spent in curacies and part-time clergy posts whose stipends were so meagre that as he and Mabel began to raise a young family their income had to be supplemented, from writing on his part and art on hers. This, and his continuing voluntary work for bodies such as the CSU, led some of his superiors to believe

Revd Percy Dearmer

he might be more interested in being a writer and a socialist than a full-time parish priest, but that was unjust. Strains on the marriage, from financial uncertainty and pressure of work, are strongly hinted at in Mabel's (only semi-fictional) novel *The Difficult Way*, where the priest at the centre of the story is asked by a doctor: 'My dear sir, why, if you hadn't private means, did you take Orders? It is a matter of common knowledge that the thing is impossible'. He replies, 'I had a call… I knew – God!'

As both historian and priest, Dearmer was professionally interested in the liturgy and ordering of the Church of England, subjects mired in controversy for much of the nineteenth-century, particularly with regard to ritualism. It was already a crowded field of research, and his intention was mostly to get to grips with the copious output of others and use his journalistic skills to synthesise and present it in a more popular voice. So the *Parson's Handbook* was derived mainly from other people's research, including the earliest publications of the Alcuin Club (estd. 1897). Arthur Duncan-Jones would later put it this way: that Dearmer 'fashioned into one sustained and impressive argument the devoted labours of so many of the first scholars of the English Church'.[1] Dearmer became convinced that vestments, ceremonial and colour in the liturgy all had lawful, and importantly *English* roots, traceable in the rubrics of the First Prayer Book of Edward VI (1549), and ultimately in the tradition of the medieval church in England. The Reformation, by associating much church practice of the day with the foreign power and doctrine of Rome and branding it superstitious, had engendered long-lasting fears among church-goers and non-churchgoers alike, that resonated down to Dearmer's time. His overriding commitment was to ensure that everything offered as a contribution to the worship of God must be a thing of beauty. None but the finest craftsmen in their respective fields should be employed.

* * *

St Mary's Primrose Hill was High Church, certainly, but by no means Rome-ward leaning, thanks to Spencer's work of building and consolidation. It must have seemed to Dearmer a suitable setting for testing the ideas in his *Handbook*. But it would be cynical to see that as his primary reason for wanting the preferment. He had already made abundantly clear that if Christianity were to have any contemporary meaning it must be rooted in social justice, through which all must receive due reward, respect and recognition for their labour, and this had to be reflected even in the liturgy and ornaments of the Church. So he was first and foremost a man with a Gospel to proclaim, not simply one with a *Handbook* to promote.

To many a priest sizing up St Mary's in 1901 it would surely have seemed that, after Spencer's noble efforts, nothing much else needed to be done by way of building or furnishing. To Dearmer though, the work of beautification still had to *begin*. Quite a few things made him shudder on sight – the monumentality of Bodley's reredos and the way it cut out light from the chancel; the plain, dark brick walls which were at best a poor backdrop for the ornaments and works of art he hoped to introduce; the ugly gas heating equipment that not only generated dust but also left an unpleasant smell in the air. There were practical niggles too, such as Manning 'mistake' (as Dearmer later called it) in providing not just one but two steps up at the communion rail, and the gradines (shelves for candles and flowers) introduced behind the high altar. He must have sensed straight away that it would take some time to convince the congregation about all the changes he wanted to see. But surely he could not have imagined it would take the whole of a fourteen-year ministry, that several of his dearest wishes would be thwarted, or that he would undergo bouts of depression on the way.

Implementing the *Parson's Handbook*

Nan Dearmer (his second wife), in her biography, suggests that Percy felt a pang of conscience about introducing changes too quickly for the congregation, in order to make St Mary's compliant with the *Handbook*. He did indeed introduce some changes almost from day one, such as the removal of the gradines, the recruitment of a plainsong expert as director of music, changes to the 'choir dress' of ministers at Matins and Evensong, and full attention to the rubrics of the Book of Common Prayer, to which he was attached as by an umbilical cord. Doubtless he also insisted on greater punctiliousness on the part of choir, servers and all who had a starring role in the services. Other changes we shall pick up in due course.[2] But the major changes usually associated with Dearmer's name were not in fact undertaken immediately, nor simply bulldozed through. Throughout his ministry he sought to explain and prepare the way for his proposals, and although Nan hints that he lost a few of the congregation on the way, others speak of how he earned their trust even if it took them a while to adapt.

Not everything changed. The general pattern of services laid down by Fr Spencer (who for a while remained in the parish and assisted occasionally, before eventually retiring to Malvern) was continued. And for the Dearmers' first year a lot of energy was in any case taken up with other things. As there was still no vicarage, finding a home was their first challenge. Emily Mulholland, a staunch supporter of the Christian Social Union who had already opened her home to the Dearmers in the 1890s, decided to follow them to Primrose Hill, where she bought a large house at 102 Adelaide Road and invited Percy, Mabel and their two sons Geoffrey and Christopher to lodge with her until they could find a house of their own. It was only a short stay, and as early as July 1901 they moved to 11 Chalcot Gardens, off England's Lane. But then there was the important question of how to make ends meet financially. As in Spencer's day, the vicar's stipend continued to be half the parish offerings, which now meant that Dearmer's share averaged something over £300p.a., plus a £50p.a. grant from Eton College. This was hardly enough for a family of four to live on comfortably while paying school fees and the wages of domestic staff, so Percy's journalism and writing had to be kept up despite the demands of full-time ministry.

Some hoped-for developments were always going to take time. He wanted, for example, to make the church surroundings, as well as its interior, more attractive, but first he had to enlist the help of his old friend from Oxford days, Lord Beauchamp, as an adviser and supplier of trees and shrubs from his estate at Madresfield (Worcestershire). Planning for the garden began at once, but it was 1902 before planting could begin. (That was also the year in which Lord Beauchamp married. He and Lady Beauchamp, of whom we shall hear more, would then worship regularly at St Mary's when they were in London on official business; they would remain generous benefactors to the parish throughout Dearmer's time and beyond.) Other kinds of change required careful presentation, above all the introduction of incense. And lastly, there were longer-term changes that could only be implemented when the necessary funds could be raised, and it was this that served as the most powerful brake on Dearmer's ambitions.

Although the staggering amount of fund-raising required for building the church itself was effectively over when the Dearmers arrived, and the last of the debt on the building was finally paid off in June 1901, the parish's financial outlook was not at all rosy. And quite apart from any changes Dearmer might wish to make, unexpected heavy expenditure was required in his first decade as vicar, including major outlay on the organ and on a new heating system. In 1907 the Revd J Walker, rector of St Columb Major, Cornwall, whom Dearmer described as 'a friend', generously offered his house at 7 Elsworthy Road as a vicarage for St Mary's. The negotiations by which this was vested in the Ecclesiastical Commissioners, who bought the freehold, took some time,[3] and although the offer itself was without cost to the parish, significant expenditure was incurred for decoration and fitting out. Amid such financial distractions, one of his projected reforms after another was discussed but then put on hold, including boarding the nave ceiling, erecting a chancel screen and installing electric lighting.

Percy and Mabel were both keen cyclists, and continued Spencer's policy of encouraging cyclists to ride to church and leave their machines in the vestry. Other efforts were made to welcome churchgoers and tempt passers-by to look in. While the trees were on order from Madresfield the Guild of Handicrafts was commissioned to provide new external notice boards. And, as if to counteract any impression that the church leaned towards the pious and austere, Dearmer quickly reminded everyone, through the parish magazine, that the Lenten fast did not include Sundays! Thriving social institutions, mostly inherited from Fr Spencer, continued with little change. These included the Girls' Friendly Society, the Church of England Temperance Society, the Band of Hope, Girls' and Mothers' Clubs, a Working Men's Club and (new) a Men's Guild – a Women's Guild would follow in 1906. For these, as well as the large programme of regular church services, Dearmer relied heavily on a team of up to four part-time assistant clergy, and lay assistants.

Ritual and ritualism

Incense, which had not been used by Fr Spencer, was clearly permitted under the Archbishops' new regulations. Dearmer waited almost a full year – appropriately enough until the Feast of the Epiphany 1902 – to burn incense for the first time, non-ceremonially before the service. There was no voluble protest, neither would there be any looking back, and it was used in the same way every Sunday thereafter. At around this time the Revd the Hon WE Bowen, presenting evidence on Contemporary Ritualism to members of both Houses of Parliament, alluded to the *Parson's Handbook* when he wrote: 'I question whether there would be a case against the Rev Percy Dearmer, Vicar of St Mary the Virgin Primrose Hill, who has conducted a most accurate and scientific investigation into what precisely were the externals in vogue during that greatly debated second year of King Edward VI.'

Even so, Dearmer knew that the atmosphere was still tense, and that he could be ensnared if he set a foot wrong. In 1902 the Kilburn branch of the National Protestant Church Union, without even approaching him, complained to the Bishop of London[4] about ritual practices at

St Mary's. *The Times* of 15 October 1902 carried a response from the bishop that whilst he was always ready to hear complaints from members of a parish or congregation he did not regard the NPCU as in any way representative of the church as a whole. The following February he honoured St Mary's with a whole day's visit, and it was with his express permission that the controversial service of Tenebrae again took place at St Mary's in Holy Week. In this highly charged environment members of the congregation were encouraged, as under Spencer, to sign up to the English Church Union. And since Arthur Hill, one of the Trustees and later a churchwarden, was Secretary of its Hampstead Branch it was natural that the parish should host the ECU's AGM in 1903.

From 1904 to 1906 a Royal Commission on Ecclesiastical Discipline took evidence from many witnesses. Its voluminous proceedings include page after page of reports from agents of the Church Association and others seeking to entrap ritualist clergy. Percy Dearmer would have made a good catch indeed if they had been able to trip him up, and they again tried their best, sending spies to services at St Mary's on two occasions in June and July 1904 to note down in the most minute detail everything that went on, and to add their own comments and interpretations. As in Fuller's time one marvels at their grasp of the jargon and technical language of ritual and ceremony and of the significance (real or alleged) of ornaments, vestments and gestures they so hated. Their evidence, despite errors and overstatement, provides welcome documentation of the parish's liturgy at the time. But they tended to tie themselves in knots over detail. Dearmer submitted a written rebuttal, but also attended in person to give evidence to the Commission (which included the Archbishop of Canterbury). He acquitted himself without much difficulty, deploying here and there a degree of 'fogging' that would have done credit to a modern politician, correcting mistaken observations, and even making the witnesses look foolish. In response to one charge that at a certain point in the eucharist he had placed his elbows on the altar, he quipped: 'I cannot remember the exact position of my elbows on 23rd June, but the implied suggestion that there was some kind of ceremony going on is false.'

Meanwhile at St Mary's he had started introducing changes dear to his heart. Plainsong Office Hymns were brought in at Matins and Evensong. Sunday morning services began to take significantly longer. Conrad Noel (see below), his main Sunday assistant at this time, later admitted that he found the experience 'a little marred for me by its too rigid adherence to the Prayer Book rite with its dislocated canon and Dearmer's insistence on reading one of the lengthy exhortations to Communion at every Sunday Mass, not for the beauty of its phrasing and its moving character – for these addresses are very beautiful – but to fulfil the legal point that they were ordered by the Reformers to be read.'[5]

The young and impressionable Peter Anson, who in 1908 also spent time at St Mary's, reported that 'the Prayer Book rite was carried out to the letter, with no interpolations or verbal additions'. Anson is a useful observer on other matters too: 'Two candlesticks and no more rested on the *mensa* and there were no flower vases'. 'The vestments worn by the ministers were of a shape then almost unknown – very long and ample.' 'The music was strictly liturgical, mostly plainchant. Never before or since have I heard better congregational hymn singing or Gregorian music than during my twelve months at Primrose Hill.'[6]

The thinking we now associate with Dearmer did not emerge fully-fledged in the first edition of his *Parson's Handbook*. During his time as vicar (and indeed beyond), the *Handbook* passed through several new editions, growing in size and complexity with each new iteration. So anyone using it for reference must take into account the date and context of the edition they consult. Another word of caution is that the *Handbook* does not contain the whole of Dearmer's guidance on church history, liturgy and praxis. In parallel, he wrote or edited a whole family of related publications to give further guidance to clergy, servers and congregation. Among works written while he was vicar of St Mary's the following deserve mention. *The English Liturgy from the Book of Common Prayer* (1903, in association with Frere and Munford, an altar book to complement the *Parson's Handbook*). In its wake there followed the *Servers' Handbook (1904)* and *The Sanctuary*

(1905, a companion to the Book of Common Prayer). The *English Hymnal* itself, discussed in more detail below, should perhaps also be included in this list (1906), together with the *English Carol Book* (1910). Dearmer also served as general editor for a series published by Mowbray's entitled The Arts of the Church. One of these in particular, *The Ornaments of the Ministers* (1908), was very much a St Mary's production, and some of the vestments illustrated are still in use at St Mary's; the text was by Dearmer, photographs taken at St Mary's by Violet Blaiklock (who, as well as being a member of the congregation, was one of the first women to achieve recognition as a photographer), and drawings by Clement Skilbeck, whilst the St Dunstan's Society (see below) loaned vestments. Other volumes in that series included one by Arthur Hill (churchwarden) on the *Architectural History of the Christian Church*, and two on Gothic and Renaissance architecture by E Hermitage Day.[7] *Illustrations of the Liturgy* (for the Alcuin Club, 1912) included more drawings made in St Mary's by Skilbeck. On a more popular level Dearmer also wrote *Everyman's History of the English Church* (first edition of 50,000 copies, 1909, to coincide with the English Church Pageant) and *Everyman's History of the Prayer Book* (1912).

In order to ensure a supply of church fabrics, vestments and fittings that were compliant with the *Handbook*, Dearmer founded the St Dunstan's Society with offices nearby to which he was a regular visitor.[8] Examples of its work were employed in the English Church Pageant. In 1912 the Society gave way to the more celebrated Warham Guild, founded by Dearmer 'to augment the studies of the Alcuin Club and the directives of *The Parson's Handbook,* and to carry out the making of all the "Ornaments of the Church and of the Ministers thereof" according to the standard of the Ornaments Rubric, and under fair conditions of labour'. One aim was to cooperate with artists and craftsmen to ensure that fine examples of their work could be inspected at the Guild's headquarters in order to encourage high standards in others. Dearmer became the first chairman of the Guild's advisory committee, alongside Maurice Bell, FE Brightman, E Hermitage Day, FC Eeles and G Kruger-Gray. Dearmer personally wrote its first publications, on Ornaments (1914) and Monuments and Memorials (1915), and many more thereafter. The Guild's marque quickly became a trusted symbol of quality workmanship in church fittings, and (as indicated in the table on p.96) several works from St Mary's were loaned to its first exhibition in 1913 and illustrated in the accompanying catalogue, which was followed up by another of Dearmer's publications, *Some Examples of Church Ornaments* (1914).[9] After all this, few church people of the time could have been unaware of Dearmer or of St Mary's Primrose Hill, which had been well and truly put on the map.

A number of eminent scholars and church artists were drawn to Dearmer's congregation. Two in particular stand out. The liturgical scholar FC (Francis Carolus) Eeles who had first corresponded with Dearmer from his home in Scotland, found a new spiritual home at St Mary's when his job brought him to London. Clement O Skilbeck was an artist and designer who when Dearmer had been a curate at St Mark's Marylebone Road had fallen under his spell. Both became stalwart members of the congregation, and both remained generous benefactors to the church even after Dearmer's time as vicar. Eeles was, among other things, a collector of antique church objects and artefacts, several of which he later gave to St Mary's. Skilbeck contributed much to the parish by way of art and design. He later recalled how Dearmer was a 'tremendously deep mine of information' on costume, design and music; not necessarily a pioneer because he felt that epithet was better reserved for people like Comper, 'but Dearmer always seemed to carry on the light'. As a layman Skilbeck was always confident that 'with Dearmer all would go right, no hitches or hesitations, everything "decent and in order"' without haste, fuss or unnecessary detail. 'All done in straightforward, manly spirit, most helpful to the lay mind'.[10]

Did he put in that 'manly' as a corrective to anyone who felt there was something effeminate about attention to beauty and style? Dearmer was not afraid to write and speak openly about beauty and aesthetics, and he also publicly valued the role of artists and craftsmen and offered them significant commissions. This in turn earned him a dedicated following within that fraternity. But so did his own youthful, rather theatrical personality. Norah Spowart, who lived in King Henry's Road next to the church, recalled that Dearmer, 'though not a member of the theatrical profession, certainly had a "fan" following of devoted young ladies almost equal to that of any film star.'[11] Peter Anson was only slightly caricaturing when he said:

> In a church like St Mary's, which attracted authors, artists and social reformers, some men defied Sunday conventions by wearing baggy suits of home-spun tweed, shirts with soft collars, and quite probably sandals instead of shoes or boots. Their women-folk tended to look like the models painted by Rossetti or Burne-Jones and revolted against the fashion by discarding corsets. Unlike the more fashionably dressed ladies with their trumpet-shaped skirts and swaying back carriage, they inclined to droop in a willowy manner, although some adopted a masculine costume, with a practical, though still long, serge skirt, starched blouse and high collar.[12]

Compare that with FC Eeles's reflection:

> To St Mary's came colonials, Americans, missionaries and non-Anglicans who had become interested in questions relating to public worship ... Dr Dearmer was also attracting people of another kind, the intellectual and artistic men and women who had been alienated by the dullness of so many churches at that time.[13]

So, should the congregation of St Mary's in Percy Dearmer's time be seen as increasingly a collection of middle-class aesthetes? The case is not proven. It would be not only arduous but also misleading to attempt a social profile of the congregation as a sub-set of the 2300 people who lived in the civil parish (and for whom the census returns provide some kind of a snapshot), because a majority of the worshippers lived outside the parish, as remains true to this day, and

Exterior from north east in Dearmer's time. (All the gables still have their crosses, and note the flag-pole).

conversely the majority of parish residents did not attend the church. The average number of Easter communicants throughout Dearmer's ministry remained fairly stable, at around 385, which may give some idea of the size of the core congregation. But by contrast, apart from a small and temporary dip in the years 1908-11, the total number of annual communions recorded continued the steady upward trend of Spencer's days, rising from 6905 in 1901 to 9883 in 1915. That strongly suggests that, for whatever reason, a growing number of people were finding the kind of liturgy and ministry on offer at St Mary's met their needs. Much of the circumstantial evidence, from the liturgy, music and preaching reported from Dearmer's time, does hint at a certain intellectualisation. But even that is not certain. Setting aside those eclectic visitors from further afield, we know from Geoffrey Dearmer that the congregation included large local families with children: in particular the Blaiklocks, the Avarnes, the Stutfields, the Ways and the Eiloarts.[14] Other witnesses insist on the simplicity and forthrightness of Dearmer's language, which does not suggest it was over the heads of working-class folk, although we have no way of knowing how many of them attended. According to Geoffrey Dearmer again, while the upper middle-class folk (whom he thought most typical of the morning congregations) came to church with their families, the domestic servants, of whom there were still many in the parish,[15] had to stay at home on a Sunday preparing lunch, and were not free to attend church until the afternoon or evening. We also hear of the mixing of social classes in the children's Catechism classes, whose numbers swelled to well over 100 in the heyday of Dearmer's ministry, although by 1911 he was complaining to Lord Beauchamp that: 'nearly all the parish is now boarding houses and maisonettes, and there are hardly any children left to teach'.[16] There was almost certainly a preponderance of middle-class folk in the congregation. But the long time it took to pay off the parish's debts and raise money for new projects does not suggest there were many truly rich members. Indeed, with some exceptions, even the middle classes lacked a strong culture of giving other than modestly to the church.

Dearmerisation

St Mary's is perhaps most famous internationally as the church that Percy Dearmer whitened. But that was not something that happened immediately on his arrival as vicar, nor was it all undertaken in a single operation as is often supposed. He would gladly have whitened the whole interior at one go, but that required funds, for which he needed the backing of the congregation or at least of a few principal benefactors. So a cautious, phased approach was required. When he did begin to change the interior from dark brick to brilliant white the effect must have been unsettling for some. The first phase – limited to whitening the chancel – was undertaken in the spring of 1903. Dearmer afterwards commented in the parish magazine: 'The effect is most beautiful and helps one to realize the refinement of the old architects, who always sought broad and pure effects by this method, and thus avoided the fussy ugliness of most nineteenth century interiors, while at the same time they brought out the lines of the architecture.' After a decent pause for reflection, the next part to be whitened was the Chapel of the Holy Spirit in 1905. That was made possible by a generous gift from Arthur Hill. After that, however, no further whitening took place for a whole decade, until the great 'renovation' of 1915 described later.

Not everyone shared Dearmer's taste for whiteness. TF Bumpus, in his *London Churches Ancient and Modern* (1908), took a swipe at both the whitening and Bodley's reredos, seemingly not realising these were commissioned by two different vicars:

> The red brick vaulted apse of this church was one of the most charming pieces of architecture of my acquaintance, but it has of late years been stupidly whitewashed and equipped with a painted and gilded altarpiece out of all proportion with its environments.[17]

By contrast, E Hermitage Day in his *Some London Churches* (1911) wrote:

> Formerly the interior was patchy and restless, the juxtaposition everywhere of red brick on white stone was not only unpleasant in itself, but ruined entirely the effect of the stained glass and the ornaments of the church. A very great improvement has recently been wrought by the judicious whitewashing of large spaces of the brickwork, and the interior has gained in value beyond all anticipation.

Dearmer had begun (perhaps a little impatiently) to introduce significant changes into the nave and sanctuary even before the first phase of whitening. A few chairs in the nave were removed to make a wider processional aisle down the centre. Otherwise, his attention was focussed on the sanctuary. With the gradines on the high altar gone (1901), the altar itself was re-modelled the following year with new furnishings for an 'English altar', designed and made by Messrs Rathbone and Stabler..

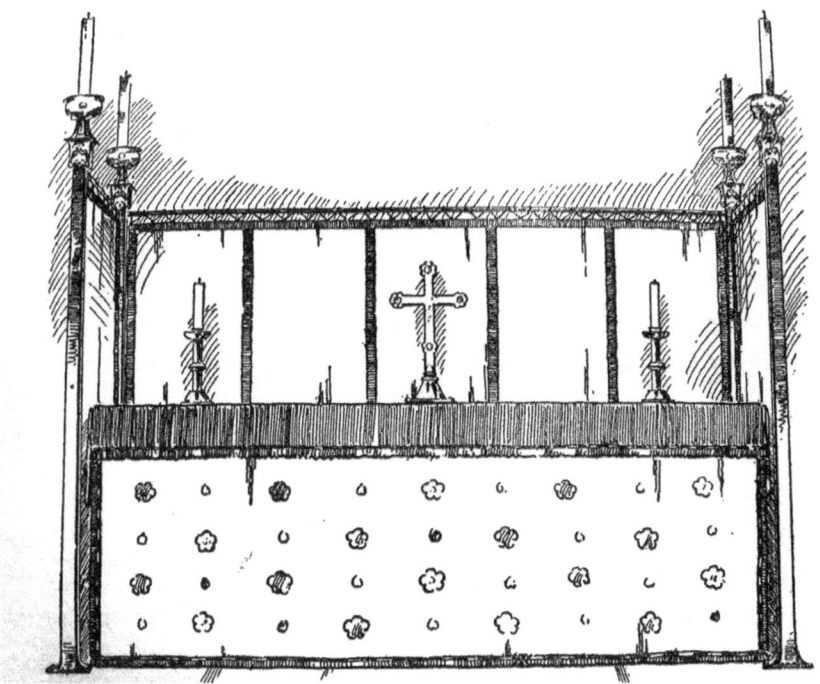

English altar, as drawn at St Mary's by Harold Stabler. Reproduced from Percy Dearmer, 'The altar and its furniture', in Essays on Ceremonial *by various authors (1904)*

More permanently than under Spencer, the table was now flanked by four 'riddel' posts, one at each corner, each having a bronze candle sconce on top. Silk curtains hung from rods at either side. (Dearmer was known on occasion to change his mind about some aspect of his colour scheme for the church, and this was a case in point: in 1909 Stabler was asked to propose a livelier decorative pattern for the riddel posts, and they were re-done, in red and gold chevrons, painted by HC Clarke, who retouched the statue of St George at the same time.)

To complete Dearmer's early work on the chancel, three Italian sanctuary lamps acquired 'by a friend' were purchased for the church by the Donaldson family and – a very English touch – by the 'Primrose Hill jam makers' (1903). And to ensure that the choir blended in with the new colour scheme they were kitted out with new blue cassocks.

Art

Taking their cue, no doubt, from the beautification of the chancel, members of the congregation now began to donate works of art to adorn the walls and pillars of the church. These include a triptych by FC Cleverly (1903), copied from a German original and mounted in a frame by AH Skipworth; and valuable reproductions of classical paintings (none of which now survive) including Angelico's *Entombment* and *Presentation* given by Mrs Crickmay (1903), Benozzo Gozzoli's *Adoration of the Magi,* presented anonymously (1904), and Perugino's *Transfiguration* given by 'two friends' (1905).

Crafts

As time went by, other new objects and ornaments – all meeting Dearmer's fastidious tastes – were acquired, to embellish the church and grace its liturgy, almost all by generous gifts or subscription from within the congregation. Some, but not all, survive, and since they were predominantly made by notable craftsmen who were then or later associated with the Guild of Handicrafts or the Art Workers' Guild, it is worth noting the main ones.

Object	artist, donor, etc	Date
Verger's wand	CR Ashbee, Guild of Handicrafts	1901
*Banner of Our Lady [Plate 3a]	Designed by CM Gere; worked and given by Miss E Batterbury	1903
Altar cross for Chapel	16th cent. Italian. Given anonymously [but by FC Eeles]	1904
Ten Commandments	Designed & painted by CO Skilbeck	1904
Table of kindred & Affinity	Calligraphy by Graily Hewitt	1904
Replica of Donatello's Statue of St George in Florence	Given by Mr & Mrs GS Walters; mounted in an oak niche designed by Thomas Falconer, replacing, as Deamer put it, an 'ancient eyesore' at the west end.	1906

Hymn Board [Plate 3b]	Metal bracket by Harold Stabler, bearing the arms of Eton College and Hampstead Borough; lettering by George E Kruger; hymn numbers by Miss Burgess.	1907
Small silver chalice and paten, and an altar book	Given by Sr Katherine (of the Clewer Sisterhood) when its school in King Henry's Road closed. *(These were taken to Serbia by Percy Dearmer in 1915 and subsequently lost).*	1907
*Gospel / Chapel Lectern	Designed by Randall Wells Painted by Alfred H Powell	1907
*Altar book, The English Liturgy	Printed by Constable. Bound by Cobden Sanderson, given by Mrs Martley in memory of her mother.	1907
Eight gilded oak candlesticks	Designed by HC King and made by Robinson, Given by Mr Knowles.	1908
Memorial tablet to Cecil Crickmay and other members of the congregation	Designed and made by Harold Stabler. Given by the Crickmay family.	1909
*Silver ciborium	Designed by Harold Stabler. Given by an anonymous donor.	
Oak benches at the back of the nave seating	Designed by Temple Moore	1910
*Men's Guild banner(s)	Designed, painted and given by CO Skilbeck.	1912
*Flags of St Mary (1) and St George (4)	Designed by George E Kruger	1913
Trendle (candelabrum)	Designed by Randall Wells. Made by F Smythe Greenwood	1915

*Items exhibited at the first Warham Guild exhibition, 1913

There was no shortage of vestments at St Mary's when Dearmer arrived, but apart from two black copes[18] acquired in 1910 after being worn for the English Church Pageant of 1909 there is surprisingly little record in the parish annals of vestments added in his time. This is partly because he tended to acquire vestments in a personal capacity to suit his tastes, some of which he presented to the parish after he moved on.

The net result of all these changes was that St Mary's became a showcase for contemporary ecclesiastical art and liturgy. Illustrations and reviews began to appear widely. The *Christian World* for 11 April 1912 ('a quarter from which appreciation is unexpected and welcome', as Dearmer put it) gave a favourable account of the Good Friday Evensong and sermon at St Mary's. Around the same time the church featured in Hermitage Day's book already quoted, with drawings of the interior by GM Ellwood. The parish wallowed in all this publicity, and in 1911 the photographer Cyril Ellis was commissioned to take a (much reproduced) photograph of the high altar. The following year Violet Blaiklock produced a postcard showing three views of the church.

Lenten Array

In his first full year in the parish (1902), Dearmer introduced the custom of 'Lenten Array', the veiling during Lent of two- and three-dimensional images such as pictures and crosses, using white or off-white cloth. The following year the same hangings were over-painted by a member of the congregation who at that stage wished to remain anonymous, but it was doubtless the Miss Burgess who would perform the same service less shyly in later years, as the number of objects to be veiled grew. Her symbols, painted in a Passiontide red, set the trend for those in use today by hinting at what lay behind each veil. For example the chapel altar hanging, as may be seen from an old postcard in the archives, bore the symbol of a dove, representing the chapel's dedication to the Holy Spirit.

Dearmer felt that his whitened chancel was nicely complemented by the Lenten Array. And when Bodley's reredos was opened up after Lent, 'the gain to the colour of the reredos will be enormous, for its red and gold will no longer be killed by red-brick.' The Array had to be completely re-thought as a result of the numerous gifts of objects and the whitening of the whole church during the 1915 renovation. Suitably plain it certainly was, but by then it looked dingy against the brilliance of the newly whitened walls and had to be replaced with fresh hangings which were again made and painted by the Misses Burgess.

One anomaly which Dearmer found vexing was that the chapel altar had an integral front panel of painted wood instead of a cloth frontal. Initially, to his strong disapproval, this remained unveiled during Lent: 'This is the reason for the Catholic custom of keeping altars plain, and for our own eighty-second Canon, which orders that the altars shall be covered with a frontal in time of Divine Service.' In order to address the problem, he had the painted panel detached in 1906 and put in a movable frame 'which, when it is not in use on the altar, can be hung up as an ornament in the church.' (The chapel itself was further adapted in 1911 when oak panelling designed by HC King was fitted along the wall.)

One pet scheme of Dearmer's which never came to fruition was for a choir screen at the top of the chancel steps. The architect Temple Moore

Temple Moore's proposed choir screen (never executed).

was commissioned (1906) to prepare an initial design for this, but for the next four years it remained no more than a dream. When Dearmer then asked him for a definitive drawing, which survives in the parish archives – a beautiful, ornate screen on medieval Gothic lines (1910) – a parish meeting (1911) voted it down before it could be used in support of a Faculty application.

Their opposition in part reflected the fact that, with the chancel considerably higher up than the nave, a screen in that position would have much reduced the people's already restricted view of choir, clergy and altar. But the more practical reason was that it was an unwise use of funds when the parish was trying to pay off its debts for the new boiler and for restoring the organ. Either way, much to Dearmer's frustration, the project was mothballed, and by 1914 it seemed more sensible, perhaps even to Dearmer himself, to put the money raised for it into a new fund then being launched to restore the Church Room in memory of Fr Spencer. Temple Moore, however, is not wholly unrepresented at St Mary's as he designed three large oak benches, one at the back of each rank of seating in the nave (1910).

Renovation of the Chancel 1914-1915

As generations of the congregation have found to their cost, whitening church walls is a process that has to be repeated at regular intervals. Even Percy Dearmer was soon awakened to this. By 1910 his white chancel walls of 1903, and even the more recent white chapel walls of 1905, were beginning to look grey with the combined effect of candle smoke, gas burners and atmospheric pollution, not to mention that old enemy, Time. Despair over the lack of progress in advancing his screen and completing the whitening of the church led him to confide in Lord Beauchamp that he was feeling thoroughly depressed with the place and had actually gone so far as to ask the bishop for a posting elsewhere. But that was not forthcoming. And as far as bricks and mortar were concerned there were no significant further developments until 1913. In that year the unexpected deaths, first of Albert Spencer and secondly of the lithographer Thomas R Way (who, with his family, was a regular worshipper at St Mary's), played into Dearmer's hands.

In Spencer's memory, the parish restored and expanded the Church Room, for which a memorial stone carved by Eric Gill (salvaged when the building was demolished in the 1960s) reads:

> This Church Room was built by the Reverend Albert Spencer, MA, Vicar, and by the congregation of the Church of S. Mary the Virgin Primrose Hill, in 1896. It was restored and enlarged in 1914, in grateful and affectionate memory of that devoted priest who passed away on Innocents' Day 1913. *Whose soul may God prosper in light.*

The Rood [Plate 4b]

Thomas R Way died at his home at 110 Regent's Park Road, aged only 51. The son and successor of another Thomas, also a lithographer, who outlived him, 'TRW' had become well known through publishing lithographs of Whistler's paintings as well as several series of popular architectural and topographical prints.[19] His requiem was held at St Mary's and was followed by burial in Highgate cemetery. His wife and family gave the church the magnificent sum of £300 for a memorial that is still one of the glories of St Mary's: the 'rood beam', the great wooden arch that presides over the chancel steps. Dearmer was particularly proud that after discussion with Sir George Frampton the family should have commissioned a sculptor of the eminence of Gilbert Bayes to design it. The central figure of Christ, reigning triumphant on the Cross (rood), is surrounded by symbols of the four evangelists. Figures of Our Lady and St John stand on either side,[20] and it has been remarked that St John bears an uncanny resemblance to Dearmer himself. The inscription in Greek reads: ΕΝΤΟΛΗΝ ΚΑΙΝΗΝ ΔΙΔΟΜΙ ΥΜΙΝ (A new commandment give I unto you), and at the foot is another inscription, *Not as the world giveth give I unto you.*[21] Barnard Way, TR's son and an accomplished illustrator, gave St Mary's at the same time a beautiful hand-written altar book crafted in his father's memory.[22]

The reredos (a) 1911 and (b) 1915

Consequentials

Dearmer now felt he had to persuade the parish that it would be offensive to Way's memory to display such a magnificent, brightly coloured work of art as the new Rood against a backdrop of shabby grey chancel walls, and a predominance of what he called 'blackish-reddy-brown' brick elsewhere. A member of the congregation, Charles Higham, put up £100 towards the £110 needed to whiten all the remaining walls, under the direction of the church's then architect, Randall Wells. But if whitening were to resume what should be done about the nave ceiling, whose exposed beams and rafters had not been touched since the building first opened? Wells rejected the idea of simply cleaning and painting all the woodwork in the roof, and decided instead to suspend a false 'ceiling', constructed in board along the full length of the nave, hoping this would serve the dual purpose of retaining heat and improving the building's acoustics. (It just about saw out the twentieth century, but then had to be dismantled when the boarding began to crumble and became a danger to people below. To general astonishment, the timbers then revealed were still in excellent condition, and after they had been preserved *in situ* the present colour scheme of the ceiling was adopted).

While all the scaffolding was up for the works in 1915 the opportunity was finally taken to install electric lighting throughout the building, another of Dearmer's long-term ambitions. Dearmer now had the bit between the teeth and pressed on with his most radical plans for the chancel, to ensure that as the eye of the observer was carried beyond the new Rood towards the high altar it would not be disappointed. Gilbert Bayes was commissioned to take down Bodley's towering reredos (which, ever since its erection, had been obstructing most of the windows in the chancel), reduce its height, clean and conserve what remained, and finally re-fit it behind the high altar. The hinged side panels were detached and taken away to be reduced proportionately and cleaned, with the help of Mr Aumonier. The central section was then taken down and its lowest panel, of the Annunciation with the motto: *Ave Gratia Plena. Benedicta tu in mulieribus. Dominus tecum,*[23] was sawn off. Bodley's angels from the very top were reverently removed and preserved. They still make ceremonial appearances on festive occasions. In 1916, just before Dearmer left the parish, and perhaps as a deliberate parting shot, he had his (and Gladstone's)[24] favourite words from Dante painted below the figures on the wings of the triptych, again by Miss Burgess: *La sua volontade e nostra pace* (In his will is our peace).

Further consequential changes were called for. New hangings were commissioned for the chancel walls, in blue silk from a French manufactory. (To make matters more complicated, this happened shortly after the outbreak of the First World War). And Randall Wells, the church's architect, designed a great brass 'trendle' (chandelier) to hang between the choir stalls and thus to be fully in view from the nave, behind the Rood beam. The chancel paving was re-laid at the same time. Lady Beauchamp gave £250 towards these improvements and the balance was raised by subscription. An Oberammergau crucifix that had belonged to Spencer, and had hung first in the nave and later in the chancel, became redundant with the arrival of the Rood, and with Mrs Spencer's consent was given to St James's Bethnal Green. The total cost to St Mary's for all these renovations was in the region of £1,000.

A third significant death occurred in 1915, that of Arthur Pollard, Keeper of Printed Books at the British Museum. This was marked by the presentation for the high altar of a copy of *The English Liturgy*, bound in red niger, by WH Smith and Sons.

Once the renovation programme was over, it was proposed that coats of arms of the principal benefactors should be painted on the plain wooden panels of Bodley's pulpit. This proved trickier than expected because one of the donors had only recently joined the congregation and felt embarrassed at the idea of being singled out, and in another case there were 'practical' problems (perhaps meaning that the donor either wished to remain anonymous or had no arms to display). The arms eventually depicted were therefore a mixture of donors and officials: those of Way, Lord and Lady Beauchamp, the Bishop of London and Dearmer. They were designed and painted by the heraldic artist and antiquary Revd EE Dorling – of English Church Pageant fame – who was also commissioned to design a new Lenten frontal for the high altar, with symbols of the passion again painted by Miss Burgess. This is still in regular use. To round off the whole process, and incidentally provide a nice coda to Dearmer's ministry, further trees were added to the church gardens.

Music

G H Palmer and Francis Burgess

Arthur Godfrey (the organist who had brought a choir with him) left St Mary's at about the same time as Albert Spencer. One immediate task facing Dearmer was therefore to find a new organist and choirmaster. Although not musical himself, he was convinced of the beauty and simplicity of plainsong (already familiar at St Mary's), and saw it as an integral part of his vision for the Anglican liturgy. So he approached an expert in its revival in England, Revd Dr GH Palmer, to help develop the music. Palmer, a prolific publisher of Gregorian plainsong in English – always in original notation with four lines to the stave[25] – came as choirmaster, bringing along his pupil Francis Burgess as assistant choirmaster and organist. Congregational plainsong practices were introduced, beginning with the psalms but gradually extending to other parts of the service so that the people might learn to participate fully. Palmer and Burgess gently began to widen the musical repertoire with occasional polyphonic music (sung by the choir alone), but their focus was always on plainsong. A report in the *Church Times* on the Easter services in 1902 commented on the boys' beautiful plainsong singing. The Maundy Thursday Eucharist was sung to the '*Orbis Factor*' Mass from the Plainsong Society's 'Ordinary'. Matins on Easter Day was 'rendered chorally to plainchant music throughout', with '*O Filii et Filiae*' as the processional hymn. But it was also noted that the setting for the Sung Eucharist was Gounod's *Messe Solenelle,* whilst at Evensong the Easter music from Handel's *Messiah* was sung as an anthem, so there was not an exclusive diet of plainsong.

Sadly St Mary's was to have these two distinguished musicians at the helm for only just over a year. Burgess, who was also Secretary of the London Organ School 1901-02,[26] left, later becoming organist at St Mark's Marylebone Road and then at St Columba's Notting Hill under Dearmer's friend and mentor James Adderley. Palmer felt unable to continue alone, and was in any case tiring of the long journey he had to make to reach St Mary's, so he left at about the same time. Despite their short tenure Palmer and Burgess left with the parish's gratitude and affection, having won over many by their championing of plainsong. From 1904 Burgess directed the choir of the Plainsong and Medieval Music Society. The music which both Palmer and Burgess continued to research, edit and promote as their careers unfolded duly entered the repertoire at St Mary's, and Palmer's edition of music for Sarum Tenebrae, was given one of its first performances there, in April 1906.

E W Goldsmith

There was now an opening – and perhaps it was always planned this way – for a pupil of Palmer's to take on the post of organist and choirmaster at St Mary's. Dr Edmund W Goldsmith was a distinguished organist and another expert in plainsong, who had studied music at the Leipzig conservatoire. As he lived much nearer to the church than his predecessors he felt able to serve in both capacities. He would remain at the helm for seven years (1902-09), re-founding a ladies' choir in 1903, reviving the church's choral society, and even mooting the idea (which came to nothing) of having a choir school. On the occasion of his full-day visit to St Mary's on Quinquagesima 1903 the Bishop of London was mightily impressed by the music, and complimented the choristers on their reverent rendering of plainchant.

The parish magazine for October 1904 carried the following announcement which illustrates the awesome discipline expected of the congregation by the vicar and organist:

It is well known that at St Mary's congregational singing is encouraged; but to be effective it needs regulating the same as choir singing. We therefore insert the following directions, the observance of which will conduce to effectiveness, and the avoidance of disturbing one's immediate neighbours.

First of all, it may be said broadly that the congregation is expected to sing all the words of the Prayer Book that are sung by the full choir, i.e. Responses, Canticles and Psalms (keeping carefully to the pause of two beats at the colon point) at the Divine Service; and at Celebrations, the Kyrie, Creed, Sanctus and Gloria in Excelsis and Paternoster; to these may be added the Agnus, and the Psalm verse and Gloria Patri in the Introit, and of course the hymns. Unison singing is essential in Plainchant. We ask everybody to join in heartily in these parts, so that the singing may be really congregational.

But there are parts which are not sung by the full Choir. Firstly, all *uneven* verses in Psalms and Canticles, and such parts as are sung by cantors alone unaccompanied or only accompanied softly, are not on any account to be sung by the congregation. Secondly, in the Office Hymn, and occasionally at other times the verses are taken antiphonally by boys and men. When this is the case obviously the *treble* voices in the congregation should sing with the boys, and the *men* with the Choir men. To do otherwise, i.e. for women to sing with the men of the Choir and men with the Choir boys, destroys the antiphonality, and the effect is spoilt. It remains to be said that there are a few things which are for the Choir alone, and are to be listened to the same as the lessons or sermon, namely, the antiphon or anthems of the Introit, carols in season, the Anthem when there is one, and, we must add, the special unaccompanied setting of the Communion Hymn No 309 by Palestrina, which is equivalent to an anthem.

No wonder that St Mary's Primrose Hill had become the 'go-to place' to hear plainsong sung in all its solemnity! Occasionally the experience was taken out to a wider audience, as in June 1905 when FC Eeles gave a public lecture about plainsong in Hampstead Town Hall, taking the church choir with him to provide musical illustrations.

The English Hymnal (1906)

Music became an essential ingredient of Dearmer's liturgical programme. When a new edition of *Hymns Ancient and Modern* appeared in 1904 he tried it out for a while at St Mary's but found it unsatisfactory. Before the year was out he convened a group of experts, mostly personal friends, to see if it might be possible to develop a supplement that would better address his own programme. As news of their work spread there was popular pressure to produce instead an entirely new book to cater better than *A&M* for the Anglican church's yearly liturgical cycle, and so was born *The English Hymnal*.

Considerable research was needed to select, edit, or where necessary write, the words of hymns which Dearmer and his team thought an appropriate complement to the *Handbook*. And although the editorial work was a team effort, Percy Dearmer stamped his personal mark on it, writing the words of seven hymns himself and editing others to make them more suitable for inclusion (including, famously but not to all the committee's approval, Bunyan's *To be a Pilgrim*). In his valuable appraisal of the *English Hymnal* in 1980, Martin Draper pointed out Dearmer's typical insistence on including the best of English poetry down the generations, even if a chosen writer – Bunyan or Blake, for example – came from outside the safe harbour of the Church of England. 'I think there was always present within him a sense of the greatness of God that made him, like many, suspicious of attempts to allow only one way of approaching him.' So an impressive list of notable English writers found a place in the book: Donne, Dryden, Kingsley, Kipling, Milton, Spenser, Tennyson and Wordsworth among them; and, among Dearmer's living contemporaries, GK Chesterton and Lawrence Housman. Contributions by Chesterton, Kingsley and Scott Holland among others ensured that those who shared Dearmer's sense of Christian social justice would find material that reflected this.

Ralph Vaughan Williams, rather to his surprise, was asked to be musical editor. With a team of researchers that included the young Martin Shaw he began work that required at least as much effort as that of the wordsmiths: identifying and selecting the best existing tunes, rejecting unsuitable Victoriana ('It ought no longer to be true anywhere,' he said, 'that the most exalted moments of a churchgoer's week are associated with music that would not be tolerated in any place of secular entertainment'),[27] seeking out new tunes including traditional folk tunes from around the British Isles, hot from the researches of Cecil Sharp and others, and composing or commissioning new tunes as necessary. Martin Shaw already knew Sharp, who had directed the Hampstead Conservatoire when Shaw and Gordon Craig had launched their Purcell Operatic Society there in 1900. He would later extend his cooperation with Sharp in the English Folk Dance and Song Society.

Dearmer told Vaughan Williams at their first meeting that he expected the work would take him a couple of months. In fact it took a couple of years, partly because of RVW's determination to make the book 'a thesaurus of all the finest hymn tunes in the world'. In this he was so successful that he occasionally had to present a tune to Dearmer and ask him to find or commission words to go with it. Conversely, where no existing tune was found to suit words which the literary editors wished to include, Vaughan Williams had either to write or commission one.

Looking back, in a broadcast to mark the hymnal's fiftieth anniversary in 1956, Vaughan Williams reflected:

> I decided that, if I was to do the book at all, I must be thorough, adventurous and honest... As regards honesty, the actual origin of the tune must be stated, and any alteration duly noted. But this does not mean that the original version must necessarily be adhered to. I always tried to find what I believed to be the best version. Cecil Sharp had just made his epoch-making discovery of the beautiful melody hidden in the countryside: why should we not enter into our inheritance in the church as well as the concert room.[28]

The hymnal's prospectus[29] set out its main selling points and called on its readers to suggest other material for inclusion. As well as the best hymns already in common use there would be some not found in existing hymnals, from specialist sources such as mission hymnals. There would be hymns for special occasions, hymns for children, and more. But ahead of all these in the prospectus came a complete set of Office Hymns and music (generally plainsong) for Introits, Graduals, Sequences and Antiphons – more than already available in *Ancient and Modern*. Accompaniments to the plainsong were provided by one of the committee, WJ Birkbeck.[30]

From today's perspective it is hard to appreciate how sensitive among the bench of bishops, and indeed among the general churchgoing public in 1906, were issues such as praying to the saints, or praying for the dead.[31] But in the prevailing climate the inclusion of some hymns with that focus caused offence and led the book when published to be proscribed for a time in some dioceses, which may even have given it added publicity and helped later sales. The publishers printed a bowdlerised edition omitting the offending numbers, but its sales were so underwhelming that it was soon forgotten. Despite this temporary blip the *English Hymnal* survived, and has even been described as 'Dearmer's best monument'.[32] It came into use at St Mary's on 30 June 1906, and many of its hymns were first sung there.

The parish's music more generally progressed well until 1907 when a couple of key singers moved away and another stood down because of pressure of other commitments. Matters were also complicated by the death of Alfred West, the organ blower. Recruitment to the choir was probably not helped by the austere announcement in the parish magazine advising would-be singers that this was not a choral society and that, for membership of the choir, 'the motive must be the devotion of our musical resources, so far as they go, to the purpose of Divine worship.' Conrad Noel had this to say about Goldsmith: 'Although his choice of music was admirable, it was above the heads of the congregation. Percy Dearmer liked congregational singing, but when I said to Goldsmith one day, "I think, at last, the people are beginning to join in that hymn", he answered, "Oh! Then I'll change it".[33]

Martin Shaw

When Goldsmith moved on in 1909, Dearmer consulted Vaughan Williams about a successor, and he recommended Martin Shaw, one of his contributors to the *English Hymnal*. The son of Dr Shaw who had been organist at Hampstead Parish Church, Martin had himself been organist at Emmanuel Church, West Hampstead, and Vaughan Williams had already confided to him how much he liked his music: 'It is individual, modern, strong and healthy – but it fits admirably with the quiet and old-established dignity of the English church ritual'.[34] Apart from his skills as an organist and composer, there were other things about Shaw that might have attracted Dearmer. He was a particular devotee of *English* music and thought it under-represented at the music conservatoires. And, accomplished musician though he undoubtedly was, he had been leading a distinctly Bohemian life among actors and performers, which (thanks to Gordon Craig) latterly included organising the music for a European tour by Isadora Duncan. Like many an artist and musician he had led a hand-to-mouth existence: so much so that on hearing he had been offered the job at St Mary's he wrote excitedly to Craig:

> I came back from Bruges and Amsterdam just lately to find £100 a year awaiting me. 'Tisn't much but it's reg'lar – Involves directing music at the very *dernier cri* in churches – Christian Socialism, Plainsong according to Solesmes, and the use of old Sarum from a XIVth cent. Tonale – etc. I like it all except the socialism, which however is quite discreet.[35]

Although he as yet knew little about plainsong, or for that matter about Dearmer's precise liturgical standards, he proved a willing learner, and a strong partnership was quickly forged between the two. And to set off on a sound footing they drew up and co-signed in September 1909 a set of Choir Rules:

ST MARY'S CHOIR, PRIMROSE HILL, N.W.

The Choir exists for leading the praises of Almighty GOD.

Those who belong to the CHOIR will naturally have a high ideal of REVERENCE in Divine Worship.

The gentlemen of the CHOIR will greatly aid the clergy and Choirmaster by insisting upon REVERENCE on the part of the junior members, & reporting any acts of irreverence, small or great, noticed by them during the service.

The BOYS of the CHOIR will remember that in future their quarterly Payments will entirely depend upon a high level of REVERENCE being maintained by them during the Services, & when in & about the Church.

No Boy need incur a single fine without wishing to do so.

The following Fines will in future be strictly enforced

ONE PENNY for: 1. Being late for Service or Practice. 2. Talking while entering Church after the Prayer has been said in the Vestry. 3. Failing to kneel upright during Divine Service. 4. Lolling about while standing or kneeling. 5. Want of smartness while standing up or kneeling down. 6. Inattention and failing to sing during the Services. 7. Unnecessary noise in replacing books or music at close of the Service.

THREE PENCE for: 1. Leaving Choir during any part of Service or Sermon.

2. Talking during any part of Service or Sermon with lips or hands. 3. Not kneeling during Prayer.

SIXPENCE for: 1. More than one boy being out of the Choir at the same time during Service or Sermon.

From the start, Shaw faced an uphill struggle. There were plenty of boys in the choir but despite regular appeals in the parish magazine the dearth of adult male volunteers already encountered by Goldsmith continued, and one of the sources of Dearmer's depression with St Mary's in 1911 was what he called the '1½ gentlemen' in the choir. Shaw aspired to widen the musical repertoire, but faced some resistance: one of the men refused to sing Merbecke instead of plainsong. Nevertheless, Giuseppe Antonio Bernabei's music for the *Reproaches* was sung at St Mary's, for the first time in England, on Good Friday 1910.

Things took a turn for the better when Martin's brother Geoffrey – another fine musician and composer – moved from a teaching post in Norfolk to become an Inspector of Schools in London and joined Martin's choir, soon to become his *de facto* assistant. He would succeed him as director of music in 1920 and remain in post until 1930. On a short-term basis, alongside such volunteers as could be mustered, four professional singers were now paid to boost the lower voices. And in November 1912, with financial support from friends, the Dearmers themselves put up the money for two further professional singers. This enabled a wider musical repertoire to be introduced. Dearmer drew back somewhat from his initial insistence on plainsong, and Shaw was encouraged to write a Modal Mass (1913) which he dedicated to the choir, and which was sung for the first time at St Mary's at the Dedication Festival the following year. It was intended for use in the penitential seasons of Lent and Advent, but was so well received that it was used even on Festival days.[36]

Martin Shaw also met with a degree of resistance from some members of the congregation who had been so well drilled in plainsong that they now had an ear for nothing else. Their protests were evidently louder than their singing, to judge by Dearmer's regular laments. Shaw explained in his congregational practices and through magazine articles that he had no intention of side-lining plainsong, but felt it

Percy Dearmer and the choir.

right to try out other music. But at the Easter Vestry meeting in 1912 Mr Ritchie drew attention 'to the elaborate nature of the polyphonic music recently introduced into the eucharistic services, to its unsuitable association with the plainsong used for the rest of the office, and to its being a cause of preventing congregational singing and to some extent a source of distraction on account of its undue predominance in the service.' A resolution in favour of reverting to the exclusive use of plainsong at the Solemn Eucharist was 'carried by a very large majority – there being an unusually good attendance.'

Joan Shaw later recollected that during Martin's time as organist Gustav Holst, John Ireland and Arnold Bax were all to be seen occasionally at St Mary's. Howard Hollis noted that Shaw detested sugary, sentimental music, which might be all right for music halls, but not for worship. 'He was not being entirely frivolous when, addressing some young ordinands, he said "any decent mother would be horrified to see her daughter behaving like Barnby in E".'[37]

The Shaws became firm friends with Percy and Mabel Dearmer, and when Mabel established a Morality Play Society to perform plays not only in the Church Room of St Mary's but more widely, Martin wrote the musical accompaniments. He also worked with Percy to do for English carols what the *English Hymnal* had attempted for English hymns. The result was the *English Carol Book* (1913). They produced *A Collection of 100 English Welsh, Scottish and Irish National Songs* in the same year.

That summer the Shaw brothers, together with Arthur Duncan-Jones, formerly dean of Caius College Cambridge, and Francis Burgess late of St Mary's, organised the first annual Summer School of Church Music, at St Stephen's House, Oxford, with 40 attendees. As the prospectus put it, 'The proceedings are to be practical and unpedantic and plainsong the principal study.'[38]

In 1915 when, as we shall see, Dearmer went to Serbia, the choice of weekly hymns fell to Martin Shaw, who implemented what he called his 'new theory of English Church Music', drawing on plainsong and traditional melodies from the Elizabethans onwards to meet, as he thought, the mood of the times.[39]

Restoration of the organ

Concerns about the state of the organ in 1909 led Dearmer to commission a detailed report from Arthur Hill, whose conclusions were bleak. Most of the instrument dated back to his father's 1873 installation shortly after the church's opening. In the intervening 37 years it had received very little attention apart from minor cleaning. Quite apart from the routine accumulation of dust, the situation had been compounded by all the building work under both Fuller and Spencer. Unsurprisingly the instrument was now badly in need of a clean, but in addition the ivories were coming away from the keys, and mechanically it was in poor shape, with much of the action worn and broken and some requiring complete renewal. For want of funds it still lacked a Choir organ and important pedal stops to complete the desired specification. Serious fund-raising was required of the parish, but in the same generous spirit towards St Mary's that had fired his father, Arthur Hill subsidised the repairs, offering to proceed by instalments and to add the missing sections anyway while the instrument lay dismantled. The job was completed swiftly and efficiently, and Martin Shaw was able to give a celebratory recital in May 1910. Further recitals followed, including a series entitled *Abendmusik* that followed the Sunday Evensongs in Advent.

Teaching and ministry

In his tribute when Dearmer left St Mary's in 1916, FC Eeles said: 'It is because the beauty of the church, its services and its music have been a true reflection of the spirit of the teaching which Dr Dearmer has given that they mean so much to so many.'

What precisely was that teaching? We know from several reports that he preached well, using stories, images and language that everyone could understand, and lacing his sermons with humour. He was exceptionally gifted in reaching out to all those embarking on a journey of faith, beginning with children. Dearmer took Catechism to new levels, still using the Saint-Sulpice method introduced by Spencer, and indeed his first Catechism classes were held during his very first weekend at St Mary's.[40] There was one important change: whereas under Spencer the children of richer and poorer families had been taught separately, Dearmer insisted they all be taught together. The number of children attending soared, which required classes to be subdivided by age, so there was a Little (or Lesser) Catechism for the younger and a Great (or Big) Catechism for the older children. This in turn meant he needed every possible assistance from his successive curates: HA King, N Newland Smith, Conrad Noel, WH Paine, JB Hunt and TW Wright. Frank Blaiklock and his daughter Violet played the organ for the Catechisms, whilst Violet's sister Elsie began a kindergarten for younger children, using a method devised by Froebel (the German educationist who invented the 'kindergarten'), and developed in Britain in a series of publications by Hetty Lee.[41]

As they were not afraid to say in later life, the children actually enjoyed Catechism, not only for the content of the teaching but also for its ambience. Nellie Starnes, who after twelve years of perfect attendance under Dearmer rose to be Head of the Great Catechism, described much of the form and ceremonial in an article in the parish magazine in 1959, including how the Catechism from the Book of Common Prayer was studied sentence by sentence in a course lasting three years: 'Looking back, it is astonishing to realise how great an influence the Catechism had had on the lives of its members, and how much what was learnt there had added to the true enjoyment of life.'[42]

Phyllis Allen Ford recalled how, as a girl, she had eagerly attended the weekly Catechism service and instruction, and how the children had been introduced to the concept of Christian Socialism. 'At first the parents of the well-to-do were anxious lest their children should catch fleas and diseases from the other children'. 'This service was treated with as much importance by the staff as the Sung Eucharist. The Vicar, and two curates, Mr Newland Smith and another, were always there…' The services were both instructive and entertaining. 'I loved them all … and wouldn't have missed it for anything and we went for years.'[43] Phyllis's mother disapproved of the socialism, and of the high-church pomp. But a deeply-influenced Phyllis would go on to become secretary of a local branch of the Christian Social Union. In the course of a sermon about Dearmer in 1987 Howard Hollis said:

> People who came to his Sunday afternoon Catechisms … learnt to do away with many hang-ups. He taught them to think intelligently about evolution, for example, as well as to know the difference between factual knowledge and what can be conveyed only by symbolism and poetic imagery. As far back as the early 1900s he could talk naturally to children about the Genesis story of creation being a wonderful myth, to picture what was beyond anyone to describe; no-one needed to be disturbed into trying to believe just how Eve was made out of Adam's rib. All Dearmer's illustrations were up to date, and his use of scientific knowledge showed a remarkable grasp of the latest knowledge of his day.

The adults in the congregation received a more serious dose of Christian Socialism. It was not party-political: Dearmer never told them from the pulpit how to vote, though he did urge them to do so, and to engage in debate from an honestly-held Christian viewpoint. Despite opposition from some quarters he was open to allowing political meetings to be held in the Church Room. Christian Socialism was to him simply a way of looking at the world through Christ-like eyes and asking with regard to every social problem, 'What would Christ do in this matter?'[44] He was as uncomfortable about party-political polarisation as about everything that divided people. He preached equal respect for all, irrespective of gender, class or wealth, and was a strong champion of women's rights and a supporter of the Church League for Women's Suffrage (CLWS). He was happy to appear as a speaker on suffragist platforms, and on one such occasion in Hampstead in 1907 said, 'It is exceedingly difficult to speak on this subject of Women's Suffrage, because it is so difficult to think of anything on the other side … I do not want to see England wasting its time in the welter of political misrepresentation which at present we call democracy.'[45] To coincide with a large demonstration in Parliament Square in November 1911 he invited the Hampstead Branch of the CLWS to hold a eucharist at St Mary's.[46]

He challenged everyone to consider how they used their wealth and managed their investments. He urged careful consideration of the relationship between capital and labour, and the end of workers' exploitation and of sweated trades, including in the production of church vestments and ornaments. He spoke out about poverty, homelessness, intemperance and vice of every kind. Two short extracts from a sermon he gave in 1906 at St Stephen Walbrook give the flavour of his thinking:

> We pray for the extinction of all tyranny, whether it be the tyranny of the few or of the many…for the exposure of all corruption … for truth in all departments of government, art, science; for honesty in trade, and forbearance in all the dealings of life. We pray that the proud may

be scattered in the imagination of their hearts, that the humble and meek may be exalted, that the hungry may be filled with good things. We pray that love may triumph over greed, meekness over malice, purity over lust, temperance over excess, God over mammon – that the Gospel of Christ, in faith and practice, may prevail throughout the world.[47]

Our trade or profession must be carried on in holy ways, looking from the gift unto the giver… All work, all service is honourable, and only idleness and thieving a disgrace. The object of all labour [is] that we may receive honourably and worthily from the great giver that which is necessary to our life.[48]

Conrad Noel

Percy Dearmer had known Conrad Noel for many years as a fellow Christian Socialist, and had officiated at his wedding. Noel's views were far more left-wing, party-political and activist, and this had made for immediate difficulties when he put himself forward for ordination (and was at first rejected), and for much of his early ministry after that. After a fragmented start to his career, he was an assistant priest at St Mary's Paddington Green when Dearmer arrived at Primrose Hill, and took a leaf out of his old friend's book by introducing Saint-Sulpice-style Catechism classes there. In 1904 Dearmer invited him to St Mary's on a part-time basis, and he soon became the main Sunday assistant, often preaching and taking one of the Catechism classes, and generally staying with the Dearmers each weekend (both before and after they had a vicarage of their own).

There were those in the congregation who could not stomach Noel's full-on socialism, which Dearmer seems to have done nothing to curb. Among these was Arthur Hill, now one of the churchwardens and, in Noel's words, 'a man of substance and an influential member of the congregation'. When handing over Noel's payment one day, Hill warned him that it would be the last he received unless he moderated his preaching. A furious Noel wrote in reply that he would rather resign than 'endure the tuning of the pulpit by an impertinent official who knew nothing about theology or politics.'⁴⁹ But he did not do so, and the storm blew over, perhaps because he diversified his preaching and included, for example a course of sermons on popular stories from literature, which were advertised in the local press. He left St Mary's in 1909, and Percy Dearmer preached at his induction as vicar of Thaxted, Essex.

Guild of Health
There were, of course, other facets to Percy Dearmer's teaching besides Christian Socialism. He was a man of prayer, with an unshakable faith in his God and a sense of spiritual depths within. This led him to take an active interest in the holistic relationship of body, mind and spirit and the place of religion in healing. In this, as in much else, he was in advance of his time. With the help of BS Lombard and Conrad Noel he founded and chaired the Guild of Health (1904) to encourage wider discussion.⁵⁰

Patriotism and Unity
On a rather different level, he also called for a broader understanding of 'loyalty' and 'patriotism'. Of course, he said, you should start with loyalty to your immediate community and country – and none could trump Dearmer's devotion to the English flag and the symbolism of St George. The death of Queen Victoria in 1901 and coronation of Edward VII in 1902 set the nation thinking perhaps as never before about its history and heritage, with a renewed sense of pride and self-confidence. For the first time a St George's flag was given to the church in 1902 to fly from the tower, and Dearmer enlisted his old friend Lord Beauchamp to speak to the people of Hampstead about the Coronation. (There would, of course be a second Coronation in Dearmer's time, that of George V in 1911). It was natural that Dearmer, who had so passionately defended the genuinely English traditions of the liturgy, should go on to champion other English symbols, ceremonies and traditions. A statue of St George was among

gifts to the church (1906). The first Guilds established for children (1909) were named in honour of St George, for boys, and St Anne, for girls. A branch of the Boy Scouts was established at St Mary's in 1913, only a few years after that movement had been founded, bringing added significance to the annual celebration of St George's Day. Four new St George's flags were commissioned for the parish (none of which has survived). In another celebration of Englishness, Rogationtide processions around the parish, more commonly thought of as rural events, were introduced in 1908. Since the procession necessarily ventured on to Primrose Hill it became a joint venture with St Mark's Regent's Park.

The English Church Pageant, 1909

Pageants celebrating the history of England and its local communities became all the rage in the first decade of the new century, and a whole new profession of 'pageant-masters' was born. Entrepreneurs like Frank Lascelles and Louis Napoleon Parker organised pageants in towns up and down the country and a kind of 'pageant frenzy' was generated, with its own summer season. As one recent writer observed, 'fashionable ladies and gentlemen would ask each other, "Do you padge"?'[51] The St Albans pageant of 1907, staged by Herbert Jarman of the Lyric Theatre, attracted particular attention, and may have influenced Clement Skilbeck and Philip Stedman of St Mary's, with the vicar's enthusiastic support and in collaboration with St Mark's Regent's Park, to produce in 1908 a parish masque entitled 'A little pageant of St George', which inter-wove a mummers' play, Morris dancing and folk songs. It was to have included a procession from the Church Room to the Church, but bad weather caused that part of the performance to be cancelled.

Revd Walter Marshall FSA, vicar of St Patrick's Hove, heard of the St Mary's Pageant while contemplating something more far-reaching for the Church of England as a whole, and wrote to Dearmer who in turn put him in touch with Skilbeck for further discussions. This turned out to be the prelude to two years of planning that, with the help of Frank Lascelles, resulted in the English Church Pageant of 1909. Although Dearmer was not its prime mover, he played a vital role in its production, and must surely have seen this, too, as complementing his *Handbook*. Held in the grounds of Fulham Palace, the Bishop of London's home, the Pageant literally had a cast of thousands, and an estimated cumulative audience of 178,000 over all the performances. Through its many scenes (some of them scripted by Dearmer), there emerged a particular 'take' on the story of the English church, from an assuredly high-church, but nevertheless firmly English, point of view. Its view of history was vigorously opposed and heckled by the same opponents of ritualism who had so recently presented their evidence to the Royal Commission. Marshall's steering committee included Dearmer, Skilbeck from St Mary's who masterminded costume design with the help of the St Dunstan Society, W St John Hope (one of the founders of the Alcuin Club to which both the latter belonged) and the heraldic artist EE Dorling (from whom Dearmer would later commission work at St Mary's). Dearmer's old boss from the Poplar Mission and Berkeley Chapel days, Revd JG Adderley, was among the performers. Representatives of Hampstead Deanery, including a select detachment from St Mary's, portrayed the bringing of Christianity to England by St Augustine, with Mabel Dearmer as Queen Bertha and Clement Skilbeck as King Ethelbert.

For all this focus on England, Dearmer would have no truck with what we might call 'Little Englandism'. The First World War would make him more, not less, convinced that a lasting settlement of world problems would only be built on Love, the sinking of prejudices and differences, and the tolerance of diversity, not on any spirit of hatred or revenge that identified people or nations as 'them', or worse, the 'enemy'. He developed an internationalist outlook, reading impressively widely in several European languages and often demonstrating in print that he was closely observing both national and international affairs, although he did not prove especially good at predicting the future course of European history. He had a particular affection for the Orthodox churches, becoming chairman of the Anglican and Eastern

Orthodox Churches Union, in which capacity he visited Russia in 1912. He felt that Christians should think beyond nation, continent or empire, and have an eye to the whole of humanity. The Christian society – the sphere of God's Kingdom and action – was no less than the whole of creation.

His overall message, while being direct and prophetic, was certainly challenging even for many committed Christians. He sought to stir people into action: 'Everyone who has a conscience must come definitely over to the side of righteousness,' he said. 'No one may think that the social duty is one that he can leave to others.'[52] He was quite prepared when necessary to speak out against the Church hierarchy for having other priorities, and even against Christian Churches collectively for partisanship and denominationalism. For if, on the secular level, loyalty and patriotism must extend outwards to all humanity, how much more within the Churches must Love and the awareness of our essential Unity in Christ pervade all our actions. His Church was 'that large and human fellowship which is inspired by the Holy Ghost, and is the Body whose Head is Christ.' Even though this did not endear him to all, he remained impatient with anything that tended in other directions, and naïvely confident that the Christian Gospel would triumph and all would come right in the end.

The kind of Unity he envisaged was not the same thing as Uniformity: 'We shall never get Uniformity,' he wrote in 1911, 'for it is against nature. But we shall recover Unity.'[53] As he wrote later, in *False Gods* (1914), 'Men occupied themselves in disputing and dividing before they had assimilated that God is love and light and life'. This last phrase might be seen as his enduring motto, and is not a bad catchphrase to remember him by.

Towards the end of 1914, Dearmer's teaching was summed up by one of his curates like this: 'That Christian principles should be applied to the relations between employer and employed, buyer and seller, rich and poor; [and] that love should dominate family life, parish life, national life and international relations.'[54] The Bishop of Willesden praised the way he had dealt with the 'open sores of life in this twentieth century… ever offering a steady opposition to all that was wrong.'[55] Nearer to home his message was simple: 'Let fellowship begin in the church, and it will spread in the parish. Our little social 'good works' will become great; for the spirit of brother-hood will be abroad.'[56] And in his parting address to St Mary's he said these words, which should probably be inscribed over the door: 'The fellowship of St Mary's will endure, and heaven and earth will always be met together within its walls.' [57]

Mabel Dearmer

Mabel Dearmer deserves special mention. Whilst she makes only infrequent appearances in the parish annals, her importance to Percy and the parish should not be under-stated. Much of her fame, both at the time and since, lay outside the parish, but she and Percy were vital influences on each other's work throughout their married life. Before they came to St Mary's Mabel, partly from financial necessity, had become a minor celebrity in her own right as an artist and illustrator for magazines, children's books, book bindings and bookplates. Jill Sheffrin, with a critic's eye, concluded that 'none of her work was of exceptional quality, and much is merely competent, but the best of her drawings and poems for children have a timeless appeal…'. She added that Mabel was a colourful and memorable personality with an enthusiasm for life which charmed her contemporaries'.[58] This was later borne out by one of Mabel's obituarists: 'She possessed in the highest degree what may be called the gift of Sunshine, and she exercised it without consciousness and without effort upon all who came beneath her spell'.[59]

After Aubrey Beardsley's departure from the *Yellow Book*, Mabel became the first female artist to have her work published on its front cover. Her work there (and afterwards) brought her into contact with a group of writers and artists who would become family friends. They included Laurence Housman, Evelyn Sharp (sister of Cecil), Netta

Syrett and Stephen Gwynne, all of whose work Mabel illustrated or interpreted. In various combinations they would usually join the Dearmer family for summer holidays, as would one of the St Mary's parishioners Mrs Knowles, with her daughter Nan (whom we shall meet again) and two sons.[60]

Percy, champion of women's rights as he was, did not wish Mabel to sacrifice her career and independence for the sake of the parish. But some involvement was inescapable. Duties began with entertaining friends and parishioners in the Dearmers' successive homes and gardens, and the change of pace in both her parish and family life from 1901 when they moved to Primrose Hill gradually led her away from illustrating into writing. She published several romantic novels for adults between 1902 and 1909. We find passing mention of her organising a fund-raising sale of work for the parish, which might suggest that what is officially recorded about her is only the tip of an iceberg. Lawrence Housman thought she had surrendered her *joie de vivre* to play her part as vicar's wife and, in his poem 'Sunday Musings', from the top of Primrose Hill, he could not resist a sideswipe at Percy:

Down there lies Mr Dearmer's church;
Alas! Through London you might search
For ritual which flaunts a front
More Popish, more un-Protest*unt*!

I'm told that there they dress in copes,
That acolytes, wound round with ropes,
Swing incense – such a dreadful smell!
And sometimes tinkle on a bell! –

An *inside* sort of bell, I mean,
With stated intervals between;
And on some queer excuse they coin
Hymn-tunes and chants which none can join!

Percy, who had trodden the boards himself from time to time while at Oxford, remained convinced of the power of drama in spreading the Christian message, although he does not seem to have had any starring role in the parish's dramatic activities. Mabel, on the other hand, with the collaboration of literary and theatrical friends (and of her two sons Christopher and Geoffrey recruited into acting roles!), began from at least 1904 to stage plays in the Church Room, the proceeds from ticket sales going to the church or the organ funds. In 1904 she co-produced with Miss Donaldson two fairy plays for children by Netta Syrett. In 1906-7 she produced further similar plays alone, *Little Bridget* and *The gift of the fairies*.[61] Much of the parish's dramatic energy for the next two years went into producing the pageants described above, but Mabel meanwhile diversified into first producing and then writing plays with a moral dimension for an adult audience. In 1909 she staged WB Yeats's *The Hour Glass*, in which she herself played the Wise Man's wife, with her sons Geoffrey and Christopher as the pupils and WG Fay, lately the manager of the Abbey Theatre Dublin, as the Fool. A second staging that year was the first production in England of Lady Gregory's *The Travelling Man*, with Fay this time taking the title role. In 1910 a Christmas mystery play for (and with) children, *The Playmate*, was mounted, with Geoffrey in the title role, and a cast that included Rosie Craig (Gordon's daughter, and thus Ellen Terry's grand-daughter). This was followed by Laurence Housman's *Bethlehem* with music by Joseph Moorat. Martin Shaw (then the newly appointed organist) was responsible for the orchestration and the direction of the orchestra, while his brother Jules, a professional actor, played Abel. Clement Skilbeck was listed among the helpers.

Meanwhile, Mabel had branched out into writing her own plays. In March 1909 her *Nan Pilgrim* was staged at the Court Theatre by Miss Mouillot for the Dramatic Productions Club. Perhaps it was Martin Shaw's arrival that gave her the idea of forming the Morality Play Society (1911) and writing a series of plays for which he composed and played the musical accompaniment: *The Soul of the World* (1911), *The Dreamer* (1912), *The Cockyolly Bird* (1913) and *Brer Rabbit and Mr Fox* (1914).

Amid all this activity Mabel was an affectionate mother to Geoffrey and Christopher (b. 1893, 1894), although there were several household servants to help with their care, and for much of their time in Primrose Hill the boys were absent from home at private schools. How close was she to Percy? Their contacts and everyday activities to a large extent diverged, and there are hints that as time went on their love may have cooled; they spent more time working (and even holidaying) apart; and there were moments of friction, or at least distractedness. Yet the shared interests and enthusiasms that had drawn them together in the first place: the love of art and beauty, the values and aspirations of socialism, pacifism and feminism, of nature and animals, and especially the sheer love of *fun*, held the marriage together.

The First World War blew things apart, however, when first their two, now adult, sons enlisted in the armed forces and then Percy, without any advance discussion, told Mabel he had accepted a chaplaincy to the forces in Serbia. This led Mabel too, despite having no prior experience, to volunteer as a nursing auxiliary there. Sadly she would meet her death there from enteric fever.[62] There is no escaping that Percy was a broken man when she died, and his heart was broken again when, only shortly afterwards, Christopher was killed in action. Percy returned to St Mary's, but scarcely knew where to turn in his grief. He was enfolded in love by the parish but needed a complete break, and very shortly afterwards resigned as vicar.

Overall assessment

As he prepared to leave St Mary's many tributes were paid to Percy Dearmer, most tellingly by his close friend FC Eeles.

> He had made St Mary's all that a London church and its services ought to be, and had gathered a devoted band of workers of every kind. But he had long ago outgrown it. The beautiful church, and the model services, the fame of which has literally become world-wide, have only been a small part of his work… Dr Dearmer trained us to think for ourselves.[63]

It was also 'about the best children's church in London'. In the parish's ceremonial and music he had defended the Prayer Book while explaining the ancient English Use. He had encouraged many who formerly saw themselves as outsiders 'to feel that they need the Church and that the Church needs them'. He had contributed much to the church and to society at large, and had shown himself to be in advance of his time in many areas, through his work with the Christian Social Union, the Guild of Health, the Anglican and Eastern Orthodox Churches Union, and most recently his self-sacrificing work in Serbia.

Eeles concluded, 'It is with no disrespect to the best of possible successors ... that we say that St Mary's will never see his like again.' And it is fair to say that several of those distinguished successors have themselves acknowledged Dearmer's greatness. GB Timms, for example, concluded that: 'History will probably say that he was one of the most influential figures in the history of the Church of England of the twentieth century.' In the course of a BBC radio broadcast about Dearmer in 1967, Colin Dunlop said:

> It is surprising how many of the details on which Dearmer laid stress have since become commonplace throughout the whole Anglican communion. I am thinking of things like the restoration of use of ample surplice, hood and scarf as the ordinary robes of the clergy; the whitewashing of the interiors of churches; altars with riddel posts and curtains (though these are going out) ... The regime at St Mary's which I remember would now seem very old-fashioned. But although Dearmer, as far as I know, was not ever involved in the modern Parish Communion movement, there were always some communicants at the 11am Sung Eucharist at Primrose Hill, which would not have been the case at other so-called 'High Churches'. To celebrate the eucharist while disallowing communicants would have been to disobey the Prayer Book, and this Dearmer would never knowingly do.

Endnotes

1. Duncan-Jones, AS; Gaselee, Stephen; and Wyatt, EGP, *A Directory of Anglican Ceremonial* (Alcuin Club, XIII, 1921), Preface. For an appraisal of the Parsons' Handbook see, for example Hughes, Dom Anselm, *The Rivers of the Flood* (1961).
2. Dearmer was 'the subject of a savage caricature in Compton Mackenzie's *The Parson's Progress* [1923], in which a thinly disguised Revd JQB Moxon-Hughes 'claimed for his pastiche fearless logic, historical accuracy, liturgical infallibility, artistic form, romantic association, loyalty to the Book of Common Prayer, practical utility, and the certainty of its overawing bishops.' See Yelton, Michael, *Anglican Papalism: an illustrated history 1900-1960* (2005), p.10.
3. CERC: Ecclesiastical Commission file 46277.
4. AF Winnington-Ingram, who had succeeded Creighton.
5. Noel, Conrad, *Conrad Noel, an autobiography* (1945), p.80.
6. Anson, Peter, *A Roving Recluse* (1946), p.31.
7. A friend and collaborator of Dearmer's, later a Trustee of St Mary's and for a time Editor of the *Church Times*.
8. Anson, 52.
9. The Guild continues today. See its website.
10. PM, Oct 1937, pp.116-18.
11. Spowart, Norah B, 'Entertainers and entertainment in Hampstead', in *Camden History Review*, 12 (1984).
12. Anson, Peter, *Fashions in Church Furnishing 1840-1940* (1960), p.310.
13. Dearmer, Nan, *The Life of Percy Dearmer* (1941), p.120.
14. A family that suffered terribly in the First World War, as testified by the war memorial.
15. For Hampstead in general, see Thompson, FML, *Hampstead…* (1974), p.50.
16. *Ibid.*, p.172.
17. *Ibid.*, p.349.
18. This is how they are described in Vivian King's parish chronicle, although he may have meant tunicles.
19. *Reliques of Old London; Halls of the City Companies;* and *The Thames from Chelsea to the Nore*.
20. A detailed description by Bayes is in PM, Jan 1915.
21. *John 14, v.27*. A pen and ink sketch of the interior by Way was reproduced and sold to raise funds at the time of the jubilee in 1920.
22. In 2014 his granddaughter, Charlotte Way, returned to St Mary's to give a piano recital in his memory.
23. Hail [Mary], Full of Grace; Blessed amongst Women; the Lord is with Thee.
24. Referred to by Dearmer in a sermon, see Hunt, Rev W H (comp), *Churchmanship and Labour. Sermons on Social Subjects* (1906), p.242.
25. See introduction by Martin Draper and Michael Willford to the CD *The St Mary's Primrose Hill tradition, Vol I* (2001).
26. Archives: Notes by John Francis Burgess on 'The Rev Captain Francis Burgess, former organist'.
27. Kennedy, Michael, *The works of Ralph Vaughan Williams* (1964), p.67.
28. Vaughan Williams, Ursula, and Holst, Imogen, *Heirs and Rebels* (1959). On the musical history and content of the *English Hymnal* see Kennedy's work cited above.
29. *CT*, 31 Mar 1905.

30 They were replaced in the 1933 edition by those of JH Arnold of St Mary's, who had by then become the leading expert in the field.
31 See, for example, Robert Atwell, 'The devil doesn't have all the best tunes…' in PM, Jun-Jul 2006, pp.5-6.
32 Dearmer's obituary, *Guardian*, 5 Jun 1936.
33 Noel, *op.cit.*, p.80.
34 BL: Shaw Archive, 13 Nov 1907.
35 Connock, Stephen and Montgomery Campbell, Isobel (eds), *'The Greater Light' – A compendium of the life and works of Martin Shaw* (2018), p.178.
36 Joan Shaw, during the 1967 BBC Broadcast 'Beauty for all'.
37 In a similar vein, Hubert Parry, wrote in 1899 that 'a very considerable proportion of the hymn tunes in many popular modern collections are as vile as it is possible for anything to be that has an excuse for calling itself artistic' (quoted by Stephen Darlington in *Cathedral Voice* 2019/1, p.18.)
38 BL: Shaw Archive.
39 Connock et al., *op. cit.*, p.88.
40 For a full account see Dearmer, Nan, *Life* p.159ff.
41 Hetty Lee, *New Methods in the Junior Sunday School* (1907), and *The Sunday Kindergarten* (1911); see Dearmer, Nan, *Life*, p.150. Newland Smith went on to write *Church Teaching for Church children* (1908) with an introduction by Dearmer.
42 Archives: History.
43 Floud, Cynthia (ed), *A Dysfunctional Hampstead Childhood 1886-1911: the memoir of Phyllis Allen Floud neé Ford* (Camden History Society 2018), p.72.
44 *The Church and Social Questions* (1910), ch. 6.
45 *Women's Franchise*, 23 Jul 1907.
46 *Votes for Women* 24 Nov 1911 [British Newspaper Archive].
47 Hunt, Rev W H (comp), *Churchmanship and Labour. Sermons on Social Subjects* (1906), p.242.
48 *Ibid.*, p. 252.
49 Noel, *op.cit.*, p.80.
50 'Health,' he said, 'is good; happiness is good; and when man loves God with all his heart, and his neighbours as himself, these things will come for us all.' *Body and Soul* (1909) p.121.
51 From an exhibit at St Albans Museum and Art Gallery, Feb 2020.
52 *The Church and Social Questions* (1910), p.22.
53 *Reunion and Rome* (1911), p.37.
54 HA King, in PM, Nov 1914.
55 Transcript from a press cutting in the parish archives.
56 'Fellowship in the parish' in *Patriotism and Fellowship* (1917), p.64.
57 Farewell letter in PM, Jan. 1916.
58 Shefrin, Jill, *Dearmerest Mrs Dearmer* (Toronto 1999) and see website http://www.teetotum.ca/DearmerestMrsDearmer.pdf
59 PM, Aug 1915.
60 She was in effect a single mother, married but living without her husband who was seriously ill. Percy took Nan as his second wife shortly after Mabel died.
61 *H&H*, 6 Jan 1906.
62 A Requiem was held for her in SMVPH on 19 July 1915.
63 PM, Jan 1916.

Chapter 5

Revd Arthur Duncan-Jones

Vicar, 1916-1928

Appointment

Percy Dearmer was bound to be a hard act to follow. He confided in Martin Shaw that he hoped his successor would be Arthur Duncan-Jones, who was well known to both of them through the Summer School of Church Music. Although they had had their differences over that, Duncan-Jones was at heart a solid admirer of everything Dearmer stood for in the Church of England. There is no evidence that Dearmer was formally consulted by the Trustees about his successor, but his views must surely have been known to the parish representatives among them, and Duncan-Jones (referred to at the time and hereafter as 'D-J') was duly presented to the bishop for induction. The succession had been sealed. He was 38, married with a family.

As in Dearmer's case, it was something of a surprise appointment because D-J had been rector of Louth, Lincolnshire for only two years, after three years as rector of Blofield, Norfolk. Prior to that he had pursued an academic career at Gonville and Caius College, Cambridge where, after graduation (1901) and ordination (1904/5), he held posts successively as chaplain and lecturer (1904), fellow, junior dean, and eventually dean (1910). On the way up that particular ladder he had married the Master's daughter (1907). They came to St Mary's with a large family.

The Duncan-Jones family by Violet Blaiklock

The offer of preferment came with the now regular warning that remuneration at St Mary's was modest, even when supplemented by Easter offerings, so he, like his predecessors, would need other sources of income to support himself and his family. Luckily, both D-J and his wife had some private means and, even with a World War raging, the chance to fill Dearmer's shoes was a once-in-a lifetime opportunity.[1]

Shortly after his appointment D-J wrote in the parish paper about Dearmer's (and his own) vision of the Church of England within the universal Catholic Church. It was, he said, a church for 'all sorts and conditions of men' ... 'nothing less than the working of God's Providence both for individuals and nations, not requiring rigid uniformity of expression but, rather, "variety", which is one of the beauties with which God has endowed the world'. It was 'the principal way in which God's Beauty and His Love are bodied forth to us English people. This is something of what St Mary's under the guidance of your late gifted Vicar has meant to me and scores of others throughout the Anglican Communion.'

One of Dearmer's final acts at St Mary's in 1916 was to officiate at the marriage of Martin Shaw and Joan Cobbold, where the composer

John Ireland was best man.² After that he was wise enough not to haunt his successor, but by request he did make several return appearances during D-J's ministry, and the parish eagerly followed his fortunes. In 1916 he quietly married Nan Knowles from the St Mary's congregation (who had shared so many family holidays), then went on successive assignments to France and India. Their return in 1919 was heralded in the parish magazine with a promise that he would pay St Mary's a visit in May that year. He was one of the preachers at the Golden Jubilee the following year, and in the same month their son Anthony was baptised at St Mary's, together with Martin Shaw's son. Nothing could better illustrate how much like an extended family St Mary's was, and is, to those closely involved. In 1925 he was back again, to give a lecture on Byzantine architecture.

The context of war

The First World War is practically unreported in the parish annals, because both the church itself and the parish as a whole remained largely undamaged. Church services (as we shall see below) continued throughout, and the number of annual communicants dropped only slightly as the war went on, before resuming its upward trend. Nevertheless the toll that the War took of the parishioners cannot be lightly dismissed, in terms of anxiety for their called-up sons and, in a few cases, grief over their death in action. More than thirty parishioners, mostly young men and women, were killed in, or as a direct consequence of, the War. For some, the story has been ably told by Martin Sheppard.³ Perhaps saddest of all was the case of the Eiloart family, which lost three of its members, Cyril, Horace and Oswald. D-J himself lost a brother, Cecil, who although not a combatant but an actor had been interned by the Germans and contracted a mortal illness from which he died while being repatriated in 1918.

The most notable physical change nearby was the appearance of allotments on the Hill from 1917 to provide an emergency source of food.

Building up the faith and the congregation

D-J found a congregation still grieving over the loss of Mabel and Christopher Dearmer in 1915, but more generally thinned, and its morale brought low, by the War. There was serious work to be done in re-energising the parish before he could improve cohesion within both parish and community. Little progress was possible while the War continued, and in some areas of activity, especially the social field, he had to proceed by trial and error and be prepared to adapt, or abandon ideas.

Children and youth
As the father of a large family himself D-J understood children well, and threw himself whole-heartedly into organising and leading activities he suspected they would find engaging. Fun was definitely on his agenda, but it was fun that was always rooted in the faith. In 1917 a children's mission was led by his old friends the Revd and Mrs SC Carpenter. Elsie Blaiklock continued to run the kindergarten as she had for ten years under Dearmer and would continue to do with 'singular charm'[4] for a further decade until 1927. Senior and junior Catechism classes continued to attract a devoted following[5] under D-J and his curates, notably Colin Dunlop for much of the 1920s. D-J's own young sons proved to be useful role models for other children in church, although Avril Wood (daughter of Sir Henry) who lived next door at 4 Elsworthy Road, recalled from her girlhood only the 'antics of the Vicar's small boys, and her dislike of the incense 'which once caused my sister to "faint" and to have to be carried very dramatically out of church'.[6]

Activities discontinued during the War were gradually started up again afterwards. In the 1920s D-J revived the Guilds of St George for boys, and St Agnes for girls, each intended to bind its members together 'for the purposes of perseverance in their religion and for instruction and social fellowship.' Each was divided into senior and junior sections (for children up to and over 14 respectively). Whilst the St George guilds each had a Master (one of these being an assistant priest of the time, and the other the Parish Clerk, Vivian H King), and a Secretary, we have it on the authority of Colin Dunlop[7] that D-J maintained personal control over their activities. The girls were convened by their guild Secretary, Miss May Jeoffroy. As well as religious events such as corporate communion services, activities included drama, dancing and 'fun of every kind that was not pure shoddy'. They got off to a good start in 1922 by winning first prize for country dancing in a competition among Hampstead clubs.

The vicar enthusiastically chose and directed guild plays, 'casting the parts with intimate understanding of the character and capacity of each player and overseeing every detail himself,' and reportedly instilling in many young people a love of Shakespeare which lay at the heart of his repertoire (*Love's Labours Lost* 1922, *Much Ado About Nothing* 1923 and *Two Gentlemen of Verona* 1924.) Other offerings included *Pilgrim's Progress* 1919, *Robin Hood* 1921 and Thackeray's *The Rose and the Ring* 1924. Costumes were made by the mothers and other ladies of the congregation, and in the 1920s musical accompaniment was provided by Geoffrey Shaw and JH Arnold – a far cry from their church repertoire! The hours spent in learning lines and rehearsing for each production were an important part of the experience for both children and parents. Other adults, including successive assistant clergy, were given front-of-house or back-stage roles so that, all-told, each production drew in a large proportion of the congregation and generated a great deal of fun alongside the sweat and tears. In 1927 the guilds were replaced by a new St Mary's Primrose Hill Club, which continued their dramatic tradition with *Romeo and Juliet*. But its activities ranged much wider, to include badminton, billiards, cricket, country dancing, lawn tennis, table tennis and boxing.

The Boy Scouts' troop (11th Hampstead) was revived, and in 1927 the 1st Primrose Hill Girl Guides and the Brownies were formed. Apart from ceremonial appearances in church, for example on St George's Day and at armistice parades, their activities have left little trace in the parish archives.

A scene from The Mystery of the Nativity as performed in 1924

Nativity plays, usually with a moral content, and/or tableaux accompanied by selected readings, hymns and carols, were performed annually around Christmas or New Year, either in church or, more commonly, in the Church Room. They became progressively more ambitious, drawing on home-grown musical and dramatic talent. In a pioneering performance in 1924, the *Mystery of the Nativity*, a medieval play of the nuns of Liège for which an English translation by Richard Aldington had only recently been published, was given its 'first performance in English dress'. Photographs of this unusual production survive in the parish archives.[8]

In January 1925 Mabel Dearmer's morality play *Brer Rabbit*, with music by Martin Shaw, was revived with the vicar's approbation. Equally well-received was the performance at the end of that year of a new *Christmas Pageant* involving 60 children, written by Joan (Mrs Martin) Shaw with music by Martin and Geoffrey Shaw. Her children's play *The Magic Fishbone* followed in December 1927. A handout survives in the parish archives for a tableau of a more secular kind in November 1923: 'A Living Library – stories in costume of life in China, India, Australia and other lands'.

Adults

For adults as for children, D-J saw spiritual growth as an important aspect of renewal. He began gently, through sermons and articles in the magazine, but from 1922 launched a fresh round of teaching on the basics of the faith, establishing 'study circles' on church history and theology with the help of two assistant clergy in particular, first Harold Anson and later Colin Dunlop.

But he also believed in social bonding. Some of that, too, would have a churchy flavour, such as the revival of the Missionary Union and branches of the Church of England Men's Society and Girls Friendly Society. But there were also activities designed for pure enjoyment and entertainment: winter social evenings were introduced from November 1920 and a Guild of Fellowship from May 1921. That same year a St Mary's Primrose Hill Society (also referred to as the Society of St Mary's) was founded, open to all on payment of a modest subscription. In addition to parties and social events it laid on serious lectures by distinguished speakers and hosted dramatic presentations by the parish's various drama groups. It was briefly moth-balled at the end of 1926, but then revived by popular demand, with an illustrated lecture on carols by Geoffrey Shaw.

The Church Room was not ideal for drama, but in the course of the 1920s it was significantly improved, first by the provision of a new platform for staged performances, built by the doughty verger, PH Bradbury; and then by the installation of electric lighting, partly with funds raised at the children's dramatic performances. There was another major limitation of the Room, namely that bookings for rehearsals had to be juggled with the needs of a Men's Club, a private badminton club, and the Scouts, Guides, Cubs, and so on. A crisis was reached in 1927 when the church's own Nativity play had to be abandoned for lack of available slots in the Room's diary for rehearsals.

At the apex of all the dramatic activities was a new parish amateur dramatic society, the Primrose Hill Players. The archives include a short history of the Players 1922-1972 and a list of the plays they performed between 1922 (when they were founded by Katherine Harvey, wife of the Shakespearean actor Rupert Harvey of the Old Vic) and 1944. The longest gap in productions was between 1944 and 1962 after which they were revived by Helen Lowry and continued for a further decade.[9]

Rupert Harvey himself launched the first season, with a triple bill of *His Chance*; *Pros and Cons* and *Box and Cox*. The Players intentionally performed mostly secular plays, the main exception being the medieval morality play *Everyman* which was performed in the Church Room in two successive seasons (1923, 1924), and again, by a visiting troupe, the St Cross Players, in 1929. The Harveys for the most part had a free hand, although there is the occasional hint of friction with the vicar, who was anxious that their plays should be suitable for an audience of church people and of sufficient moral content to give the audience food for thought. Reviews in the parish magazine, of both Guild and Players' productions, could be forthright as to short-comings such as fidgeting or line-fluffing,[10] and occasionally as to the merit (or not) of a play, and therefore the wisdom (or not) of choosing it for performance. In 1923, D-J enjoyed the farce *Postal Orders*, but its partner in that evening's double bill, Stanley Houghton's *The Younger Generation*, left him cold: 'One could only feel sorry for the producer and the actors, who magnificently attempted the impossible'. Katherine Harvey gave a robust defence of her choice, but that only stirred up more critique![11] John Masefield's *Good Friday* was performed in 1926.

Lay support

D-J inherited an articulate and loyal, but by no means subservient, laity. Martin Shaw remained organist. FC Eeles, and Vivian H King who was both Master of the Servers and Parish Clerk, were safe hands in the sanctuary. Lord and Lady Beauchamp continued their occasional visits to St Mary's when in London, and remained regular benefactors. Sir Frederick Holiday was a member of the Church of England's National Assembly, and would be elected as a member of the Parochial Church Council when it was formed. Other eminent parishioners in D-J's time included Sir Cyril Cobb, Chairman of the London County Council; Sir Archibald Bodkin, public prosecutor; Judge Shewell Cooper; Henry Pegram, sculptor; and occasionally Sir Henry Wood who lived next door, in Elsworthy Road.

Towards a Parochial Church Council (PCC)

Parochial Church Councils came into being in 1919.[12] St Mary's was thus ahead of the general tide when, at the Easter Vestry of 1917 it instituted a 'Voluntary' Church Council (VCC) which, in addition to the two churchwardens and the vicar, comprised 14 elected members: initially 7 men and 7 women.[13] Its Minutes provide a welcome additional strand for this history.

The VCC met for the first time in April 1917. Inevitably it discussed housekeeping matters, but it also concerned itself with liturgy, times of services, special preachers, fund-raising for specific objectives, payment of clergy, church officers and choir men, and the use made of the Church Room. While the War continued, with a reduced congregation, a tight lid had to be kept on outgoings and there were strict limits to what the council could afford even for basic housekeeping. As it turned out (though they were not to know this at the time), St Mary's would face no physical threat in the First World War, in stark contrast to the Second,[14] and services were able to continue as usual throughout. On the Day of National Intercession for the end of the war, 6 January 1918, a Litany was sung in procession round the parish,[15] and the Council voted in favour of singing in church the additional, bullish, verse of the National Anthem that had been omitted from the *English Hymnal*.[16]

The blueprint for PCCs[17] required incumbents to consult them on any changes they proposed to make. Conversely, the PCC might suggest its own changes, subject to the proviso that: 'All such changes, by whomsoever proposed, must be in accordance with the Canons, Constitutions and Customs of the Church of England'. The vicar was not obliged to accept PCC proposals, but in the event of a dispute they could appeal to the bishop. Nor was he entitled to dispose of church property without the PCC's consent, and he must consult the council before introducing any new ornament. If the PCC considered the incumbent (its Chairman) to be negligent, the Vice Chairman (a layman), on the request of two-thirds of the council, could convene a meeting in his absence to discuss the matter; if it was not then resolved they could appeal to the bishop. Provision was also made for the PCC to 'have a voice in the appointment of the incumbent, but not that the appointment should be entirely in their hands'. Churchwardens and Incumbent were to consult the PCC annually on the church's budget and the means of meeting it.

The VCC took all this in their stride and, having metamorphosed seamlessly into a PCC in 1919, continued to operate in much the same way as before apart from meeting more frequently – usually about 8 to 10 times a year. It paid more attention to the intricacies of finance and budgeting. From the start, agendas for its meetings were posted in church in advance, but the Council was adamant that attendance at its meetings should be limited to the *ex officio* and elected members and not be open to all, although a report of its proceedings might be published in the parish paper after each meeting. One interesting feature of the St Mary's PCC was that there was from the start a strong cohort of women among those elected (as opposed to those serving *ex officio*), and by 1928 women were in the majority (10:7 of elected members, although the offices of churchwarden and sidesmen continued to be an exclusively male preserve).

Church building, maintenance and outreach

As the church lacked any endowment, funding remained a perennial problem. Maintenance of the building and the boiler were inescapable charges, but since the sum required was never predictable in advance there was a regular note of foreboding in successive treasurers' pronouncements. Financial recovery after the war had been spearheaded by Arthur Babson Horton, an American citizen working in London, who was elected churchwarden in 1918 and established a new Fabric Fund. He died of a serious illness, aged only 50, in 1920. Bricks-and-mortar issues were to remain a major element of PCC business.

As early as 1918, the VCC turned its thoughts to cleaning, decluttering and refurbishing the church, although it was the following year before they were in a strong enough financial position to embark on serious maintenance work. The roof needed repair and there was now the further question of erecting a war memorial. Inside the building, a good clean-up and redecoration were unavoidable. The ledges below the clerestory windows – high up, inaccessible and always neglected – were filthy, and the Scouts were put on stand-by. The font also needed a good clean, but to save expenditure, that job too was delegated to volunteers (July 1918). The organ required repair after a major leak in the roof in 1917, and to prevent its further deterioration the council gave the vicar discretion to restrict the hours, other than services, at which it could be played. When (much later) it came to really expensive projects such as re-whitening the church in 1926, special appeals were needed. And in that particular case one thing led to another: during the work the builders discovered that the clerestory windows were in a parlous state, so yet more fund-raising was needed to put that right, as it was again the following year to repair the west end.

Unsurprisingly, if a little embarrassingly, in the years before Frank Marriott took over as Treasurer, contributions to the Diocesan Fund (quota) tended to be paid late or withheld altogether, and it was a matter for celebration when payments were up to date, as in 1923. More commonly, yearly ad hoc appeals were made to balance the books, and special collections were taken, over and above the weekly offertories. Under the Clergy Pensions Measure, provision was made in 1927, for the first time, to formalise a parish pension contribution for both vicar and curate, with a further regular contribution towards dilapidation costs at the vicarage so that those no longer had to be met entirely from the vicar's pocket.

Encouraged by their new representation, the laity proved eager to discuss matters of national and even international concern as well as parish-pump issues. When someone protested about the use of the Church Room for a political meeting, it was robustly pointed out, as it had been under Dearmer, that, there being no other public meeting place in the vicinity, political meetings were as acceptable as any other. In September 1920 the council asked to be briefed on the Lambeth Conference; and from 1921 Sir Frederick Holiday reported back to them after each National Assembly meeting, particularly on the Education Act 1922. Informed discussions also followed the vicar's briefings on the successive proposals for revision of the Prayer Book.

Guilt over spending the lion's share of a church's income on maintaining the building, was as evident then as it is today, but the newly-born PCC was determined that charitable and outreach work would also be strongly supported. From 1921 the council set a target of giving a quarter of its annual income to external objectives. And the scale of need was very considerable. After a brief post-War economic boom the 1920s was a decade of mass unemployment. How far this directly affected the congregation is not clear, but there was plenty of awareness of other people's sufferings and a desire to help. The Church Room, for example, was deployed in May 1922 for collecting clothes destined for the Mayor's Fund for the Unemployed in London, and in November 1924 the PCC expressed concern about the over-crowded housing in some parts of the parish, and urged the congregation to let out their spare rooms to ease the problem. Nor was concern limited to Great Britain: following the Russian famine of 1921-22, for example, money was raised in the parish in June 1922 for Russian soup kitchens.

War memorial

Even before the end of the First World War,[18] a temporary 'war shrine' designed by Clement Skilbeck was placed outside the south wall of the church. It comprised a crucifix behind closable wooden doors, and bore the names of fallen parishioners. Once the War ended, the PCC, which included Skilbeck himself, first considered whether some altogether different form of commemoration would be more appropriate, such as adding a wooden tower to the church with the original shrine figure attached to it, or providing a more ornate memorial with additional figures. But on cost as well as aesthetic grounds they settled instead for a simple memorial, and commissioned a design from Gerald Cogswell

ARIBA for a 'wayside crucifix' on which, they felt, the figure should be 'that of the suffering Christ'. This went through several modifications as they changed their minds about the kind of figure they wanted and even the format in which the names should be written. Most significantly, the figure was changed to a Christ 'triumphant', as on the great Rood. After further delays to await fund-raising, it was only in April 1921 that a Faculty authorising the final scheme was granted, with the figure of Christ carved by A. Marus. There was then another argument about how it was to be protected from the elements. That was never properly resolved, and ominously, even before the memorial was formally unveiled its stonework had already suffered some frost damage. Over the succeeding generations the weather caused erosion to both the figure and the names, which necessitated their periodic re-incision and eventual replacement.

The memorial, eventually costing a little over £200, was unveiled by Lord Beauchamp on 13 November 1921. As reported in the *Church Times* and parish magazine, the ceremony fell into two parts: inside the church, a Commemoration of the Departed based on the Vespers of the Dead, then, outside, an Act of Consecration, with special emphasis on Victory and Resurrection, 'the two being joined together by the singing of the Psalms of faith and triumph to which the field of Agincourt resounded. The prayers were based on an old English source, the Canterbury Benedictional. The ceremonial and the music were carried through with a dignity and order and simplicity which reflect great credit on all who took part, but most of all on those who were mainly responsible – Mr Vivian King and Mr Geoffrey Shaw'.

Golden Jubilee (1920)

Silver, Golden and Diamond Jubilees (not to mention sesqui-centennial ones) are, of course, sent from Heaven! They provide excuses for fund-raising, planning great works for the future, and partying. The Golden Jubilee of commissioning the original iron church fell in 1917, but with

War in progress celebration that year was unthinkable. When hostilities ceased the next sensible date to be classed as a 'jubilee' was 1920, to commemorate the start of building on the permanent church in 1870.

Ahead of that there was much preparation to be done, beginning with de-cluttering, and in that respect the first thing on most people's minds was what to do with the lowest tier of Bodley's reredos, sawn off on Dearmer's instructions in 1915 and still awaiting disposal. The council felt that it, together with a processional cross no longer required, should be offered to a poor parish, but no clear decision was made on this until 1925 when, following a preaching visit by the Bishop of British Honduras (who was a former vicar of St Paul's Avenue Road), they were given to him for use in Belize cathedral.[19] We also learn from a letter of thanks from Revd JW Massingham, assistant priest at St Nicolas, Guildford and a friend of JH Arnold, that the PCC had presented a frontal to his mission. The sale of a number of Arundel prints from the nave to raise funds, and even the sale of the vicarage at 7 Elsworthy Road (presumably as a step towards acquiring a more suitable residence), were both considered but not acted on.

As the Jubilee approached, a commemorative booklet, *St Mary the Virgin Primrose Hill after Fifty Years*, was put together. With a cover design by Clement Skilbeck, it included photographs of the interior by the parish's own distinguished photographer Violet Blaiklock, and an essay on music by Geoffrey Shaw. Profits from sales went towards a jubilee Thank Offering Fund, for which a £500 appeal was launched. For those unable to afford major donations, a picture of the exterior of St Mary's by TR Way (the lithographer commemorated by the Rood), was printed for sale, as were studio photographs of some of the church officials.

Jubilee services

D-J's links with academe enabled him to attract an impressive list of preachers during the festival, including the Revd EG Selwyn (Editor of *Theology*), Percy Dearmer (of course); FA Iremonger (the Chair of Life and Liberty); and the Revd SC Carpenter of Trinity College Cambridge.

Jubilee 1920. Group photograph outside the Church Room.

An unfortunate clash of dates with the Lambeth Conference prevented the bishops of both London and Willesden from attending, but a number of clergy previously associated with St Mary's returned for the occasion.

By the time of the festival the sum raised towards the Thank Offering Fund stood well below the hoped-for £500, but it was enough to pay off the debt on the Church Room, buy a new best frontal for the High Altar and have something in hand towards repairing the organ. The appeal was kept open, but in a clear affirmation of its concern for the wider church, the PCC voted to 'tax' contributions by 5%, to raise money for foreign missions.

Gifts to the church

We saw what a treasury of decorative ornaments, as well as more utilitarian furnishings, was acquired in Dearmer's time, with the emphasis always on the finest craftsmanship for the House of God. The same standards were maintained under D-J, and gifts came in, at first slowly on account of the War but later at an accelerating pace. When it came to textiles, the parish was fortunate in having skilled practitioners in its own ranks, like Mrs Eeles (FC's mother) of the Royal College of Needlework, the Misses Jones of King Henry's Road, and Miss Burgess (who re-painted the Lenten hangings and the reverse of the reredos doors). Mrs Eeles added to her already generous donations a new frontlet for the high altar, decorated with shields designed by EE Dorling, the heraldic artist (Dec 1916). Among other gifts in D-J's early years were a silver stand for Christmas decorations (Lady Beauchamp, 1917), a pyx in memory of Mabel Dearmer, Violet Hallam and Mary Janssen (Girls' Friendly Society 1918), and a silver Russian icon, which will make further, rather dramatic, appearances in this story under both Fr Hardcastle and Fr Timms (Evelyn Cooke 1920).

The 1920 Jubilee encouraged many more gifts, and its effects continued to be felt right down to the end of D-J's ministry, with altar linen, choir robes, hymn books, pictures, vestments and furniture.[20] Mrs Eeles worked two new chanters' copes (given by Geoffrey Shaw) and a black velvet frontlet for the high altar (given by JH Arnold). Possibly with the Jubilee in mind, Percy Dearmer generously made an outright gift to the church of some of his own personal vestments which he had left at St Mary's and never reclaimed.[21]

Other gifts and acquisitions under D-J which are still to be seen today include: the two **cherubs** on the organ case (given by Mrs Armstrong in 1921, probably originally from a church near Vienna); a larger **pyx** for the reserved sacrament (given by JGB Dick 1923), designed by WE Hardcastle, silversmith, and made, like the one given in memory of Mabel Dearmer, by Smythe Greenwood; and **a bishop's chair** for the sanctuary, made and given by Grace Jones, a copy of a 17th-century chair in the V&A, which displaced the earlier one made for Spencer by Harry Hems.

St Mary's was still being looked to by the wider Anglican church as a model of good taste, and was occasionally asked to lend items for use or exhibition elsewhere. A set of red vestments was loaned to St Barnabas, Norwich for the Anglo-Catholic Congress (1922), and a cope and censer loaned for a parish tableau in Welwyn (1926).

A gift that caused more vigorous argument than anything else before or since was **Henry Holiday's** Crucifixion *[Plate 4a]*. Holiday (1839-1927), an eminent Hampstead artist and designer of stained glass and mosaics, embraced pre-Raphaelitism in the circle of William Morris, Burne-Jones, Holman Hunt and Rossetti. He was a passionate Liberal, and supporter of women's suffrage, and died at Chesterford Gardens, where the Crucifixion had been displayed on an outside wall of his house.[22] Made in a technique known as 'opus sectile', it was not to everyone's taste. It was given to the church in 1927 by his brother Sir Frederick. As a result of its previous exposure to the elements it first needed specialist restoration at the British Museum. When it returned, the PCC could not agree where best to display it, and had to apply repeatedly for amended Faculties as they kept changing their minds. It first found a home in the transept, with a view to being eventually fixed to the exterior of the west wall at the end of the north aisle so that passers-by on King Henry's Road would see it, but conservation experts advised against that. The council became so exasperated that it even considered asking Sir Frederick to take it back! In the end it resolved (although not until Fr Harcourt's time, and not a moment too soon as Sir Frederick himself was to die in 1930) that the work should remain inside the church. After some peregrination it was displayed for several generations beside the font, but since the opening of the St Mary's Centre it has been displayed in the glazed atrium there, at the other end of the church.[23]

Unfortunately, some losses have also to be recorded. At the end of 1916 JA Little of Easington Colliery, Co. Durham, wrote explaining that a chalice from St Mary's lent to him in Serbia by Percy Dearmer had been pilfered by the Serbian authorities. In November 1919 the PCC heard that vestments it had loaned to the South Kensington Museum for its War Memorial exhibition had been damaged. In July 1920 the church was broken into via the south door at about 4 a.m. and £5 cash stolen.[24] And in October 1921 a careless workman dropped a light on the sacristy roof and started a small fire that damaged the roof lead. The water used to extinguish it in turn damaged items in the sacristy below.[25]

Colin Dunlop

Arthur Duncan-Jones would not have been able to maintain such a vigorous programme of activities throughout his ministry at St Mary's without a regular succession of able assistant clergy. Of these, none so won the hearts of the congregation, first as deacon and then as priest, as Colin Dunlop (1922-27).

As a young man he had lived in Hampstead, and during the War had at least once visited St Mary's when Percy Dearmer was celebrating and Martin Shaw playing the organ. The boys' singing of the hymns became imprinted on his memory: 'It seemed that the English language had had a spring cleaning, so clear and ringing were its vowel sounds'. Through his brother Walter, he also came to know at least one of Arthur Duncan-Jones's sons (and perhaps D-J also). At any rate D-J already knew him when he was preparing for ordination (after Oxford, war service and theological studies), and head-hunted him to be his new assistant. Having achieved the highest marks of his cohort in the examinations he would normally have been chosen to read the Gospel at the diocesan Ordination service at St Paul's cathedral, but by a special dispensation he was instead allowed to be ordained deacon at St Mary's by the Bishop of Willesden on 29 October 1922.[26] This was unusual enough in those days to merit coverage in the *Church Times*, where the music under Geoffrey Shaw and ceremonial under Vivian King drew particular praise: 'It was all very dignified and yet so simple, so direct, so personal, so intelligible, that it was plainly a religious act, the deep significance of which must have been grasped by the youngest worshipper in the

Revd Colin Dunlop

church, and it was good to see how many young people were present.' Dunlop was priested at St Paul's cathedral the following year, on 23 October 1923, and to mark that event his sister Sybil Dunlop, a renowned art deco jeweller, presented St Mary's with a jewelled morse for its best cope.

Dunlop showed himself to be very much in the Dearmer/Duncan-Jones mould by writing an Alcuin club pamphlet very shortly after his ordination, entitled *What is the English Use?*[27] With PCCs in need of reference material, especially during the long-drawn-out debates on Prayer Book reform, this was a timely offering. It explored the divide among loyal High-Church Anglicans between those like Dearmer, who followed the 'English' Use and those who, partly for want of timely direction to the contrary but partly as a claim to liberty of expression in the face of persecution, followed the 'Western' (Roman) Use.

Dunlop's job description included taking on the 'Mastership' of the Junior Guild and leading the junior Catechism, but being still a bachelor with little experience of dealing with children, as distinct from soldier subordinates, he confided to his diary that fear of his own limitations in this kind of work first terrified and later depressed him.[28] But he soon won over the boys, not least by introducing cricket as one of the guild's summer activities, and perhaps also by replacing the guilds in 1926 by the new Social Club for both sexes.

Fortunately he had much else to divert him, including preparing sermons and writing articles for the parish magazine about aspects of the liturgy and vestments. When, through pressure of work, D-J resigned as Secretary of the Alcuin Cub in 1923 (remaining a member of its Committee), he shoed-in Dunlop in his place, where he remained until he left St Mary's in 1927.

At the end of 1925, when D-J accepted an invitation to visit the Berkeley Divinity School in the USA for three months, he had sufficient confidence in Dunlop's abilities to request that he be made priest-in-charge (with other clergy available to assist) during his absence, and the bishop approved. A grateful parish awarded Dunlop an honorarium to cover the extra responsibility.

Dunlop naturally came to know Geoffrey Shaw (and through him Martin) and Jack Arnold and their respective families. He became godfather to Jack Arnold's son Colin, named in his honour, and remained firm friends with the Arnolds right up to Jack's death in 1956, when he presided at the requiem.

In May 1927 after more than four years at St Mary's, Dunlop was appointed chaplain to the bishop of London at Fulham Palace, although he took two short postings on the way there, at St George's, Paris and in St Moritz. D-J's appreciation thanked him for 'the loyal comradeship of these last four years. We are such old friends that the parting will be particularly severe. And there are many who, though they have not known him as long as I have, will have very much the same sense of personal loss.' In a letter from Paris thanking the parish for his leaving present, Dunlop wrote, 'I shall always regard St Mary's as my home in a way which no other parish can ever be – for it was you who trained me to be a priest of God.' After a spell in Baghdad (see below) he served as chaplain to Bishop Bell of Chichester, then as vicar of Henfield, Sussex where he introduced a moderate form of the English Use,[29] then became Bishop of Jarrow and finally Dean of Lincoln. His work in Chichester kept him in close touch with D-J (who by then had become dean of the cathedral) and he also met once again his old friend from Oxford, Dr E Martin Browne, the first Diocesan Advisor on Drama, who in his turn would later move to London and become a parishioner and Trustee of St Mary's. *O Fortuna*! We shall meet Dunlop again as a frequent visitor and friend. His associations with St Mary's, as priest and then bishop, continued right through to the 1960s and his last official act at St Mary's was the dedication of the new high altar ornaments in memory of Arthur Duncan-Jones, Martin Shaw and Jack Arnold in 1960.

Liturgy

D-J had no wish to make serious changes to the liturgy at St Mary's so soon after the reign of Percy Dearmer, and in any case placed great faith in Dearmer's judgement in matters of both liturgy and art. He was particularly enthusiastic about Dearmer's introduction at St Mary's of the 'English altar' with four corner-posts and curtains.[30] And although, over the course of his ministry, D-J did indeed introduce changes, often encouraged by the musicians and the congregation, they were broadly in line with either the Dearmer tradition itself or evolving Anglican practice as illuminated by the ongoing publications of the Alcuin Club of which Dearmer and a number of others with past or present associations with St Mary's (Sir Cyril Cobb, FC Eeles, Revd JN Newland Smith) were still key committee members, with D-J himself as Secretary and later Vice President. D-J's own important addition to the Club's output, which confirmed his standing as a liturgist, was the *Directory of Ceremonial* (1921),[31] which was seen through the press by Vivian King and illustrated by Clement Skilbeck, both of St Mary's. Amid much else, it included ceremonial provision for Candlemas (introduced at St Mary's in 1919) and the liturgy of Holy Week. All of the changes, as well as much of the regular practice, were explained through articles in the parish magazine, written by the vicar and others including FC Eeles and later Colin Dunlop. According to one estimate[32] there were at this time about 50, mostly adult, servers, a tally that has probably never since been matched.

Lenten Array

Percy Dearmer's introduction of the Lenten Array has already been described, but the great Rood with its figures had been erected only in 1915, shortly before he left St Mary's. A decision therefore had to be made early in D-J's ministry about how, if at all, to veil that during Lent. Its size and height from the ground were significant challenges, and it was four years before a solution was found, by means of ropes and pulleys, to hoist in front of the cross a piece of unbleached linen (the original donated by Mr Eggleton), painted by Miss Burgess with a plain red cross.[33] This in turn led to the introduction of a ceremonial (new to St Mary's) for the unveiling of the Rood at the end of the Palm Sunday procession. As new pictures were acquired or presented, the Misses Jones supplied appropriate veils, with images again stencilled by Miss Burgess.

High and Low

No more than Dearmer did D-J hold with bowing and scraping, but he did expect uniformity of movements and gestures by the clergy, servers and choir, at the Sung Eucharist in particular, and encouraged the congregation (though not at all heavy-handedly) to follow suit. In choir and sanctuary he could scarcely have had a more devoted and expert team than Eeles and King.[34]

If the congregation remained split over what church observances to tolerate (and whether it mattered!), the PCC on their behalf grappled with even the most arcane of liturgical questions: whether flowers might be placed on the altar (rejected, November 1917); whether the feast of Corpus Christi commemorating the institution of the Blessed Sacrament should be celebrated and whether a bell should be rung to mark the Angelus (both rejected, July 1920). In 1926 a revived proposal to celebrate Corpus Christi with a eucharist was again roundly rejected, and the vicar explained that he would in any case not have celebrated it, as it was not an approved feast of the Church of England.[35] Veneration of the Cross on Good Friday, by those who wished to do so, was accepted in March 1921, but the service of Tenebrae, which had taken place several times before at St Mary's, was rejected in February 1922, and the censing of objects and people was rejected in March 1923.

It remained the custom of many at St Mary's to receive communion fasting, and therefore at the early Eucharist at 8 a.m. Those who intended to communicate instead at the Sung Eucharist were not chided, but simply asked to take a place in the chapel by the time of the Offertory so they could be counted.[36] Many other traditions were kept up, including the outdoor Rogationtide procession with St Mark's. That, however, lost some of its poignancy once the wartime allotments on Primrose Hill were discontinued.

For much of the 1920s all eyes were on the Church Assembly as it struggled to agree the form of a new Prayer Book to lay before Parliament. Duncan-Jones was a strong supporter of the Assembly's direction of travel, and explained the successive stages of debate in the magazine and in more detailed briefings held in the Church Room. In preparation for the expected arrival of the new book he also worked with Jack Arnold to publish a scheme of liturgy for the Three Hours' Devotion on Good Friday.[37] But the House of Commons refused to approve the 'Deposited Prayer Book', thus in effect rejecting the Church's claim to settle its own doctrine and practice. On the last Sunday of Advent 1927 a bitterly disappointed D-J preached a sermon branding the Book's opponents as people with little knowledge of theology, who in some cases were trying to bring about the disestablishment of the Church. The PCC took the unusually forthright step of writing to Hampstead's MP complaining that, by voting against the Measure, he had gone against the 'united wishes of the churches in his constituency'.[38]

From at least 1923 it had been customary at St Mary's during the Three Hours on Good Friday to sing the Passion Gospel to plainsong. In the 1662 Prayer Book the narrative is split between the readings at Matins and Holy Communion, but the 1928 Prayer Book offered it as a single narrative, and with the Bishop of London's permission that was the version sung at St Mary's in 1928.

Preaching

D-J was a good preacher, firmly in the Christian Socialist tradition of Dearmer but with a distinctly modern edge and, like his predecessor, never allowing party politics to intrude into his sermons. Colin Dunlop recalled after D-J's death in 1955 how

> almost every Sunday morning of the year he would be the preacher at the Solemn Eucharist at 11.15. It was usually his practice to preach on the collect, epistle or gospel for the day, and everything he said was firmly based upon sound theological principles clearly and attractively expounded. But like the great Fathers of the Church he brought within the orbit and judgment of these principles the every-day events of his time, the public controversies of the hour and the political and international happenings. No one who regularly 'sat under' D-J at St Mary's can ever forget that wonderful series of sermons, addressed mostly to the head and the will but occasionally, and with great power, to the heart. … As one friend

of St Mary's once [said]: there was always fresh air blowing through St Mary's. His congregation was mostly resident within a mile of the church but others came regularly from considerable distances. What everyone learned from D-J was to love Catholic worship, both through the dignity of its presentation and through the doctrinal principles on which it rested, and to see in Catholic worship the pattern of the Christian life.[39]

That may have been the regular pattern, yet D-J also introduced the parish to many illustrious visiting preachers, especially at festivals, as we saw in connection with the 1920 Jubilee. Among those whom Dunlop recalled hearing while curate were Walter Frere, Bishop Winnington-Ingram, Kenneth Kirk, William Temple and Bishop Gore.[40] The Patronal Festival each July continued to be celebrated in style, and the mood it invoked can be judged by the resolution of the PCC after the 1923 Festival, recording 'their appreciation of the work of the Rev Dr Dearmer and the Rev AS Duncan-Jones in building up and maintaining a ceremonial based on loyalty to the Prayer Book and in accordance with the ancient usage of the English Church.'

Another jubilee, but this time given only low-key treatment on 28 April 1927, was the 60th anniversary of the opening of the iron church. It fell on a weekday but was marked by a Sung Eucharist at 7 a.m.

Among other liturgical observances, Duncan-Jones also saw to it that the Armistice was properly recognised at St Mary's year by year.

Music

As Martin Shaw had been disqualified from the military call-up on health grounds, music at the church was maintained throughout the War, even though enlistment took its toll on both choir and congregation, and it became increasingly difficult even to find an organ blower, let alone singers. In spite of everything, a high standard was maintained, and in October 1916 the vicar was proudly able to quote from a recent church newspaper that:

...there are churches where a higher standard exists, where there is an atmosphere of sanctity, of repose, of a grave and ordered comeliness, of a classic healthiness of the senses, where beautiful objects may be found set in a certain austerity, and where beautiful music can be heard. In London, for instance, there is St Mary's Primrose Hill, where Mr Martin Shaw is organist. Here the *English Hymnal* is used and beautiful hymns as well as Sequences and Antiphons, whose existence is never suspected by the majority of church-goers, can be heard every Sunday. In addition, plainsong is used throughout. Now plainsong, which is the old modal church music, is not to be appreciated at a first hearing; but if any reader who goes to St Mary's (Chalk Farm Tube) any Sunday at 10 a.m. comes away after service without experiencing that joy which comes in taking part in really beautiful work, and comes from that alone, I shall be much astonished.

A Choir Fund was established from voluntary contributions, divided into Men's and Women's sections. From it, the choir men who remained, and others recruited to fill vacancies, were paid a small stipend, and from 1917 Geoffrey Shaw was paid £30 p.a. as assistant organist, half-and-half from each of the two funds. Martin Shaw composed a new Folk Mass which was given its first performance at Septuagesima 1918. With the vicar, he also helped to organise a meeting of the Church Music Society at St Mary's in April that year.

With the ending of the War both Martin and Geoffrey Shaw took active steps not only to boost the church's music, but also to raise money for the church's (and the organ's) refurbishment. Martin put out press advertisements for more men, and appealed in the parish paper for new boy choristers (May 1919). He affiliated the choir to the League of Arts. Meanwhile, in aid of the Fabric Fund, Geoffrey gave a lecture about national music (1918), and a series of fund-raising organ recitals in the autumn of the following year. Congregational practices of the hymns were revived.

In December 1919 Martin Shaw resigned in order to become director of music at St Martin-in-the-Fields. A later press tribute said of him:

'Experimenting and developing, he obtained a grasp and experience of church music that has made him indispensable in Anglican propaganda. Congregational singing was specially cultivated in the church, and plainsong thereby was popularized and made attractive.'[41]

D-J continued to chair the Summer School of Church Music, and with Joan Shaw was invited to lecture to the Welsh National Music Festival in Aberystwyth in 1916. He brought his thoughts together in a book entitled *Church Music* (1920), which explored the role of music in the liturgy both historically and for his own day. It was a timely contribution, given the rising national popularity of Holy Communion as the focus of Sunday worship, and a growing awareness (promoted by the likes of Martin Shaw and Vaughan Williams) of what was distinctively English and what, within that, was the best. Music, he said, was an offering to God and should therefore be of the highest possible standard in the local context. That would mean different things for a cathedral compared with most parish churches, and in the parish there was much to be said for keeping things simple. To D-J's mind a diet of plainsong and home-grown English music by the likes of Merbecke was ideal – certainly preferable to Victorian saccharine, but he was open to a wider repertoire. The people should be encouraged to participate, and PCCs too should have a say. Everything must contribute to praise and edification, and the music should assist the natural flow of the liturgy – so, for example, anthems and settings should not drag on to the detriment of the liturgical action. The parson must maintain a lively interest in the music, but without seeking to usurp the organist and choirmaster's roles.

Geoffrey Shaw, by now well-known at St Mary's, was welcomed as his brother's successor, at a salary of £100, while £50 was made available for an Assistant Organist, this post eventually being offered to JH (Jack) Arnold. The treble line was steadily built up, and their routine was rather strict, with three evening practices a week which included lessons in reading music in both conventional and plainsong notation.[42] Congregational concern in 1919 about the boys' restless behaviour in church was resolved quite simply, by allowing them to slip out for a break during the sermon. By February 1922, in addition to the boys, the choir comprised 2 cantors (one of them Geoffrey Shaw himself); 6 men; and 2 women, one of whom was Mrs Dick, the wife of the churchwarden Bernard Dick.[43] Relations between the music department and the vicar had never been better. Shaw wrote in the Jubilee booklet in 1920:

> How fortunate we are in possessing a vicar who is a recognized authority on Church music ... Our ideals are identical with his. His sympathy with our efforts is unfailing. In his hands our traditions are safe; and he has in addition that modern spirit that enables him to appreciate to the full any new work that is good.

According to Jack Arnold, D-J as a singer was 'able and fluent and a pleasure to accompany.' Even though he knew nothing about the organ, at children's services he would still sit at the keyboard to provide the accompaniment.[44] He took considerable pains to ensure that the congregation understood the English liturgical tradition.

To encourage better participation, and help the congregation *enjoy* the services more, details of all the musical and liturgical books in use were printed in the parish paper so that those so minded could buy their own copies and bring them along each week. But this stirring of interest carried a measure of risk. It encouraged the PCC to set up a Music Committee which occasionally flexed its muscles to keep the music department in check. During one discussion in 1922 Bernard Dick, who had recently completed a term as churchwarden, called for simpler music at Evensong, better-known tunes for the hymns, and 'the disuse of the pulpit gown', but the PCC disagreed and resolved that (1) the choir should sing throughout; (2) there should be congregational practices and (3) the black gown should be retained but explained.

The solid diet of plainsong developed in Dearmer's early years had already been moderated by Martin Shaw's introduction first of Merbecke then of his own two mass settings. Under Geoffrey Shaw and D-J, plainsong retained its primacy, and Jack Arnold became an expert in its accompaniment. In 1927 he published his definitive work

Plainsong accompaniment (OUP). In a letter used as the preface to the book, Geoffrey Shaw wrote to Arnold:

> You and I, as fellow workers at St Mary's, share together a privilege so lovely that we cannot imagine that the bond between us could ever be broken. We have grown to think alike in our work, though I own I have not yet grown to the measure of your strong principle and considered judgement in the matter of the right place for my organ music, nor even, alas, for the key of the cupboard in which I ought to put it away.

The Martin Shaw masses continued to feature regularly as settings at the Sung Eucharist. Rather gingerly, Geoffrey introduced an occasional motet for the choir, at the very end of the service, but this was not universally appreciated. Mr Lyster-Smythe objected to the choir's singing a Byrd motet in Latin, even though a translation of the words was available in the *English Hymnal*. The Music Committee, without in so many words seeking to prohibit it, let it be known that it would think it inappropriate to fund the purchase of any more Latin music!

Shaw and Arnold began giving short organ recitals before Evensong: at first with a rather conservative, Bachian repertoire, but soon more wide-ranging, including works of the great English composers from SS Wesley to Vaughan Williams, and of the recent great wave of Parisian organists such as Vierne and Widor. Lists of the weekly hymns and musical settings were published in advance. Some practical experiments were tried. Alongside the revival of congregational practices already mentioned, Shaw published in the magazine a set of 'directions' to encourage a better ensemble:

Congregational singing

1. The Congregation is asked to sing heartily the Responses, Hymns, Kyrie, Creed, Sursum Corda, Lord's Prayer and Gloria.
2. The third and fifth verses of a hymn will be sung by the congregation alone; except in a hymn of only three verses, when the congregation

will sing the second verse. The choir alone will sing the fourth verse of a hymn unless the fourth verse is the last verse of the hymn.
3. Occasional practices for the congregation will be held.
4. Remember (a) to sing with conviction and meaning; (b) to take plenty of breath, so as to sing one phrase in one breath wherever possible; (c) To stress the syllables that require stress; (d) To keep the rhythm going. *Do not drag.*

The singing of the Creed and Lord's Prayer at Evensong on a monotone was dropped in favour of plain speech, with only the last phrase in each being sung. The congregation, however, does not seem to have lived up to the clergy and musicians' hopes. In January 1925 D-J complained that the clergy often felt nobody was joining in, even with Amens. At Geoffrey Shaw's suggestion Matins was begun a bit later to reduce the gap between it and the Sung Eucharist.

In September 1922, there was further evidence of the high esteem in which music at St Mary's was held nationally, when no fewer than three representatives of the parish (Lord Beauchamp, Geoffrey Shaw and the vicar) were chosen to serve on a new Archbishops' Commission on Church Music.[45] From 1924, it became the practice for four boys from the choir to stand round the cantor's lectern at the end of the Sung Eucharist to sing the plainsong Communion proper, and for this Arnold prepared a large manuscript book, the 'Book of Communion Anthems'.

More ambitious musical programmes included in June 1925 a special service, talks and a recital in honour of the tercentenary of the death of Orlando Gibbons, and in December the same year a grand carol service. By then the urgency of repairs to the organ was becoming more apparent. Norman and Beard were called in to examine the instrument for mechanical defects, and estimated that its repair would cost £122 and take five weeks. As £58 was already available in the Organ Fund and an anonymous donor had offered another £50, the PCC approved the expenditure, but the work could not be carried out for a further year because of a builders' strike. It was then decided that services would be unaccompanied during the work, in the course of which pipes for three of the organ stops that were never used were removed and two others re-voiced.

D-J's external involvement

Although D-J had put a university career behind him in favour of parish ministry, he continued to study and write on English liturgy and church music. His work in connection with the Alcuin Club has already been mentioned. Before he came to Primrose Hill he had been approached to deliver the 1916 Hulsean Lectures in Cambridge, a series that resulted in his book *Ordered Liberty* (1917) which gave him the opportunity to show his mettle in the Dearmer tradition, defending the Anglican church: against Rome, certainly, but as part of the one true Church of God. In the Preface he wrote, 'I have discovered at the Church of Our Lady by Primrose Hill that when the Church of England is allowed freely to express itself, and just itself, that is a thing of austere and virile beauty, whose notes are joy and praise and hope.'

During the 1920s it became more necessary for him to earn additional income, and he undertook paid work for a church newspaper, *The Guardian,* which occasionally impinged on the time he had available for the parish. 'Without it,' he wrote in self-defence, 'I could not very well continue at St Mary's'. He also found time to contribute a biography of Archbishop William Laud (1927) to a series on 'Great English Churchmen' edited by Sidney Dark and published by Macmillan. Written from a fairly sympathetic point of view, befitting a liturgist interested in maintaining the dignity of worship, it was nevertheless a well-argued piece.

Resignation

The 1920s, and especially the period when Colin Dunlop was D-J's assistant 1922-1927, were both happy and successful times at St Mary's.

The rising yearly total of communicants tells its own story: 11777 (1923); 11769 (1924); 12442 (1925) and 12906 (1926).

At the beginning of 1928 D-J resigned in order to move on, to St Paul's Knightsbridge. At a special church meeting on 7 February, the congregation presented him with an oak writing desk, a chair and a cheque for £130 'to mark their appreciation of his 12 years ministry at St Mary's', and the women of the congregation gave his wife a wrist watch, lacquer toilet articles and the balance 'in a purse.'[46] In his farewell letter to the parish, after what he described as twelve years of 'almost unmixed happiness', D-J said it had left him feeling delighted to be a member of the Church of England. The 'sense of corporate life and churchmanship' was now so strong that the vacancy to follow would be no problem, and 'the composition of the board of Trustees who exercise the patronage of St Mary's makes it certain that my successor will be a man who can be relied on to continue the principles and practices that have proved their worth for twenty-seven years'. As to that, time would tell!

The sense of loyalty to the church which he engendered comes across in two later tributes by Colin Dunlop, who remained a friend for life. D-J's days at St Mary's, he said, were the happiest of his [D-J's] life, and whilst, intellectually, he appealed to one slice of the congregation, he was down-to-earth enough to be well liked also by 'many plain folk'.

> It was … his teaching and leadership rather than his personality which brought the people together. Quite a number of the firmest adherents of St Mary's were extremely critical of their vicar, and a few were antagonistic to him, but it did not occur to them to go elsewhere (so easy in London), for it was D-J's teaching and leadership that they valued… [47]

The most valuable things he did were his work in teaching and commending the Catholic faith to a large, regular and distinguished congregation, and in his pastoral work among what would now be called 'teen-agers'.[48]

After only a year in Knightsbridge, D-J was appointed Dean of Chichester. Throughout his ministry he remained closely in touch with St Mary's, and he will make regular further appearances as the story unfolds.

* * *

Other lives

Blaiklock family

Frank Blaiklock, who lived at 18 Elsworthy Road, was one of Spencer's first churchwardens, elected in 1889 and serving right through his ministry and on until 1902 when he became Treasurer. Arthur Duncan-Jones would later describe him as a 'devout Anglo-Catholic of the old school', but despite all the changes he lived through he remained loyal to his parish church and provided stalwart support to three vicars. He served as a Trustee from 1898 to 1916 (in which capacity he would have had a say in appointing Percy Dearmer), and as trustee of the Church Room from 1895 until his death in 1926. A former parishioner from Fr Fuller's days, Geoffrey Austin [GHA], paid this tribute after Blaiklock's death:

> When the Revd A Spencer came as 2nd Vicar, he was faced with very considerable difficulties, principally an incomplete Church, an unhappy balance sheet, and a ritual which was colloquially known as 'Fuller's mixture', and naturally he had to look out a suitable man as his warden. Few men would have cared to take office under such conditions; the responsibility was very great, but the man was there, the right-hand man, tact and sense and business capacity united in him... We do not forget the great gifts of Revd A Spencer; but we doubt whether he would have succeeded so well without Frank Blaiklock's valuable and faithful aid all those wonderful years ...

Violet Blaiklock, his daughter, assisted her father in playing the organ for Dearmer's Catechism services, while her sister **Elsie** ran the kindergarten, a role she performed for two decades. Violet was an accomplished photographer whose work was extensively used by St Mary's in its publications and postcards, copies of some of which survive in the archives. But she achieved wider prominence in the 1920s, as one of the first female, nationally-rated colour photographers. (Fellow of the Royal Photographic Society, 1920). She was among the founders of the Society's Colour Group in 1927.[49]

PH Bradbury

One particular person who provided robust support to D-J was his Verger, PH Bradbury. He was later remembered by Colin Dunlop:

> Though short and stocky of frame, his calm, steady eye set beneath a massive forehead and over a fine beard revealed the essential dignity of his personality. No one dared take liberties with him, not even D-J. Bradbury's attitude to his Vicar was a blend of bewilderment and intense loyalty. He could never thoroughly understand him, but he instinctively trusted him and secretly admired him. At the giving of an order or the inauguration of some change in the way things were to be done, Bradbury would apparently bristle with opposition, but in a week's time any critic of the innovation could receive very short shrift from the Verger.[50]

Dick family

Bernard (JBG) Dick, proprietor of a celebrated 'crammers',[51] served two terms as churchwarden, 1918-21 and 1929-30, and was the anonymous donor of a pyx for the communion of the sick in 1923. His wife **Mary** was one of the first female members of the choir under Geoffrey Shaw, and according to one witness[52] since women were not allowed to go hatless in church right up to the Second World War, wore 'a fetching little tricorne'. She served on many church committees until the family moved away from the parish in 1953. Their son Godfrey, who had Down's syndrome, was a keen server and thurifer (not afraid to tackle the 360-degree loop, with spectacular consequences on at least one occasion!)[53] After Bernard's death Mary presented the oak case for the memorial book in 1965, at which time she and Godfrey were worshipping at All Saints' Margaret Street.

Endnotes

1. See, in particular, Carpenter, SC, *Duncan-Jones of Chichester* (1956). In 1922 the PCC voted to raise the vicar's stipend to £300, and aspired to make it £400. As well as taking on paid work for a church newspaper, the *Guardian*, he undertook some marking for the Oxford & Cambridge examination board.
2. BL: Shaw archive.
3. *Primrose Hill, a History* (2013), ch 12.
4. Carpenter, *op.cit.*, p.98.
5. *Ibid*, p.42.
6. PM, Nov 1980.
7. PM, Feb 1955.
8. An advertisement (?*CT*) for this is pasted into VH King's parish chronicle, p.81.
9. There were no plays in 1926-27; 1930-34; 1936; 1939-41; 1944-61. For the Group's later history see Part Two.
10. See, for example, *Love's Labours Lost* in PM, Jun 1922.
11. PM, Apr 1923.
12. Through the Church of England Assembly (Powers) Act or 'Enabling Act' which was consolidated by the Parochial Church Councils (Powers) Act, 1921.
13. The legislation was thoroughly overhauled and updated by the PCC (Powers) Measure 1956 which has itself been amended by a number of subsequent Measures.
14. It was a near thing: Ainger Road was damaged by bombing, PM, Oct 1917.
15. PCC, Dec 1917.
16. PM, Apr 1918. The verse in question can only have been one that never appeared in the successive editions of the *English Hymnal*: 'O Lord our God arise, Scatter our enemies, And make them fall; Confound their politics, Frustrate their knavish tricks; On thee our hopes we fix: God save us all.'
17. Pasted into LMA: P81/MRV/91.
18. PM, Jan 1917.
19. PM, Oct 1908: Report that the vicar of St Paul's Avenue Road, Rev Herbert Bury, has been appointed Bishop of Honduras. The same faculty authorised disposal of a dark blue altar frontal, three frontlets and the temporary war shrine.
20. In the wake of subsequent changes in liturgical fashion and the use of church space, some items of undoubted historic and artistic value have since been lost, or disposed of: including a chanter's lectern (designed by Skilbeck, 1921), two 15th-century oak chests (given by Eeles, 1922) and a set of crib figures by Miss Rope – probably Dorothy Ann Aldrich Rope, niece and assistant of the more famous Ethel Mary Rope (given by Lady Beauchamp, 1924). These may have been the figures smashed by a demented vandal one Christmas in the 1970s, as reported in Part Two.

21 PM, Dec 1920.
22 See Christine Mill, 'Henry Holiday – an eminent Hampstead Victorian', in *Camden History Review*, 6 (1978).
23 CERC: CARE 23/329.
24 Archives: VH King Chronicle p.73.
25 Ibid., p.77.
26 This was the first ordination ever to take place at St Mary's.
27 Alcuin Club pamphlet 11 (Mowbrays,1923).
28 Dunlop, Francis, *From London to Lincoln via Baghdad. The life of Bishop Colin Dunlop 1897-1968* (2019). pp.83-84.
29 Information from John Hawes.
30 PM, Jun 1922 remarks in passing that the altar at SMVPH has four corner pillars and curtains. Introduced as English style by Dearmer and sometimes opposed on precisely those terms. 'We certainly owe Dr Dearmer a debt of gratitude, in that he was one of the people who saw most clearly the religious and artistic rightness of the Christian tradition in this matter'.
31 John Hawes in PM, Feb 1993.
32 Carpenter, *op. cit.*, p.98.
33 PM, Mar. 1920.
34 Carpenter, *op. cit.*, p.33.
35 Neither, for that matter, was the feast of All Souls, but as that was already being observed when D-J arrived at St Mary's he did not change it.
36 PM, Nov 1921.
37 Duncan-Jones, A and Arnold, JH (eds), *A Liturgical Service for Good Friday*. [c.1927].
38 PM, Feb 1928 p.19.
39 PM, Feb 1955.
40 Dunlop, *op. cit.*, p.91.
41 *Suffolk and Essex Free Press,* 13 October 1920 [British Newspaper Archive].
42 Information from Norman Smith, 2006.
43 See Kit Ruggles in PM, Jul/Aug 1989.
44 Carpenter, *op. cit.*, pp.34,35.
45 PM, Sep 1922, p.3.
46 Archives: V H King Parish Chronicle p. 87.
47 Carpenter, *op. cit.*, p.45.
48 PM, Feb 1955.
49 See, for example, 'Violet Blaiklock's *Lead Kindly Light*', in Royal Photographic Society Journal, April 2015 p.320.
50 Carpenter, *op.cit.*, p.46.
51 Information from Peter Heathfield.
52 PM, Jul 1989.
53 John Arnold, 'St Mary's – a focus on childhood', in PM, June-July 2005, p.16.

Chapter 6

Revd Hubert Harcourt

Vicar, 1928-1933

The setting
In the parish magazines for 2008-2009, Roger Langrish wrote of his childhood memories of the area in the 1930s: quiet streets with little motorised traffic and few parked cars (because they were mostly garaged or kept in Oppidans Mews); still plenty of horse-drawn delivery vehicles bringing, for example, coal from Chalk Farm railway yard, milk from United Dairies, bread from the local baker; the muffin man ringing his bell as he walked along the street, or that other bell so eagerly anticipated by children, from the Walls Ice Cream box tricycle. The 31 bus along Adelaide Road was open-topped with solid tyres on spoked wheels, and although all was business-like, life was less hurried and frenzied than in our computer-driven age.

Appointment of the new vicar, and early concerns
Arthur Duncan-Jones gave ample warning of his impending departure. Hoping to avoid any significant delay in finding another candidate, the Trustees held several meetings even before his last service on 5 February 1928,[1] but in the end a short vacancy became necessary and the Revd EW Sara who had been assisting D-J at St Mary's since 1923 was temporarily appointed Priest-in-charge. Sara had scarcely warmed the vicar's stall, however, before the Trustees came forward with the name of the Revd Hubert Harcourt, the recently married senior curate of Dorking, aged

40, who had spent his early ministry in Armenia. He was instituted as fifth vicar of St Mary's on 11 April 1928 by the Bishop of Willesden on behalf of the Bishop of London. Shortly afterwards Sara moved on to another parish, leaving Harcourt without an assistant. After a deacon withdrew on health grounds, and then a newly appointed assistant had to move on after just a few months, it was to be February 1929 before Harcourt regularly had an assistant.

Financial reforms

Harcourt had no previous connection with the parish or its clergy, but was aware of its traditions and of the esteem in which it held Percy Dearmer, so that liturgically his was a safe pair of hands. But it was not so much liturgy as finance that demanded his immediate attention. The bill he faced for 'dilapidations' (necessary repairs and redecoration) as he moved into the vicarage came to over £300. The PCC went some way to helping, by giving him that year's Easter offerings of £77 (taken during the vacancy). In addition a loan of £54 was secured from Queen Anne's Bounty. But Harcourt still had to find £150 himself. This he generously did, and then went even further by giving back to the PCC £20 *per annum* from his still only modest stipend in order to launch a Vicarage Fund to enable running repairs to be carried out as they arose rather than mounting up until there was a change of incumbent, as had happened to him.

Luckily he had a good eye for financial management, and within just a few months had persuaded the PCC to set up in addition two Endowment Funds, one for the church fabric and the other for the augmentation of the living itself. Contributions to these by parishioners were generally quite small (although in 1932 the Augmentation Fund received a major boost with a legacy of £2000 from Lt-Col Lee),[2] but as they were later matched by the Ecclesiastical Commissioners and other grant-awarding bodies they gave useful underpinning to the living and made a lasting contribution to the running of the parish during and after Fr Harcourt's time. The PCC voted to raise the vicar's net stipend to £400 p.a. including the £50 grant from Eton College and the income from the Endowment Fund (averaging £67), as well as providing for dilapidation costs on the vicarage, repayment of the loan from Queen Anne's Bounty and a pension contribution.[3]

Church maintenance

Harcourt was also conscientious in organising the maintenance and decoration of the church. No large-scale building work of the kind undertaken by the first three vicars was called for during his time, but considerable attention was paid to the building's upkeep. Among other projects, expert advice was sought on restoring the War Memorial in 1928, the external brickwork was repointed in 1929, and the clergy vestry re-whitened in 1931.

Parish social life

Harcourt's first priority was to get the measure of his new parish, and he quickly registered that its make-up was rapidly changing as people moved out of the area and many of the larger houses were divided into flats. This in turn suggested that some of the old ways of doing things might no longer be appropriate. His wife played a major role in getting to know the ladies of the parish, through a series of weekly 'At Homes', one outcome of which was the establishment, for the first time at St Mary's, of a branch of the Mothers' Union. However, the 'St Mary's Society' founded under DJ was mothballed, and in its place an events and social committee was established. For young people, what sounded like a substantial new programme of activities was launched in the Church Room, but they included much that had been tried and tested, such as the Cubs and Brownies, and in 1931 (once again) a troop of Girl Guides. Badminton was also on offer for young adults, in the Church Room. What was notably lacking, however, was a leader with the drive and imagination of Colin Dunlop to take forward this work with children and young people, and as a result much of Dunlop's work, as he himself would later lament, withered on the vine.

Amateur dramatic performances by the St Mary's Players were encouraged, and in addition to Passion plays and children's nativity plays the offerings included a new outing for the medieval morality play *Everyman* (1929, performed in church with the bishop's permission); Housman's *Five Little Plays of St Francis* (1930), and a version of *Pilgrim's Progress* (1932, both in the Church Room).

Liturgy

After the 1928 Prayer Book failed to receive Parliamentary backing Harcourt spent some time weighing up options before deciding in December to draw selectively on the new book, as permitted at the bishops' discretion, to revise the eucharistic liturgy at St Mary's. Jack Arnold, the assistant organist, gave the church a liturgical copy of the 1928 book. Harcourt, as we shall see below, was ostensibly sensitive to the liturgical needs of his congregation, even at the risk of upsetting his organist and choirmaster. In 1929, after consulting an unnamed theologian 'friend of the parish', he decided that the feast of Corpus Christi, which had not been observed by Duncan-Jones, could now be celebrated without impropriety.

A number of ladies in the congregation, particularly the two Misses Jones, made and presented new vestments, including surplices and copes (one red and gold, one white).

Fire

Only three months after the Harcourts' arrival disaster struck when the main electric cable to the church blew, causing a fire in the ambulatory which destroyed much of the roof there as well as a cupboard containing four thuribles and an incense boat. Fortunately the alarm was raised in time for the brigade to prevent the adjacent sacristy and its contents catching light, otherwise the entire building might have caught fire. The church's insurers paid for the damage in full. Meanwhile St John's, Red Lion Square, made a short-term loan of a thurible, but an anonymous donor quickly put up the money to commission a brass thurible and incense boat from the Warham Guild, based on a 14th-century thurible and a 16th-century incense boat found in Whittlesea Mere in 1850 and thought to have been originally from the medieval abbey of Ramsey.

The vicar's authority

It was the undoing of Fr Harcourt that he took a distinctly authoritarian view of the vicar's role, in a way that belied his public assurances that he was keen to hear suggestions and take advice from his congregation. He got off to a shaky start by writing to the press, and again in the parish magazine of October 1928, publicly opposing a united service with other Christian denominations, arguing that the Church of England must maintain its distinctive and separate witness. He would never worship, he said, with any body that had deliberately cut itself off from the Church of England, nor with the Roman Catholics (to whom, like many of his contemporaries, even including Dearmer before him, he was all-but allergic.) The majority of his PCC strongly disapproved of his stance and felt some kind of public distancing from his views was necessary, though not such as to advertise to the outside world that there was a rift between the council and the vicar. Without consulting him, they corporately drafted for the press a letter of dissent from his views, signing it, however, as if it came merely from 'A Member of the Church Council'. A furious Harcourt came to the next meeting saying that whilst he had no objection to the public expression of views contrary to his own he felt very strongly that the writer should not hide behind a mask of anonymity. One of the most senior members of the council, Judge Shewell Cooper (vicar's warden, 1923-29), then revealed that the letter had in fact been the work of no fewer than 11 members, and added that there was a well-established tradition of anonymity in press correspondence. After an uncomfortable discussion they accepted a challenge from the vicar to make a public statement in the parish magazine, which they did as follows:

> We, the undersigned eleven members of the Parochial Church Council, wish to inform the congregation of St Mary's that we accept full responsibility for the subjoined letter, which we thought right to send to the local press. JH Arnold; F Shewell Cooper; I Shewell Cooper; DH Dent; LC Henderson; MS Jeoffroy; F Learner; Grace E Pulling; Clement Rosselli; Joan Shaw; FPB Shipham.

Was it just this incident or something more sinister that then provoked a new comment from the vicar that he had started receiving poison-pen letters? As for their writers, he said, 'if this meets the eye of any of them, will they note that my wastepaper basket is the immediate receptacle of all such correspondence.'[4]

At the next Annual Meeting of the parish, in February 1929, the first Harcourt had to chair, he fanned the flames still further by saying that it was the duty of PCC members to support him, and that those who felt unable to do so should do the honourable thing and stand down 'for a time'. It was unfortunate that at about the same time the Trustees of the living had to consider how best to fill two vacancies in their own number, arising from the death in 1923 of Dr Arthur Hill and the resignation in November 1928 of the Revd E Hermitage Day who had moved abroad. Hill in particular had been a stalwart member of the congregation since Fuller's time and knew the church's traditions inside out. Instead of seeking someone with comparable inside knowledge of the parish the Trustees mysteriously approached two prominent outsiders: Sir Walter Robert Buchanan Riddell, (principal of Hertford College Oxford and a member of the Church Assembly); and the Revd Canon Francis Underhill (warden of Liddon House and Chaplain of the Grosvenor chapel, who would later become dean of Rochester). This led the PCC to fear that, were there to be another vacancy any time soon, the vicar chosen by the Trustees might prove to be someone still less in tune with the St Mary's tradition. Jack Arnold accordingly put to the PCC in April a resolution regretting that the Trustees had not thought fit to add to their number a person who was, or had been, in intimate touch with the parish.

Harcourt's stand on his rights stirred up other problems too. When a member of the drama group loaned costumes to another parish without his knowledge he suggested that the lender, who was a lynch-pin of the group, had acted improperly. In his view such items belonged to the church and could therefore not be sent off site without his permission. He proceeded to draw up new rules whereby if the recipient of loaned items were to use them for a paying entertainment a fee would be payable to St Mary's. The PCC did not agree, and minuted that no impropriety had taken place over the loan of costumes.

Resignations of Geoffrey Shaw and JH Arnold

The most unfortunate débâcle, however, came over the music. Geoffrey Shaw, the director of music, whilst maintaining an outward show of civility towards Harcourt, never got on well with him, and the blissful partnership between the vicar and the music department that had made St Mary's such a harmonious place under Duncan-Jones fell apart. In 1930 a prickly situation arose. As far as can be judged amid the heat of the controversy, Shaw wanted the organ not to be used during Lent, even for accompanying the hymns, and took advantage of the vicar's absence one Sunday to try this experimentally without his permission. It provided scope for more plainsong and unaccompanied music, to the delight of the choir perhaps, but not to that of all the congregation, some of whom protested to the vicar on his return. Harcourt's reasonably-held but opposite view was that in a parish church it was essential to have organ accompaniment to sustain the congregation. On his return he insisted on this in the most peremptory fashion, apparently refusing either to see Shaw face to face or even write to him to discuss the matter. 'If he could not see me,' wrote Shaw to his sister-in-law Joan, 'there is ample evidence that pen, ink and paper are not wanting in the vicarage'.[5] Both Shaw and his assistant JH Arnold took umbrage. Who was responsible for the music: was it the organist and choir master or the vicar? Shaw submitted his resignation, closely followed by Arnold. Harcourt made some slight attempt to retrieve the situation, and indeed their resignation was probably the last thing he really wanted.

Rumours began to circulate: that Harcourt was ruling like a dictator; that he was hell-bent on radical reforms to the music; and that he had refused to meet Shaw and Arnold for discussions. Harcourt denied all of this in an article in the parish magazine, but its unfortunate tone can have done nothing to heal a desperate situation. Joan Shaw later charitably suggested that he was possibly already in pain from what proved to be a terminal illness.

> Personally [he wrote], I am not interested in authority. I find decisions often very difficult and I would rather dig potatoes than strive for authority. The Church has seen fit to commit to me as incumbent of this Parish, certain responsibilities and duties, one of the most important of which is the ordering of the services of the Church, in respect of ritual, ceremonial and the use of music, [which] I hold as temporary trustee only. These responsibilities I refuse to abdicate or to entrust to anyone else because my abdication would not only hamper my own plans and work but would impair the freedom and hinder the work of my successor who will, no doubt, have his own ideas and policy. That sphere of responsibility which I received at my acceptance of the cure I intend to hand on free and unprejudiced to him who succeeds me as Parish Priest of St Mary's.

A petition urging Shaw and Arnold to withdraw their resignations attracted almost 300 signatures from members of the Electoral Roll, and Lady Beauchamp mustered another 40 from external supporters of St Mary's. But the two were adamant and left their posts. There were no words of thanks or appreciation from the vicar, but a groundswell of genuine sympathy and affection from the congregation, which raised a handsome £100 and more from 100 people to buy each of them a set of Grove's *Dictionary of Music*.

On 13 July 1930, Shaw wrote to JBG Dick, the churchwarden, thanking the congregation:

> It is a great grief to me to give up my work at St Mary's. It was always a joy, pure and unalloyed, and I am delighted to think that so many of those who heard Mr Arnold's, and my, endeavours Sunday by Sunday were so much in sympathy with us. We had but one thought – to make the music suitable and beautiful. I don't think we always succeeded, but that was our aim… I shall always remember my twenty years connection with St Mary's as the best part of my life, spent as it was in working with such sympathetic friends.[6]

Two days previously Arnold had written to Frank Marriott:

> Few can be more conscious than I of debt to St Mary's, and few can realise the utter misery of ceasing to serve 'the Church of one's dreams' through work that has been almost as dear as life. In a preface that Geoffrey Shaw once wrote for me, he used these prophetic words: "You and I, as fellow workers of St Mary's, share together a privilege so lovely that we cannot imagine that the bond between us could ever be broken". There must, indeed, be a link between all who have really loved St Mary's…[7]

This deeply sad chapter in the parish's history did not cover any of its protagonists in glory. It would be hard to name two people more committed to St Mary's both musically and spiritually than Shaw and Arnold. And the situation was made all the worse by the fact that this episode came within a month of Geoffrey Shaw and his wife's giving to the church a new aumbry for the reservation of the Blessed Sacrament in the chapel, inscribed to the memory of their eldest son Peter. It was made by Smythe Greenwood, and supplied through the Warham Guild.

Both Shaw and Arnold continued to be heavily involved in church music at national level. Geoffrey Shaw and his brother Martin were both honoured in 1932 with Lambeth doctorates of music. Jack Arnold put his expertise in plainsong and its accompaniment to very good use as a member of the team revising the *English Hymnal* for its new edition in 1933. Under Harcourt's successor, once the dust had settled, Arnold succeeded VH King as Master of the Servers,[8] and remained an occasional organist at St Mary's.

Many were embarrassed more than they could say by these events, not least Arthur Duncan-Jones, now Dean of Chichester, who had been booked to preach at the Patronal Festival in July 1930 marking the Diamond Jubilee of the church's initial dedication in 1870. He now felt that (particularly as he was an old friend of the Shaws) he had to withdraw.

Changes of personnel

The Diamond Jubilee year of 1930 saw some sad farewells, with the death of Sir Frederick Holiday, for whom a solemn requiem was sung, and the retirement of Miss Burgess after a long time in charge of the kindergarten. It also marked the completion of 25 years' service by PH Bradbury, the formidable verger appointed by Dearmer in 1905, an anniversary he later marked by the gift of an ivory crucifix for the high altar.[9] Bradbury, who was 68, continued in office for a further two years until the PCC ruled that he must retire at the age of 70. He was succeeded (1933) by Robert Fake.

The music, however, was quickly put back on an even keel, with the appointment in June of Cyril Knight FRCO as organist and choirmaster, with Patrick Harvey holding the fort until Knight was free to come. There was not the mass defection by the choir that some had feared, and later that year, possibly as a practical contribution to the Diamond Jubilee, the PCC voted £100 (from an anonymous well-wisher) towards the installation of a mechanical blower for the organ. As the vicar would later report, the provision of steady wind power had 'improved our rather antiquated instrument', but it was only the first stage of what really needed doing: 'There are some very excellent parts in our organ but the mechanical side is very out of date. Two manuals are operated by [tracker] action nearly fifty years old, and a great many of the movements of the levers are very noisy.'

Jubilee 1930 (a) Group photograph outside the Church Room.

Jubilee 1930 (b) Street procession

Knight made a determined attempt to strengthen the choir, according to one report trying much new music and giving organ recitals after evensong, introducing each piece himself. But he was hampered, as so many successive choirmasters at St Mary's have been, by a shortage of volunteers to sing. By 1933 he was also trying to drum up support for a completely new organ.

Meanwhile, Fr Harcourt, seeking to stem the tide of hostile rumour and gossip about his intentions, proposed that PCC meetings should be open to all. This sounded democratic and was no doubt well-meant, but it did not meet with the approval of the elected council and had to be shelved.

Harcourt's resignation and death

Calm was restored for a time, but by late 1932 Fr Harcourt was in great pain and had become so seriously ill that he had to be admitted to hospital for tests. Early the following year (1933) he had a major operation after which his health sadly declined and became the cause of his resignation in June. Three months later, on 10 September, he died, aged only 46, leaving a widow (Charlotte Mary) and three young children. During this period of his illness, and again during the vacancy

Plate 1

Plate 2

Plate 3

Plate 4

Plate 5

Plate 6

Plate 7

Plate 8

that followed, it fell to the assistant priest, Sidney Crouch, to run the parish. With the PCC's consent he introduced further modifications to the liturgy in line with the 1928 recommendations, although his emphasis on fasting communion was not well received.[10]

On the day after his death Fr Harcourt's body was taken to St Peter's Chalvey, Slough, where he had been priest in charge between 1915 and 1920.[11] A large congregation attended his funeral,[12] and the people of St Mary's raised over £200 to support Mrs Harcourt and family. The Blessed Sacrament altar and tabernacle at Chalvey are dedicated to his memory.[13]

Endnotes

1. PM 1928, p. 17.
2. CERC: Ecclesiastical Commission File 46277.
3. These payments threatened to land the parish with a surcharge towards his pension from the Clergy Pensions Board when he retired, but his early death meant that this issue died with him. LMA: P81/MRV/95, Letter of 25 July 1933.
4. PM, Nov 1928 p.107.
5. Shaw family papers, seen courtesy of Isobel Montgomery Campbell.
6. BL: Shaw archive 1767/6/3.
7. Ibid.
8. PM, 1934 p.102.
9. LMA: P81/MRV/94.
10. I owe this point to John Hawes.
11. PM, Oct 1933.
12. *Uxbridge and West Drayton Gazette,* 15 Sept. [British Newspaper Archive].
13. A cutting of the *CT* obituary on 22 Sept 1933 by the Bishop of Gibraltar is pasted into VH King's Parish Chronicle in the Parish Archives.

Chapter 7

Revd Anthony Hardcastle

Vicar, 1934-1952

1. Before the Second World War

Appointment

With Harcourt's lengthy periods of illness and then his death, and the anxiety already mentioned over the composition of the body of Trustees, St Mary's briefly became a jittery and unhappy place. Jack Arnold and Geoffrey Shaw confided in their old friend Colin Dunlop that they feared the parish might enter 'the bondage of conventional and legalistic Anglo-Catholicism'. In a deliberate attempt to prevent that, his friends at St Mary's sounded out Dunlop (who was then building up a new church as chaplain in Baghdad) to see if he would allow his name to be put to the Trustees for consideration. The Chairman of the Trustees, Francis Underhill, wrote to him on those lines and the PCC mounted a petition in his favour. Joan Shaw went so far as to write to the Archbishop of Canterbury asking him to intervene, but the Archbishop's chaplain replied that he had no jurisdiction in what was essentially a diocesan matter, and in any case had no wish to disturb Dunlop's work in Baghdad. Joan Shaw worried that St Mary's 'has had its historic past so jeopardized – I had almost said smashed – that it seemed impossible to sit watching any longer'.[1]

For Dunlop in Baghdad this presented a most unwelcome dilemma. He knew the parish intimately. He had friends on both sides of the Harcourt divide, and had been told by some who had been boys and girls during his curacy, that most of his own painstaking work with the young people in D-J's time had been dropped. He sensed he would be capable of bringing about the much needed reconciliation. And St Mary's was one of the places dearest to him in the world. On the other hand he was horrified that (as he put it) so 'vulgar' a thing as a petition should have been got up, and his ministry was now developing on rather different lines. But, above all other considerations, he was about to get married: to Mary O'Malley whom he had met at St Mary's while curate, and who was still (though only just) a member of the congregation. She had been keeping him informed of developments, including her own increasing fear and depression about the place, and he was not at all sure he could ask her to begin married life as the vicar's wife in such troubled circumstances. So, after some agonising, he declined the approach, and instead recommended two other names to the Trustees.

A lengthy delay followed, which Dunlop (being a former chaplain to the Bishop of London) was inclined to lay at the door of the diocesan authorities. But part of the trouble in fact lay with the Trustees. In September 1933 they committed a *faux pas*, in this new era of PCCs, by simply informing the churchwardens without any prior consultation that they had offered the living to Revd JC Moore, assistant priest of St Michael's Highgate, who had accepted. After a protest from the PCC, probably more over the process than the man, the Trustees felt obliged to withdraw their offer to Moore, and after a further delay proposed in his place – but this time with the PCC's approval – the Revd JAL Hardcastle. A single man who was previously unknown to Dunlop, he had won the affection of both young and old in his previous posts. After graduating from Jesus College, Cambridge, he had trained for the ministry at Wells theological college and then taken his AKC in 1922. Prior to his ordination in 1923 he had worked in a lay capacity at St Thomas's, Bethnal Green. His first curacy had been in Southampton, after which he moved successively to St John's, Red Lion Square (1924-

7) and St John-the-Divine, Kennington (1927-9), gaining significant insights into the London religious scene. He then became priest-in-charge of St Francis, Sandycroft, Hawarden, Flintshire (1929-33). He was instituted to St Mary's in May 1934 by Bishop Perrin, in the presence of the Deans of Rochester (Francis Underhill, Chairman of the Trustees), and Chichester (Arthur Duncan-Jones).[2]

Harmony restored

The turmoil during Harcourt's time as vicar had not surprisingly led to a falling-off in church attendance. In the course of discussion with the Clergy Pensions Board in 1933 the PCC estimated there had recently been a fall of 25% in collections, although it attributed some of this to 'a marked and continuing deterioration in the social status of the district'.

Hardcastle quickly restored a good working relationship with the PCC, and whilst much of the council's business was necessarily devoted to bread-and-butter issues, its Minutes continue to reveal a wider awareness of issues besetting society and the world at large. In July 1934, for example, the council discussed modern slavery, and Hardcastle agreed to preach a sermon on it. VH King's Chronicle also shows that in November 1935 Michael Seymour, head of the Oxford House settlement in the vicar's old stamping-ground of Bethnal Green, addressed the congregation after High Mass, and a generous collection was raised in support of his work.

In the Dearmer tradition

Hardcastle was fully aware he was walking in the footsteps of Percy Dearmer, and indeed seems to have taken him as something of a personal role-model. Not long after arriving he took down Dearmer's portrait from the Church Room, had it restored, and then re-hung it not where it had come from but in the Sacristy, to serve as a daily inspiration to the clergy.[3] As under D-J, Dearmer was invited back to St Mary's several times during Hardcastle's ministry: in the autumn of 1934 to give an illustrated lecture in the Church Room on the great Venetian masters (with the aid of a lantern projector donated for the occasion), and again in 1935 for the church's Golden Jubilee celebrations. In the course of a conversation during that festival, Hardcastle asked Dearmer what improvements or additions he would like to see at St Mary's, and he suggested extending the kind of panelling used in the Chapel to other areas, especially around the font, although this never came about. Whilst still broadly approving what he saw at St Mary's twenty years after his departure, Dearmer added: 'That west wall was my one bad mistake; fussy and messy; do try and clear all those shelvings away, and substitute or adapt to a worthier scheme'. Dearmer died in 1936. Two years later, with the help of funds left over from the parish's Dearmer memorial appeal and a further donation in memory of VH King, new panelling, designed by Frank Knight and incorporating a verger's stall and hymn book racks, was fitted at the west end.

Hardcastle sometimes felt he was being bullied in liturgical matters by FC Eeles and VH King. He certainly came under their watchful eye as he stamped his own mould on the liturgy, but he took the congregation with him in the traditional way by writing explanatory articles in the parish magazine (for example defending his celebration of the feast of the Assumption on 15 August). Hymns were no longer announced during the services; the outdoor Rogationtide procession was revived and, in time-honoured fashion, support was again encouraged for the Church Union. In the autumn of 1934 (when there was still a paid curate), in addition to the regular daily mass he introduced a new (Sarum-style) system of daily 'votive' masses using the 1928 rite. The separate Sunday morning service for children was, however, discontinued. For Hardcastle's first Christmas midnight mass (1934) the church was exclusively candle-lit, as in Dearmer's time.

There was some ruffling of feathers among the more liberal element of the congregation, for example when he reminded them of the traditional policy of fasting before communion,[4] or when he let it be known (1935) that whilst there seemed to be no reason in principle why women should not be among the readers for the Epiphany service of Nine Lessons and Carols, it would not be happening that year.

Two glorious years

For liturgy and ceremonial, the two years 1935 and 1936 were among the most memorable in the parish's annals. Hardcastle had a particular interest in the Orthodox churches, and new ground (for St Mary's) was broken in March 1935 when he invited a Greek Orthodox Archimandrite, James Virvos from the cathedral in Bayswater, to preach at Evensong, cense the church's (Russian) icon, and give the blessing. On 1-2 May 1935 the Golden Jubilee of the building's consecration was celebrated, with as many of the parish's former clergy in attendance as could be mustered. After the Sunday High Mass, Percy and Nan Dearmer were the guests-of-honour at a luncheon held in the Church Room, where the tables were decorated with 50 lighted candles and primroses. One of the speakers was Mr W L Cook, who had been crucifer at the consecration service on 2 May 1885. The day was rounded off by Evensong at which the preacher was the Dean of Chichester (D-J). Nor was that the end of festivities that month. A special service was held on 12 May in honour of the King's Silver Jubilee, and on May 27 the people of St Mark's Regent's Park joined those of St Mary's at the summit of Primrose Hill for the Rogationtide procession, and then walked down to St Mary's for a combined service.[5]

July 27th saw the marriage at St Mary's of Colin Dunlop, by then at St Thomas's, Hove, and Mary O'Malley. Hardcastle stood aside to let the Dean of Chichester celebrate the nuptial mass, and the Bishop of Chichester gave the blessing. As the press delighted to report, the service followed the 1928 rite in which there is no promise for the wife to obey her husband. Martin Shaw's *Folk Mass* was the setting, with anthems by Gustav Holst and one of his pupils, Jane Joseph; the faux-bourdon of the Communion Hymn *Tantum ergo* was written by Geoffrey Shaw.

In May 1936, at Hardcastle's invitation and under the auspices of the Anglican and Eastern Churches Association and the Russian Church Aid Fund, a Russian Orthodox priest, Fr Alexis van der Mensbrugghe, celebrated the Orthodox liturgy of St John Chrysostom at St Mary's,

Visit by Russian Orthodox choir, 1938

partly in English but with choral contributions in Slavonic. This event was organised to coincide with the visit to London of the student choir of the Russian Orthodox Theological Academy in Paris, led by Ivan Denissov. As it was such an exotic event for many English readers it was reported in the press in considerable detail. Prayers were offered for, among others, the Archbishop of Canterbury and the Bishop of London. The Epistle was sung in English, in a return visit to St Mary's, by Archimandrite Virvos (of the Greek Cathedral, Bayswater). Minor adaptations were made to the church furniture for the occasion but 'the absence of an ikonostasis gave an unimpeded view of the clergy at the altar, and enabled the congregation to see and follow much of the service which is normally hidden in an Orthodox church.' Hardcastle entertained all the visiting clergy and choir to luncheon afterwards. In 1938 more Russian Orthodox music was heard when St Mary's was one of the stops on a concert tour by a choir of seven men and five women from the 'Action Orthodoxe' church in Paris, under the direction of Theodore Potorjinsky, and a collection was taken for Russian refugees in Paris.

Death of Percy Dearmer

Percy Dearmer, then a Canon of Westminster, died on 29 May 1936. On the day of his funeral at Westminster Abbey (3 June, 1936), a High Mass of Requiem was first sung at St Mary's, which included the hymns sung at the requiem of his first wife, Mabel. The vicar, churchwarden Marriott, FC Eeles and a number of other prominent members of the St Mary's congregation from Dearmer's time then represented the parish at the Abbey ceremony.[6] In Dearmer's memory, Hardcastle personally made a gift to the parish of a silver incense boat and spoon, and after some discussion about other possibilities the PCC agreed to add to this a new silver censer, again based on the Ramsey censer but at 2/3 scale, to the design of Greenwood and supplied through Watts. In recognition that parishioners might themselves wish to provide some lasting memorial to Dearmer an appeal was then launched to buy a new Bible for the eagle lectern. They had in mind one of the limited run, on hand-made paper, of 'the greatest edition of the Holy Scriptures produced in modern times: The New Oxford Lectern Bible … a landmark in the history of fine printing.' Allowing for a binding worthy of the book, it was thought this might cost £70. But that proved to be beyond the amount subscribed, so instead they settled for the standard edition (price £28), still a handsome book. It was bound in the finest morocco with an embossed memorial inscription and gilt-edged pages, and was entirely worthy of the man it commemorated. It was solemnly carried up to the altar during the offertory procession at the High Mass on the Dedication Festival 1937, and censed with the oblations. There it remained until Evensong when, for the second lesson, it was escorted down by taperers and thurifer, and placed on the lectern. The parish's old Bible – after 46 years' service – was 'reverently burned'. (A similar fate did not befall the Dearmer Bible itself when its own turn came to be retired in recent years: although now in a fragile condition, it survives in the parish archives.)

Gifts

When Hardcastle was appointed vicar, the Golden Jubilee (1935) of the church's consecration was fast approaching. With the churchwardens and other leading members he made a determined push to spruce up the building, dispose of clutter, and replace some of the older ornaments. The jubilee itself occasioned a great shower of gifts that continued well into 1937. They included vestments, linen, hangings, kneelers, plate, pictures, service and music books and wooden furnishings. Among the more notable were an **English alabaster of Christ the King**, given by Mrs Trotter in 1936, and a small **16th-century chalice** that had belonged to Mrs Eeles. After her death (1934) it was given to St Mary's, for which she had done so much work. A **board bearing the names of the vicars** of St Mary's to date was inaugurated for the jubilee and is still in use. Also worthy of mention are an Arundel Society reproduction of **Memling's** *Crucifixion*, given by FC Eeles (1935), and a 16th-century Spanish **processional cross**, an **alms dish** and a pair of Renaissance **standard candlesticks** (also given by Eeles in memory of his mother, 1936); two **oak benches** in the Sanctuary for servers, one **oak stool** and one **oak prayer desk** (1937, designed by the church's then architect, Frank W Knight, the gift of Mrs VH King in memory of her husband); and an antique Welsh **corner cupboard**, originally kept in the sacristy to house sacred vessels but now situated beside the font. The figures of Mary and Joseph from the crib set by Miss Rope were repainted in 1935 by the original artist, and the great hanging trendle in the chancel (now no longer in existence) was restored in 1936. In 1940, JH Arnold gave a **silver paten**.

Disposals

As gifts flowed in, older furnishings and fittings that had become surplus to requirements were disposed of. Two chanters' copes were given away in the autumn of 1934, one to a country parish and one to the Windward Islands. In 1937 a modern brass processional cross was given to the Diocese of Gibraltar for the use of Bishop Sara (formerly an assistant priest at St Mary's) in Jamaica, whilst an old white chasuble, several used skull caps, burses, an old altar cross, a wafer box and two other chasubles were given to the Kelham fathers for their missionary work. When a set of new kneelers had been worked, the old ones were given to the Church Army.

Maintenance and finance

Hardcastle, rather like Dearmer, had an artistic eye. The one bit of St Mary's he could not abide was the bleak north transept, and he wrote in 1935 that he hoped to set up there a Chapel of the Holy Angels: it was, he admitted, just a dream, but 'far pleasanter to contemplate than the present appearance of the transept, which has almost the actual presentment of a nightmare, compared with the beautiful and reverent appearance of the other parts of St Mary's'. It also offended him that from certain angles (as early photographs testify) it was not possible to see the feet of the figures of Our Lady and St John which stood either side of the great Rood, so in 1937 he personally put up the money to call back the original designer, Gilbert Bayes, to fit small blocks beneath the figures to raise them by six inches, bringing their feet fully into view.

The vicar, PCC and architect did what they could with available resources to keep the building properly maintained and watertight in the 1930s, though with finances always stretched it was unquestionably a struggle. The Service Registers, although incomplete, confirm that attendances were falling. The average number of communicants on Easter Day in Fr Spencer's time had been around 400, and for the first six years of Dearmer 375. By the years 1935-39 it had fallen to 210. Daily and weekly services showed much the same downward trend. The consequential decline in income meant that by February 1936 there was insufficient money to pay a stipendiary curate, and that from then onwards, Hardcastle would have to rely on clergy friends and volunteers for any assistance.

Even when there was little money in hand, some expenditure was urgent. Leaks in the main body of the church had to be fixed, most seriously one in the zinc roof around the tower, which in 1935 again damaged the organ. A major crack in the wall of the choir vestry was repaired in the same year, and the vestry itself re-whitened and cheered up with two artworks (both since lost): a plaque of the crucifixion and a reproduction of Raphael's Madonna.

Social

Hardcastle was keen to revive social events for both young and old. He arranged successful young people's summer outings to Eton (1934) and

Chichester (thanks to the St Mary's old boys, D-J and Dunlop, 1935). Joan Shaw made a valiant effort to organise other social activities, and the chance survival of a programme for a series of Wednesday evening entertainments that she put together in the Church Room from January to April 1935[7] shows Colin Dunlop (returned from Baghdad) talking on the Assyrian church, lantern-slide lectures about zoo animals (by David Seth-Smith, curator of mammals and birds at the London Zoo), and on the Eastern Orthodox Church; a practical talk on 'How the telephone works'; and the play *The Other Half* by Myra Lovett, produced as in earlier times by Katherine (Mrs Rupert) Harvey. A note in the parish magazine in 1936 also records that a small parish library of sorts had been established, comprising 'several modern theological books and others of more general church interest'.[8] Kathleen Beck later recalled as one of the highlights of Hardcastle's ministry the annual 'Missionary Sale'. 'There would be a lunch and there would be, I should think, a hundred people there: a wonderful thing every year.'[9]

The vicar, however, soon found to his dismay that the numbers attending social gatherings were just as seriously in decline as those attending services. In the case of the younger element of the congregation that was not at all surprising. One generation had grown up and moved on, and without an assistant like Dunlop to organise youth activities there was not much prospect of enticing another generation in to replace them, especially at a time when there was a growing reluctance on the part of young people to attend church anyway, which made it impossible to contemplate a return to the glory days of Dearmer's Catechism classes.

Music

Cyril Knight had given notice in Harcourt's time that a new organ was needed. An estimate from Walker's arrived in time to be presented at Hardcastle's first PCC meeting, but there were naturally other pressing matters to discuss at that point, so it was deferred, although as a first step an organ fund was again launched. Meanwhile, perhaps in honour of the Golden Jubilee celebrations, a new piano was given in 1935 by a member of the congregation.

The core tradition of using plainsong for the psalms and propers was maintained, albeit supplemented by other mass settings and anthems. Fuller analysis is hampered by the omission of music lists from the parish magazines from 1935, when savings had to be made. In Holy Week that year, however, we read that the service of Tenebrae was revived, as a tribute to EW Goldsmith, the earlier master of music, who had died in 1934. Copies of the revised Wantage Press edition of *Sarum Tenebrae* were presented anonymously in his memory.

That same year the practice was introduced – to some, 'antiquarian' or ridiculous (or both), but very likely approved by the sanctuary hawks – of singing the full, very lengthy plainsong *Exultet* at the Easter Vigil service. A regular 'deacon' for this role was found in Fr [Francis] Noel Davey, who, after a curacy at St Chrysostom's, Victoria Park, Manchester, had moved to St Deiniol's College, Hawarden. He was therefore a near neighbour of Hardcastle's during his time at Sandycroft. Hardcastle, having encouraged Davey to learn the *Exultet*, invited him to earn his spurs by singing it at St Mary's in 1935. That was probably not Davey's first visit to the church, for as a young man he had greatly admired the work and teaching of Conrad Noel (vicar of Thaxted and a former St Mary's curate), so coming to St Mary's was for him something of a pilgrimage. Davey's singing, even though it must have considerably extended the length of the service, was evidently appreciated because he was invited back at Easter each year until war intervened, by which time he had become a Fellow of Corpus Christi College, Cambridge and lecturer in theology. In 1935 he sang the *Exultet* in English, but in 1936,

The beginning of the Easter Exultet (in Latin) from the Sarum Manuale

more audaciously, he ventured into Latin providing the congregation with an English translation.

(After the Second World War, having now moved to London as Editorial Secretary of SPCK, Davey sought Hardcastle's help in finding a house, and since by chance he knew of someone about to sell, the matter was quickly sorted. A grateful Davey offered his services to Hardcastle, as an occasional (unpaid) assistant priest at St Mary's, which gave Hardcastle some welcome time off and cover when sick.[10] In 1947 he was co-opted to the PCC, and he would see St Mary's through the vacancy after Hardcastle's resignation.) The War left Hardcastle with no option but to sing the *Exultet* himself. One of the parish's rarely-seen treasures is an original Sarum *Manuale* of the early 16th century, a manuscript book in Latin acquired privately by Hardcastle. Although incomplete and therefore of little commercial value, it nevertheless includes the full Latin text of the *Exultet,* so could be used for its singing.

In 1936, after five years in the parish, Cyril Knight moved on to St Stephen's, Bournemouth, and was succeeded by Arthur Clarke, FRCO, who came from St Paul's, Vicarage Gate. An early experiment of his was to have the Creed and Gloria sung antiphonally, but that discouraged the congregation and was soon abandoned. Later that year the choir made its first gramophone record, of four office hymns, for Columbia records. According to VH King's Chronicle it was well reviewed and 'largely stocked by the trade'. Plainsong's continuing dominance is confirmed by a note in the Chronicle for Holy Week 1937 that the polyphonic choruses in the Passion were dropped in favour of plainsong. Among the gifts recorded that year were 12 copies of JH Arnold's edition of *The Ordinary of the Mass*, presented in appreciation of his services to the music at St Mary's. This coincided with the Arnold family's moving away from the parish, to Stanmore. He then became closely involved with the music at the new church of John Keble, Mill Hill.[11]

Drama

Unless it has simply been under-reported, drama seems not to have held quite the same sway under Hardcastle as under his predecessors, in part no doubt because rehearsals and dramatic performances still had to compete with other bookings of the Church Room. But, as we have seen, there is mention of the occasional play mounted by Katherine and Rupert Harvey (1935, 1936), and of a reading of Harley Granville Barker's *Rococo* (1937), as well as Nativity Plays and children's Christmas entertainments. The *Church Times* of 20 December 1935 carried an announcement that the Nativity Play *Holy Night*, 'from the Spanish of G Martinez Sierra', was to be performed in the church on 22 December immediately after Evensong. The parish continued to hold an Epiphany Party, and in 1937 this included a star turn offered by the ballerina Lydia Sokolova who at certain hours rented the Church Room to practice. Other entertainments included a musical lecture on nursery rhymes by Martin and Geoffrey Shaw (1934). What a pity that was not recorded for posterity!

In the wider church, religious drama was being given a new impetus; and nowhere more so than in the diocese of Chichester where E Martin Browne was appointed as the first diocesan Director of Religious Drama in 1930 by Bishop George Bell. As Browne was an Oxford contemporary and friend of Bell's chaplain (none other than Colin Dunlop), and as the Dean was Arthur Duncan-Jones, there was no risk that St Mary's would be left in ignorance of developments at the cutting edge of religious drama. The parish magazine informed the congregation of works produced by Browne, especially TS Eliot's church pageant *The Rock* (1934) at Sadler's Wells, with music by Martin Shaw (also late of this parish), and more importantly Eliot's *Murder in the Cathedral* (1935), with music arranged by JH Arnold. JH's son John, then a young boy, later recalled Eliot playing with him and his Hornby trainset during one of his many visits at this time to the Arnold household in Elsworthy Terrace.[12] After the Second World War, as we shall see, Martin Browne moved to London, became a devoted member of the congregation at St Mary's and eventually a churchwarden and Trustee.

Time for reflection
Dearmer's death in 1936 marked the end of an era, and may have been among the factors triggering something like a mid-life crisis for

Hardcastle. The Abdication of King Edward VIII at the beginning of 1937 cannot have improved his mood. But there were factors closer to home disturbing him. The churchwardens had already articulated that the decline in attendances and income was to some extent due to wider developments in society at large and was common to many churches. All the same, it must have given the vicar pause for thought. But was he referring just to that dwindling attendance or to something more when he wrote cryptically in the magazine that 'there are many decidedly perturbing things about the corporate spirituality of St Mary's'? Whatever lay behind that remark, he told the congregation he was seriously considering an inner call to serve the church overseas.

Something held him back, but as he then ran into serious challenges over the buildings and plant at St Mary's one wonders if he feared he had made the wrong decision. The Church Room, of whose 'disgusting' state he had felt ashamed at the time of the Jubilee celebrations, was belatedly repaired and re-whitened. Then, in the course of an inspection of the church itself in 1938, the architect identified further work in need of attention, to the massive tune of £3000. Nearly a third of that was for repairing or replacing defects in the brickwork caused by air pollution, some of it from smoke from the nearby railways. (A later Archdeacon was heard to say that the Victorian brickwork of many of his churches was one of the greatest crosses he had to bear). But also required were the relaying of roof-slates, and replacing old downpipes with new copper ones. Not included in the total was the cost of re-whitening the interior, which was again looking shabby, but some whitening was evidently done, because John Arnold (son of JH) recalled his mother taking the lead in fund-raising for it by making and selling many hundreds of pounds of marmalade. JH himself used to quip to his friends, 'Olive actually whitewashed the walls of St Mary's with marmalade'.

Grants were applied for, and at the annual parish meeting in the Spring of 1939 the architect reported that the work might just about be postponed for one further year, but not longer. How wrong he was: the outbreak of the Second World War just a few months later put paid to all that. And it also meant that Hardcastle now knew beyond doubt that he was going to have to stay, for no-one knew how long, to lead parish and people through this new crisis. Shortly after the outbreak of the War, Hardcastle announced his engagement to Ruth Seth-Smith, whose father David (curator at the London zoo) we have already met. They were married quietly on 16 January 1940[13] and spent their honeymoon in Wells where he had trained for the ministry.

2. The Second World War[14]

War begins

Preparations for war had been taking place on Primrose Hill in 1938, with the crown of trees removed from the top, gun emplacements set up and trenches dug. As war became a reality other changes took place in the parish, including the requisitioning of some of the houses in Elsworthy Road, just next to the Hill, for military use. During 1940, as in the First World War, parts of the Hill would again be turned over to allotments.[15]

From the day war was declared, Sunday 3 September 1939, St Mary's was on alert. Air-raid warning sirens were being tested even as the High Mass was being celebrated that morning. Even so, most of the congregation stayed put. The following Wednesday, when warnings again sounded during the early mass at 6.45 a.m., the vicar recorded simply that he 'carried on'. That was to be his heroic default position throughout, though his periodic and highly personal notes in the service registers trace many sleepless nights during waves of relentless bombing of the city and the neighbourhood.

Blackout and running repairs

Robert Fake, the verger, lost no time in fitting blackout blinds, and by the second week of December 1939, 'by the expenditure of an incredible amount of his time and a very small sum of our money'[16] he had set them up in the south aisle and chapel in such a way that that part of the church at least could be lit for evening and early morning services without contravening the blackout regulations. Fake again proved his worth as a handyman when the fencing round the garden at the east end had to be repaired the following year.[17]

Air Raid Precautions (ARP)

The Bishop issued general instructions to the diocese that no objection should be made to requests from the civil authorities to use church premises for emergency purposes, subject to his being kept informed. St Mary's, as the largest public building in the vicinity, was on the civil authorities' short-list for such use. Mr Lias, the Chief ARP warden and a parishioner,[18] asked if the church itself might be used as an emergency casualty station, and the vicar went so far as to offer the Sacristy also, as an ARP post, but there is no sign that either offer was ever taken up. The Church Room was assessed as a possible billet for troops manning the guns on Primrose Hill, but was discounted on the rather surprising grounds that it was too far away to be useful. As the war went on and incendiary bombings increased, arrangements were made for one of the church doors to be left unlocked to enable the fire wardens' patrol to carry out inspections.

'Keep Calm and Carry On'

At the suggestion of the PCC a notice was posted outside the church inviting passers-by as well as the regular congregation to use the building as a place for quiet reflection and prayer for the nation and the local community. We can scarcely begin to imagine what it must have been like to conduct or attend services amid air-raid warnings, let alone during actual bombing. It was hard to determine what was the safe thing to do – or what was God's will in such a situation. But Hardcastle's determination was rock solid, even to the extent that after one prolonged period of sleepless nights, having overslept and missed a morning service, he still recorded a *mea culpa* in the service register!

Despite his best resolve, some disruption was inevitable. The first Sunday in October 1939, which at that time was normally kept as the church's Dedication festival, coincided with a Day of National Prayer, so the Dedication was commemorated only at Evensong.

Removal of valuables

The most precious items of the church's plate – mainly crosses and candlesticks – were sent off for safe keeping to a store in the crypt of Salisbury cathedral, and some of the vestments to another safe location in Guildford. Smaller items, including five antique sanctuary lamps given by FC Eeles, were simply stored in the crypt, which the vicar thought as safe a place as any. His optimism was rewarded, and they came to no harm.[19] At Christmas 1940 a new wooden altar cross with a copper figure made its appearance on the chapel altar, replacing an antique latten crucifix sent off into storage.[20]

The Blitz begins

It was to be August and September 1940 – a year after the outbreak of war – before the worst fears of aerial bombardment were realised and the Blitz began in earnest, but before that there were plenty of alarms. A surprising number of the regular daily services still took place, albeit with much reduced congregations. On Sunday 1 August services began as usual with Matins and the Litany; mass was then sung in the chapel, to the background of an air-raid warning, though fortunately the All Clear sounded during the Gospel and the service was completed. A fortnight later Armageddon seemed to be just around the corner. A bombing raid on the city on the night of Saturday 14 August caused huge fires in the East and South East which were clearly visible from Primrose Hill,[21] and windows of houses in Primrose Hill Road were shattered by vibrations from the guns on the Hill. The PCC meeting of September 1940 had to be postponed when too few members could attend because of an air-raid warning. The noise of sirens could no longer be assumed to be either tests or false alarms, and in the ensuing week, after the vicar had begun to record in the service register the local bomb damage as well as the loud (if not particularly effective) anti-aircraft fire from the Hill, several of the weekday services were curtailed or cancelled. A dreadful reminder of the danger very close to home came in the early hours of 22 September 1940 when St Mark's Regent's Park was gutted by an incendiary bomb. On Friday 27th at 3 a.m., after a landmine was dropped on the Hill but did not detonate, some 90 people had to be evacuated from houses in Primrose Hill Road and Elsworthy Road – including of course St Mary's Vicarage – until the area had been declared safe. For a short time that day the church itself was declared out-of-bounds, and the daily service could not be held. On Sunday 29th the vicar recorded that he had the smallest congregation on record, 'except perhaps during "Ritual" War!' The following Tuesday, no daily mass could be said because the few servers theoretically still available had all been recruited to make munitions. For the second year running, the Dedication festival was under threat. It went ahead on Sunday 6 October, but the number attending was too small to warrant holding the traditional outdoor procession. A Warning sounded during the Preface, but once again Hardcastle was able to enter in his register: 'Mass completed'.

There followed an illusory night of absolute calm, with neither warnings nor bombings. But any hope that the worst might be over was soon shattered. At 10 a.m. on Sunday 20 October the Vicar decided, for the congregation's safety, not to hold either Matins or the Litany. Two stalwarts stayed behind with him so that mass could be celebrated even as Warnings were sounding, but as no actual bombing or aircraft were heard he once again persevered to the end of the service, and by Divine Providence the All Clear sounded just as he was giving the Blessing. All Saints' Day (1 November) 1940 saw another great fire-raid on the city which destroyed the Guildhall and many churches but did not directly affect the Primrose Hill area. Then, alas, on 21 December 1940 another neighbouring parish church, St Paul's Avenue Road, received a direct hit which rendered the building unusable. So began the lengthy process whereby, almost two decades later, St Paul's parish would be united with St Mary's.

The first major damage to St Mary's itself occurred in the Spring of 1941 when the vicar's report for 16/17 April ran: 'Fearful raid previous night. Windows in north transept and aisle shattered. Many churches destroyed'.[22] The transept windows (of plain glass) were probably the more badly damaged. The stained glass windows of the aisle, to judge by their present appearance and the fact that their iconography seems to be exactly as described when they were first installed, may not have suffered such serious damage, or alternatively some whole windows may have been blown out more or less intact. The War Damage Commission made a grant towards the cost of reinstating all the damaged windows.

By 1942 it had become a real issue whether it was worth the effort and risk to hold a midnight mass at Christmas. Hardcastle let it be known he was willing to do so if he could get between 24 and 30 people to sign up for it and to help, but he warned that, as he could not expect the organist and choir to turn out, it would have to be a simple affair with hymns. Among many other necessary changes, sermons were discontinued from Advent 1943 until further notice, in order to keep the services short and the exposure of those present to a minimum. Even when there was no direct bombing in the area, the tension was still palpable. The Patronal Festival in July 1944, for example, included yet another service held against a background of air-raid Warnings.

The worst day, 25 November 1944

As far as the parish was concerned, the worst bombing came on the night of St Catherine's Day, 25 November 1944, when the church roof and windows were badly damaged. Hardcastle later wrote to FC Eeles who was now in charge of the Council for the Care of Churches:

> It was a Fly-Bomb – not V2 – which hovered uncertainly over us on St Catherine's Day (the 75th anniversary of the 1st opening of the Church for worship), finally falling at 5.5 a.m. in a garden between King Henry's and Oppidans Roads, completely obliterating 3 houses in the former. Out of the 27 persons living in these, 11 were buried and 6 being later discovered dead, 2 died later in hospital, the remainder extricated by the extremely prompt and efficient ARP. Actually it was Oppidans Rd which suffered the worst material damage, and some

of our oldest established and most faithful parishioners escaped with their lives and little else. None of the fatalities were 'faithful' – though the parents of a server now in [the] RAF perished, and an esteemed Doctor was among the victims. All our faithful casualties have gone on well, and some had quite miraculous escapes.

The spirit of all was amazing and magnificent. It was a pathetic sight ... and has to be seen to be believed. Some 50 houses are condemned and there are as many again empty; I reckon about one third of our small parish may be said to have been devastated. The Church has virtually lost its three boarded-up windows again, and the 3 stained glass windows of the apse are damaged – the NE one the worst, which was the first stained window ever put in – the SE pretty bad (the most recent), the middle (& last) slightly.[23]

Damage to the roof and glass, 1944-45

A working party rigged up a tarpaulin to cover the breach in the roof as a temporary measure until remedial work could be undertaken. The windows high up in the clerestory and those behind the altar were worst affected, the stained glass windows in the two aisles apparently being largely spared. The initial work on re-glazing the boarded-up clerestory windows (which were always of clear glass) took two months and was completed in March 1945; but just days later a further series of V2 raids nearby first broke some of the newly installed panes and then shattered most of the rest, although luckily this time there were no further human casualties in the parish.

The Easter Vigil of 1945 was held, and the *Exultet* sung as usual on Easter Even, 31 March, but the vicar noted that there was a 'tremendous gale' blowing through the unglazed windows. This unfortunate exposure continued for much of 1945, and Frances Wilton later recalled having seen Hardcastle celebrating mass 'with thick jersey cuffs showing, and hands blue with cold'.[24] In June the Treasurer reported to the PCC that he had been pressing the Diocese for a licence to apply for a grant for temporary glazing repairs, but was told that the labour situation was very difficult and St Mary's would have to wait its turn. The PCC appealed on the grounds that the church seemed to be the only damaged building in the parish that had not had at least first-aid repairs, and that dust and damp were causing progressive deterioration. But this too fell on deaf ears, and in October the vicar reported that St Mary's had been 'virtually open to the elements since November 27th of last year', windowless, with the cold and damp getting in', and as a result the condition not only of the organ but also of the piano had been badly affected by damp.

Governance during the War
With men from the congregation enlisting or being called up for military service, it was not surprising that, at the APCM in 1940, women took 11 of the 12 elected positions on the PCC, although the two Churchwarden posts, as well as that of Treasurer and all the sidesmen were still exclusively a male preserve.[25]

On the outbreak of war FJ Marriott, who was both People's Warden and Treasurer (see **Other Lives** below), enlisted temporarily as a Colonel in the army, and was replaced as Warden by FB Benthall and as Treasurer by William Henderson. In 1941, the Vicar's Warden, Mr Lyster Smythe had to resign and move to Watford when his London house was damaged. By September that year, however, Marriott had returned to civilian life and resumed his old job as Treasurer, before also being re-elected as People's Warden the following spring.

Philip Bradbury, the former verger, died in 1943.

The vicar's work-load, both pastoral and practical, increased hugely during the War, yet both he and Mrs Hardcastle out of necessity somehow also found the time to help with routine cleaning and maintenance.

Numbers attending the church, of course, fell steeply. To pick just a few indicators, the number of Easter communicants recorded was 174 in 1939, falling to 145 in 1940 and 69 in 1941. Treasurer Marriott on his return to the parish reported in 1941 that the congregation had fallen by two-thirds as a result of the War. The Electoral Roll was down to 161 in 1943 and 140 in 1946. By 1944 there was only one person available to serve at the daily mass. Cash-flow, which had been proving difficult even in peacetime, became extremely challenging, compounded by the very circumstances of the war which much reduced the scope for special collections and appeals. Offerings, which had totalled around £10 a week before the war, had fallen to under £3 by September 1941, but in that year the Ecclesiastical Commissioners gave the parish a grant of £60 to tide it over, and the War Damage Commission's grant, to meet the costs of repairs directly attributable to the War up to that point, amounted to £47.

Successive treasurers imposed strict economies and postponed even priority work, but some expenditure could not wait, including, for example, roof repairs and a new boiler in 1942. It became impossible to meet the parish's full contribution to the Diocesan Fund, and funds supposedly ring-fenced for other specific purposes had to be raided to meet basic running costs, pared to the bone though these were. By the spring of 1941 the use of electric lighting had been reduced to a bare minimum and the boiler was only being lit at weekends, except when necessary to prevent the pipes freezing. It was hard to think of other economies. An experiment was tried in 1942-43 of sharing the cost of an assistant priest with St Saviour's, but that proved short-lived. Noel Davey (he of the *Exultet*) provided sterling ad hoc assistance. From 1943 the PCC regularly questioned whether the occupancy of 'Church House' next to the Church Room by Robert Fake (Bradbury's successor as verger) represented value for money in return for his opening the church and supervising the Church Room which was being let on 3 evenings a week. That arrangement continued, but the fact that it was under discussion must have worried Fake and his wife.

Even amid all the financial worries of the war, the small congregation still made donations to support the mission field as well as the wider church at home. Of the church's total income of £1090 in 1942 between a fifth and a quarter was spent on objectives outside the immediate needs of the parish: £45 to the diocesan fund, £193 to missions and £6 to charities.

Music

In the autumn of 1939 the vicar told the PCC 'he wished to be responsible, should it be necessary, for the stipends of the gentlemen of the choir, at any rate until the end of this year, as he thought they had made a most valuable contribution to services in the first Sundays of War.' Relatively little is recorded about the church's musical life thereafter, but it must have been severely constrained as adult choir members enlisted for war service. Arthur Clarke remained Master of the Music until 1941, and tried against all the odds to keep up the parish's interest in its music. In April 1940 he gave two lectures on the subject, and in the course of that year wrote several articles in the parish magazine.

Under the War Damage Act, church buildings were insured by the government free of charge but congregations had to insure contents, including organs. Two years into the war, in the autumn of 1941, the vicar advised the PCC to take out specific insurance for the organ, to enable a temporary electronic instrument to be provided should that become necessary. It comes as no surprise that they could not afford it, but they would have occasion to rue that decision. Even before the great bomb of November 1944 the church roof just above the organ, adjacent to the tower, had been badly damaged by shrapnel, and serious water ingress after heavy rain in the summer of 1944 ruined the Choir Organ. The PCC of September that year received an estimate of £50 for its repair, plus a further £150 for a much needed thorough clean of the instrument, but it had to defer this work on both financial and practical grounds until the following year 'if war and other conditions permit'. The rest of the instrument hobbled on, and although by the week before Christmas it was said to be on its last legs, it had evidently dried out sufficiently to make just enough sound on Christmas Day.

The vicar's letter to FC Eeles in November 1944, quoted above, continued:

> St Mary's people have been really quite wonderful. The congregation have kept up, considering, remarkably well ... We have 4 very sweetly singing boys who are continually receiving astonished praise from strangers, and we have revived some of the former plainsong. And the singing of 'Rocking' at the Crib on Christmas Day moved many to tears, I hear. It was so really exquisite and touching. Nothing short

of complete annihilation will, I think, defeat us; and indeed we have more than 'kept up' our tradition – ceremonial and musical – under the most difficult circumstances.[26]

Geoffrey Shaw, the former Organist and Choir Master, died in the spring of 1943 and a tribute by Arthur Duncan-Jones was printed in the parish magazine. His son, Flt-Lieut. James Shaw was to die in action in August 1944.

Salvage drive

Hardcastle, who throughout his ministry seems to have had a particular aversion to clutter and to the accumulation of ornaments and objects that were never used, responded enthusiastically to the government's drive to salvage paper for the war effort, by rounding up large parts of the parish archives and sending them off for salvage. The core records and registers of legal significance, including all the registers of baptisms, marriages and funerals, were spared destruction, as was most but not quite all of the master set of the parish magazines, some of which were later returned to the parish by a waste paper merchant, having been found awaiting recycling. But among items sent for salvage were some of the service registers and much historic correspondence. Since no list of the disposals was kept, we can only imagine and bewail the loss. Hardcastle defended what now seems an act of sheer vandalism to the parish's corporate memory by noting that the items sent away had in any case been thoroughly gone over in the past by Percy Dearmer and Vivian King for articles in the parish magazine and for the compilation of the parish Chronicle. But how different this book might have been if that culturally costly sacrifice had not been made. The scale of Hardcastle's actions is clear from a memo he wrote in the parish magazine for December 1941, which makes chilling reading:

> Nine tenths of our 'rubbish' has gone to the furthering of the War effort. It would seem that nothing in the way of MSS, let alone of several specimens of printed leaflets, has ever been destroyed at St

Mary's for seventy-five years. ... If there is something sad in consigning these ancient volumes to the salvage van, there is much more of relief; more than enough still remains for that posterity, which, we trust, will care at any rate to glance at such and, perhaps, make, as we have done, a transcription here and there, before consigning even this reminder to a Peace Time Salvage; the War will not have been fought in vain if the destruction of such books and papers, secular and religious, becomes compulsory at least after a quarter of a century's storage.

Other items continued to leave St Mary's, but in a more controlled way to meet the needs of other churches. In 1942 the PCC approved the vicar's suggestion of lending to St Mary's, Humbledon, Sunderland, a small thurible that was no longer in use. Theatrical costumes held for use by the Primrose Hill Players, who were not meeting during the war, were loaned to a country parish wanting to put on a Nativity play.

Social life

Whilst a number of the parish's children were evacuated from London, some remained, and the PCC was anxious to lay on activities for them. The choir vestry was made available for handicraft sessions led by two ladies from the congregation, and a house in Fellows Road for other children's activities. For the remaining adult members of the congregation it was (understandably) well-nigh impossible to maintain any social activities.[27] At the end of 1939 it was still possible to hold the usual Christmas party. The money collected round the crib in church that year was sent to support the work of the Salvation Army in Finland.

3. The aftermath of war

Service of remembrance, November 1945

With the ending of the War, Hardcastle organised a special commemorative service on St Catherine's Day, 25 November 1945, on the site in the parish where the fatal bomb had fallen exactly a year before.

The aim was not only to remember the fallen, but also to give thanks for those whose lives had been spared and 'for the further opportunities of service that remain to us.' At 12.30, straight after the High Mass at St Mary's, a procession comprising verger, crucifer, 'a chorister', the vicar and members of the St Mary's congregation made their way to the site, where others including members of the Chalk Farm Baptist Church joined them.

Efforts towards recovery

The St Catherine's Day bomb had left many houses in King Henry's Road and Oppidans Road either flattened or so badly damaged as to be uninhabitable. The rubble and scars remained visible for years, and must have been a depressing sight, with no small effect on the parish's morale. A few houses in Elsworthy Road and Primrose Hill Road, too, had been destroyed by bombs. But many more had suffered blast- or collateral damage, so in a large part of the parish there was a general air of dereliction. Recovery was to be neither immediate nor spectacular. Rather, it was a gradual process, measured in many years, with the top priority being to make the buildings properly fit for use again.[28]

Roger Langrish, a former resident of Elsworthy Road, returned in 1946 from war service in the Royal Navy: 'I found a very different Elsworthy Road. Houses appeared very run down, with windows boarded up here and there, all the railings removed to be melted down for armaments, and street lighting dimmed because of the national fuel shortage.' In the severe winter of 1947 there was such deep snow that 'there was just one motor track in the middle of the street which such motors as there were negotiated cautiously in second gear.' Houses were almost impossible to heat at an affordable cost: gas was supplied at reduced pressure. Strict food rationing was enforced. 'We all suffered from war-weariness and general malaise'.[29] A large quantity of the rubble from destroyed properties was piled up on the Hill; those working on the project were temporarily accommodated in the requisitioned houses in Elsworthy Road which returned only slowly to more normal residential accommodation, and in a few cases were unfit to do so. In July 1946 the Vicar reported that he had been 'approached by several people with regard to the continued presence of the military on Primrose Hill which prevented the public having access to the summit'. After discussion it was agreed that he should write to the local MP about this, on the parish's behalf.

And what of the church itself? The Annual Meeting in 1947 heard that there had been a small increase in attendance including children, but even by 1950 the Electoral Roll still stood at only 88. People had understandably had the wind knocked out of their sails by the War, and as late as 1951, six years after the War's end, the vicar was still having to encourage his congregation to put behind them the time of 'survival' and adopt a new mind-set to start a time of 'revival'. In fact, revival efforts had begun much earlier, with a Social Committee, chaired by Mrs Hardcastle, which by 1950 had become an Entertainments Committee.

Anxious for the Church Room to be used to the benefit of the wider community, as well as to be self-supporting with a guaranteed income-stream, the PCC in November 1945 once again authorised its use for political meetings, and from June 1946 it was regularly let for weekday use by the Sadler's Wells Ballet School. For a time a Men's Club also met there. Robert Fake was sufficiently keen to continue in office as verger that, when the parish decided in 1946 it could afford no more than £2 a week towards his wages, he agreed to take on additional part-time work elsewhere to make ends meet. As finances slowly improved and bookings (and therefore revenue) for the Church Room increased he was able to return to full time employment in the parish. By January 1949 a Boys' Club with about 50 members was meeting there and the Room had truly come into its own as 'not only an asset but of great financial value in other ways.'

After a campaign by Councillor Bucknell, who with his wife had lived in one of the shattered houses on the site of the V1 strike, the devastated properties in King Henry's Road and Oppidans Road were eventually demolished by the Borough and replaced by Primrose Hill Court, with its 102 flats, at a cost of £228,000. They were officially opened in 1951 by the Mayor of Hampstead. By the vicar's tally when he wrote up the event for the parish magazine[30] there were 11 one-roomed; 15 two-roomed; 24 three-roomed; 35 four-roomed and 17 five-roomed flats. 'Here,' he said, 'is an opportunity for neighbourliness ... It is up to St Mary's people to do anything they can to say to these people, "There is your Church".' Whole new challenges of ministry lay ahead.

Organ and music

Remedial work on the organ had been on hold for a decade and a half when, in the autumn of 1945, Messrs Hill, Norman and Beard who had maintained the instrument since it was installed, were asked to make a full report. Jack Arnold, who knew the instrument well as a former assistant organist and occasional deputy since his resignation from that post, suggested that the PCC ought to get a second estimate from Smith and Foskett, of Lisburn Road, Hampstead, from whom he had had good service in the restoration of another organ. By November, Hills had reported back that a full repair would cost £350 to £400, whereas Smith & Foskett quoted £205, with an additional £25 for replacing the swell box, which had not even been mentioned by Hill's. The Vicar threw a firecracker into the discussions by writing in the parish magazine in December that he thought the organ would be better placed at the west end of the church, but he knew he was in a small minority and this was not taken further.

The PCC inevitably accepted the lower quote, but Hill's were understandably put out after their long association with St Mary's and in January 1946 complained to the Diocesan Secretary that St Mary's arguably had a contractual arrangement with them. The Diocese, however, supported the parish in its acceptance of the lower tender. As Smith's proceeded with the work the parish magazine for February 1946 described how the organ 'lies in the North aisle in its disintegration...'

Mr Spencer, now the organist, somehow kept services going throughout the restoration work, but then stood down in 1951, with Arnold (once again living in Elsworthy Road)[31] again stepping in for a time until a replacement could be appointed.

Post-war repair grants

The contribution the parish itself could realistically make after the War towards repair of the damaged fabric, windows and organ was small in proportion to the need. A Restoration Fund was launched, but a great deal of time and energy still had to be spent by the vicar and church officers in fund-raising within the parish and pursuing grants from the War Damage Commission and other bodies.[32] The Commission had been set up precisely for this purpose, and as we have seen had already made one grant to St Mary's in 1942. But after the War the long queue of applicants meant that its grants were neither prompt nor automatic, and in fact it was to be three full years (September 1948), before the architect was given the green light even to submit estimates, which by then were: £2293 for reinstatement of war damage (including the clerestory windows); £600 for replacing the stained glass windows at the East end; and £1200 for urgent essential repairs other than war damage.[33]

Whilst the Diocesan Secretary freely admitted that there was no immediate prospect of obtaining a licence anyway, he asked the parish whether it might be able to cover the last element (the £1200) if a licence could then be procured for the rest. But as the congregation had already raised £300 for the most urgent repairs, every possible external aid was still required. By April 1949 the Bishop of London's Reconstruction Fund had promised £500 (which, by the way, was considerably more than St Mary's had itself paid into that Fund), and the City Parochial Charities £300, to which in August the Incorporated Church Building Society added a further £75. Even so, the Treasurer still urged the parish to find ways of raising another £500 itself, if necessary by means of a loan from the Diocese.

Experts were consulted in 1946 and 1947 about replacing the church's worn-out gutters and restoring the war memorial, but in both cases the work was postponed on cost grounds. When the guttering was finally tackled in May 1948 the work exposed defects in the drains, and it was reported ominously that 'some heavy expenditure would be incurred in meeting the requirements of the Borough Sanitary Inspector'.

In January 1950 the Diocesan Advisory Committee approved designs by Leonard Mathews for new stained glass windows to replace two of those destroyed behind the high altar, and for the restoration of such other glass at the east end as could be rescued. The themes chosen for the new windows were the Annunciation, and the boy Jesus in the carpenter's shop. The style was completely 1950s with no attempt to mimic the Clayton and Bell glass in the other windows, and is at first sight rather startling. The artist, EJ Lucas, incorporated local character into his design by inviting some of the parish's scout troop to act as models (partly so that the boys' knees could be accurately portrayed), and by sneaking in a portrait of Hardcastle's cat![34] Of the £603 required, the War Damage Commission eventually agreed to pay £464 and a donor covered the rest. Only one of the restored windows was in place by the time of the Bishop's visit in June 1950, and somewhere along the line a most unfortunate misunderstanding of the collected fragments from the Victorian glass seems to have led to the insertion of a new glazed inscription in one of the windows, stating that it had been given in memory of a James Peter 'Arthur'. No such person existed! The surname should have read 'André', for it was the caption to the first window ever given to the church, by the foundress Emily André in memory of her late father. To make matters worse, it is now not at all clear that it was placed under the correct window, as much of the glass was recycled and reused wherever it would fit.[35] Apart from that, Mathews's helped the parish well beyond the call of duty, replacing the plain glass in the clerestory windows at the same time and, while they had the scaffolding up for that, re-whitening the nave and chancel, using discretionary money provided by the Vicar from two legacies to the church. As the parish then began to hesitate over whether it could afford the cost of leasing the scaffolding for any further work, Mathews also agreed to bear the whole additional cost of whitewashing the transept and chapel as an advertisement of his firm's capabilities, whilst Bob Fake, whose cottage had recently been repaired using moneys in the Church Room fund, assisted by whitewashing the nave pillars.

The redecoration of the chapel necessitated dismantling the reredos behind its altar, which was found to be in a 'seriously dilapidated condition'. Frank W Knight, the architect, submitted plans for its restoration, but there was a 'general disinclination to consider any scheme for its eventual restoration,' and it silently disappears from the record.

Thefts

In the post-war years there was a distressing upturn in the number of thefts and attempted thefts from the church. In 1945 the chapel's red altar frontal was stolen and an attempt was made to take the silver Russian icon. In the latter case the thief must have been disturbed half way through his work: the space on the wall where it had hung drew attention to its disappearance, and a search of the building located a hidden bundle containing the icon, presumably ready for collection at some future time. Almost everything in the church was a potential target for theft: just a few months later the riddel curtains of blue silk and silver thread given by Lady Beauchamp also disappeared. Also stolen was a pair of antique brass candlesticks from the Chapel altar. They had been purchased in Bournemouth by the vicar about ten years previously, and were of little financial value, although he reported rather waspishly that they were 'immeasurably superior to those surprisingly tolerated by Doctor Dearmer which were of the poorest "church-furnisher" description and which they replaced.' The church's insurer reimbursed this loss, but when the congregation of the new church of John Keble, Mill Hill (perhaps through JH Arnold) heard of the crime they generously presented St Mary's with a new pair of oak candlesticks designed by an architect member of their congregation. After that the vicar became used to moving anything valuable, when it was not in use, into the sacristy behind locked doors, rather than keeping the whole church locked.[36]

Refitting the church: gifts and disposals

By December 1945 there was glass of some kind in all the windows, although no restoration had yet taken place. While the scaffolding was up for this, the Rood was cleaned. With a reduced congregation, fewer seats were now required. Damaged chairs from the north aisle were thrown out, and some undamaged ones were loaned to St Mark's. Towards the end of 1946, Geoffrey Shaw's widow offered a new set of wooden communion rails in his memory for the chapel, in place of the brass ones then in place. Designed by Frank W Knight, who was one of the servers,[37] they had a bronze plate affixed to the upper surface inscribed with the words: 'In remembrance of Geoffrey Turton Shaw, Doctor of Music, Chanter, Asst organist and master of the Music of this Church from 1912 to1930, who died April 14 1943 and of his youngest son James RAF killed on active service July 8 1944 these Altar Rails are given by their family.' In 1951 the council approved a faculty application for Hardcastle's long dreamt-of chapel in the north transept, again to the design of Frank Knight, but its commissioning would come only after Hardcastle's departure from the parish.

Liturgical highlights

In the immediate post-war period, amid all the uncertainty and restoration work, there were still moments of liturgical glory in the finest St Mary's tradition. The Lambeth Conference of 1948 occasioned several of these. Two photographs in the archives show episcopal processions on two Sundays during the Conference, one featuring Bishop Thorne of Masasi, nephew of May Thorne (a member of the St Mary's congregation); the other Bishop Colin Dunlop who was staying at the vicarage while Hardcastle took a holiday. At the close of the Conference, St Mary's was invited to supply a crucifer (John Bolton, with the parish's festal processional cross) and two taperers (Harold Robinson and Peter Heathfield who recalls this occasion) for a service in St Paul's cathedral.[38]

Hardcastle's sudden departure

Late in 1951, Anthony Hardcastle abruptly resigned from St Mary's. The sad circumstances are undocumented in the parish archives but, according to Somerset newspaper reports he had been charged by the police with indecently assaulting four boys earlier that year while on holiday in Wells. When he appeared before Wells City Magistrates in November, in return for pleading guilty to one of the charges and thus saving the boy a court appearance, no evidence was presented in the other three instances, and those other charges were quietly dropped. The Bishop of Willesden and Dr FC Eeles both appeared personally to give character testimonials. The bishop supported Hardcastle by saying that he was 'well known as a very fine and hard-working parish priest' who had done particularly fine work during the Blitz; and Eeles, recalling that he had known Hardcastle throughout his ministry at St Mary's, added that he had a thoroughly sound and good reputation and was respected by both his family and the congregation as 'a man of the highest integrity who did exceptionally good work under trying conditions during the war years.' On being sentenced by the magistrates to three months' imprisonment Hardcastle resigned from St Mary's 'on account of illness'.[39] On appeal to Somerset Quarter Sessions his sentence was commuted to a fine. He never again held a benefice, but completed his ministry as a minor canon of Carlisle cathedral.

Hardcastle's integrity in his work at St Mary's was never in doubt, and it seems likely that the congregation, if indeed they ever learned the true circumstances, would have shared the view of his lawyer at the Wells hearing that his experiences during the war 'had in some way affected him.' There is no record of what the Bishop told the congregation when he came to take a service in Hardcastle's absence and presumably to explain his sudden departure, but according to one tradition he was said to have suffered a breakdown, and it was perhaps on that understanding and in genuine ignorance of the facts that the PCC agreed in December to a proposal from FJ Marriott to send him a 'letter of sympathy and regret'. This was echoed by a similar proposal at the parish's annual meeting the following April. Hardcastle returned to St Mary's only once, twenty years later in 1972, to help celebrate the church's centenary. Following his death in 1973 a donation to the church by his widow, Ruth, in his memory, paid for the south porch, which is surmounted by a memorial inscription.

St Mary's owes Anthony Hardcastle a great deal. After he had passed through his own personal doldrums in 1937 and contemplated a spell of ministry overseas, something about St Mary's – quite possibly the Dearmer tradition which he cherished and wanted to uphold – held him back. Noel Davey, preaching after Christmas 1951 after Hardcastle had left the parish, remembered the happier times in the 1930s when he had come annually to St Mary's to sing the *Exultet* at the Easter Vigil service:

> On every one of these visits there was some fresh evidence to be seen, in the furnishing of the church or in the ordering of its services, of Father Hardcastle's exquisite taste and care, and some fresh evidence, too, both in the vestry and in his house, of his capacity for making friends.

When the War broke out in 1939 Anthony Hardcastle had known in his heart that he had to stay, to lead his parish and save the church he loved. To Davey the Blitz seemed like Hardcastle's 'final preparation for the heroic years during which he and his wife remained to tend a shrinking parish and congregation; years during which he allowed no difficulty or excess of fatigue to interrupt the Sunday, or even the daily, services of the church.' 'Heroic' is not too strong a word, even if that heroism occasionally verged on the foolhardy, but always in the name of his Lord and Saviour.'

The post-war years required continuity and reassurance alongside new birth, and this he quietly provided in the final years of his ministry, seeing the church restored once again to its former glory. Peter Heathfield, a young member of the choir in those post-war years, then a server and for one year a PCC member, recently recalled: 'When I first went to the church it was war-damaged, many windows being blasted out and of course … it was dingy and a bit run-down – not dirty or uncared for, simply showing the effects of wartime shortages and difficulties. I remember our great joy when the stained glass windows were restored in the apse.' 'The choir was very small but competent. We always sang the office hymns to the correct plainsong melody and at Mass, at festivals, the proper sequences too… The very efficient verger, Robert Fake, came to our rescue in the sacristy when difficulties arose!' Mr Ansell taught him to play the organ. Hardcastle, he pointed out, conducted services in a devout manner and with a fine voice, although his sermons tended to be lengthy and rambling (and, according to Kathleen Beck, difficult to understand).[40] At PCC meetings, if people did not agree with him he would hurry on to the Blessing, signifying the end of the meeting!

But perhaps we should let Howard Hollis, a later vicar of St Mary's, have the last word on the Hardcastle years. In an appreciation published shortly after Hardcastle's death in 1973 he wrote: 'No Vicar of St Mary's has served in more difficult times or with greater devotion, and we will always be grateful to him for his valiant ministry through the desperate days of the last war.'[41]

* * *

Other lives

Vivian H King, Parish Clerk since 1916, a familiar and much loved figure in the church, who by reason of his office had his own stall in the chancel, retired on health grounds in the summer of 1934. As a member of the congregation for many years before becoming Clerk, and eventually Master of the Servers, he knew more than most about the history, liturgy and records of the parish. He compiled a 'Chronicle', still in the archives, listing the principal dates and personages in the parish's history. It was later updated by JH Arnold. After King's death in 1935, Hardcastle noted that 'a great figure passed from St Mary's; and a greatly loved and honoured master, servant and friend… In the Eternal mindfulness we pray that he will often remember for good the best in us he so kindly, graciously helped to call to the faith'.[42]

JH Arnold, who appears many times in this book, was by profession not a musician but a banker and rose to be Secretary of the Westminster Bank. It is, however, for his music, particularly his devotion to and expertise in plainsong, that he is chiefly remembered. He was, as George Timms put it, 'the foremost student and teacher of plainsong whom the Church of England has produced.'[43] This expertise earned for him a Lambeth doctorate of music after the Second World War. Arnold was a great servant and benefactor of St Mary's, to which he and his wife Olive (d1952) had first become attached when Martin Shaw was organist. His devoted service as organist, head server, subdeacon and a PCC member was sadly interrupted by the débâcle already recorded under Fr Harcourt which led to his resignation, at least from musical duties. Later in the 1930s Arnold and his family moved to Stanmore, and worshipped at the church of John Keble, Mill Hill (consecrated in 1936), of which O.H.Gibbs-Smith was the first vicar. The special title was created for him there of 'Counsellor in music and liturgies'.

The 1920s, when Arnold was assistant organist, saw the forging of a lifelong three-way friendship and artistic partnership between himself, Arthur Duncan-Jones (vicar) and Colin Dunlop (curate). They kept closely in touch through thick and thin even after all of them had left St Mary's. D-J as Chairman, recruited Arnold to both the Church Music Society and the Alcuin Club, and in due course Arnold became Secretary of the latter. D-J and Dunlop both settled in Chichester, and through them Arnold came to be further enlisted in the 1930s as a musical adviser and arranger for both Martin Browne and TS Eliot. He used to visit Chichester regularly, to help D-J with the Holy Week liturgies. His service to St Mary's, alongside that of Martin and Geoffrey Shaw and Arthur Duncan-Jones, is commemorated in the plaque in the choir mentioned below (ch. 12).

Arnold never ceased to regard St Mary's as his spiritual home, and frequently returned. After the Second World War, when he lived intermittently in Elsworthy Terrace while retaining his Stanmore home, he again helped out with St Mary's music. Even when less mobile in later life he would insist on being brought back to St Mary's for the major festivals.⁴⁴ His requiem in a full church at St Mary's in 1956, was sung by his old friend, Bishop Colin Dunlop.

Lord and Lady Beauchamp

William Lygon, Lord Elmley and subsequently (1891) 7th Earl Beauchamp, was a friend of Percy Dearmer's from Oxford days, always known to him as 'Elmley'. His principal residence was at Madresfield (Worcs), where Dearmer was a regular visitor. He is thought to have been the model for Lord Marchmain in *Brideshead Revisited*. Percy and Mabel were among friends and artists depicted in the chapel there.⁴⁵ In 1902 he married Lettice Grosvenor, sister of the second Duke of Westminster. Both have already made several appearances in this book as regular attenders at, and benefactors to, St Mary's.

A member of the House of Lords and a loyal Liberal, Beauchamp was made a Privy Counsellor in 1906 and became successively Lord Steward of the Household (1907-10); Lord President of the Council (a Cabinet post, 1910 and 1914-15) and First Commissioner of the Office of Works from 1910. In 1913 he was appointed Lord Warden of the Cinque Ports, where his flamboyant parties led to well-founded gossip that he was a homosexual. By 1930 this had become undeniable (and, in his day, scandalous) after he openly went on a world tour with a male lover. The following year Beauchamp was denounced to George V by the Duke of Westminster, his brother-in-law. Having been privately warned to flee the country or face immediate arrest, he fled first to Europe then successively to Sydney and San Francisco. The news drove Lady Beauchamp to a nervous breakdown and, seeking to evade public scrutiny she took refuge with her brother, but was in the news again when she successfully sued Beauchamp for divorce. Their children refused to testify against their father and remained broadly supportive of him. Lady Beauchamp never fully recovered. She died in September 1936, just two months after Percy Dearmer. As the warrant for Beauchamp's immediate arrest if he re-entered the country was still in force he was refused permission to attend her funeral. The warrant was, however, lifted shortly afterwards, following the death of

George V, and he returned to Madresfield where he removed from the house everything that reminded him of his wife. He died of cancer in 1938.[46]

Endnotes

1. Shaw family papers, seen courtesy of Isobel Montgomery Campbell.
2. The following year, a new band of Trustees was appointed, including three prominent members of the congregation: Sir Cyril Cobb, JH Arnold and Frank Marriott. In 1944 Bishop Colin Dunlop and Arthur Duncan-Jones, Dean of Chichester were appointed Trustees in place of Cobb and Underhill who had both died.
3. PM, Dec 1934 p.181.
4. This evidently changed later. In his sermon on Percy Dearmer (1987), Howard Hollis would write, 'I remember how criticized St Mary's was, even in the 40s, as being out of step, because it was a church where, at its splendid Sung Eucharist, everyone received communion… fasting communion was one of the sacrosanct rules of piety.'
5. Archives, Vivian King's Parish Chronicle p.105.
6. Archives: Order of service for the burial of Percy Dearmer.
7. Shaw family papers, as above.
8. Archives: Parish Chronicle p.111.
9. Archives: audio tape.
10. Hardcastle to Timms, 3 Nov 1955: Archives.
11. See his obituary in PM, Aug 1956.
12. John Arnold, 'St Mary's – a focus on childhood', in PM, Jun-Jul 2005, p 15.
13. PM, Jan 1940.
14. For more, local detail including the presence of the military on the Hill itself and the development of allotments to grow food, see Sheppard, Martin, *Primrose Hill, a History* (2013).
15. Sheppard, *op. cit.*, ch. 12.
16. LMA: P81/MRV/95   PCC Minutes, APCM, 1940.
17. LMA: P81/MRV/95   PCC Minutes, Jun 1940.
18. Francis James Lias (1869-1952), in whose memory one of the communion rails was subsequently donated.
19. At some point, however, they were misguidedly lacquered, which ruined their appearance. As the metal was fragile, Greenwood advised after the War that they should be re-lacquered. PM, Sep 1945.
20. Reported only in Apr 1941.
21. Sheppard, *op. cit.*, pp. 201-2.
22. LMA: P81/MRV/9.
23. CERC: CARE 23/329.
24. Wilton, Frances, 'A few memories of Fr Hardcastle', in PM Jul-Aug 1984.
25. This remained the case for a considerable period after the War, the corresponding proportion of women being 8/10 in 1946, 10/12 in 1950 and 14/16 in 1951 when the number of elected positions was increased.
26. CERC: CARE 23/329.
27. Archives: audio tape.
28. For more detail see Sheppard, *op.cit.*, ch. 13.

29 PM, Apr-May 2009, p.23.
30 PM, Aug 1951.
31 See his obituary in PM. Aug 1956.
32 Hardcastle complained privately to FC Eeles in 1944 of the bureaucracy of the diocesan authorities.
33 PCC, Sept 1948.
34 The original designs submitted in support of the faculty application are in LMA: DL/A/C/02/096/055
35 Kitching, Christopher, 'Not a place for the Archers', in PM, Dec 2019-Feb 2020, pp.36-9.
36 APCM, 1948.
37 Archives: Supplement to VH King's Chronicle.
38 Archives: notes by Peter Heathfield.
39 Archives: Supplement to VH King's Chronicle.
40 Archives: audio tape.
41 PM, Feb 1973.
42 The office of Parish Clerk was revived in 1938 for Mr H Webber who had succeeded JH Arnold as Master of the Servers.
43 A copy supplied by the late John Arnold is in the parish archives.
44 See his obituary in PM, Aug 1956.
45 Jane Mulvagh, *Madresfield, the real Brideshead* (2008).
46 Information from Historic England website and Wikipedia.

Key to the Colour Plates

With particular thanks to John Salmon (JS) and Steve Reynolds (SR)

Plate 1. Stained glass: (a) St Cecilia by HV Milner, 1893 (JS). (b) St John the Baptist by Bucknall and Comper, 1893 (JS). (c) Angel from Kempe's West window, 1895 (Vanessa Berberian).

Plate 2. (a) One of Thomas Earp's four evangelist corbels, 1883 (JS). (b) North porch, showing Samuel Fry's tympanum of the Annunciation, 1893 (CJK).

Plate 3. (a) Banner of Our Lady designed by CM Gere, executed by Miss E Batterbury, 1903 (CJK). (b) Hymn board, lettered by GE Kruger, 1907, but subsequently adapted (CJK).

Plate 4. (a) The Rood by Gilbert Bayes, in memory of Thomas R Way, 1915 (JS). (b) The Crucifixion, in *opus sectile* by Henry Holiday, donated 1927 (CJK).

Plate 5. Statue of St Paul designed by Francis Stephens and executed by Siegfried Pietszch to commemorate the union of St Mary's parish with St Paul's Avenue Road, 1957 (JS).

Plate 6. Celebrating the seasons: (a) Christingle. (b) The Palm Sunday procession, 2018 (SR).

Plate 7. Youthwork: (a) The youth club at play. Preparatory sketch for a larger scale picture by Dorothy Ralphs, 2005 (CJK). (b) Group photograph 2018, with Jason Allen, Youthwork manager. (By kind permission of *On the Hill*).

Plate 8. Bishops: (a) Rt Revd Rob Wickham, Bishop of Edmonton, celebrates the launch of St Mary's Brewery, 2016. (b) Rt Revd Sarah Mullally at the top of Primrose Hill, 10 May 2018, her first day in office as Bishop of London, flanked by Bishop Rob Wickham and Preb. Marjorie Brown (SR).

Part Two (1952-2022)

VICARS

Revd Preb George Timms (1952-65)

Revd Howard Hollis (1965-76)

Revd Richard Buck (1976-85)

Revd John Ovenden (1985-98)

Revd Robert Atwell (1998-2008)

Revd Preb Marjorie Brown (2009-)

Chapter 8

Introduction to Part Two

If we wish to discern the angel of a church we first need to *see what is there*. Once we have become acquainted with its personality we can ask about its vocation. We can start from the visible, isolating the manifest characteristics of a church and asking what each reveals about its angel. We must attempt to grasp the angel whole, to gain a felt sense of its spirit or energy as a totality. Even the most meticulous analysis sometimes overlooks the most important qualities.

Walter Wink, Unmasking the Powers *(Philadelphia, 1986)*

The 'angel' of St Mary's

On taking up office, all the recent vicars have asked themselves and their PCCs what it is that God is seeking to do through the life and witness of the parish, and how the distinctive character of St Mary's Primrose Hill might best be defined, championed and carried forward. The vocabulary has varied, from identifying the 'charisms' of the parish, to finding its 'angel', or driving force. But the underlying quest has been the same, namely, to identify how God's will has been done – in this place and through these people – in the past; how it is being done today; and how that should guide what is to be done in our own generation. That is not to deny a role for divine providence, but on a day-to-day level it is what the worshipping congregation, clerical and lay, does with and for the 'angel' that gives concrete expression to the daily prayer 'Thy Kingdom Come'.

***

Some attributes of the 'angel' of St Mary's emerged in Part One of this book:

- The pioneering spirit of the church's founders in ministering to the poor and under-privileged and raising money in support of charitable and evangelical activities of the wider church, both in the mission field and closer to home.
- The regular ministry of Word and Sacrament, heroically maintained even throughout the Second World War; to provide spiritual food to the congregation, with preaching that was stimulating and often radical, yet capable of being understood by people of all ages and classes; and through structured teaching of the faith to the young.
- A dignified liturgy rooted in the authorised prayer books and rubrics of the Church of England.
- Good music to sustain that liturgy, beginning with plainsong but extending into a wider repertoire.
- The beautification and maintenance of the building for the worship of God, with particular attention to fine artistry and craftsmanship.
- The cultivation within the congregation of a sense of the church being a family, uniting its members in a common bond of witness, love and service.

***

All the above continue to be influential down to the present day, but in the years covered by Part Two (1952-2022) some new features have emerged, through:

- The comprehensive banishment of old prejudices against the deployment of women, in every aspect of the congregation's work and witness.
- The progressive empowerment of the laity.

- The integration of children into the worshipping community.
- The development of a liberal, progressive, non-judgemental ethos with a commitment to equality, inclusiveness and openness in shared witness to the Kingdom of God.
- The realisation that the whole church space is an asset that can properly be placed at the service not only of the congregation, but of the wider community.
- The urgent expansion of solidarity with, and services to, that community beyond the church doors. As the weekly service sheet has it: 'Our worship has ended. Now our service begins'.
- The adoption of stricter financial and management practices and a professional approach to staffing, budgets, accountability and legislative and regulatory compliance.

One of Bodley's angels originally from the top of the reredos. (Image courtesy of The Courtauld).

* * *

Part Two is all about transition: how the parish got from where it was in 1952 to where it finds itself today. The next chapter offers short overviews of the successive vicars and of key developments during their respective periods of office, in order to provide a framework for the thematic chapters that follow.

Chapter 9

Clergy

Revd George Timms, vicar 1952-65

George Timms was an Oxford graduate who, after training for the ministry at Mirfield, held successive curacies in Coventry and (for eleven years) at St Bartholomew's, Reading.[1] After a spell as the Oxford diocese's Inspector of Schools (1944-49) he moved to Southwark cathedral as Priest-Vicar and Sacrist. Southwark's English-style ceremonial fed his already strong interest in liturgy and equipped him well for a church like St Mary's. He was 42 and single.

His time as vicar saw:

- The return of stipendiary curates after an absence of two decades.
- The union of the parishes of St Mary the Virgin Primrose Hill and St Paul Avenue Road.
- Liturgical reforms to put St Mary's on a less antiquarian footing and refocus the liturgy for a new generation.
- The first Stewardship Campaigns, to improve the parish finances.
- The appointment, for the first time, of a woman – Sister Joanna DssCSA – as a member of the ministry team.

* * *

While still vicar of St Mary's, Timms was elected in 1955 as a Proctor in the Convocation of Canterbury, and in 1964 installed as Prebendary of Totenhall in St Paul's cathedral. From 1959 to 1965, he also served concurrently as Rural Dean of Hampstead – the best for 50 years according to Violet Tatham.[2] He then left St Mary's to become vicar of St Andrew's Holborn where he was able to devote time to study and writing, especially on liturgical matters. From 1971 until his retirement in 1981 he was also Archdeacon of Hackney. He returned to St Mary's on Trinity Sunday 1975,[3] to celebrate the fortieth anniversary of his ordination to the priesthood, and from the following year was invited to become one of the church's Trustees. Later, as Chairman of the English Hymnal Company, he stepped into another Primrose Hill tradition by becoming a major contributor to the *New English Hymnal* (*NEH*,1986, musical editor Anthony Caesar). When the *NEH* was published, it became the hymnal of choice at St Mary's. On its committee sat two others with St Mary's connections, the Revd Martin Draper (curate 1975-78, who would eventually succeed Timms as the Hymnal's chairman), and Michael Fleming (organist 1978-80).

Francis Stephens, in his *Guide and History* (1972) wrote of Timms:

> A great pastor, teacher and organiser, his significant contribution was to change St Mary's from a somewhat eclectic, even esoteric, church for a particular congregation into a warm and vital family, outward-looking and serving the community at large.

* * *

Assistant clergy, and stipendiary curates

When Timms joined the parish there had been no stipendiary curate since the mid 1930s, but he was able to draw on occasional assistance from, among others, Revds Noel Davey (until 1955) and John Satterthwaite (later Bishop of Fulham). As the union of St Mary's and St Paul's almost trebled the size of the parish's population, the diocese agreed to support first one, and later two, stipendiary assistant clergy.[4] In addition, in 1960 Arthur Fyfe, a late vocation to the ministry, joined the team as a deacon and remained as priest until 1965 when he became vicar of Bardwell, Suffolk. For some two decades St Mary's then had two paid assistants concurrently, and the diocese allowed the united parish the use of the former St Paul's vicarage at 8 Adamson Road for assistant clergy.[5]

Revd Howard Hollis, vicar 1965-76

On Timms's departure one of the curates, Revd Bruce Addison, became priest in charge.[6] The PCC made detailed representations to the Trustees about the kind of man they wanted as vicar. In view of the local Council's plans for major demolition and new house-building, not to mention the regular turnover of parishioners common to most London parishes (estimated at between a quarter and a third of the congregation each year), the man chosen should be both energetic and pastorally-minded. He should be intellectually versatile in order to be able both to nurture mature Christians in their faith and yet preach and teach simply when it came to engaging children and young people. He must be a 'Prayer Book Catholic', aware of St Mary's liturgical traditions, and have a knowledge of music 'not excluding plainsong'. 'He should not be narrowly traditional, but alert to contemporary liturgical thinking and theology, open-minded and aware of present-day pastoral needs'. All such wish-lists begin to look like the job description of a saint! But, in what may have been a first, the PCC then actually recommended a specific candidate for consideration, the Revd Howard Hollis, aged 48, married with two children. And he it was whom the Trustees, now chaired by Dr Eric Abbott, dean of Westminster Abbey, presented to the bishop.

Born and educated in Australia, Hollis had graduated in music before training for ordination (1945-46). In 1947 he came to Britain and served successive curacies in Croydon and at St Stephen's Gloucester Road, before being appointed a minor canon of Westminster Abbey (1951-59) and chaplain at Westminster School. In this latter capacity he coached the scholars in their singing of the 'Vivats' in Parry's *I was Glad* at the Coronation of Queen Elizabeth II in 1953.[7] In 1959 he returned to Australia as chaplain of Geelong Grammar School and domestic chaplain to the Bishop of Melbourne, and it was from that position that he came back again to London six years later as vicar of St Mary's. His wife Margaret was a fellow musician.

* * *

His time as vicar saw, among other things:

- The large-scale demolition and rebuilding of much of the parish's housing.
- The introduction at St Mary's of the successive new liturgies published by the Liturgical Commission.
- The arrival of the parish's first self-supporting ('non-stipendiary') minister, Revd Francis Stephens.
- The opening of St Paul's School on its new site in Elsworthy Road.
- The celebration of the centenary of Percy Dearmer's birth (1967) and of the church's own centenary (1972).
- Strong support for the church's music.

* * *

Diocesan reorganisation

Significant social changes throughout north London, as well as the hard-pressed finances of the diocese, were triggering new thinking about both diocesan and parochial structures. Towards the end of 1970 the deanery of Hampstead, in which St Mary's was situated, was moved from the jurisdiction of the Bishop of Willesden into the new episcopal area of Edmonton under its first bishop, Alan Rogers. Shortly after that, responsibility for running the parish of All Saints' Finchley Road was split experimentally between All Souls' Loudoun Road and St Mary's, with one of St Mary's curates, John Wainwright, acting on behalf of St

Mary's.[8] However, that arrangement was short-lived as All Saints' was formally attached to St John's Wood church in 1974.

* * *

In the autumn of 1975, after a decade in the parish, Hollis made a return visit to Australia, after which he announced he would be returning there in 1976, as rector of St James's, Sydney. St Mary's, he said, was 'unquestionably the most loved and lovable community I have known.'[9] For its part, the parish saw him as a diligent man of prayer, with a life rooted in the sacraments; but also as a practical, hands-on helper; a good listener; a supportive trainer and colleague to successive assistant clergy (even those with a more elevated churchmanship); a strong encourager of music, drama and the arts; and an outgoing and hospitable man. Martin Browne, who had known St Mary's for 40 years, felt it had 'never been more fully, more vividly alive than under Fr Hollis'. In later years Hollis made occasional return visits to St Mary's, including one in 2003 when he was back in England to attend the celebration of the golden jubilee of the 1953 Coronation (as one of the priests who had assisted on that occasion).

* * *

Curates and other assistants

There continued to be two full-time paid curates, plus several part-time or short-term assistants.[10] To house the second curate the parish secured from Eton College the lease of a small flat in Elsworthy Rise. Also on the staff, following in Sister Joanna's footsteps, was Sister Geraldine, DssCSA. Their work is described in the next chapter.

The clergy team was further energised by the arrival of Francis Stephens, a church artist and designer with a late vocation to the ordained ministry. Deaconed in 1970 and priested at Michaelmas 1971, he was the first self-supporting minister on the staff of St Mary's. This meant that he offered his services to the parish on a part-time, largely unpaid basis while continuing the professional work that was his source of income. This pattern of ministry, innovative at the time, would become, as we shall see, increasingly familiar at St Mary's in the next generation. From 1974, additional part-time assistance was provided by Revd Michael Vine, a former naval chaplain who taught at the Hall School.

Revd Richard Buck, vicar 1976-84

Apart from the two *ex officio* Trustees (the Provost of Eton and the Vicar of Hampstead), only two of the other five were able to participate in the presentation process that followed Howard Hollis's resignation. They were the Chairman (still Dr Eric Abbott) and Dr Martin Browne of the congregation. They (but in all probability their Charman) steered the Trustees towards the Revd Richard Buck, another Australian who had come to England in 1959 to test his vocation to the religious life, leaving behind an early career as a journalist which powerfully honed his communication skills and awareness of the world beyond the Church. Having decided that the cloister was not for him, he trained for ordination. After successive curacies at John Keble Mill Hill, and All Saints' Margaret Street, he became Canon Treasurer of Truro cathedral, but his acceptance of that post[11] was coloured by what turned out to be the mistaken understanding that it would bring some responsibility for post-ordination training. When that turned out not to be the case, and also because he freely admitted to missing the cultural stimulus of a big city, he soon sought a return to London.[12]

* * *

Reform of the Trustee system
This presentation exposed an obvious weakness in the Trustee system, in that, apart from the two *ex officio* Trustees, over half were too elderly to act. Once the appointment had been determined, all except

Martin Browne and the *ex officio* Trustees followed Dr Abbott's lead in resigning, which left Browne as *de facto* Chairman. After his long association with the parish he had a good grasp of its traditions and ethos and was well up to the task. He began by asking the PCC if it would prefer to see the Trustee system abolished altogether, which would mean entrusting future presentations to the bishop. But, wishing to keep appointments independent of the bishop (perhaps calling to mind the sometimes uneasy relations between previous vicars and their bishops), they endorsed the Trustee system, with all its faults. So, with the help of the *ex officio* Trustees, Browne recruited new blood to restore the complement to the full number of seven. The new Trustees were George Timms (by that time Archdeacon of Hackney); two members of the congregation, Laurence Gillam and Margaret Plouviez; and one independent figure, Anthony Lloyd, QC (a Fellow of Eton College, later Lord Lloyd of Berwick). This set the pattern down to the present: namely that four of the seven Trustees should be either members of the congregation or, as in Timms's case, closely connected with it, and one an independent person.[13]

* * *

Richard Buck's time as vicar saw, among other things:

- The introduction at St Mary's of the *Alternative Services Book*.
- Outreach to the community on a scale that had never before been attempted, through the work of Sister Judith, OHP.
- The re-whitening of the church and installation of its first sound system.
- The merger of the two main Sunday congregations into one.
- The introduction of westward-facing celebrations of the Sung Eucharist at the high altar.

* * *

In 1984 a chapter of Howard Hollis's history seemed to be repeating itself when Buck, during a period of sabbatical leave, made a return trip to Australia for the first time since coming to England. Taking stock of his eight-year ministry at St Mary's he decided, like Hollis before him, that it was time to move on, and in October he resigned in order to take on an experimental role in a Dulwich parish, working alongside Roman Catholic monks from Worth Abbey, with a title invented for him: Ecumenical Adviser to the Bishop of Southwark.

* * *

Ministry team

Francis Stephens continued in post. Martin Draper, who had arrived as deacon in Hollis's last year, celebrated his first eucharist at St Mary's in the same month as the new vicar's institution in 1976.[14] The diocese,

Revds Richard Buck (centre), Michael Johnson (left) and Francis Stephens (right) with choir and servers, c.1980. (Stanley Taylor, crucifer, centre of back row; Michael Willford, organist, seated front row)

which was under increasing financial pressure, was no longer in a position to support two paid curates, and when the senior curate, Revd John McKay, moved on in the course of the following year he was not directly replaced. Instead, Revd Winston Ndungane, a married South African priest undertaking a BD at King's College London, became an honorary curate and he and his wife Nosipho lived in the curate's flat.[15] He was the first black member of the ministry team. Having been imprisoned, like Nelson Mandela, on Robben Island for his outspoken opposition to apartheid in South Africa, he provided a fresh global perspective for the St Mary's congregation.[16]

Subsequent stipendiary curates were Revds Michael Johnson (1978-81);[17] and Jeffrey (Jeff) Heskins (1981-85). The latter had already been attached to St Mary's as a pastoral assistant while testing his vocation to the ordained ministry, and to the parish's delight was permitted to return to serve as curate after his ordination. James Roose-Evans, the theatre director perhaps best known for *84 Charing Cross Road,* who had a late vocation to the ordained ministry, was also licensed at this time to assist at St Mary's as a self-supporting minister.

Revd John Ovenden, vicar 1984-98

George Timms, now Chairman of the Trustees, drew on his experience as an Archdeacon to ensure that the appointment process for the new vicar was both robust and transparent, and also that the Trustees paid full attention to the wishes of the PCC. The vacancy was openly advertised, and candidates were selected and interviewed, not simply head-hunted as had often been the case in the past. The Trustees presented Revd John Ovenden who had trained for the ministry after initially embarking on a career as a teacher. After curacies in Handsworth (Sheffield) and Uckfield he became Precentor and Sacrist of Ely cathedral, and was thus the fourth vicar of St Mary's in a row to come directly from a cathedral or great church background, bringing a strong awareness of liturgy and music at the highest level. Caroline Dunn, one of the Trustees, remarked with relief and delight after his first mass (as she would also after the next two appointments): 'Well, we've got a good singer!' He and his wife Christine came to St Mary's with two children, and a third was born during their time in the parish.

* * *

During his time as vicar:

- Encouraged by the appointment of a married priest with young children (a significant new experience for St Mary's), other young families began to join the congregation.
- The church building was made more user-friendly, with the construction of a 'Parish Room' extension at the west end, and the opening up of the whole church space when necessary, for wider use by the parish and the community.
- The ordained ministry of women was strongly affirmed, even in the face of episcopal opposition.
- The organ was rebuilt, following a major fund-raising appeal.
- An annual Christingle service was instituted, which to this day has remained the best-attended service of the year.
- The first steps were taken towards diversification of Sunday evening worship, including Taizé prayers with an ecumenical flavour, and Contemplative Prayer.
- Closer ties were developed with the Liberal Jewish Synagogue.

Ovenden resigned from St Mary's in 1998 on being appointed a Canon of St George's Chapel, Windsor.

* * *

Ministry team

Jeff Heskins moved on shortly after John Ovenden's arrival at St Mary's, and was not immediately replaced as a paid curate. He has spoken of the 'good models of ministry' which encourage people to discern a possible vocation, and to judge by the numbers coming forward, Ovenden like his predecessor was strikingly formative in this respect. Francis Stephens, who continued to assist until his retirement in 1992, became a role-model for others who, despite having secular employment, were considering a call to the ordained ministry. Lyndon van der Pump and Sally Webster (two churchwardens in a row), and Joanna Yates, PCC Treasurer, all followed him on the Southwark Ordination Course. After ordination, Lyndon van der Pump joined the clergy team as a self-supporting minister (deacon 1988, priest 1989).

Rt Revd Brian Masters, who had become bishop of Edmonton shortly before John Ovenden's institution, hoped to steer the parish towards the extreme heights of Anglo-Catholic worship that he himself favoured and which had become typical throughout his episcopal Area, but which by no means accorded with the English Use, Prayer Book Catholicism so cherished at St Mary's. He had the idea that he might achieve this, and at the same time satisfy St Mary's need for a curate, by offering the parish a deacon of his own persuasion. And the lot fell on Revd Stephen Masters who joined the clergy team in 1987 fresh from training at Mirfield. His pastoral gifts were appreciated from the start, and he made some good friends within the congregation. But liturgically he was of much higher churchmanship than the parish he had been appointed to serve, and his single-handed attempts to import a number of Roman observances (such as a high mass for the Feast of the Assumption, celebrated complete with propers from the Roman Missal, during the vicar's absence on holiday and without his sanction) put him at odds with the clergy and many of the servers, and caused much unease. Bishop Masters's relations with the parish became frostier as his awareness grew that Ovenden, and St Mary's in general, strongly supported not only the English Use but especially women's ministry. Eventually he took the extraordinary step of severing his ties with the parish completely and placing it for the time being under the episcopal oversight of the Bishop of Willesden, who in 1998 came to take the annual Confirmation service. After Ovenden's departure, however,

Bishop Masters again took responsibility for St Mary's, which has since remained in the Edmonton episcopal fold.

After Stephen Masters moved on in 1990[18] it was to be more than a decade before St Mary's would again have a stipendiary curate, but the deficit was more than made good by the arrival of several further self-supporting ministers (SSMs). Sally Webster, after her ordination as deacon in 1991, was allowed to return to St Mary's as a SSM, and to remain after her priesting in 1994. From late 1991 she was joined by another SSM, the Revd David Jones (in secular life a business executive), who as well as preaching and presiding at the eucharist became particularly active alongside Sally Webster in developing youth work and parish house groups, and in 1998 led a pilgrimage to the Holy Land which is still remembered as a powerful influence on the spiritual lives of those who participated. Several other clergy and ordinands also assisted on a short-term basis, including Revd Susan Chrystal from the USA (see next chapter).

Revd Robert Atwell, vicar 1998-2008

At the time of John Ovenden's departure the parish had no fewer than four self-supporting priests in post simultaneously.[19] They worked collegially with the churchwardens during the vacancy. From a strong field, the Trustees selected the Revd Robert Atwell, a single man in his mid forties and so a complete contrast with his predecessor. Their choice was warmly endorsed by the parish representatives.

A graduate of Durham University (1975), he trained for the ministry at Westcott House, Cambridge and the Venerable English College in Rome where the Church of England sent him on an ecumenical scholarship. After ordination he served (like Richard Buck before him) a curacy at John Keble, Mill Hill (1978-81) before becoming chaplain of Trinity College, Cambridge (1981-87) where he taught Patristics. He next spent ten years (1987-97) as a monk of Burford Priory, an Anglican Benedictine monastery, before deciding to return to secular life. While awaiting the right moment to seek a return to full-time parochial ministry he spent a year working on two anthologies of readings, at the request of the Liturgical Commission of the Church of England, which were later published as *Celebrating the Saints* (1998) and *Celebrating the Seasons* (1999). Bishop Masters formally approved his presentation to St Mary's, but died before the induction service, which was therefore conducted by the Bishop of London.

Robert Atwell was determined at the outset to find a vision for St Mary's that would be true to its essential charisms. Two in particular stood out for him: its commitment from the very earliest days to reach out to the socially excluded young people in the community; and its renowned liturgical and musical traditions.

* * *

Among highlights from his time as vicar:

- Women's ministry continued to be affirmed.
- The parish's administration was overhauled, with increased professionalisation including a paid secretariat, the first paid youth worker, and the church's first website.
- The new Anglican liturgies which culminated in *Common Worship* were introduced.
- The new Millennium (2000), and the centenary of the *English Hymnal* (2006) were both celebrated.
- The highly successful Blueprint Appeal resulted, *inter alia*, in the restoration of the nave roof, extensive redecoration of the church, the building of St Mary's Centre as a new powerhouse for community outreach, and the institution of an organ scholarship.
- The Primrose Hill Lectures were launched, to engage local people of all faiths and none in the big issues confronting society.
- Closer ties were established with St Paul's school, and the vicar became chair of the School Governors.

- A stipendiary curacy was again revived, partly to compensate for time Atwell himself gave to the diocese in his responsibilities as Director of Post-Ordination training for the Edmonton Area.
- The Friends of St Mary's was established to capitalise upon the goodwill of many in the local community and further afield towards the church.

Robert Atwell left St Mary's in 2008 on being appointed Bishop of Stockport, from where he was translated to Exeter in 2014.

* * *

Ministry team

What had previously been known as the 'clergy team' was now re-named the 'ministry team' to allow for the inclusion of lay leaders such as pastoral assistants, Sunday school teachers and youth workers. A trusted external adviser was engaged to enable the team to take stock of its own direction and effectiveness.

There was no shortage of additional help, both lay and ordained. Sally Webster was able to time several of her return visits from the USA to assist in the parish while the vicar took a holiday. In 2001, while awaiting selection and training for ordination, Sarah Eynstone served as a pastoral assistant. She too played an important part in running youth activities, as subsequently did the Revd Paul Nicholson who in 2002 became the first paid curate at St Mary's for over a decade. He served, as deacon and then priest, until 2006 when he was appointed vicar of St Saviour's Chalk Farm (Eton Road) with St Peter's Belsize Square. Linda Dean joined the team as a self-supporting minister following her ordination as deacon in 2004. The team was further expanded following the licensing as a Reader first of Roberta Berke, and then of William Morris, the latter subsequently training for the ordained ministry. In 2007 another self-supporting minister, the Revd Mark Wakefield (deacon 2007, priest 2008), also joined the team.

Revd Preb. Marjorie Brown, vicar 2009-

The vacancy following Robert Atwell's resignation was in effect the first opportunity for ordained women of sufficient experience to apply for the post. But, as there were at that time no female incumbents in the Edmonton episcopal area, the environment for women was, to say the least, challenging. The Trustees nevertheless gave notice to the Bishop of Edmonton that they were minded to proceed without any gender discrimination (but without positively discriminating in favour of a woman either). Although he and the Bishop of London were not personally committed to the priestly ministry of women, they graciously agreed that they would accept a woman if one were presented. From a strong field of both men and women the Trustees selected for presentation Revd Marjorie Brown, vicar of St Thomas's Clapton Common since 1999 and priest in charge of St Matthew's Upper Clapton since 2006. She had been a Reader in the Edmonton area in 1992, the year that Synod approved in principle the ordination of women, and at that point had enrolled for training at the Southern Ministry Training School in Salisbury. Having been ordained deacon in 1995 and priest in 1996, she served her title in the Stepney episcopal area, for which she became Dean of Women's Ministry in 2002. She was married with three adult children.

* * *

Marjorie Brown's time as vicar has seen, among other things:

- The closer integration of the congregation's children into the worshipping community.
- Enhanced congregational understanding and ownership of the parish's outreach to the wider community, especially through the work of the St Mary's Centre with young people at risk.[20]
- The participation of the parish, alongside other Camden churches, in the Cold Weather Shelter scheme run during the winter months.

- Support for other specific community and citizens' initiatives, as well as front-line pastoral response after a number of local crises.
- Empowerment of the laity in a wide range of ministries and activities.
- Renewed focus on the care of the elderly, including healing ministry.
- The use of young volunteers and sponsored workers including pastoral assistants, some from mainland Europe, and Time for God volunteers.
- The development of a pastoral link with the evangelical churches of Berlin, and the twinning of St Mary's with the parish of St Luke in the Fields, New York City (in addition to its existing partnership with St Peter's, Cazenga, Luanda, Angola).

Marjorie Brown served successively as Assistant Director and then Director of Ordinands for the Edmonton Area. She was appointed concurrently as the Prebendary of Portpool in St Paul's cathedral in 2017.

* * *

Ministry team

After Paul Nicholson's departure St Mary's for a while once again had no paid assistant. Mark Wakefield and Linda Dean (until her retirement on health grounds) remained as SSMs and Lyndon van der Pump (though now retired) offered occasional assistance. Mark Wakefield was particularly influential in stimulating discussion forums, including a men's group (from 2009),[21] a group addressing faith in the workplace (from 2012), and above all introducing and chairing many of the Primrose Hill Lectures. One after another, leadership of these enterprises was handed over to the laity.

With the outreach work of St Mary's assuming ever growing importance, and in view of Marjorie Brown's responsibility for ordinands, St Mary's was once again designated as a training parish for newly-ordained clergy. The successive curates since that time have been the Revds Timothy Miller (2014-2017), Nick Walters (2017-2020), Emily Kolltveit (2020-) and Rupert Jones (2021-). A number of other ordinands and pastoral assistants have also had short-term attachments to the parish in the course of their training.

Endnotes

1   A church in the Alcuin Club tradition and featuring in Part II of its *Directory of Ceremonial*. He appears in some of the illustrations.
2   Peter Heathfield to Francis Stephens, 1972: Archives.
3   An extract from Ven Clive Young's address at Timms's funeral is printed in PM, Dec-Jan 1997/8.
4   The first paid curate was Paul Jack (1955-57), followed by Peter Thackray (1957-59). Emrys Evans then served briefly (1959-60) pending the arrival of John Crane (1960-64), who in turn was succeeded by Bruce Addison (1964-66).
5   And, later, by lay workers.
6   He retired the following year and went to live in South Africa (Supplement to parish chronicle).
7   His red cassock as a priest of that royal foundation, came out of the wardrobe when he was entertaining as vicar!
8   PM, Jan 1972.
9   PM, Jan 1976.
10 The curates were: David Gerrard (1966-69), Peter Jermyn (1967-70), Peter Lang (1969-73), John Wainwright (1970-73), Andrew St John (1973-75), John McKay (1974-77) and Martin Draper (1975-78).
11 Encouraged by the Bishop of Truro, Dr Graham Leonard, formerly Bishop of Willesden.
12 PM, Jul-Aug 1976.
13 Since the retirement of Lord Lloyd, the latter position has always been held by a senior Anglican priest from outside the parish.
14 PM, Sep/Oct 1978.
15 PM, May 1977.
16 After completing his studies he returned to South Africa where he later became Bishop of Kimberley and Kuruman and then Archbishop of Cape Town in succession to Desmond Tutu. For his memorable final sermon at St Mary's he took as his text some words from Timothy, 'God has not given us a spirit of timidity'.
17 PM, Dec 1978.
18 He eventually became vicar of St Anne's, Alderney.
19 Lyndon van der Pump, Sally Webster, David Jones and Susan Chrystal.
20 PM, Aug-Sep 2009.
21 A separate women's group ran for a while, convened by the vicar.

Chapter 10

Women in the Church

In strongly favouring the ordination of women, Percy Dearmer had been well ahead of his time, but after him no further clerical champion of that cause emerged at St Mary's for 60 years. When George Timms became vicar in 1952, women's ordination was not even a topic of discussion in the parish. Perhaps more remarkably, little or nothing was being done even to cater for women in the congregation, and for the first seven years or so of his ministry that remained the case. But then came several important break-throughs.

Although women continued to be in a considerable majority among elected members of the PCC after the War, they had as yet never been put forward for election by the Vestry as churchwardens nor by the PCC as Treasurer or sidesmen (stewards). But the first tentative step towards changing this mind-set was now taken, when Kathleen Beck, the parish librarian and historian,[1] became one of the 'sidesmen', to the dismay of the verger Robert Fake who gave her a hard time of it! It was as if an unspoken taboo had been broken, and other women followed in her footsteps.

In April 1959 Sister Joanna of the Deaconess Community of St Andrew came to the parish as a member of a very successful mission team that sought actively to involve many of the laity. This would lead in turn to their greater involvement in parish visiting. It struck Timms that if her Community would allow Joanna a longer attachment to St Mary's she might develop a specific ministry to women. She was permitted to stay on, at first on a wholly unofficial basis, but in September she was seconded to the parish on a part-time basis that still allowed her plenty of time with her Community. She established at St Mary's a women's Fellowship,[2] and also a new post-confirmation group for girls, the Quest. But she also gradually took on a wider ministerial role, including developing annual retreats.[3] Since deaconesses were not the equivalent of ordained male clergy, she sat during services with the congregation in the body of the church.[4] Joanna remained on the staff until 1965 when she was called back to her Community full-time upon her election as its Mother Superior.

Mother Joanna (as she now was), having seen how valuable a woman's presence could be at the centre of things at St Mary's, generously allowed this part-time work to be continued by another member of her Community, Sister Geraldine, who continued to assist in the parish until her death in 1971. Her work concentrated more on outreach, and she was instrumental in raising the congregation's awareness of poverty and isolation on the church's doorstep, and in keeping them informed of social changes taking place around them, in particular the building of the tower blocks along Adelaide Road. To give some idea of the scale of the changes taking place, in October 1972 she reported that 72 new flats had been completed but a further 600 were under construction.[5]

* * *

Women's ordination became more of a hot topic under Howard Hollis, amid long-drawn-out discussions on this subject in the Church Assembly and its successor the General Synod in the 1960s and 1970s. Neither Hollis nor most of his curates openly supported women's ordination, although they believed it should be seriously debated. The notable exception was Francis Stephens, whose highly public support for women's ordination became a costly commitment as it lost him a number of artistic commissions from churches that were unsympathetic to the cause. He saw to it that the ordination of the first women priests in Hong Kong was marked in an article in the parish magazine for

April 1972. On 26 November the following year, largely because of its Dearmer connection, St Mary's also featured in a BBC *Open Doors* programme, about women's ministry.

In 1974 the Hampstead Deanery Synod, on which St Mary's was represented, formally passed motions in favour of women's ordination, but the cause was still well short of gaining national approval. The case for and against was argued in articles in the parish magazine in October and November 1975, with the vicar attempting to hold some form of middle ground – in God's good time, but not yet – and John McKay (curate) arguing against. Women were gradually welcomed into the teams of servers, stewards and readers, but still not as thurifer or subdeacon.

* * *

Richard Buck was not a born supporter of women's ordination, and was happy to argue against it in the parish magazine,[6] while not being completely deaf to the arguments of supporters like Francis Stephens who, together with Leo Shirley, Kathleen Beck, Dorothy Ralphs and a number of others from the congregation, was active in the Movement for the Ordination of Women. Buck came gradually round to the view that the ordination of women to the diaconate might be acceptable: but not to the priesthood. After leaving St Mary's, however, he dropped his objections to their ordination as priests and when at that stage Sally Webster, one of the churchwardens, who was a staff member at the American School in London, visited him to discuss the possibility of training as a Lay Reader, he advised her instead to consider aiming for ordination. That turned out to be the most definitive step yet for women's ministry at St Mary's.

An almost equally important psychological barrier was breached when Joanna Yates, despite some opposition, became the first woman to serve as thurifer and subdeacon at St Mary's.[7] 'I have often reflected,' she says, 'that once women were allowed to handle the incense it was only a matter of time before we became priests.' When, as subdeacon, she was eventually licensed to assist with the chalice,[8] a tiny minority of the congregation could not accept it. She remembers that 'one old gentleman would hop along the line at the communion rail to avoid receiving the wine from a woman.'

Following the tradition set by Sisters Joanna and Geraldine, in 1977 Richard Buck asked Sister Judith of the Order of the Holy Paraclete, who had worked alongside him at Margaret Street, to join the staff at St Mary's, with a specific brief to reach out to the local communities.[9] Over the next six years she forged many grass-roots links, establishing for example a community garden, a group of Adelaide Neighbours and a Bangladeshi mothers' group, the two latter meeting in the basement flat of the vicarage which she used as her HQ. Through detailed articles in the parish magazine, as well as in occasional sermons and addresses, she kept the congregation informed of what for many – especially the large proportion of the congregation that lived beyond the parish boundaries – was a mostly unknown world.

In 1980, when the PCC had to turn to the pressing internal matter of re-whitening the church, which was bound to require major financial outlay, Judith assumed the mantle of an Old Testament Prophet, warning St Mary's against becoming merely a 'liturgical ghetto' oblivious of the community it was called to serve.[10] But she need not have feared: in 1981 the parish held a day conference on its community involvement, and gave strong backing to her initiatives. One tangible result was that in 1983[11] St Mary's paid for the foundation stone of the new Swiss Cottage Community Centre.

On a lighter note, one witness recalls Sister Judith's rather particular style of driving:

> Many of the clergy have a reputation for fast driving, as if they were trained at the Jehu, Son of Nimshi School of Motoring,[12] but Sister Judith outclassed them all. There was a memorable staff outing, a day trip to Boulogne, which ended with a car-load of people speeding through the Kent countryside in the small hours, Sister Judith at the wheel, singing the Angelus at the tops of our voices.

* * *

It was in John Ovenden's time that the conclusive national moves were made towards the ordination of women, moves from which in the long run St Mary's would benefit enormously. Synod approved women's ordination as deacons in 1985 and the first were duly ordained in 1987. It then took a further five years to approve their ordination as priests (1992, Royal Assent 1993), with the first being ordained in 1994. Sally Webster, ordained deacon in 1990,[13] joined the clergy team as a SSM, initially without knowing whether or when she might be allowed to progress to the priesthood (for which, as it transpired, she would have to wait until 1994). By contrast, Lyndon van der Pump, who had had a very similar trajectory to the ministry, was ordained deacon in 1988 and, without any hiatus, priest in 1989. Sally Webster's ordained male colleagues at St Mary's, however, welcomed her into the clergy team from the start, and there was general rejoicing when she celebrated her first eucharist on 24 April 1994.[14]

Sadly, it has to be recognised that these decisions hurt some members of the congregation who remained opposed to women's ordination, and a few left the parish. But there was to be no looking back. A number of other women from the congregation now offered themselves for ordination training. They included Joanna Yates (former Treasurer and a subdeacon), Liz Piercey (former PCC Secretary), Linda Dean (churchwarden), and Ruth Lampard. In 1997, Revd Susan Chrystal, a priest in the Episcopal Church of the USA, came to London with her family during her husband's posting to a job in the City. But London was a far cry from her own liberal diocese of Newark NJ, and she was surprised how difficult it was for a female priest to find acceptance. She

Revd Sally Webster.

found her way to St Mary's and was quickly invited by John Ovenden to become a SSM in the ministry team. Thus for a short time, which included the hand-over from John Ovenden to Robert Atwell as vicar, there were two ordained women priests simultaneously, both American, on the staff. That, however, was short-lived because when her husband's posting to London came to an end Susan Chrystal returned to the USA with her family.

* * *

At all levels of ministry in the parish, lay and ordained, women were at last fully accepted on equal terms with men. Symbolically, from 1996 the 'sidesmen' (coordinated by a woman, Marie Alexander) were restyled as 'stewards'.

Roberta Berke, a member of the congregation, was licensed as the parish's first Lay Reader (of either sex) in 1998. In 2004 Linda Dean was ordained deacon and joined the staff in a self-supporting capacity. Her previous experience as a teacher equipped her well for preaching and training children for the children's choir of the time. She was ordained priest by Bishop Edward Holland at St Mary's in 2006, and would go on to play an important role in the ministry team, and in running the parish during the vacancy following Robert Atwell's elevation to the episcopate. She continued to serve under Marjorie Brown, until ill health led to her retirement.

* * *

Marjorie Brown's appointment as vicar was a huge milestone in the history of both the parish and the area. The bishops of Edmonton and London both accepted the presentation without demur, and the parish, which by then had had long experience of women's ministry in assisting roles, was delighted. She was instituted as vicar of St Mary's on 28 January 2009 by the Bishop of London (Dr Richard Chartres), with the Bishop of Edmonton (Peter Wheatley) as preacher.

During her time as vicar, women have been further empowered, especially in the sacristy and serving teams, with Kimberly Gilmour becoming the first female Head Server as well as leading first communion classes for children. Miriam Rinsler, another former teacher, became a Licensed Lay Minister (Reader) and, having been ordained deacon in 2020, went on to serve in another parish. Emily Kolltveit, who had served as a pastoral assistant in the parish before her ordination training, returned as stipendiary deacon in 2020 and was priested in 2021.

With St Mary's now widely known to be a training parish supportive of women's ministry, several other women, including trainees from the Diocese of Europe, have successively had short attachments to St Mary's in the course of their ministerial formation. A number of young lay women have also served as pastoral assistants, particularly in the light of the new partnership with the church in Berlin.

Endnotes

1. In 1955, with the help of a grant from the Rebecca Hussey Book Charity (and a bookcase donated by JGV Bolton to mark his 21 years in the parish), the PCC set up a parish library which she ran. She also wrote a long series of articles in the magazine about the parish's early history, on which subsequent guides as well as the present work have freely drawn.
2. Later opened to men as well.
3. Timms in PM, 1991.
4. John Ashby, 'Up-steps, down-steps', in PM, Jun-Jul 2009, p.20.
5. PM, Oct 1967.
6. PM, Nov 1978.
7. She also became Treasurer and Sacristan.
8. Bishop Brian Masters had initially restricted permission to administer the chalice to ordinands, see PM, Jan-Mar 1986.
9. For a profile see PM, Mar 1978.
10. PM, Jun 1979, Sep 1983.
11. PM, Nov 1983.
12. 2 Kings 9, v.20.
13. For her personal memoir see PM, Jul 2001.
14. In spite of initial reservations, Robert Wills served as subdeacon for both Sally Webster's first eucharist and later for Marjorie Brown's institution.

Chapter 11

Sacred and secular spaces

The Church Room (to the 1960s)

As the borough's post-War housing development plan took shape in the 1960s it became clear that Eton College, despite everyone's earlier expectations, would not be in a position to renew the parish's lease on the Church Room off Oppidans Mews when it expired in 1964, because it was now clear that the whole neighbourhood was scheduled for demolition and redevelopment. Eton at first thought it might be able to find a replacement site in Oppidans Road, on the first floor of another property, and this seemed a sure enough prospect for Timms to report it to the parish meeting in 1963. An ominous silence then descended, and nothing had been agreed before he left the parish in 1965. Negotiations then went downhill, until it became clear that the building Eton had had in mind was no longer a starter. Camden proposed instead a completely new hall, but at a cost well in excess of anything it could afford to pay St Mary's as compensation for eviction from the Church Room. If the parish had accepted, it would have had to find bridging loans to make up the difference, and although the PCC did seriously consider that, it knew it was about to incur major expenditure on the church building itself (see below) so reluctantly decided against.[1] A third suggestion was that St Mary's might share a community centre with one of the new tower blocks, but that too was rejected because it would have left the church unable to guarantee access to the premises whenever it wanted. Altogether, negotiations dragged on for something like a decade until in 1973 the parish agreed to release Eton College from its undertaking to find alternative accommodation, in return for a cash settlement which it was hoped might provide the seed-corn for some future church hall.[2] By 1975, there was around £15,000 from this settlement in the bank, and discussions began on how best to invest or use it,[3] but these remained unresolved for another decade, with the real value of the money steadily depreciating.

So, from the mid 1960s, St Mary's had no hall. In its absence, the church building and to some extent the vicarage had to be called into play to host many of the meetings and events that had previously taken place in the Church Room. Some activities could not be so easily re-housed, and a number of sports clubs as well as the ballet school that had hired the Church Room were cut adrift. From 1972, when the new St Paul's School was built just across Elsworthy Road from the church (see below), and its hall made available for church use, the loss of the Church Room was less acutely felt.

Union with St Paul's Avenue Road (1957)

The damage to St Paul's church, Avenue Road, during the Blitz[4] was severe, but not so severe as to make its rebuilding impossible ... until a contractor sent to deal with another damaged property in the vicinity mistook his instructions and began to demolish the church! And, alas, he had made all too good progress before anyone realised he was not acting on diocesan instructions. This unintended vandalism left St Paul's in an even more parlous state than before, and was enough to tip the scales against rebuilding. Pending a decision on the church's future, the vicar (Revd Leycester Malet) and his congregation held their services in the hall of their parish school in Winchester Road. Only when Malet retired in 1955 was the much-heralded decision finally taken by the London Diocesan Reorganisation Committee to merge

St Paul's Avenue Road

St Paul's with St Mary's as soon as the necessary formalities could be completed. The two congregations had been given ample notice, and the last St Paul's service was held in September 1955, although it was not until 1957 that the necessary Order in Council was secured, creating the united benefice of 'St Mary the Virgin Primrose Hill with St Paul's Avenue Road'.[5] On 22 October 1957 George Timms was formally instituted as Vicar of the united parish. Whereas St Mary's parish before the merger had an estimated population of only around 2,800, the combined total was, as Timms put it, 'a more economic unit of 7,500.'[6]

The churchmanship of the two was rather different, with St Mary's being the more high-church. Some of the 40 or so regular congregation of St Paul's in effect feared they were about to be 'sold to Rome', but one of them, Caroline Dunn, who would later become a Trustee of St Mary's, remembered Timms leaving a very favourable impression when he addressed a meeting at St Paul's. That did not reassure everyone, and some went off to other nearby churches, in particular St Peter's Belsize Square. In the end only about half moved to St Mary's, where the 9.45 a.m. liturgy was re-modelled as a less formal service in the hope of making them feel welcome (see p.). Several of the St Paul's congregation went on to play an important role at St Mary's, including Stanley and Sylvia Taylor, Caroline and Brian Dunn and Frank and Mary Ward. The united parish inherited sponsorship of St Paul's School, which would remain in Winchester Road for a further fifteen years.

St Paul's School (since 1972)

That original school building had been condemned by the Board of Education as far back as 1913, but had somehow staggered on for almost sixty years with no viable alternative being proposed. Indeed, further classrooms were still being added in the 1960s. At the beginning of 1970 official approval was finally given for a new building to be constructed opposite St Mary's, in Elsworthy Road. As it was a church school, the parish was expected to meet a modest proportion of the costs, and fund-raising efforts began in a distinctly St Mary's way with a Drama Group presentation in the church of JB Priestley's *They came to the City*.

So unsuitable had the Winchester Road premises become that a plan was hatched to bus students every day to another school pending completion of their new building, but that was never implemented. Building work on the new premises was completed in 1972, and in the autumn term staff and pupils finally moved in and parishioners were invited to take their first look around.[7] For St Mary's this marked a new beginning, with a church school intimately bound-up with parish life for the first time since Charles Fuller's days. And, as a token of the new partnership, successive head teachers generously allowed the church, as its sponsor, to use the school hall for functions outside school hours.

St Mary's church

Works on the church building in the time of George Timms, in addition to the organ restoration separately described, included the installation of a new boiler (1958), renovation of the choir vestry (1960) and the eviction of 'old, unused church furniture and furnishings that had filled every available nook and cranny'.[8] A more major overhaul came when new electric lighting was installed and the church was once again re-whitened (1961). It may seem inconceivable today, but the PCC discussed whether the Mary and John figures of the Rood, which some thought excessively sentimental, should be removed, to leave only the central crucifix.[9] Fortunately they drew back from the brink. Otherwise, there was only some modest re-ordering. In September 1954 Sebastian Shaw, Geoffrey's son, paid for a stone credence in the Holy Spirit chapel. That was also the year when a new altar in the north transept, a scheme so earnestly hoped-for by Hardcastle, was at last dedicated (to St John the Evangelist).[10] After the merger with St Paul's, one of that church's altars was brought to St Mary's for use in the new chapel (1959), and Robert Fake, the verger, remodelled the earlier transept altar as a portable one for use in the nave at the 9.45 service.

Under Howard Hollis there was no major building work, although significant outlay was required for the renovation of the roof and brickwork following architect's inspections. The parish chronicle records that 'the whole church [was] cleaned and redecorated by Mr & Mrs Frank Ward and helpers.' There were three notable changes in the church's internal appearance. In 1973 the return stalls at the top of the chancel steps were removed,[11] thanks largely to pressure (as he proudly admitted) from Francis Stephens. In 1974 Martin Browne sponsored new lighting for the chapel, in memory of his wife Henzie Raeburn. And in 1975 an internal south porch was erected as a memorial to Fr Hardcastle. As well as an inscription in his memory, the porch incorporates small panes of glass inscribed with the signatures of Howard Hollis (vicar), Charles Plouviez and Eric Whiteley (churchwardens), Francis Stephens (designer of the screen) and Stanley Taylor and Elizabeth Webb (who made it). St Mary's formally became a Listed Building in 1975.[12]

* * *

Under Richard Buck two far-reaching bricks-and-mortar decisions were taken: the re-whitening (yet again) of the church from top to bottom, and the long-deferred acquisition of a new Vicarage to replace 7 Elsworthy Road.

Early enquiries about the cost of re-whitening concluded that it might far exceed the parish's budget. And that was in any case not the only major item of expenditure falling due. After much thought, a cost-effective though not risk-free alternative was chosen, namely to contract the whole operation to Community Service Industries: in effect 'volunteer' young offenders working under professional instruction while serving community service sentences. The massive job was undertaken at remarkably little cost to the parish (other than materials, supervision and the hire of scaffolding), but even that required Sally Webster to mastermind a military-scale operation to raise £10,000 in only nine months, with the biggest fairs and bazaars St Mary's had ever seen! So grey and grimy had the church already become since its last re-whitening under Timms that much of it required four coats of paint. While the work was in progress, the church had the use of St Paul's school hall for its services.

Other renovations followed, including cleaning and re-gilding the reredos (1982). The fabric of the tower was repaired and its spiral staircase cleaned, to evict pigeons that had been getting in and nesting, and to deal with the unpleasant consequences. The south aisle was given a new fitted carpet, to make a better environment for concerts, and for young children attending the services.

Vicarage

No 7 Elsworthy Road, acquired in 1907 as the vicarage, had never been ideal for its purpose, and indeed its sale had been discussed as far back as Duncan-Jones's time. It was a large building and difficult to maintain at the best of times, so it was scarcely surprising, given the Second World War and its aftermath, that when George Timms arrived the vicarage had had no major work done on it by either the Church Commissioners or the parish for more than twenty years. It therefore needed a complete refit. While that was being done Timms, for his first six months, lodged with Evelyn Brough at 115 King Henry's Road.[13] On his return to the vicarage, which was far too large for a single man, he took in a married housekeeper and her husband, as well as a succession of lodgers, some of them priests assisting with the services at St Mary's on what would now be called a house-for-duty basis, and also his life-long companion and soul-mate, Jim Holden.[14]

Even though Timms was uneasy with crowds, he allowed the vicarage and its garden to be used for parish parties. Memorably, when the wall separating the garden from Primrose Hill collapsed in 1955, he had a self-locking wooden door incorporated into the new wall – quite contrary to local custom – taking a stand on 'the ancient privilege of clergy whereby the lawful incumbent of a parish is permitted the easiest access to all parts of his parish', which in his case included the major portion of Primrose Hill.'[15]

By Richard Buck's time the vicarage was suffering from rising damp, dry rot, a leaking roof and faulty electrical wiring, and had become a health hazard for the vicar and a constant worry for the parish.[16] For a time, efforts were made to keep it viable, with piecemeal adaptations to provide office and meeting space. In an article in the parish magazine for January 1978 Buck spoke of how, in the absence of a church hall, it was having to be used to host committees and social events. But, he added, 'because it is a lovely house I want to do it justice by making it as attractive as possible. I could, I suppose, sit on orange boxes and have sacking at the windows, but I don't. Like most priests of today, I don't have private income but, through the generosity of friends over the years, I have acquired some good pieces of furniture and have managed to put a home together.' Later that year the basement was adapted to include a room large enough for youth and community activities and to provide a base for Sister Judith.[17]

In 1982 the Church Commissioners agreed in principle to sell the property if the parish could find another suitable house nearby that met their criteria for parsonage houses, which included having five bedrooms. The churchwardens identified 44 King Henry's Road which was ready for occupancy subject to redecoration and fitting-out, and this was accordingly purchased by the Commissioners. They reserved for diocesan use an existing flat in the basement, which did not technically become part of the 'parsonage'. For the short term, however, they allowed lay workers from the parish to occupy both that and a newly converted flat on the top floor of the main building. A team of lay volunteers helped the vicar with both his house-move and the renovation of the garden, for the improvement of which piles of manure were delivered to the front door, whence they had to be man-handled (more truthfully, woman-handled!) down the steps and out to the back of the building.[18] The garden would be further developed by subsequent vicars, in particular Robert Atwell.

Changing attitudes to the church building

The last half century, at St Mary's as elsewhere, has seen a shift in attitudes towards the use of church space. Right up to the 1970s St Mary's was regarded as an inviolable sanctuary where nothing other than worship and church-related business should take place, and where the staging of secular entertainments (and to some even the provision of refreshments) was seen as irreverent or improper. The development of an alternative vision, whereby the building's whole space might be dedicated to both church and community use, was severely constrained by the simple fact that Manning's footprint for the building (as completed under Spencer) occupied very nearly the entire site donated by Eton College, with the exception of small gardens on the east and south sides and the apparently unusable strip of land at the west end that separated the church from the adjacent houses in Elsworthy Road. Whereas many other churches of the period were set in grounds spacious enough to allow for extensions and adaptations, and not a few had the space for a church hall, and car parking, that was never true of St Mary's, where there were not even public WC facilities let alone an office, kitchen or meeting room.

Some preliminary thought was given under Richard Buck as to whether the space at the west end might prove sufficient for an extension but, after the re-whitening already described, funds were not available and there was no appetite for another major appeal. Nevertheless that earlier vision of an unchanging, inviolable, sacred church space did begin to crumble. A first modest step was taken with the erection of the 'Dearmer screen' across the transept (which was no longer being used liturgically), to enclose a small parish office. Originally designed by Francis Stephens and built by Stanley Taylor, the structure has since been adapted and improved several times to include a rudimentary ceiling and (optional) windows on to the church. It is inscribed in memory of Percy Dearmer and was dedicated when the congregation moved back into the church after its exile for the re-whitening of 1980-81.

An early social innovation in the time of John Ovenden was the regular provision of refreshments in the body of the church after the Sung Eucharist on a Sunday. It became immediately apparent to the organisers why this had not been the norm before! The only available source of water was a tap in the choir vestry, which was through two doors and down several steps from the level of the church, all of which had to be negotiated with trolleys, crockery and jugs of water. The only WC was still situated off the ambulatory at the east end, and that was reserved for clergy, choir, and Stanley Taylor (see ch.12).

Parish Room extension (1988)

As these arrangements were patently unsatisfactory, with John Ovenden's encouragement, the PCC and congregation undertook a more radical re-think of the use of the building. Attention was again focussed on the small strip of land between the west end of the church and the boundary of the neighbouring properties. Long overrun by weeds and scrub as well as the inevitable accumulations of litter and detritus, it was not an immediately promising prospect. Nor was that its only limitation: the site was narrow and tapering, and would only be able to accommodate small rooms. Nor could any extension rise above the height of a single room without offending the neighbours, who were already uneasy about even a low-rise extension. Perhaps most challenging of all, if an extension were to be accessed from the church, Manning's original west wall would have to be breached. Other ideas were considered, including a gallery at the west end (for which Francis Stephens drew up provisional plans); but it was eventually decided to limit the operation to what seemed the most manageable option, a westward extension, and this was built in 1988 at a cost of around £75,000. The small sum then still left in the bank from the surrender of the Church Room represented no more than a starter for the fund, and to add to the challenge a further £20,000 had to be raised simultaneously for essential repairs to the south aisle roof. Mary Jean Pritchard recalls that 'planning, fundraising, and building was a huge community effort. We had a ball (as in a real dancing ball!) at the zoo; art auction; endless jumble sales and I don't know what else.' Among the many fund-raising efforts, John Ovenden invited parishioners to contribute literary offerings towards an anthology, *England's Lane.*

The extension provided a 'Parish Room' for social gatherings and small meetings, an adjacent kitchen – the most awkward part of the plan, on account of its constricted, tapering shape (since re-designed) – a small room for flower-arranging, and two WCs (again subsequently re-designed, to comply with accessibility requirements). Whilst the last two functions are accessed through a door inside the north porch, entry to the Parish Room and kitchen did indeed require two new doorways to be knocked through the west wall, with consequential changes to the interior panelling. The extension was dedicated in 1988.

Flexible use of the church interior

A much bolder question was how to make better use of the large internal space of the church itself. The congregation's preference (right from the start) for chairs rather than fixed pews did at least mean that it was perfectly feasible to open up an impressively large space by moving the seating aside. Richard Buck tried this experimentally, in order to provide an open worship-space for use by the large numbers of young people who attended the international Taizé meeting in London in 1981, for which St Mary's was one of the host parishes. Moving aside the seats became a more frequent occurrence under John Ovenden, but now for a wider range of secular activities: concerts, parties, and socials such as the Barn Dance that became a regular accompaniment to the parish's harvest celebrations. Whilst the western extension transformed the building's potential, this new-found freedom to use the full interior space was in some respects the more dynamic long-term development. A psychological threshold had been crossed; and it later became the norm to clear away all the seating for large events such as Designer Fairs and the many banquets and festivities organised by the Friends. In 2020 most of the seats had to be removed anyway, and for a more sombre reason: to restrict the number of seats available, in a controlled configuration aimed at enforcing 'social distancing' in accordance with the regulations during the coronavirus epidemic. That in turn cleared the way for the acquisition of new seating for the church's 150th anniversary.

'Blueprint': nave roof and St Mary's Centre (2000s)

Unsuspected by the congregation, Percy Dearmer's boarding suspended below the nave roof had become brittle with age. Shortly before the millennium, pieces of it started to fall down into the church, posing a threat to life and limb. Pending its removal, the nave was equipped at just below ceiling height with fine-meshed netting to prevent pieces of board falling on those below. Its repair became a new priority, but that was by no means the only item on the agenda for capital expenditure. On his appointment as vicar Robert Atwell had been quickly struck by the continuing lack of space on site for the kind of activities many parishes take for granted. Working parties were once again established to see how, if at all, this might be addressed, and fund-raising began in earnest.

Stage One of the 'Blueprint' Appeal (2001) raised in one year something in excess of £200,000 (from grants, individual donations and, once again, a host of fund-raising events including an art exhibition and a series of concerts). This, among other things, enabled the nave roof to be repaired. Once the boarding was dismantled the wooden roof above was found to be in near pristine condition, and at the architect's suggestion the panels between the timbers here and in the north aisle were painted (for the first time) in a pink and blue typical of Bodley's palette. A partial re-whitening of the church was undertaken while the scaffolding was up, and the church was re-wired and a new sound system installed.[19] In the same stage of the Appeal one of Kempe's windows at the west end was re-leaded and restored.[20]

The second, more ambitious, phase of Blueprint ran from 2003 to 2007 and created (on the site of the old choir vestry, ambulatory and part of the garden at the east end of the church) the St Mary's Centre, designed by Margaret Davies. Like the earlier extension at the west end, this has proved transformative for parish life. The Centre comprises a Community Room with supporting facilities including improved WC arrangements, and a kitchen to make the Centre self-sufficient for catering. A small room for counselling and one-to-one meetings was also funded, through the estate of the late Christina Barth, a former member of the congregation. The suspended ceiling of the old vestry was taken down, revealing a fine cross-beamed roof, and a new floor was fitted. The new room provided much improved meeting space, including a more pleasant environment for choir practices, with dedicated storage for both music and choir robes.[21] But its most important use is for outreach activities such as youth work and hosting the Cold Weather Shelter. The Centre is lettable, and a small but steady income contributes towards its running costs, from bookings as varied as nursery, playgroup, yoga classes, language teaching and AA meetings.

St Mary's Centre was officially opened by the Bishop of London, Dr Richard Chartres, on 25 April 2007. He was accompanied by the Archbishop of Nigeria who happened to be staying with him during the Lambeth Conference of that year.[22]

* * *

Several further improvements have been made in the past decade. With the Cold Weather Shelter particularly in mind, the Centre's

WC facilities were upgraded and a shower added in 2010. To make the church compliant with national regulations for access by disabled people, a ramp was built in 2014 to replace the steps leading to the church door from Elsworthy Road. The garden along the south side of the church was then completely redesigned, on the initiative of Malcolm Craddock, one of the churchwardens. This too has since been further developed, with both a seating area and a small memorial garden for the interment of ashes. When the weather-worn inscriptions on the existing war memorial at the south east corner of the church site were in danger of becoming illegible, the PCC decided to commission a completely new, plaque-style war memorial, which was affixed to the exterior of the south wall in 2018. Meanwhile, the bleak aspect of the church on the north side, where there had never been a garden, was cheered up, on the initiative of churchwarden Casey Oppong, by establishing in the spaces between the buttresses a self-contained garden and planters. To the surprise of many, despite its shady north-facing location, both flowers and vegetation have flourished there. The main change to the interior was the installation, from 2013-14 onwards, of new, energy-efficient, LED lighting throughout.

At the time of writing, plans for the further redevelopment of the building, in connection with its 150th anniversary, were under active consideration.

Crypt: St Mary's Brewery

The space below the chancel, among the foundations of the church as reinforced in 1883, had never found a use other than as storage for furniture and movables no longer in active use, which in practice meant an indiscriminate mixture of junk and items of historic interest. This space principally housed the gas boiler, but had uneven floor footings and an inconveniently low ceiling, and consequently had never been used for (and was never intended for) any liturgical purpose. In 2014-15 the old boiler, which had failed, was removed and replaced by fan-assisted gas fires throughout the church, which opened up the possibility of the crypt space being used for some other purpose. In 2016 two members of the congregation (Roddy Monroe and Steve Reynolds) obtained permission to establish a micro-brewery in the crypt with a trinity of aims: to make good beer, to provide a service for the community, and to help the parish assist the St Mary's Centre youthwork. The brewery was launched and blessed on 15th October 2016 by the Bishop of Edmonton who presented an icon of St Arnold, the patron saint of brewers. Both the bishop and the archdeacon attended a beer-tasting to mark the brewery's public launch.

Endnotes

1. LMA: P81/MRV/98, PCC Minutes, 12 and 26 Oct 1971.
2. Ibid. PCC Minutes 20 Mar 1973.
3. Ibid. PCC Minutes Sept 1975.
4. Built by SS Teulon, it was remembered by Sir John Betjeman, who used to worship there, as 'weird within and without', with its many gables and turrets, its strident polychrome interior and tile reredos. Archives: C Plouviez notes.
5. CERC, NB23/359.
6. Archives: *St Mary's Primrose Hill: the Parish and its Vicars* (1955).
7. The official opening ceremony did not take place until 13 July 1975. See also PM, Jun-Nov 1975: Short history of St Paul's school by Ronald Simmons.
8. PM, Oct 1960.
9. Archives: audio tape.
10. LMA P81/MRV/145: PCC Minutes, 9 May 1954.
11. Ibid.
12. LMA: DL/A/C/MS19224/449.
13. For his appreciation of her see PM, May 1970.
14. See PM, 1997/8: extract from an address by Ven Clive Young at Timms's funeral, Nov 1997.
15. TNA, WORK16/1604 quoted in M Sheppard, *Primrose Hill: A History.*
16. PM, Sept 1982. Poem: PM, Mar 1983.
17. PM, Mar 1978, Jun 1979.
18. Information from Sally Webster.
19. The first deaf loop system had been installed in 1994.
20. For more information on the Blueprint appeal see PM, 2001-2 (*passim*) and appeal literature in Archives.
21. The space below the organ was also converted to provide a new servers' vestry and further storage space.
22. It poured with rain during the service, and during the sermon the thurifer and crucifer were deployed behind the scenes, mopping up water pouring through a defect in the new roof! Information from John Hawes.

Chapter 12

The beauty of holiness

Gifts and disposals

Each generation has sought to continue the tradition of generous donations towards the beautifying of the church, and whilst in some ways the process can be seen as continuous, key anniversaries and jubilees have always inspired the flow of new gifts.

Gifts (1950s-60s)

In 1952 St Mary's was offered some fittings from the bombed-out church of St John's Red Lion Square, including a hanging wooden pyx by FE Howard. This was tried out in the chapel pending a faculty application[1] which, however, was never forthcoming, perhaps because the pyx was out of scale with its surroundings. A chastened Timms told the PCC in January 1953 that he felt any future changes to the church's fittings should be considered only after taking the professional advice of an architect, and suggested Randall Blacking (a pupil of Comper and close friend of Jack Arnold), who was then the consulting architect to the cathedral in Salisbury where he lived. In the short time that Blacking assisted St Mary's he designed oak kneelers and a credence table, the Shaw memorial inscription, and a desk for a benefactors' book. But he found his remoteness from London too inconvenient, and London-based architects were soon engaged in his place.

Frank Knight of Wellingborough, the silversmith[2] who had already crafted several items for St Mary's, was consulted over the best fate for ageing sanctuary lamps, crosses and candlesticks. He recommended disposal of those in poor condition or of poor design. At the same time Knight offered to restore two candlesticks given to the church by FC Eeles,[3] but the cost was more than the church could afford.

The merger with St Paul's brought further movables to St Mary's, most of them surplus to requirements. Of five chalices, three were offered to the mission field. Knight accepted the fourth, a small silver one, as payment in kind for restoring the fifth, a medieval one which St Mary's retained.[4] In 1959 Mrs Watson and her brother donated a larger wafer box, in memory of Dorothy Mathew, to serve the enlarged congregation.

Deaths during Timms's ministry included those of several stalwarts from earlier pages of this history: in 1953, Bernard Dick, a former churchwarden; WL Cooke who was old enough to remember the church's consecration; in 1954, FC Eeles (to mark whose national importance as Secretary of the Central Council for the Care of Churches a memorial service was held at St James's Piccadilly); FJ Marriott, churchwarden, treasurer and Trustee; and [Grace] Mary Shaw, Geoffrey's widow; in 1955 Arthur Duncan-Jones, former vicar, and subsequently Dean of Chichester; in 1956 JH Arnold, organist, choirmaster, server and benefactor of the church; in 1958 Ralph Vaughan Williams, Martin Shaw and May Thorne. They were respectively commemorated in gifts to the church. **Two kneeling benches** for communicants at the High Altar, were designed by Blacking and given in 1954: one by the Shaw family in memory of Geoffrey, his wife and their son James; the other in memory of Francis James Lias (1869-1952) by his widow. The Shaw gift also included a **credence table** for the sanctuary which, however, was soon superseded by a stone slab fitted by the Warham Guild. In memory of FC Eeles a new **green frontal and dossal** were given by May, Cecilia and Edith Jeoffroy and Miss Judith Scott, his Secretary.[5] In grateful memory of Frank Marriott and his immense work for the parish a new **sanctuary lamp** was subscribed to by the congregation in 1954.

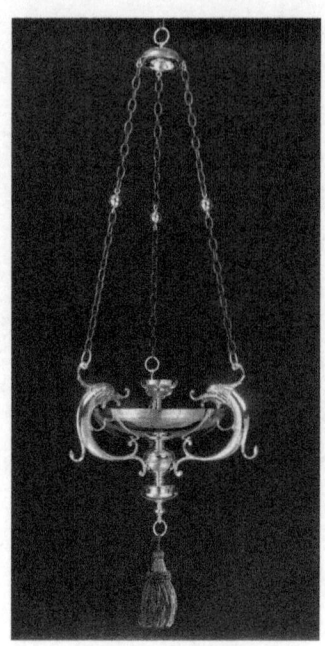

Sanctuary lamp designed by Frank Knight 1954. (WF Knight)

Of fire-gilded bronze, it was designed by Frank Knight. A memorial fund in Marriott's honour remained open and continued to fund additional acquisitions including a new **festal altar front** in 1957. An **oak desk with a glass top**, to contain the parish's memorial book, was given in memory of Bernard Dick, and very appropriately a new **vestment press** for the sacristy was given in memory of May Thorne who had been associated with St Mary's for 55 years, and had latterly taken charge of repairs to the church vestments and linen.[6]

So closely identified were Duncan-Jones, the Shaw brothers and JH Arnold that it seemed best to have a single memorial to all of them. The first suggestion was simply for a Processional book, but the congregation's response was so generous that a new **High Altar cross and candlesticks** were purchased instead. The cross, again by Frank Knight, is of silver, partly gilded, with enamel inlays of the four evangelists. The silvered and gilded bronze candlesticks which originally accompanied it were stolen in 1968. Dearmer's aesthetic standards had resulted in the walls of St Mary's being thus far free of any memorial tablets and monuments. It was therefore a mark of the unique esteem in which this distinguished foursome were held that a discreet **memorial plaque** recording the benefaction was permitted to be fixed to the wall on the south side of the choir. It was carved by John Skelton, a nephew of Eric Gill.[7]

In 1955 St Mary's added to its collection of 'episcopal' chairs, with one originally given to Mr and Mrs VH King as a wedding present, made in 300-year-old oak, 'from the belfry of the old church in Bridgwater'.[8] Among vestments and textiles gifted or purchased at this period were, a new **green chasuble** (purchased 1953); and a **gold damask humeral veil** (made and presented by Mrs Audrey Browne, Martin's second wife, in 1955).

In the aftermath of the church's 90th anniversary, further significant gifts were recorded in 1963: a 'new **festival frontal**' for the chapel;[9] and a **two-sided frontal for the nave altar**, red on one side and printed with a stencilled design on the other for use in Lent.[10] Revd CM Lamb, sometime vicar of St Mark's Marylebone Road, donated a set of **Passiontide-red eucharistic vestments** made by the St Dunstan's Society for Revd JN Newland-Smith, one of Dearmer's assistant curates, whilst, in memory of her sister Jessie, Miss Swain paid for a new festival **tunicle** for the Clerk.[11]

The further adventures of the Russian icon (1963)

The most remarkable story – the reader must decide whether it suggests divine intervention, coincidence or cock-and-bull – surrounds the silver icon of Our Lady, given to the church in May 1920 by Dr Evelyn Cooke who was then a member of the choir. He had purchased it in Novorossiysk while serving with the Royal Navy in the Black Sea. As we saw in Part One, it was very nearly stolen from the church in 1945. But in October 1963 it disappeared for real. Timms told how, not long after its disappearance, he called at an antique shop in England's Lane and casually mentioned it to the proprietor, who sheepishly admitted he had the very object but insisted it had passed through other hands in south London before coming to him. Timms was able to produce a photograph showing the icon in position on the wall of the Chapel of the Holy Spirit, which clinched the matter, and it was restored to the church.

The eagle spared

Timms himself proposed to the PCC in February 1956 that the brass eagle lectern, which he had never liked, should be replaced by a wooden one, but the doughty old bird survived this attack. In 1957, however, the PCC did agree to give a number of unused brass candlesticks to a church in Hong Kong.

Legacies

The parish chronicle records a number of legacies to the church at this time, of which the most striking was that of Beryl Oswald who had been a member of the parish since Albert Spencer's time and for a time the PCC Secretary. She left her entire estate to the church, amounting to some £1700.

Further gifts and renovations (1960s-70s)

Among notable gifts in Hollis's time were an **oak chest** that had housed the altar vessels in the iron church (1967).[12] Francis Stephens, very soon after his arrival as a non-stipendiary minister, became the resident design guru and arbiter of taste. In 1972 he repainted the **figures on the Rood** and went on to design several noteworthy items for the church including the **statue of St Paul** which occupies the niche in the west wall *[Plate 5]*.[13] Carved by Siegfried Pietzsch, it marks the union of St Mary's with St Paul's Avenue Road. St Paul holds a representation of that church. The same duo were responsible for the **crucifix** (1973) that hangs in the chapel.[14] In 1975 a new festal **super-frontal**, which Stephens thought one of the most impressive pieces of modern embroidery he had ever seen, was completed by Dorothy Moore. Other significant gifts at this time are shown in a Table at the end of this chapter.

Embroidered kneelers (1960s-80s)
In January 1967, a team of skilled volunteers under Mary Whiteley embarked on what was to prove a long programme of embroidery to work new kneelers for the church. Elizabeth Elvin of the Royal School of Needlework, their consultant, produced four designs; Frank Ward and Stanley Taylor made the embroidery frames; and the canvas and wool were bought by the volunteers themselves. Sylvia Taylor and Dorothy Moore carried on the project after the Whiteleys left the parish in 1983.[15]

Thefts and damage (1960s-70s)

The sad price for keeping the building open for prayer and drop-in visits, with too much reliance on the goodwill of visitors and too little on security, was a particularly galling series of thefts and damage at the hands of criminals and the insane. Losses included a sanctuary lamp from the chapel (1967) and Frank Knight's high altar candlesticks, dedicated only as recently as 1960 as part of the Shaw-Arnold memorial set. In an unusual act of sacrilege, a silver ciborium – one of the items that had come from St John's Red Lion Square – was stolen from the aumbry, with the consecrated host still inside it. A brass lamp which had hung over the font was stolen in 1970, and the valuable 15th-century English alabaster plaque of Christ the King (given in 1936 by Mrs Trotter) disappeared from the north aisle in 1973. These incidents eventually led to the church's being temporarily closed except for services.

Stanley Taylor as church watcher

A solution of sorts involved Stanley Taylor, one of the former parishioners of St Paul's, who in his retirement was allowed to use a section of the choir vestry as his workshop for carpentry and cabinet-making. Under Hollis and later vicars he proudly made many fixtures and fittings for the church, including the doors of the internal south porch, a portable nave altar, a set of 14 candelabra for festivals, a plain cross for use at Passiontide, and the Dearmer screen. He also undertook paid work towards some of Francis Stephens's professional commissions, as well as private work for members of the congregation. As he was present most weekdays (drinking legendary quantities of tea and inviting favoured parishioners to join him in the vestry for a chat), he became the church's informal watchman in return for his use of this free work-space. If anyone entered the building he would down tools and emerge to establish their *bona fides*, looking as fierce as an elderly gent in a brown dust-coat could. In spite of this renewed vigilance, a deranged person still managed to set fire to the crib in the north transept at Christmas 1975 and in the process destroyed a cupboard containing a few vestments and the original framed portrait of Percy Dearmer. The blackened transept had to be redecorated, and the following year Messrs Rushworth and Dreaper had to give the organ a major clean to remove soot. An almost copycat incendiary outrage just a few years later is recorded below.[16]

In response to pleas from the choir, John Ovenden had Taylor's part of the vestry screened off to reduce its encroachment on the choir's vestry ('The Great Wall of Stan', as the screen was affectionately referred to in the sacristy).

Renovations and gifts, 1970s-80s

During Richard Buck's time as vicar, a number of practical and aesthetic improvements were made to existing fittings. The hinged panels of the reredos, which had become cracked and warped, were repaired in 1979 by Stanley Taylor and Elizabeth Webb under the direction of Francis Stephens,[17] and while the scaffolding was up to re-whiten the church in 1980-81 the Rood was cleaned for the first time in a decade, revealing more clearly its inscription in Greek: *A New Commandment give I unto you* (John 13, v.34).

Despite Stanley Taylor's continuing vigilance, the church was again vandalised more than once in Buck's time. In 1977, in an unpleasant echo of the earlier incident recorded above, a deranged visitor who claimed to have heard voices telling him to wreak havoc on Roman Catholic (*sic*) churches, again smashed the Christmas crib. Replacement (though much smaller) figures were found by Sally Webster at very short notice, from a redundant church.[18] Further damage occurred two years later, also at Christmastide, when among other things the holder for the church's Paschal Candle was destroyed.[19] The following spring, however, the vicar purchased an ornamental Victorian cast-iron drainpipe in a shop in Portobello Road. After a new wooden base and top had been made for it by Stanley Taylor it was commissioned as the Paschal Candlestick and is still in use today. Early in 1984 Francis Stephens designed a pair of silver candlesticks for the high altar, which were given in memory of Raymond Suffield (d.1981) by his widow Lesley.

In time for the centenary of the church's consecration in 1985, two new tunicles for the Clerk and Crucifer, in blue and gold, were made by Margaret Humphries and Tanya Okorji out of the old High Altar dossal curtain no longer in use. Shortly afterwards a new set of blue vestments for Advent was donated, and a new portable nave altar made by Stanley Taylor, was given in memory of Hubert de Jersey Hunt and dedicated by the bishop during the centenary festival.

Francis Stephens's taste (as well as a degree of mischievousness!) could at times provoke controversy. With a team of volunteers he cleaned and regilded the reredos in 1982. 'With the Archdeacon's permission,' (as he put it, but evidently without a faculty), he took the opportunity to change the reredos's background colour from its original pink to ivory. This caused offence to some prominent members of the congregation who cherished its high Victorian colouring. In 1991, in another improvised experiment, he 'refreshed' – or was it tweaked? – the Lenten Array, with the aid of nothing more than a red felt pen.[20] In 1992, in more sensitive vein, he again cleaned and restored the Rood figures.

A living tradition

Under both Robert Atwell and Marjorie Brown, with the help of successive sacristans, comprehensive efforts have been made to review and replenish the vestments. Whilst some entirely new items have been acquired, including a new set of green high mass vestments, the process has also involved retiring those that had become too damaged or fragile to use, and where possible incorporating material from them into new items. A similar approach was applied to the most impressive portion of the Lenten Array, the huge drape for the Rood, which, in a heroic piece of needlework, was comprehensively resewn by Miriam Rinsler in 2017. Other gifts have included a new blue sanctuary carpet for the High Altar (2019), given by Christopher and Ruth Kitching.

The church bell

St Mary's original bell, cast by Warner's of Cripplegate, had been in place since the church's opening, but was cracked and had stood idle for many years, so in 1983 a Faculty was procured for its removal. Almost a decade later, through the good offices of two members of the congregation who were keen bell-ringers (Philip Gray and John Hawes), a replacement was acquired through Whitechapel bell foundry. The sand-cast bell had originally been the tenor of a chime of three made for St Alphege, Southwark (once very high-church, now demolished), where, coincidentally, JH Arnold had held his first organist post. The foundry provided a new headstock and chiming lever, and the bell was re-dedicated on All Saints' Day 1992. Despite its great weight, it was then hauled up the spiral staircase and fitted into position by a team of three including the vicar and the head server.[21]

* * *

Appendix: Table of gifts 1965-76

	Artist	Notes
Textiles and linen:		
Festal gold cope	Winifred Bettridge	1967
Linen cloth for nave altar	Dorothy Moore	1968
Gold aumbry cover	Dorothy Moore	1968 gift of Miss Jermyn
Lenten chasuble	Irene Hales	1969
Green brocade frontal for chapel	Sister Geraldine	1969
Tapestry kneelers	[ladies of the parish]	1969
Fair linen cloth for nave altar	Sister Geraldine	1969
Humeral veil in needlework	Dorothy Moore	1972
Festal gold chasuble	Irene Hales	1972
Set of green vestments	[woven in France]	Gift of Miss Webber in memory of her husband
Sanctuary carpet		Gift of Marion West in memory of her mother
Reversible frontal for nave altar		Mary Dick in memory of her son Godfrey 1973
Turkey rug for chapel		Malleson family 1973
Lent cope (fire replacement)		1975

Furniture:		
Communion benches for nave altar	Stephen Dykes Bower	Lansdowne family in memory of Margaret Lansdowne 1968
14 candelabra	Stanley Taylor	1970
Glastonbury chair		Given by Miss Miller
Plate and metalwork:		
Silver ciborium	Montagu Malleson	1969
Hexagonal lantern for font		Brass repro of a Georgian original 1970

Endnotes

1. LMA: P81/MRV/145, PCC Minutes July 1952. It is now in the church of St Agatha, Portsmouth. (Information from John Hawes).
2. Not to be confused with Frank Knight FRIBA the architect.
3. Ibid.
4. LMA: P81/MRV/96, PCC Minutes Sept 1958,
5. PM, Nov 1956. For faculty see LMA: DL/A/C/MS18319. May Jeoffroy wrote to Judith Scott, 'Their ferial frontal is awful': CERC: CARE 23/329. So, according to John Hawes, was its replacement. produced towards the end of the Warham Guild's existence. It has since been replaced.
6. See Supplement to Parish Chronicle, March 1957.
7. Archives: Faculty correspondence and Order of Service for the dedication.
8. PM, Jan 1955.
9. Warham Guild, given in memory of Amy Lefroy by Miss Hull.
10. Given by Mr and Mrs MJ Moriarty.
11. The present one, known in the sacristy as the "coat of many colours", belonged to Dearmer but has long been unusable. Information from John Hawes.
12. Given by Miss McNally, to be kept in the vicarage, but no longer extant.
13. Replacing a statue of St George which had suffered 'accidental damage'.
14. Donation of Miss Weber and Miss West, in memory of Reginald and Gertrude Pullen-Baker.
15. PM, Mar 1987.
16. The parish had discussed with the Dearmer family in 1973 the idea of scaling down this large portrait, but that was apparently never done (LMA: P81/MRV/98, PCC Minutes 20 March 1973). After the fire Francis Stephens began work on a Dearmer memorial plaque, a scheme which also came to nothing (LMA: P81/MRV/98, PCC Minutes Feb 1976.
17. PM, Apr 1979.
18. PM, Feb 1978.
19. PM, May 1980.
20. As Dorothy Ralphs, another resident artist in the parish, would remark: 'Francis always has a pencil in his pocket, ready to alter something'.
21. John Hawes, 'The tower and bells of St Mary's', in PM, Oct-Nov 2007, pp.6-7, and additional information from John Hawes.

Chapter 13

Training for lifelong discipleship and mission

Prayer, preaching and instruction have always gone hand in hand as the means of building the faith for members of the congregation and equipping them to come of age in their Christian life and witness. Apart from sermons delivered during services, the pattern of instruction on offer has varied in accordance with the needs and imperatives of particular generations and the insights and initiatives of individual leaders, both clerical and lay.

In a church like St Mary's it is a given that not all spiritual needs can be met directly in the scripted services of official prayer books (the *Book of Common Prayer* and *Common Worship*). For those serious about deepening their faith – which is probably the majority – additional disciplines are available: Bible study; spiritual direction; the sacrament of Penance; discussion groups; instruction in (and practice of) different forms of prayer; personal or group retreats; pilgrimages to holy sites; and more. For some this deepening of their faith has led to a discernment of a call to the ministry, lay or ordained, and the consistently strong number of people from the congregation offering themselves for ordination or Reader training, from the time of Richard Buck right up to the present day, is testimony to the parish's thriving spiritual life.

There was always something of the monk about Richard Buck. For some he opened new windows on to spirituality and the devout inner life. People not just from the congregation but further afield, perhaps especially single people, found him a sympathetic counsellor and spiritual director. He was hospitable in the best Benedictine tradition, allowing his vicarage to be used on a Sunday once a month for a parish lunch (cooked by volunteers). A communal Christmas Dinner was similarly hosted, for those who would otherwise be alone, which of course included himself. 'I learned,' says Jeff Heskins, one of his curates, 'that hospitality was how you let people into the windows of your life.'

As Buck had himself experienced a late vocation, he was alert to the possibility that others who appeared to be settled in secular occupations might yet have a vocation to explore, and was quietly on the alert for the first signs, some of which flowered immediately, others only some years later.[1] That same openness and perseverance in discernment has been continued by all the subsequent vicars.

Preaching

Since at least the days of Percy Dearmer St Mary's has been a church where good preaching, often in a challenging and radical vein, could be heard. It must be admitted that today's sermons lack the fire and brimstone of a Conrad Noel (and are considerably shorter), but a number of contributors to this history have stressed how consistently engaging and thought-provoking the weekly sermons have been. Occasionally this has been put to the test, by holding discussions with the preacher after the service, or, as in Timothy Miller's innovation 'Preaching and Pints', by hearing an evening sermon and then adjourning to a nearby hostelry to discuss it.

In the past, individual sermons were often printed in the parish magazine, to be re-read at leisure, although none of the vicars of St Mary's – not even Dearmer – kept whole series of sermons with the intention of publishing them. Today, sermons (and variants such as dialogues with lay people) reach a wider audience, through the parish website and online streaming.[2]

Preaching: Revd George Timms (L). Revd John Ovenden (R)

George Timms's press profile suggested that 'the social significance of the Christian gospel, preached by his predecessors, is certainly preached by him.' His bold manner of tackling key moral issues, such as apartheid in South Africa or the death penalty in Britain, through both sermons and articles in the parish magazine, attracted a following well beyond the congregation and was reported and discussed in local papers such as the *Hampstead and Highgate Express*. Famous figures invited to preach at St Mary's in his time included Fr Trevor Huddleston, CR.[3]

A good example of the way in which the tradition of focussing on the most urgent priorities of the day has been continued would be the series of sermons and dialogues delivered in the autumn of 2020, attempting to see the world through the eyes of three sometimes marginalised, isolated or under-heard sections of the community: children, the elderly, and (in the wake of the Black Lives Matter campaign) people from a black or minority ethnic heritage.

Through preaching and action, John Ovenden strongly encouraged everyone to accept people of all sorts and conditions, no matter what point they had reached on their Christian journey, and to walk alongside them without judgement. 'Everyone was welcome,' he reflects, 'and everyone's contribution of value.'[4] This ethos came as no shock to an already liberal congregation, but it had never been so clearly articulated. And the welcoming of newcomers irrespective of age, race, gender or sexual orientation paid immediate dividends. Some, like the divorced and re-married, who had feared they might be ostracised by a church, found St Mary's to be a place of welcome.

Sermons, of course, can take many different forms. Richard Buck and Robert Atwell drew on their respective wells of monastic experience to bring fresh spiritual focus to the worship and witness of St Mary's and to their sermons, which were widely cherished. But introverted they certainly were not, and indeed the congregation's awareness of the imperatives for Christian action was continually honed.

Spiritual discipline

Whilst Bible-reading for individuals has always been strongly encouraged at St Mary's, and a structured approach to this has long been on offer through readily available published guides, the enthusiasm for Bible-reading as a group activity has waxed and waned. Highlights in this period included the Lectionary Group, convened by Oliver Smith under Robert Atwell, to study in advance the passages of Scripture set for upcoming services; the 'Bible in one year' project under Marjorie Brown, stimulated by Kimberly Gilmour; and the Bible Book of the Month discussion group that followed. A small group based on *lectio divina* principles – the meditative study of the Scriptures – has also met under Marjorie Brown.

Other typical discussion groups have included house groups meeting in the homes of members of the congregation. In their original manifestation these comprised small groups of friends and neighbours living in the parish who, particularly in the time of Timms and Hollis, agreed to get together occasionally for refreshments and an informal discussion on a serious theme. That kind of gathering began to wane in popularity as members aged, and in any case it did not serve the needs of the many members of the congregation who lived outside the parish (who throughout this period have always accounted for between two-thirds and three-quarters of the congregation).[5] Something of the same spirit, however, came to pervade the rather different discussion groups originating under Richard Buck and reaching the height of their popularity (to date) under Robert Atwell, and which continue down to the present. Meeting in Lent, and sometimes also in Advent, they normally discuss either a Scriptural or religious book or a seasonal theme. In 2021, in the midst of the coronavirus restrictions, a new approach was tried. The Lent discussion moved online and was a joint enterprise by St Mary's and the neighbouring parishes of St John's Wood, St Mark's, St Peter's and St Saviour's.

Parish retreats, to a number of Retreat Houses in this country, are recorded in the annals, and in the same vein should be mentioned organised foreign pilgrimages (to the Holy Land with David Jones as previously mentioned, and again in 2014 with St John's Wood parish; to Bec with Robert Atwell, to Taizé for young people with Marjorie Brown, and later to Assisi and Ravenna in partnership with St John's Wood church), all of which have challenged and deepened the faith of those who participated.

The sacrament of Penance (confession to a priest, followed by absolution), which since Charles Fuller's time had only been spoken of *sotto voce* at St Mary's, was perhaps more openly mentioned in Richard Buck's time – albeit always on the Anglican principle that 'some ought, all may, none must' – and a devout few availed themselves of it. A nice story is told of an elderly lady who usually came to church to make her confession but who on one occasion asked Richard Buck whether he would kindly visit her at home for this purpose. Inside the front door, silence reigned but he was met by a sea of hand-written notes: 'tea', 'coffee', 'milk', 'sugar', 'seat' … It emerged that she was by no means sure of the etiquette of speaking (or not) to a priest before he heard one's confession![6]

Ever-changing dynamic

It is inevitable that over a period of seventy years some activities for the building up of the worshipping congregation have come and gone, particularly those that relied on the support, enthusiasm or organising skill of one or two individuals. In some cases increased pressure on the time of would-be organisers, participants and their families have meant that some groups have found it hard to continue; in others the call for a particular activity has evaporated. A few examples will illustrate. Drama, which was so important in the social life of St Mary's until the 1960s, no longer holds such a central place today, but it has nevertheless been enthusiastically picked up from time to time.[7] House groups, which continue to meet, especially in Lent, are much less popular than they once were. Scout, Guide and Cub troops have disappeared, as have the St Mary's branches of national organisations such as The Mother's Union and the Church of England Men's Society. Even within this period, the Friends of St Mary's have come and gone, as have the Taizé Prayers that ran for two decades.

The same pressures have affected some aspects of public worship. The ability, or willingness, of people to turn out for services on weekdays has dwindled. As a result the eucharist is no longer celebrated every day of the week, nor is there a sung eucharist on most red letter saints' days that fall on a weekday.

In a rapidly changing world, frequent adaptation of the church's activities has become the norm, whether to address new needs or as an emergency response at short notice. The constituency and focus of discussion groups has been fluid, to allow for new initiatives on, for example, the environment, debt management or death, or new ways of exploring the Bible; or to provide a forum for people from a particular group (men, women, young workers). At the time of writing there are continuing programmes of bible study, book groups, and thriving activities such as a weekly tea-room for the elderly and isolated, the Designer Fair, the Primrose Hill Lectures and the St Mary's Brewery, but the next generation will almost certainly address its needs in different ways.

Mission

Parish 'missions', in the strict sense of the word, have fallen out of favour today, but were still *de rigueur* up to at least the 1970s.[8] They had several aims: to rally the faithful, to stir up interest in the church within the general population, and to map out a future path of commitment. Under Hollis St Mary's reached its centenary in 1972, and a fresh attempt was made to take the Gospel message out beyond the church doors. Preparations included a week of 'Mission and Music'. The mission, a Christian wake-up call to the parish (churchgoers or not), was conducted by a six-strong team drawn entirely from outside the parish: a mixture of men and women, ordained and lay, with a notable monastic input. Headed by Fr FWB Perkins of the Order of the Good Shepherd (Senior Lecturer in Divinity at the Institute of Education), the team also included a deaconess from the Community of St Andrew (Sr Denzil), two nuns from the Society of St Margaret, East Grinstead (Srs May Cecilia and Rachel Margaret), a deacon (William Beer from Torquay) and a layman (Peter Tabernacle, an insurance broker).

The week culminated in not one but two triumphal processions around the parish, with a float bearing children from the school, in fancy dress as animals, accompanied by adult members of the congregation, and the mission team. This was certainly designed to be attention-grabbing! Unfortunately it rained heavily as the processions followed two different routes, morning and afternoon, in order to cover the whole parish, but the intrepid (and wet) team still sallied forth, equipped with wellies and umbrellas, led by a policeman and escorted by a police car. Religious songs (such as *Kum Ba Yah* and *Shout for Joy*) were sung lustily, and bystanders were encouraged to join in. As Sister May Cecilia described it in the parish magazine:

> The more it rained the more lustily everyone sang. The spirit was tremendous!
>
> As we went slowly along the streets, some broke away from the procession to give out leaflets. The children were especially good at this: if the leaflets were refused they were popped into shopping bags or put through car windows.

For the Dedication Festival in July there were special services and events, parties, a renewal campaign (Renew '72)[9] and the publication of *St*

Mary's Primrose Hill: A Guide and History. Edited by Francis Stephens but drawing on the earlier labours in the parish archives by Bernard Stutfield and Kathleen Beck, this would remain the definitive account of the church's history for three decades.[10]

The sheer scale and exuberance of these festivities has to be admired. On the eve of the festival the Hollises entertained 200 guests to a party in the vicarage garden. The Festival Eucharist was concelebrated by nine priests, with Dr Alec Vidler as distinguished preacher. It was followed by a lunch for 300 people in the new school hall – a special dispensation, as it had not yet been officially declared open. Later in the week, Tony Greening gave an organ recital of music written over the centuries in honour of the Blessed Virgin Mary, taking his inspiration from the ancient Marian plainsong antiphons. Over the course of the next two weeks there were friendly pastoral visits by both the Bishop of Edmonton and the Bishop of London.

Processions

In the earlier part of this history, one of the ways in which the church had tried to advertise its message beyond its walls was through outdoor processions. Some were little more than a walk round the outside of the church, as part of the festivities associated with a festival or an episcopal visit. Others were altogether more ambitious. They included the Rogationtide processions already mentioned which, as they climbed on to Primrose Hill, became a joint venture with St Mark's parish. Their aim was to 'beat the bounds'[11] and pray for God's blessing on the parish and its people. In a similar vein, to mark significant jubilees more spectacular processions were held, complete with fully vested clergy, choir and servers, churchwardens with their staves, banners and (when practical) candles. From the 1950s, and more particularly after the loss of the Church Room in the 1960s (which removed one of the obvious termini, or 'stations', of an outdoor procession), these manifestations slowly fell out of vogue. The one remaining vestige of this form of outdoor witness is the Palm Sunday procession in which, weather and plague permitting, the service begins with prayers and readings at the top of Primrose Hill, then the fully vested clergy, choir and servers, and the congregation, process slowly down to the church to continue the solemn liturgy of the day. On one famous occasion – perhaps the only one in which it has been possible for everyone in such a long, straggling crowd to sing in synch – the Salvation Army band from the Chalk Farm Citadel was recruited in 1989 by John Ovenden to lead the descent. In recent years it has become the tradition to join with the clergy and congregation of St Mark's for the preliminaries at the top of the Hill, and then, in alternate years to march to St Mark's or St Mary's, to the general amazement of Sunday morning by-standers who – this being Primrose Hill – probably think that it is some form of Druidic event, at least until they hear the hymns!

Ecumenism

The parish chronicle records that in the autumn of 1955 George Timms invited first a priest of the Orthodox Church of India and then a Russian Orthodox priest to preach at St Mary's, and that a Russian orthodox choir came to sing in St Mary's (an echo of the similar events in Hardcastle's time two decades earlier).

St Mary's is in the relatively unusual position of having no building of another Christian denomination, or indeed of another religion, within its parish boundaries. This, however, did not deter Howard Hollis (whom Andrew St John describes as 'a natural ecumenist at heart') from encouraging friendly relations with other religious traditions locally. As the respective Church hierarchies tied themselves in knots over practical and theological details of ecumenism, much of the day to day initiative was left to parishes or even individuals. In the wake of Vatican II[12] it seemed most appropriate to seek closer relations with the nearby Roman Catholics of St Dominic's Priory in Kentish Town, with whom joint Lent Groups were held, as well as annual pilgrimages, for example to Canterbury Cathedral and to an Orthodox Monastery in Essex. Hollis took seriously the Week of Prayer for Christian Unity each January, and in 1968 for example, invited one of the (RC) Marist fathers as preacher. He also began to interest the parish in the work of the Council for Christians and Jews, and on one occasion a group from the Hampstead Synagogue came to the Candlemas Eucharist at St Mary's. The discussions at this time on the possible union of the Anglican and Methodist churches (into which George Timms had personally put much effort) foundered, to the great sadness of Hollis and many in the congregation.[13] Nevertheless, as he looked back at the time of his retirement, Hollis could reflect with some satisfaction that, on the ecumenical front, this had been a time of 'quiet cooperation' and mutual acceptance.

The main ecumenical event under Richard Buck was the hosting of the Taizé youth meeting of 1981, but in general neither ecumenism nor inter-faith dialogue was high on the agenda at that time. John Ovenden strongly revived the momentum. Joint discussion groups and exchange visits to one another's liturgies were arranged with the Liberal Jewish Synagogue in St John's Wood. Friendly relations were also re-established with the Roman Catholics of St Dominic's Priory; and the launch at St Mary's of a monthly Taizé-style service of chants and prayers, which would continue for two decades, provided a context in which Anglicans and Roman Catholics in particular, but also at various times Baptist, United Reformed Church, Methodist and Quakers could worship together.

Cordial relations have been maintained with other denominations and faiths down to the present, and the local Jewish community has been very supportive of the Cold Weather Shelter. A particular highlight was the visit of Rabbi Mark Solomon in 2019 to give a Jewish insight into St John's Gospel.

Children in the congregation

When George Timms arrived as vicar, some 30 children were attending the church. There was no Sunday School, though the Sunday afternoon

Catechism continued. Only slowly was the point was reached (1954-56) when it was worth re-establishing troops of cubs, scouts and guides.

Hardly any trace of these activities has been left in the church's annals, but they should not be overlooked on that account, as years of hard work were expended on them, among others by Jim Holden, Scout Master from the inception of the troop until 1960 when he was succeeded by Mr A McIntosh.[14] The mention in the parish chronicle for 1964 of a 'new' scout troop being formed under Mr P Thorne might suggest that it was difficult to maintain momentum.

After curates were added to the ministry team, activities for the church's youth and young adults began to gain some credibility – perhaps especially so after one of the curates dared to dress down in jeans ready for action.[15] Badminton was organised in the Church Room and, in the run-up to the merger with St Paul's, St Mary's youth participated in a youth group there, in Winchester Road, where Stanley Taylor proved a dab hand at table tennis! It is pleasing to learn from Jim Jelley that, in those days long before *Strictly*, a lady came along to teach the boys the rudiments of the Waltz and the Cha-cha-cha: skills which one imagines must soon have become redundant, with the advance of Rock! The boys of the choir came to account for a large proportion of all children in church, but they mainly formed a separate cadre, with their own organised outings as a reward for the hard grind of choir practices. When the Church Room was closed, the youth activities that had been hosted there were split between the St Paul's site (for 8 to11-year olds) and the curate's flat in 8 Adamson Road (for 11 to 18-year olds).[16]

Partly on account of the population movement resulting from all the demolition and re-building in the parish, the number of children attending church again declined under Howard Hollis, and organised group activities once more died out, to the extent that youth and children's work are scarcely mentioned in the records. An informal Sunday School was run by a member of the congregation, but had very few takers. No account of youth work, however, would be complete without a mention of the important contribution of Ron Holding, the St Paul's school caretaker, who organised an out-of-school club – the

Horseshoe Club – on school premises one evening a week for older children, mostly from the school. Under Richard Buck the church lent its strong support to that Club, which came to include over 60 children (who were generally not from the congregation). A number of senior laity led by Sally Webster, as well as successive members of the ministry team, helped in the organisation of activities and outings. It was not a proselytising activity and did not result in additional children attending the church services. Later, Michael Johnson (curate) and Jeff Heskins (as pastoral assistant) hoped to organise a youth group for older children; but without professional input they soon had to admit defeat. Some support was instead offered to the Winchester youth project at Swiss Cottage.

Slowly, from the early 1980s (driven in part by the growing attendance in church of would-be entrants to St Paul's school), new initiatives were taken, with a small Sunday school initially run by Christine Macsween which grew into a youth group run by her and Pippa Gaines with the help of the curate, Jeff Heskins. One of its more memorable activities was a 'sleep-over' in the church, a first in its day though not at all unusual now in the wake of the Cold Weather Shelter. Sally Webster and successive lay helpers then took on the Sunday School, which met in St Paul's school, with opening prayers led by a member of the clergy, and piano accompaniment by one of the music team (often Dorothy Southern). As the original cohort of children grew older, and as more joined, they in turn metamorphosed into a new youth group, for which additional activities and outings were laid on by Sally Webster and assistant clergy, including notably David Jones.

Under John Ovenden and Robert Atwell, with a growing Sunday School roll – which peaked at an impressive 140 under Robert Atwell (though fewer than half appeared on any given Sunday) – a structured programme of learning and activity was developed by teachers drawn from the congregation, and this tradition continues today. One constraint was (and is) that the fluctuating levels of attendance week by week made it difficult to provide an equal level of instruction for every attendee.

For older children (in general those who had been confirmed), there has been a shifting pattern of activities, depending on the number in the group, and the availability and enterprise of the leaders. A succession of curates, youth leaders, pastoral assistants and Time for God volunteers has helped develop and run both the Sunday School and church youth activities, and the group for older children has changed its name and scope several times. Under Paul Perkins, for example, when the group met at the old vicarage of St Peter's Belsize Park (then being used to house the youth team and pastoral assistants), a more informal act of Sunday worship, 'Blue Sky Think', was staged, its content being shaped largely by the young people themselves. From it emerged Skeptikos, a discussion group for young people. Marjorie Brown later introduced a teenagers' Film Club, meeting monthly at the vicarage to watch and discuss classic films.

She also introduced the practice of admitting children, after a course of instruction, to receive Holy Communion before Confirmation and thus to share more fully in eucharistic worship with their families. The structured course, with themes such as prayer, sharing, callings, belonging and the church family, as well as Communion itself,[17] was developed by a lay member, Kimberly Gilmour. Children have been further integrated into the main congregation by being enlisted in larger numbers as servers at the Sung Eucharist; but in addition a less formal, and definitely more family-friendly service (compared with the 9.45 service under Timms and Hollis) has been introduced on two Sundays a month. As with the 1030 service, this was further revised by Emily Kolltveit during the pandemic of 2020-21 as a streamed, on-line resource for those necessarily having to join in the worship at home. In 2021, for the first time, a group of children were commissioned by the bishop as Young Worship Leaders.

Endnotes

1   The numbers might have been still higher had not the wider Church's discernment processes denied several others the green light to proceed with training.
2   Or, during the coronavirus epidemic, its You Tube channel.
3   21 Oct 1956. See Supplement to Parish Chronicle.
4   See also his final sermon, in which he said that St Mary's 'is a non- judgmental place, open to all who feel inclined to come in… It takes people gently by the hand to seek the God within.'

5   Based on annual electoral roll figures.
6   Information from Martin Draper.
7   See Chapter 17.
8   The element of mission associated with the Stewardship campaigns under George Timms is described separately in ch 16.
9   This was the model for similar Renewal campaigns in 1984 and 1988.
10 It was then superseded by *The Parish Church of St Mary the Virgin Primrose Hill: History and Guide* by John Hawes, Christopher Kitching, and Bryan Almond (2002, 2009).
11 Follow the parish boundaries.
12 The second Ecumenical Council of the Vatican, held between 1962 and 1965 on the initiative of Pope John XXIII.
13 PM, Jan 1969.
14 Archives: Supplement to VH King's Parish Chronicle.
15 Jim Jelley recalls David Gerrard being the first priest at St Mary's to do so.
16 PM, Jun 1970.
17 Based on Diane Murrie and Steve Pearce, *Children and Holy Communion*. Information from Kimberly Gilmour.

Chapter 14

Maintaining and developing the St Mary's tradition

1. Liturgy[1]

Chronological overview

In 1951 Frank Marriott concluded that up to that point there had been a 'strikingly complete continuity of liturgical and ceremonial behaviour', and that despite 'ebbs and flows' of liturgical preference, 'never has the fundamental principle of complete loyalty to the rite and ceremony of the English church been in question. In brief,' he said, 'the outward forms of worship conform to the English Use'.[2]

George Timms, already a published liturgist when he arrived as vicar, remained essentially true to that St Mary's liturgical tradition. A faded cutting in the parish archives of a press profile of Timms from near the end of his days as vicar,[3] insisted that:

> He is not fanatical about 'the Sarum use'. He does not even like the term, which he regards as something of a misnomer. What Percy Dearmer did, he explains, was simply to clothe the Anglican rite in an aesthetically fitting Catholic ceremonial that would satisfy the ornaments rubric …[4] The 9.45 Sung Mass, which has a strong family flavour, now sometimes exceeds in numbers the more magnifical High Mass at eleven.

Overall, Timms was content to strip away Hardcastle's antiquarianism, and most of the changes he introduced were probably noticed only by a few *cognoscenti*, given that there were no more liturgiologists of the stamp of Eeles, King and Arnold in the congregation. He discontinued singing the Litany on Sunday, except for Lent, Rogationtide and Advent, on the grounds that the Intercessions at the Sung Eucharist made it redundant. Ceremonial changes tended to reflect his training at Mirfield: for example, the thurifer immediately followed the taperers in the procession; the celebrant genuflected at the consecration of the elements (– one witness remembers there being *rather a lot of genuflections!*); and ablutions were held after the communion rather than after the blessing.[5] One significant set of liturgical innovations (1955), perhaps inspired by similar changes taking place at the time in the Roman Catholic church, concerned the Holy Week services, which were expanded, with Compline sung on the Monday, Tuesday and Wednesday evenings; whilst on Maundy Thursday an evening Eucharist was celebrated, followed by a Watch before the Blessed Sacrament,[6] although there was no administration of Holy Communion on Good Friday.

As explained elsewhere, the 9.45 eucharist on Sundays became more like a 'parish communion', intended to include children, although in practice those who attended were mostly adults who preferred it to the more 'magnifical' Sung Eucharist. At that 9.45 service, which was now held in the body of the church rather than in the chapel, the celebrant (for the first time at St Mary's) faced the people from behind a portable altar. For celebrations at the High Altar, however, an eastward-facing position was retained.

Major festivals in Timms's time included the 70th anniversary of the church's consecration in 1955, attended by the Bishop of London, and a memorable Confirmation service with 36 candidates, taken in July 1958 by Bishop Colin Dunlop, who was staying at the vicarage while attending the Lambeth Conference.[7] Writing some years later to Mary Dunlop after Colin's death, Timms recalled this as 'everything that a Confirmation should be – and Colin was so evidently an apostolic minister of our Lord in all that he said and did.' Among other appointments while in residence, Dunlop met Vaughan Williams to discuss a shortened version of the *English Hymnal* with 300 hymns and psalms for use at Parish Communion services.

Also in Timms's time, St Mary's made its mark on television. The Sung Eucharist was broadcast for the first time, by the BBC on 16 August 1959; the Solemn Eucharist with Confirmation by the Bishop of London by ATV on 4 December 1960; and the Good Friday 10 a.m. service in 1963 by ITV.[8]

* * *

Howard Hollis's time as vicar coincided with the development of provisional new liturgies for the Church of England. The rejection of the revised Prayer Book in 1928 had set back liturgical reform and renewal at national level, and it was not until 1955 that a Liturgical Commission had been established to work up new forms of liturgy to be debated and approved in the General Assembly, and then tried and tested at parish level. Its first chairman was none other than Colin Dunlop. The authorising legislation, the Prayer Book (Alternative Services) Measure, was laid before Parliament only in 1965, and this time approved. Over the next two years the first services were published, for experimental use alongside the Book of Common Prayer. Entitled Series 1 and Series 2 – with Series 3 in more modern English appearing in 1973 – they were all put through their paces at St Mary's, with consequential (but mostly minor) changes in the liturgical choreography. Under the Worship and Doctrine Measure of 1974 work would then begin on what became the *Alternative Services Book* of 1980.

Hollis, although steeped in the Anglican liturgical tradition, was not a specialist like Timms, and allowed himself to be guided by others. Francis Stephens later remarked that Timms still occasionally returned to haunt him! But the mainly modest changes he did introduce were occasionally subjected to surprisingly informed critique from within the congregation.[9] Among the more significant innovations was the giving of communion (in both kinds) during the Three Hours service on Good

Friday from 1970.[10] At the Centenary eucharist, for the first time at St Mary's, there was concelebration by several priests (a practice which, for a time under Richard Buck, was extended to Maundy Thursday).[11] The Book of Common Prayer was still used for the 8 a.m. Holy Communion service. Series 3 was introduced at the 9.45 service, but the Series 2 texts of the Gloria and Creed were retained in order that the settings by Merbecke and Martin Shaw which were familiar to the congregation could still be sung.[12] Series 1 was used at the Sung Eucharist, although the sermon continued to be preached after the creed. A small choir of ladies sometimes led the singing at Choral Evensong.

In the course of his farewells to the parish, Hollis would remark that the eucharist had lain at the centre of St Mary's work and worship 'with a diversity which has made no one feel alienated from the Lord's table or from our welcoming and accepting community. Side by side we have been able to use modern and traditional liturgies, whether simple and unadorned or with the enrichment of music, colour and ceremonial to provide a worship real and acceptable to all.'[13]

* * *

Under Richard Buck the heralded *Alternative Services Book* (*ASB*) appeared. He established a Liturgy Committee, with the head server Robert Wills and other lay members of the congregation, initially to determine how the new book might best be put into use at St Mary's. It included revised rites for the eucharist, adapted from the earlier Series, and like them was intended for use alongside the *Book of Common Prayer*. The *ASB*'s emphasis on distinguishing the Ministry of the Word (readings and sermon) from the Sacramental part of the eucharist that followed required further choreographic changes. For example, since the ministers sat for the first part of the service in stalls on either side of the crossing, in order to be close to the proclamation of the Word, the censing of the high altar was postponed until they moved there at the Offertory. As for the music, Richard Buck would comment in 1984 that it had 'undergone many changes as our liturgy has reflected the trend towards greater congregational participation'.

The exile in the school during the re-whitening of the church in 1980 led to the merger of the 9.45 and 11.15 services in a way that had only previously been tried on certain high Feast Days, but the clergy in particular had long been hoping to bring this about in order to unify the hitherto separate congregations. In the artificial context of the school hall, the liturgy necessarily had to be simplified. A piano replaced the organ, and the celebrant had no choice but to face the people, who were seated very close to the makeshift 'altar'. Apart from one unfortunate incident in which one of the clergy set fire to his alb while standing with his back to a lighted candle, all passed off smoothly and everyone took it in good part. Preaching just a few feet away from the audience required a rather different technique than preaching from a pulpit, and a more *ex tempore* approach was called for. On one occasion, Sister Judith indeed had no option: her sermon notes inexplicably (?) disappeared from the lectern before she rose to speak. She responded with an impromptu, heartfelt account of her work with the poor and underprivileged in the parish – surely one of the most rousing addresses anyone could have hoped for.

Services moved back into the re-whitened church on 2 November 1980, and on 18 January 1981 a Sung Eucharist of thanksgiving and re-dedication was celebrated by the Bishop of London (Rt Revd Gerald Ellison), at which the 'Dearmer screen' was also dedicated. There was no appetite for a return to the previous two-service regime, so a compromise time of 10.30 was agreed for a single Sung Eucharist. Much of the ceremonial and music familiar to the former 11.15 congregation was retained but, for the first time at St Mary's, the high altar was moved forward from the reredos so that the celebrant could face the people, as had been done in the school (and at the old 9.45 service). Genuflections were impractical, and would have looked clumsy, in the small space behind the altar.[14] Jeff Heskins recalls that some of the congregation who did not welcome the changes left, but the great majority squared up to the 'discomfort of change' and stayed on.

Much discussion then ensued over how the church and its liturgy could be made even more accessible. A prototype sound system was introduced to support the voices of ministers, readers and intercessors without falling foul of the building's natural resonance,[15] but this proved more intractable than expected and the system has since had to be upgraded several times. Challenges of a wholly different order were experienced (and surmounted) in the course of live-streaming services on the internet during the pandemic of 2020-21.

By the late 1970s few among the congregation knew the name or fame of Percy Dearmer, and most of those present on a Sunday either did not notice, or were no longer troubled by, changes in ritual and ceremonial. There was no longer any great loss of sleep over liturgical minutiae such as whether the thurifer preceded or followed the crucifer; or whether and when the celebrant genuflected or made a reverent, Dearmer-style low bow; or, for that matter, whether he called the communion service the 'Sung Eucharist' or the 'High Mass'. Moreover, everyone involved had learnt to take liturgical mishaps in their stride, with much less sense of guilt or fear of recrimination than might have been the case in a previous generation. A server at that time, whose anonymity should perhaps be preserved, recalls that:

> People tend to think of church as being a bit stuffy, but what I remember is that it was fun! We laughed over my walking in in procession with the white girdle thrown over my shoulder (where I had temporarily put it while getting the thurible ready) and another server walking in procession with a pencil tucked behind her ear (she had been making notes!)

The parish was treated to an entirely different style of worship at New Year 1981 when the Taizé community held its annual youth meeting in London and chose St Mary's as one of the base parishes for scores of its participants, mostly young Germans, Spaniards and Italians. The church, together with the London cathedrals and larger churches which hosted many of their services, resounded to Taizé chants. By way of thanks the young pilgrims gave the church a copy of Rublev's icon of the three angels visiting Abraham.

* * *

By the time John Ovenden became vicar the form of the liturgy had become more settled. Special celebrations in his time included the centenary of the building's consecration (1985) and a eucharist televised by ITV (19 June, 1988). For Ascension Day 1985, an ordinand from the parish, David Michaels, with support from the clergy and serving teams, coached the Youth Group in mounting a eucharist in a style as close as possible to that of Percy Dearmer's day. An advertisement in the *Church Times* ensured that there were many visitors, but Joanna Yates remembers that one man, 'seeing me vested in a tunicle, ready for my role as clerk, turned on his heel and walked straight out again, saying: "I don't like to see a woman in vestments". By contrast, when Percy Dearmer's granddaughter Juliet came in, her reaction was: "This church is fizzing".' Further Dearmer-style sung eucharists according to the Book of Common Prayer were celebrated yearly during John Hawes's time as head server, a post he held for some twenty years and to which he brought wide-ranging knowledge of the liturgy and its history, and a determination to protect and promote the Dearmer tradition.

Liturgically speaking, perhaps the most striking innovation under John Ovenden was the introduction of a Christingle service on Christmas Eve. From the start this proved so popular that it was common (right up to the time of the pandemic of 2020 when it had to be cancelled) for every seat in the church, as well as many imported extra ones, to be occupied.

Since the 1980s there has been a marked shift in patterns of attendance at services other than the Sunday eucharists. Regular attendance at Sunday evensong had even by that date become sparse, and a review concluded that this might be the time to diversify the kinds of evening worship on offer. Choral Evensong was retained once a month, whilst on other Sundays there were, for example, Contemplative Prayer, ecumenical Taizé-style prayers,[16] or themed discussions. A similar diversity of provision, though with different options, is evident today.

As for weekday observances, an older generation that was used to turning out for daily celebrations and evening sung eucharists on major feasts had slowly died out, whilst the much-changed work and family commitments of a younger generation had made their attendance on weekdays well-nigh impossible. Robert Atwell addressed this by reducing the overall number of week-day eucharists (while retaining a daily celebration), and that process has gone further under Marjorie Brown, where full advantage has also been taken of revisions in the lectionary permitting the celebration of certain major feasts such as Epiphany, Candlemas and All Saints on the nearest Sunday.

* * *

Drawing deep on the wells of spirituality from his time as a Benedictine monk, and at the same time conscious of the Dearmer tradition, Robert Atwell paid close personal attention to detail in liturgy and ceremonial to ensure that the worship at St Mary's continued to reflect the 'beauty of holiness'. Perhaps nowhere was this better demonstrated than in the liturgy for Maundy Thursday, ending with the procession to the 'altar of repose' and the watch before the Blessed Sacrament.

The Church of England had travelled beyond thinking (if it ever did) that its needs could mainly be served by a single *Alternative Services Book*, and in Atwell's time the Liturgical Commission was working its way through new and revised rites for every occasion, in a gradually-accumulating, encyclopaedic publication, *Common Worship*.[17] Introducing these at St Mary's as they came off the press involved determining which of many permitted options were actually going to be deployed. To make things easier for the congregation once the choice had been made, new service booklets were printed, one for each liturgical season. These served until under Marjorie Brown the order of service, readings and notices were all merged into a single weekly handout.

Marjorie Brown has been equally devoted to maintaining the liturgical traditions of St Mary's and developing them for a new generation, with a deliberate emphasis on inclusiveness (lay and clerical; black and white; male and female; children and adults). A few highlights will give the flavour. A limited number of lay members of the serving team have been licensed by the bishop to administer Holy Communion to the sick and housebound on an occasional basis. Together with the parish's Licensed Lay Ministers (Readers) they also assist in the liturgical role of 'deacon' at the Sung Eucharist. A lunchtime celebration of the eucharist once a week, aimed particularly at the elderly, includes the laying on of hands and prayers for healing: a ministry which at St Luke's-tide is extended to all the congregation. Foot-washing at the Maundy Thursday eucharist, long a St Mary's tradition, is now offered to anyone who wishes to participate. And after the Christingle service on Christmas Eve carols are sung on Primrose Hill.

The Hill itself, which of course is an unmistakable feature of the geographical parish, still provides inspiration. The old Rogationtide processions may have fallen into disuse, but there is a close relationship with St Mark's Regents Park and St John's Wood parishes which share the Hill. Sarah Mullally, the first woman to hold the office of Bishop of London, on the first day of her new ministry (Ascension Day 2018) invited the local parishes to join her early in the morning at the top of Primrose Hill to pray over the city and diocese. She then joined parishioners in St Mary's for breakfast.

In order to make good a shortfall in the number of adults volunteering to act as servers, both Robert Wills and John Hawes (successive head servers) recruited younger members of the congregation in this role. That policy has been taken further under Kimberly Gilmour, with a renewed emphasis on integrating children into every aspect of worship.

In 2010 St Mary's held it first Jazz Eucharist.

The Dearmer continuum

St Mary's Primrose Hill is still often associated with the name of Percy Dearmer, and in spite of many differences of style and detail in its liturgy compared with his original precepts, the parish still honours his name, still uses his *Parson's Handbook* as a point of liturgical reference, and still offers worship with un-fussy ceremonial in the English-Use tradition, and in close accord with the rites and ceremonies formally approved by the Church of England, which now include the vast edifice that is *Common Worship*.

Some of Dearmer's innovations specific to St Mary's are still in evidence to this day. The walls are still whitened, incense is still used (more amply now than was permitted in Dearmer's day), his scheme of liturgical colours for vestments and altar hangings is still followed, give or take a few changes in line with the lectionary,[18] and the Lenten array, although much altered since his time, is still in use from Ash Wednesday until Good Friday each year.

Whether for practical reasons or following changes in liturgical fashion, or simply because things wear out with time, many of Dearmer's original fixtures and fittings, such as the elaborate Kruger hymn board designed for masses with Plainsong propers, the sanctuary lamps and the great trendle that used to be suspended in the chancel behind the Rood, have been removed by later generations. One of the last major physical changes to his scheme of things was the removal by George Timms in 1952 of the 'English altar' with riddel posts and curtains, in favour of a simple altar.[19]

Probably in the wake of discussions held with Colin Dunlop when he came to take the Confirmation service in 1958, Timms and the PCC started thinking about creating some memorial to Percy Dearmer that would be more demonstrative than the great lectern Bible purchased at the time of his death. On being asked to suggest the wording for a memorial (whose exact form was yet to be determined), Dunlop tentatively proposed the following:

Remember with thanksgiving Percy Dearmer, Master of Arts, Doctor of Divinity, Vicar of this church from 1901 to 1915: who made St Mary's Primrose Hill a centre of Church life which has influenced the worship of the whole Anglican Communion. + "The hill of Sion is a fair place, and the joy of the whole earth": Ps: XLVIII.2.

Perhaps because no-one could think how and where such a memorial could be displayed without offending Dearmer's own loathing of monuments on white walls, no further action was taken. The idea resurfaced from time to time, in various forms, right up to 1980 when the screen already mentioned, designed by Francis Stephens and built by Stanley Taylor was erected and named in his memory. The celebration at St Mary's of Dearmer's centenary in 1967 was spread throughout the year. An appreciation of his life by George Timms appeared in the parish magazine,[20] and Howard Hollis preached a series of sermons on Dearmer's books. A commemorative service was organised by the Hymn Society of Great Britain and Ireland at which Christopher Herrick directed a choir of a hundred singers from St Mary's and other neighbouring churches in a selection of Dearmer's hymns. Other festivities included a vicarage garden party, a parish outing to Westminster Abbey, and Martin Browne's staging of three medieval plays. On 12 February the BBC broadcast a celebratory radio programme, 'Beauty for all', with contributions from many who had known Dearmer, including his son Geoffrey, Joan (Mrs Martin) Shaw who was another long-standing parishioner, and Colin Dunlop.

Such celebrations became all the more needful when, with the passing of the years, fewer and fewer, especially of the younger members of the congregation, knew of Dearmer at all, except as a name on the lips of others. Yet, in one form or another, the parish has faithfully kept his memory alive. In May 1986 a festival eucharist was held to mark the golden jubilee of his death, and sermons about him were preached by Francis Stephens and Howard Hollis and printed in the magazine.

Percy and Mabel Dearmer's son Geoffrey continued to worship at St Mary's right up to his death in 1996, and in 1980 Geoffrey's daughter Juliet was married in the church to Rt Revd Kenneth Woollcombe. Geoffrey had been a much loved member of the congregation, always ready as his years advanced to contribute to the parish magazine either avuncular reviews of drama group productions or (in several instalments) his own reminiscences of Primrose Hill in earlier times. On reaching his 100th birthday in 1993 he was suddenly 'discovered' as an unjustly neglected poet of the First World War. He died in 1996 and a requiem mass was held at St Mary's on 21 November that year.[21] A plaque in his memory was later affixed to the external wall of the church above the parish garden.

The centenary in 1999 of the first edition of Percy Dearmer's *Parson's Handbook* occasioned several re-assessments of Dearmer and his *chef d'oeuvre*, and was commemorated at the parish's Patronal Festival. But the biggest recent Dearmer celebration at St Mary's occurred in 2011 to mark the 75th anniversary of his death. On 29 May that year there were addresses at the Sung Eucharist about both Percy and Mabel Dearmer and a small commemorative exhibition was arranged in the church. The extended Dearmer family and close friends were well represented, and his biographer, Canon Donald Gray was among those present. In the afternoon a ceremony was held in the Great Cloister of Westminster Abbey to lay a wreath on his tomb. John Hawes, the former head server who was now working at the Abbey, made the arrangements and acted as verger.

Most recently, in Percy Deamer's honour, one of the beers produced by the St Mary's Brewery bears his name![22]

Endnotes

1   I am particularly grateful to John Hawes for sharing his expert knowledge in this field.
2   A detailed description may be found in *A Directory of Ceremonial, Parts I and II* issued by the Alcuin Club.
3   Undated and from an unidentified newspaper.
4   John Hawes adds that Dearmer never claimed to be reviving the Sarum Use. 'He understood, as so many Anglo Catholics never did, that reformed services needed simpler rather than elaborate ceremonial.'
5   Information from Martin Draper.
6   Information from John Hawes and John Rutter.
7   Dunlop, Francis, *From London to Lincoln via Baghdad. The life of Bishop Colin Dunlop 1897-1968* (2019), pp.348-9.
8   Archives: Supplement to VH King's Parish Chronicle.
9   eg PM, Feb 1970, where Grace E Pulling criticises Series II communion service for omitting the *epiclesis*.
10 Supplement to parish chronicle.
11 Information from John Hawes.

12 The 9.45am celebration was the one at which those who lived in the tower blocks worshipped. It was the only mass after which refreshments were served.
13 PM, Jan 1976.
14 John Hawes points out that the high altar was also shortened to its original length at about this time.
15 A faculty for this had been granted in 1978.
16 With friends from the congregations of St Dominic's Priory and a number of Anglican and other denominations. This became a tradition for almost twenty years.
17 Robert Atwell explained *Common Worship* in an article in PM, Oct 2000.
18 John Hawes in PM, Dec 1994, pp.6-8.
19 The framed portrait of Dearmer that had been so significant to Hardcastle was no longer kept on display, but was stored – it was thought safely – in a cupboard in the Transept. Together with other contents of the cupboard it was destroyed by fire in 1975.
20 PM, Apr-May 1967.
21 PM, Oct 96 memoir by Helen Stutfield.
22 Archives: correspondence on fixtures and fittings.

Chapter 15

Maintaining and developing the St Mary's tradition

2. Music

No estimate of the whole worship could be formed without an awareness of the remarkable quality of the liturgical music which has been built up during the successive masterships of Dr Martin Shaw and Dr Geoffrey Shaw. It might be briefly characterised by words such as 'catholic', 'national' and 'parish church'. The strains of war and the changed circumstances of the parish have reduced the music both in its capacity and in its personnel, despite the devoted labours of the last incumbent, but the substratum of Plainsong still clearly underlies the whole structure… A new young organist, who has been trained in the musical tradition of the church, is collecting and training choirboys.

Frank Marriott's memorandum for the new incumbent, 1951

* * *

Choir

George Timms's time as vicar saw the gradual build-up of a men's and boys' choir, although there was a rocky start because that 'new young organist', RW Ansell, resigned in October 1952 and his successor,

Graham Sudbury, who had been recommended by the RSCM, left after only two years (1952-54) to become organist at Wimborne Minster. Like many organists before and since, they both found it an uphill struggle to recruit enough volunteer singers.

But it could be done! Timms next persuaded EH Warrell who had been assistant organist at Southwark cathedral during his own time there, to come to St Mary's. Warrell (who would become Honorary Secretary of the Plainsong and Medieval Music Society) was an expert voice trainer and took the choir in hand, reviving the plainsong tradition though apparently not extending the repertoire very far into polyphonic music. He was so successful in recruiting boys that by the end of 1956, when there were as many as twenty of them in the choir, the supply of surplices ran out. However, when Warrell then had to resign on doctors' orders momentum was again lost.

Was it a definite new strategy at that point on Timms's part to seek as his organist an aspiring student from one of the London conservatoires? Whether it was a brainwave or a stroke of luck that paid off, the strategy was a success, even allowing for the fact that an appointee with that sort of background would surely move on to higher things after only a few years. The result was that for over a decade St Mary's became a training-ground for talented organists who went on to enjoy wider fame in cathedrals or large parish churches. One could turn that round and say that the fine organ at St Mary's helped them to advance both their technique and their career. By contrast, what they made of the choir was essentially a matter of personal commitment.

David Gedge (organist 1957-62),[1] a student at the Royal Academy of Music and just 17 when appointed, remembered being instantly impressed by the liturgy and general ambience of St Mary's: 'The services were stunning, so well-ordered, but unobtrusively so. The church itself was indeed colourful, but it was spotlessly clean and kept so by Bob Fake, the verger with a pronounced Yorkshire accent.'[2] Gedge literally walked the parish, knocking on doors in order to build the choir back up to a dozen boys and 'a few' men by his first Christmas. A demanding regime of regular choir practices was re-established and (no doubt

David Gedge at the organ.

because his recruits were raw and still had much to learn) there are tales of him losing his temper, sending hymn books flying and even tearing up the music. But they loved it, and he is remembered affectionately as not only a great choirmaster but someone deeply committed to bringing out the best in young people.

From May 1959 the Parish Chronicle records that the psalms and canticles at Sunday Evensong reverted to Anglican chant. Two of his choristers were Nicholas and Tony Taylor. After one Christmas Midnight Mass, Gedge was invited back to the Taylor household for a 'first breakfast'. At dead of night he then went back to the choir vestry to attempt some sleep (with the fire on) before the morning services.[3] It was reported in the magazine for August 1958 that he had introduced an anthem at Evensong for the first time in twenty years. It is difficult to believe that could be correct, but if so it shows how far the music had declined since the days of Shaw and Arnold. In October 1960 he took the choir to sing Evensong in St David's cathedral, Wales.[4] After completing his studies at the Academy, Gedge trained as a teacher at the Institute of Education then left St Mary's to become organist at Selby Abbey (and later Brecon cathedral).

St Mary's had only a single bell, and that was cracked! During the parish mission of 1959, a recording of bells from another church was evidently played from the tower to announce services and events, as happened in some other, generally more modern and suburban churches around the country. Perhaps surprisingly, the congregation rather liked this, and some would have had it continue: at any rate, research was undertaken to establish how much it would cost. News reached the Central Council for the Care of Churches in the form of a complaint from Eric Slater of 36 Oppidans Mews, a local resident and one of the choir. FC Eeles must surely have turned in his grave. But Judith Scott, who had been his secretary, flew the same colours, and wrote in response: 'I am indeed horrified to hear that this proposal for canned bells comes from St Mary's Primrose Hill, a church which I was always taught to regard as being the very model of all good things, ecclesiologically and liturgically as well as on the artistic side.'[5] The idea was quietly buried. Among other notable liturgical and musical events in Gedge's time was a visit by the Bishop of London in 1960 for a Confirmation service which was televised.

Anthony Greening (1962-64) was a student at the Royal College of Music, and would in due course become sub-organist at Ely cathedral. John Rutter, then a pupil at Highgate School and living near Finchley Road, tells how one day in about 1962 while walking past the church with his schoolmate John Tavener he heard the organ being played. They went in and found Greening practising. Rutter struck up a conversation with him, which resulted in Greening's allowing him to use the organ for his own practice. As a *quid pro quo* he was recruited to fill a vacancy in the bass line, and remained in the choir for three happy years until he went up to Cambridge. 'I became,' he writes, 'quite a faithful back-row member of what seemed to me at the time a rather fine boys-and-men choir of maybe 25 or 30 voices'.

Christopher Herrick (1964-67), formerly Organ Scholar at Exeter College, Oxford, was embarking on three years' postgraduate study, also at the Royal College, when he was appointed to succeed Greening. He inherited a good men's line but, like some of his predecessors, struggled to find and keep boys for the choir.[6] Although plainsong was new to him, in general he embraced it, but when one day he decided to introduce a bit of variety by using Vaughan Williams's setting of 'Hail Thee, Festival Day' rather than the plainsong version, he received 'a very firmly worded letter from a gentleman in the congregation' explaining that he was 'going against the St Mary's ethos and tradition.' He did not fall into the same trap again! He would return to St Mary's to give the opening recital on the restored organ in 2012, when he noted: 'It was very nice to be asked back to play the Hill organ which I had spent untold hours practising in my early 20s. It is a beautiful and historic instrument'.

Howard Hollis (vicar 1965-76) had imbibed from his years at Westminster Abbey a love for dignified but un-fussy liturgy. As an accomplished musician himself he took a keen interest in the parish's music and insisted on the highest possible standards of performance, whether by clergy, choir or congregation, and could be quite forthright with the organist or clergy colleagues if the music was not up to scratch. He loved the traditional hymnody of the *English Hymnal*,[7] and insisted that the choir and congregation sing even the less familiar hymns and tunes in the book. He would occasionally take to the organ himself if the organist was absent for whatever reason – Christopher Herrick on one occasion forgot he was due to play for a wedding, and later learnt that the vicar had not only conducted the service but played the organ as well. Herrick continued as organist until the summer of 1967, giving regular recitals himself and occasionally inviting famous recitalists to perform, among them Dr Francis Jackson of York Minster.[8] In a manner of speaking, Herrick's 'last service' at St Mary's was his own wedding, for which Anthony Greening returned to play the organ, and the men of the choir sang the Byrd 3-part Mass.

Herrick went on to be assistant organist at St Paul's cathedral, where he had been a chorister, and was succeeded at St Mary's by Malcolm Hill (1967-74) of the Royal Academy of Music. Under his direction the choir was reduced to men's voices only (ATB), with a necessarily more austere repertoire of plainsong and early music (which, it should be said, some of the congregation preferred). For the church's centenary year in 1972 he organised a programme of organ recitals featuring former St Mary's organists (Gedge, Greening, Herrick and Warrell), as well as a joint recital by Howard and Margaret Hollis on keyboard and flute respectively. Warrell, who was by then Musical Director of the Gregorian Association, also arranged for the Association's 1972 festival to be held at St Mary's in October that year.

When Hill moved on, to Holy Trinity Prince Consort Road and a fully professional choir, Hollis appointed in his place Ivan Fowler, a student at the Royal School of Church Music (RSCM), who was ably assisted by Dorothy Southern, a devoted member of the congregation and accomplished organist, who had begun to deputise under Herrick and would continue until ill health forced her to step down. As he inherited hardly any choir, Fowler had to do something radical. After discussion with Dorothy Southern who had been the lynch-pin of the ladies' choir at Evensong, he decided on one occasion to put together a ladies' choir to sing the Fauré *Messe Basse* at the Sung Eucharist. A shocked Hollis, quite mistakenly taking this to be a deliberate assault on the St Mary's choral tradition, summarily 'sacked' him after the service, but after learning later that day how much the congregation had appreciated it, he contritely reinstated him before Evensong! Although the ladies' performance was a one-off event rather than a permanent *démarche*, it did now seem sensible, even to the vicar, to set about recruiting a mixed choir of men and women, and that has been the basis on which the choir has operated ever since.

Despite what a disgruntled few clearly thought at the time, a mixed choir was not something new to St Mary's – as these annals have shown. But some in the congregation had become so attuned to male-voice plainsong and early music that it took them a while to adjust. Pending the enlistment of sufficient volunteers for a new choir, a generous member of the congregation put up the money to employ a small number of paid singers on a temporary basis.[9] That was something else that had been tried before, although St Mary's has never been one of those London churches to have an exclusively professional choir.

Ivan Fowler tells an amusing story. As the organ lacked a much-needed humidifier:

> I procured some plant trays and, on the advice of the organ builder, put them in the organ chamber and filled them with water. I put towels into them and strung the towels up so that the water would rise through the towels and produce some moisture. When asked by two ladies who were in the vestry doing the flowers what I was doing with the buckets of water, I replied that I was growing tomatoes in the organ. Within minutes the Vicar arrived in a tizzy, wondering if I had gone mad. However, Howard was an organist; he realised that this water was necessary. He actually went along with my joke and after a little while he returned and produced, I assume from a local shop, some tomatoes, to give to the ladies, that I had supposedly grown in the organ!

In October 1975 Hollis marked the centenary of Martin Shaw's birth with a long article in the parish magazine and a commemorative Eucharist. The following spring Lyndon van der Pump, then a lay member of the congregation and a professor of singing at the Royal College of Music, gave a song recital ranging from Purcell to Vaughan Williams and Shaw. Shaw's Christmas mime *At the Sign of the Star,* with original and folk songs, was performed by singers and members of the parish Drama Group in December,[10] with accompaniment provided by Dorothy Southern (who could always be relied upon to find appropriate incidental music for Drama Group productions).

Ivan Fowler resigned as organist in 1977 after three years, and was followed, though only for a brief two-year spell, by Michael Fleming (1978-80), staff tutor at the RSCM and organist of Croydon Parish Church. He had been attracted to St Mary's by its plainsong tradition and the Dearmer heritage, but was quickly disappointed not to have a stronger choir at his disposal, and lacking the time to recruit one he moved on to St Alban's Holborn where there was an established professional choir.

Michael Willford, an engineer by profession, but also a capable organist, had joined the St Mary's choir as a tenor in 1976 and, alongside Dorothy Southern, assisted Fleming. On the latter's departure he was invited by Richard Buck to step up and become organist and choirmaster. This was a departure from the 20-year tradition of having as organist either a student or staff member at one of the London conservatoires aspiring to a career as a professional musician. But Willford was no less strongly committed to the St Mary's musical tradition, and remained at the helm under three successive vicars for almost three decades, until 2008. Assisted first by Dorothy Southern (d.1994) and later by Bryan Almond,[11] he determinedly built up a strong and loyal SATB choir, encouraging and promoting them by broadening the repertoire, and through regular concerts, both in the church and further afield. For festive occasions masses with orchestral accompaniment were introduced.

Concerts included, in 1989, a 'choral peregrination' of six City churches, master-minded by Andrew Alexander, a member of the congregation, with bell-ringing for the event arranged by John Hawes. A cassette recording and several CDs were produced, of which perhaps the most relevant for this history was *The St Mary's Primrose Hill Musical Tradition* (2001), with Bryan Almond, organ. It featured music by, or arranged by, GH Palmer, Martin and Geoffrey Shaw, and JH Arnold, as well as hymns from the *English Hymnal*, Arthur Clarke's faux-bourdon setting of the Magnificat and Nunc Dimittis written for the choir in 1939, and Alan Ridout's 1962 anthem, *O glorious maid*, premièred for the church's 90th anniversary. In 2000 and again in 2002, highly successful choir visits were made to St George's, Paris, where St Mary's former curate Martin Draper was then chaplain. Both visits included informal, but well-received concerts at the Madeleine, the first consisting of 'Hymns to the Virgin', the second of settings from the Psalms. To herald the new Millennium a performance of Messiah was mounted in December 1999, the choir's CD of 'Music for a Summer Evening' was released, and in June 2000 there was a week-long festival of liturgy and music. In November 2002 John Rutter returned to conduct a choral workshop.

The centenary of the *English Hymnal* in 2006 was marked nationally by a volume of celebratory essays and a book entitled *Strengthen for Service: 100 years of the English Hymnal*. Writing à *propos* the latter, Robert Atwell commented:

> Every book is the product of its age and the *English Hymnal* is no exception. Archbishop Rowan Williams, whilst celebrating its achievement, admits that it is a monument to a particular set of North London suburban tastefulness, 'the Edwardian ecclesiastical equivalent of sun-dried tomatoes in Islington'. So let's hear it for sun-dried tomatoes, I say.

The choir and congregation also played their part in the *EH* celebrations, notably through a special edition of BBC Television's *Songs of Praise*. The programme was recorded at St Mary's in the depths of winter for broadcast later in the year, so in order to enable the congregation to appear in bright summer clothes on a cold winter's day the church heating was turned up to maximum. Other tricks used in the production had better remain Commercial in Confidence! Extracts from this recording have often appeared in subsequent episodes of the programme.

Tony Henwood, the present organist and music director, like Herrick a former Organ Scholar of Exeter College Oxford, and a professional music teacher, was appointed in 2008, but the number of volunteer singers able to commit to regular weekly attendance began to fall once again, so an application was made to the Hampstead Church Music Trust to fund the appointment of four choral scholars, one of each voice (SATB) to sing alongside the regular volunteers in order to guarantee a quorum of singers each week. When the scheme began it was not foreseen just how important the scholars would become in keeping up the church's music throughout the coronavirus pandemic of 2020-21. To abide by the successive regulations in force, they either had to record anthems from their own individual homes, which were then brought together on screen for the on-line Sung Eucharists streamed each week from the church, or (later) to sing live in the church, but with no more than two other singers present. Singing by the congregation – surely one of the most fundamental aspects of Christian worship today – remained prohibited throughout the pandemic.

Organ

During David Gedge's time as organist a major re-fit of the organ was commissioned. It fell into two phases. After a temporary blip in the post-war years when the organ was maintained by Messrs Bishop,[12] regular upkeep of the instrument had returned to Hill, Norman and Beard, and in 1958, after the union with St Paul's Avenue Road, that firm was invited to examine what if anything might be saved from the St Paul's organ. That too had been a fine instrument but had suffered serially from war damage, theft, and then the building's neglect and exposure. The firm was able to add to its stock a small proportion of re-usable pipe-work from the St Paul's instrument, and by treating that as a part-exchange, was able to provide a new pedal-board for St Mary's organ (1958) in return for a modest additional contribution. The congregation was advised (for the umpteenth time) that 'before long we must consider opening an organ fund, so that when repair and renovation becomes necessary we may have money to meet it.' However, in the early 1960s, just in time for the commemoration of the 90th anniversary of the church's opening, the organ was substantially and sensitively rebuilt, this time by NP Mander Ltd, with tracker action for the Great organ and electro-pneumatic for the rest. It was over half a century since the last major intervention, and the diocesan organ adviser was firmly convinced that the instrument had soldiered on for so long only because of the 'very sound and conscientious manner in which the original work was carried out' by Hill's. Mander respected Hill's original tonal character, and retained as much of the Swell and Great as possible, while providing additional mutation stops to give greater tonal brilliance. A *Ham and High* reporter noted that, like many 19th century organs, it was better suited to Romantic than Baroque repertoire but, for all that, was a fine instrument. Costs rose steeply during the work, and (not for the first or last time) funds proved insufficient to cover all the desirable improvement work, so some stops were merely 'prepared for'.

Greening was fortunate to take up his post as organist in 1962, soon after this rebuild, and just in time for the church's 90th anniversary Festival. Within a month of his appointment a grand opening recital was given on the restored instrument by Dr Sidney Campbell of St George's Chapel, Windsor, and at the Festival itself an anthem newly commissioned by Timms in honour of Gedge and the choir, *O Glorious Maid* by Alan Ridout, was sung for the first time.

After the 1962 rebuild little further work was carried out on the instrument for several decades, save that in the autumn of 1969 (Malcolm Hill organist) a bequest from Garda Hall enabled a new 16ft double clarinet stop to be added in her memory by Messrs Rushworth and Dreaper, and in 1983 a new humidifier was provided by an anonymous donor. By 1990, however, after a number of malfunctions, further major work was found to be necessary, for which it was estimated that £50,000 might be required. Sir Charles Groves agreed to become patron/president (with Lady [Evelyn] Barbirolli and Lady [Valerie] Solti as vice presidents) of what proved to be a highly successful Organ Appeal, although the final bill, this time from Messrs Harrison and Harrison, was for £65,000. In July 1992 Jennifer Bate gave the opening recital on the restored instrument.

One of the objectives of the church's Blueprint Appeal under Robert Atwell (see ch17.) was to establish an organ scholarship to give aspiring young players practical experience of liturgical accompaniment. This scheme was duly implemented, with tuition and oversight being provided to the scholars by successive organists, Michael Willford and (from 2008) Tony Henwood, and by their Deputy, Bryan Almond.

A fundamental rebuild of the organ loomed in the early 2000s, and fund-raising began from 2008, which included a major series of concerts from autumn 2008 to spring 2009, put together by a committee under the chairmanship of Keith Hill.[13] The work was again contracted to Harrison and Harrison in 2012, with an initial estimate well into six figures. (The cost rose steadily during the operation, not least when a recent fiscal change meant that organ repair was no longer exempted from 20% VAT). The PCC explored cheaper options, including the installation of a permanent electronic instrument, but decided that to maintain the fine musical tradition of St Mary's and make the most of the building's acoustics there was no realistic option but to raise, from grants and another major appeal, the huge sum necessary to restore the original instrument, which came to well over £200,000. The organ was therefore dismantled, pipe by pipe, and taken away to Harrison's works in Durham. Pending its return an electronic instrument was indeed installed, but only on a temporary basis, and there was general rejoicing when the pipe organ was re-commissioned. On Michaelmas Day 2012 the inaugural recital on the restored instrument was given by Christopher Herrick, and in January the following year Jennifer Bate paid a return visit to give a recital in memory of John Horder, a much loved local GP and amateur organist.

Endnotes

1. Gedge (2005). [See Bibiography].
2. Ibid, p.107.
3. Information from John Ashby who was then one of the choir. He also recalls occasional choir outings, such as that to the Balham and Tooting music festival, and Gedge's use of both the vestry and the church itself for rehearsals of the Thomas Morley Chamber Orchestra of which he was conductor.
4. Supplement to Parish Chronicle.
5. CERC: CARE 23/329.
6. Christopher Herrick, 'Three years at St Mary's', in PM, Apr-May 2013, pp.8-9.
7. He was a Director of the English Hymnal Company.
8. Advertised in *Church Times*, 3 Feb 1967. See Herrick article cited above.
9. Information from Ivan Fowler.
10. PM, Feb 1976.
11. Jack Wells, a choir member, was also an occasional assistant.
12. LMA: P81/MRV/145, PCC Minutes, Jan 1958.
13. Brochure in the parish Archives.

Chapter 16

Empowering the laity

If, by focusing on the successive vicars of the parish, Part One of this story appeared to under-play the role of the laity, that was certainly no part of its intention. In fact, the laity have been ever-present in the story: as founders, builders and benefactors of the church; leaders of the congregation; and ardent supporters of the faith and of the St Mary's way of doing things. And from at least 1917, with the establishment of the first church Council (even though it was chaired by the vicar), the laity had developed an increasingly important voice in the running of the entire parish enterprise.

In the period since the 1950s the influence of the laity has increased enormously. The transformation has been gradual rather than sudden, and has been so trouble-free that even long-standing members of the congregation may have been unaware that they were living through what, with hindsight, seems to amount to a revolution. This chapter focuses on areas of activity where the laity have exerted particular influence, but since that theme is interwoven throughout Part Two a few cross-references to lay activities mentioned in other relevant sections of the text are given at the end of the chapter.

* * *

When George Timms became vicar in 1952 St Mary's, like most other churches, was clergy-dominated. The vicar and his assistants had always been if not the prime movers then at least the key overseers of every strategic aspect of the parish's life. We need think only of Spencer and Dearmer determining fixtures, fittings and iconography; of Duncan-Jones influencing drama, or Dunlop the youth work; or almost all the vicars seeking to influence the music – with varying degrees of success or ignominy.

The contrast with today is palpable, and anyone who doubts it has only to look at the reports presented to recent Annual Parochial Church Meetings, which overflow with evidence of lay-led activities. How surprised the parishioners from those earlier generations would be to see the range of today's parish activities, both inward- and outward-facing, and to see how many of them are lay-led. And what questions they would have about how the very nature of church and congregation could have changed so much over the last seventy years.

* * *

Indicators of change

The following may serve as indicators of how things have changed in this period. Some are explored in greater detail in other chapters:

- **Liturgy.** With the introduction by Timms of a less formal eucharist in the nave, at which the celebrant faced the people from behind a free-standing altar, and the extension of the same principle to the High Altar by Richard Buck from 1981, the parish priest seemed a much less remote figure. Another trend in the same general direction might be noted. The more modern, almost every-day language of the new liturgies that were progressively introduced under Howard Hollis and later vicars right up to the present, together with the more modern translations of the Bible used,[1] have made the liturgy itself more accessible.
- **Ministry**. A steady questioning, by clergy and laity alike, of clergy-focussed assumptions about the nature and meaning of 'ministry' has led to a wider understanding of how the term

might embrace lay activities too. This affirms – one might even say 'sanctifies' – the contribution of the laity. The entire *laos*, or People of God, works towards a common purpose.

- **Stewardship and representation**. From the 1950s, new teaching and exhortation about Christian Stewardship encouraged the laity to think not only in terms of their financial commitment to the church, but also their commitment of time and talents. That in turn encouraged more of them than ever before to participate in the church's non-liturgical activities, and perhaps as a result to expect their views to carry more weight. This gave more purpose and influence to the deliberations of the Parochial Church Council and its Committees, and to participation in outside bodies such as the Deanery Synod, as was particularly apparent over the latter body's discussions concerning the ordination of women as deacons, priests and bishops.

- **Outreach and evangelisation.** National and diocesan directives about evangelisation and an outward-looking ministry have been taken to heart, and have profoundly influenced the way St Mary's operates within the wider community. But more proactive outreach has only been possible through significant additional fund-raising and the involvement of more lay people, from both inside and outside the congregation. The church building, too, has been re-purposed to provide better, dedicated space for staff, and more particularly for community activities, with improved amenities ranging from kitchens, showers and WCs to internet access and (most recently) cameras and broadcasting equipment.

- **Clergy self-awareness.** All of the above factors have required fundamental changes in the self-awareness of the clergy, who have become increasingly keen and willing to share or even devolve some of the control that in previous generations had always been assumed to be vested in the vicar. Paradoxically though, the role and responsibilities of the clergy have at the same time also grown inexorably, as more projects have been added to the parish's portfolio of activities and responsibilities and more legislation, regulations and central directives have had to be complied with. A typical parish is now a big business, operating under new imperatives of accountability and efficient management. Happily this burden falls just as much on the laity as on the clergy.

Lay responsibilities: overview

Unpaid officers

Looking back over Part One, some things remain constant down to the present, including the essential role of the (unpaid) elected officers. The two Churchwardens and sidesmen, the Treasurer and, from 1919, the PCC Secretary have always provided crucial support and advice to the vicar, as well as continuity during a vacancy in the living. The duties of Churchwardens and sidesmen include the ancient legal requirements to answer to the bishop for the proper maintenance of the building itself and its fixtures and fittings, and to keep order among those who attend (which had become a particular issue during the Ritualist controversies described in Part One). Those are only the minimum job requirements. Others include maintaining harmony within the congregation, ensuring (with the Treasurer) that the parish meets its financial obligations towards the wider church, and keeping a weather eye on income and expenditure to avoid unserviceable debt. All this work (which of course continues) was and is done by lay members of the congregation on a purely voluntary basis: those involved give their time and wits for the benefit of the church and its people. Without the tireless dedication in different generations of, say, a Thomas Hill, a Frank Marriott, or a Ronnie Fuller, this might have been a very different story.

Paid staff

Throughout Part One, the only paid lay people at St Mary's were the organist (and deputy when there was one), occasional professional singers, and the church's verger who often doubled as caretaker and odd-jobs man.

Bob Fake, the verger whose sterling wartime effort for the church has already been recorded, successfully negotiated a much needed increase in his wages under Timms, in return for taking on additional cleaning and gardening duties. After ill health compelled him to retire in 1963, shortly after he had celebrated thirty years of service, Mr A Hadley took on the job, at least for a short time, but it is not clear whether he was paid. No other lay people were paid by St Mary's until the arrival of the first paid Parish Secretary/Administrator and Youth Workers in the early 2000s.

Other ranks

Apart from the officers, many other lay members gave voluntarily and copiously of their time: as choir members, members of church committees (for fund-raising, mission and the like), teachers at Catechism and Sunday School, poor-visitors, organisers and helpers for social activities and drama, cleaners, flower arrangers, caterers, and much else. Above all, lay people (– up to the 1950s it was always men) played an indispensable part in the liturgy, as taperers, clerk, thurifer and subdeacon. Several of them had almost as good a grasp of doctrinal and choreographical *minutiae* as the clergy.

Liturgy, lay preaching and prayer

The process of lay empowerment, beginning right at the heart of the church's preaching and worshipping ministry, has accelerated markedly under the last three vicars. St Mary's first Lay Reader, Roberta Berke, was licensed in 1998, and others have followed: William Morris under Robert Atwell; Clement Hutton-Mills and Miriam Rinsler under Marjorie Brown.

Other lay people have been actively enlisted for roles in the ministry of prayer and teaching, including readers and intercessors, roles which in a previous generation might have fallen to the clergy. John Ovenden gave lay members completely free rein to organise some of the Sunday evening services such as Taizé Prayers and Contemplative Prayer.

Licensed Lay Ministers (Readers). Roberta Berke (L), St Mary's first Lay Reader. Clement Hutton-Mills (R), Licensed Lay Minister and, from 2021, a lay canon of St Paul's cathedral

Robert Atwell, as well as continuing those activities, gave the youth coordinators scope to arrange special liturgies for the church's young people. The role of subdeacon at the Sung Eucharist, which used to be restricted to a small handful of lay people, has been opened up to many more – men and women, young and old alike, and under Marjorie Brown four of these have also additionally received the bishop's licence to assist with the administration of the Holy Communion 'by extension' to the sick and housebound. Along with the Licensed Lay Ministers they also act as liturgical 'deacon' at the Sung Eucharist on a regular basis.

In recent years the clergy have deliberately devolved to lay leaders some of the social and outreach activities that were initially clergy-led, including the Primrose Hill Lectures. At the time of writing one of the churchwardens, Roddy Monroe, was leading the major 2022 Capital campaign to revitalise the church for its ongoing ministry and outreach beyond its 150th anniversary.

Since at least the time of Richard Buck lay people, with guidance from but not oversight by the clergy, have organised some of the parish retreats and led house groups and book groups, and most recently on the initiative of another churchwarden, Casey Oppong, a monthly fasting and prayer group.

Finance

The management of the parish's finances has always been one of the areas where lay members of the congregation have carried most responsibility, and it is fitting to pay tribute to the long succession of Treasurers, Auditors/Independent Examiners and Stewardship Recorders who have helped in this way.

At the point when the coronavirus pandemic dramatically shut off several of the main sources of income in 2020, St Mary's finances were on an even keel.[2] This had not always been the case. We saw how long it took the then small congregation, after the church's opening, to pay off its debts on the building and the organ; how it struggled (ultimately victoriously) to raise the massive sums required to build Spencer's extensions; and how the sacrificial giving of the early clergy, and the positive expectation that they would bring or seek additional means of financial support for themselves and their families, had no small part to play in the parish's overall financial viability.

For all that, in the absence of any significant endowments there were many times when St Mary's still struggled to meet its outgoings year on year. Under the watchful eye of Treasurers, and most particularly the long-serving Frank Marriott, spending was carefully prioritised and projects put on hold when necessary.

Frank Marriott

Marriott is a giant among the lay-folk of St Mary's. Serving the church for three decades, with a very short interruption of less than a year during the Second World War, he was concurrently Treasurer for thirty years (1923-53), Churchwarden for 28 years (1925-53), and a Trustee from 1935 until his death in 1954. In the sanctuary he was a server, and frequently subdeacon.[3] He was a senior civil servant at the Exchequer and Audit Department, rising to become its Deputy Secretary, and also served as Chairman of the London Diocesan Fund. A profile in the *London Churchman* noted that for thirty years he kept St Mary's free of debt, ensured that it paid its diocesan quota 'or more' and gave £200 to £300 annually to the mission field. Without his considerable financial skills St Mary's during and after the Second World War would have been in dire financial straits.[4]

On Marriott's retirement, which sadly was closely followed by his death, he was honoured with a CMG. The *Church Times* of 22 January 1954 described him as a faithful servant just as much of the Church as of the State. An extract from his overview of the parish in 1951, could well stand as his own memorial: 'There are no debts, and no major expenditure is likely at the moment … The buildings are in good condition and the whole cost of the recent restorations has been met by grants and contributions. The parish has a good record for gifts to the missionary work of the church and to the Diocese.'

Vicar's stipend (1950s-70s)

In 1953, Marriott as Treasurer also compiled a helpful memorandum on the vicar's stipend. Before the War it had reached around £400 plus Easter Offerings, a pension contribution and the cost of dilapidations at the vicarage. The parish's contribution to this from offerings amounted to £283; Eton College still paid £50 p.a.; and the Church Commissioners a further £67 from the additional endowment set up in Harcourt's time. During the Second World War, as regular income declined, the parish's contribution sank as low as £233 but both the Church Commissioners and the London Diocesan Fund gave more in order to maintain the level of vicar's stipend they had set for London. After the War, the London diocese set a minimum target of £600 (plus rates) for a vicar's stipend, but stepped in to assist parishes unable to meet this. St Mary's stepped up its own contribution to £263 but even so found itself unable to meet the new total without assistance. It was materially helped by a legacy of £2,000 from Colonel Lee which was immediately put into the endowment fund and generated some £80 p.a. The Diocese came to its aid with an augmentation of £167.[5]

When the financial position was explained to Eton College on the appointment of Howard Hollis, the College gave him a personal grant of £250 p.a. in addition to its existing stipend.

Stewardship (1950s-present)

After the financial shock of the Second World War the diocese sought urgently to persuade congregations of the need to become more self-reliant and less dependent on the diocesan central fund. Christian Stewardship was not a wholly new concept, but it had not yet been articulated and promoted in a way that made the laity take stock of how, and how much, they contributed individually to their church, in terms of money, time or talents. The most basic challenge was to get parishes to meet their own reasonable running costs, but it was important also to emphasise their need to contribute to the costs of the wider diocese through the common fund (now the 'parish contribution').

A first full-blown Stewardship Campaign was launched at St Mary's under George Timms in 1959; a second would follow in 1962. In 1959, after detailed central briefing, the campaign was meticulously planned by a parish committee, with almost all the effort devolved to the laity. The PCC was briefed at an away-day, after which lay volunteers were recruited to speak to their fellows in the congregation and parish about the potentially sensitive matter of giving. Nothing quite like it had ever been tried before. Following an explanatory letter from the vicar to all parishioners, the campaign proper was launched with exhortatory speeches at a public dinner (attended by 212 people including the Bishop of Willesden),[6] again requiring lay volunteers. In the following days the volunteers knocked on doors. Fund-raising and social events were held in tandem, and the campaign concluded with a special eucharist. A quarter of a century later, in a memorial tribute to Charles Vaughan-Lee who had chaired that first stewardship campaign, Timms recalled it as 'a venture of faith, for such programmes were in their infancy, and a good deal of prejudice had to be overcome… The programme went smoothly, and was successful beyond all our expectations.'[7] In fact, it was largely the increased giving resulting from these campaigns that enabled St Mary's to meet its heavy outgoings in the years that followed. At the Annual Parish Meeting in 1962 the vicar could proudly boast that the church was better off than ever before.[8]

Similar campaigns, but directed now almost exclusively at the congregation itself rather than the wider parish, continued to be held every three or four years well into the 1980s, and sporadically thereafter, each time with a slightly different *modus operandi*. The 1972 campaign, for example, was associated with the church's centenary celebrations and, for the visiting, enlisted the help of an external team. The campaign of 1984 was prefaced by a day conference and had input from a number of working groups.

Stewardship continues to drive people's regular giving today, and the effort is still lay-led. Since at least the 1990s one aim has been to encourage regular and tax-effective giving in a manner that reduces the amount of cash put in the plate. (Keith Hill, Treasurer in the early 1990s, still remembers cycling to the bank 'with a panier weighed down with sacks of coins to deposit'). The old three- or four-yearly structured campaigns have been replaced by detailed annual presentations to the congregation about the financial health of the parish, through a combination of sermons and separate after-service talks, with an appeal for members to review and renew their giving. Fund-raising for major objectives beyond the church's running costs is handled through separate appeals, such as those for the Parish Room extension in the 1990s, the organ appeals of 1990 and 2012 and the Blueprint Appeal (see ch17). Under John Ovenden an 'auction of promises' was also held, organised by Peter Symonds, with John Inman as the auctioneer. Although this was a one-off event it served to focus people's minds on how it might be in their power, even in small ways, to be of service to others.

Cash-flow challenges

St Mary's has no endowment, and to avoid external debt it has to rely on balancing its income and expenditure year on year. At various times over the past 70 years, even when there has been healthy stewardship giving, income has fallen well short of expenditure, for example because of unforeseen building maintenance costs. [9]

Almost every Treasurer has had to face this challenge, and responses have varied with the gravity of the situation. The inevitable first response has been to rein in expenditure. A second has been to increase income by laying on special events like the jumble sales and bazaars of the 1980s and 1990s (including a still-legendary International Evening with a troupe of Brazilian Lambarda dancers), and the Designer Fairs from 2000 onwards. Thirdly, the Churchwardens and Treasurer have from time to time approached members of the congregation for interest-free loans to prevent the church defaulting on its debts. And finally, in past generations though not lately, *in extremis* the churchwardens sometimes had to inform the diocese that the parish was unable to meet in full its common fund contribution (a requested sum determined centrally, rather than a mandatory tax). The whole Church of England would collapse if these payments were widely withheld, and today the payment of the parish contribution is a major priority of the parish's finances.

Administration and accountability

Increased role for the laity

Next to the elected Churchwardens and the Treasurer, the office of PCC Secretary is perhaps the most important for the smooth running of the parish, and St Mary's has been fortunate in having a succession of dedicated and long-serving members in this role, including in this period Frances Wilton, Leonore Shirley, Robert Wills, Pauline Collett and most recently Amanda Martin. Richard Buck freely admitted that he was not a born administrator, and happily entrusted to the churchwardens,

PCC and parish officers much of the day-to-day running of the church. Subsequent vicars have tended to do the same (irrespective of their administrative skills!).

Quite a few lay people have filled more than one role, and it is right to recall a particularly colourful group of senior characters from Buck's years. Walter Joslin, a retired civil servant, as well as being the PCC Treasurer, was also a poet much admired for his wry and highly pertinent verses for the parish magazine. Stanley Taylor we have already met as carpenter and church watchman; he was also a conveyor of cash to the bank and an amateur thespian. He was given the honorific titles of Parish Clerk, and in later life Verger. Randall Ellison, stewardship recorder, was also a strong defender of Prayer Book-style worship and language. And Tom Copeland, another witty poet on a par with Joslin, was the retired manager of a building firm who famously remarked that he 'loved every brick' of St Mary's, of which he set himself up as the self-styled 'Clerk of Works' or, as he always abbreviated it in his magazine contributions, CoW. (See Appendix to this Chapter).

Parish Office

Up to the time of Richard Buck the vicars had no regular secretarial help, nor was there any Parish Office in the church itself, although some secretarial space was set aside in the vicarage in Elsworthy Road. The erection of the Dearmer Screen (1981) for the first time enclosed the north transept for this purpose, and Dorothy Southern, the assistant organist who had recently retired from a secretarial post at the Tavistock Institute, offered her part-time assistance on a purely voluntary basis which continued for seven years until ill-health compelled her to stand down.[10] With her retirement a first attempt was made to employ a paid 'Parish coordinator',[11] Paula Greenley, but sadly, this soon proved at the time to be financially unsustainable. She was followed by two successive volunteers from the congregation, Julia Smith and, under Robert Atwell, Pauline Collett (the latter serving for seven years from 1999 to 2006).

Parish magazine

It was a classic symptom of the clergy trying to do too much that George Timms, like some of his predecessors, edited the parish magazine himself until 1960 when he finally admitted that 'the grace of ordination does not necessarily confer editorial ability.'[12] At that point he handed it on to a layman, and with the exception of a period when it was edited by Revd Francis Stephens, its editorship has (without censorship by the vicar) remained in lay hands.

Website

As the world moved into the Internet Age, Robert Atwell saw that St Mary's had to adapt to survive. In order to equip the church for a new Millennium, the first parish website was set up. This has now grown into the principal vehicle for the church's communications, both internal and external. It combines a memory bank of historical and archival data and documentation, a first point of entry for many enquiring about the church and its activities, an up-to-date means of communicating news of services and events, the gateway to the church's on-line services, and much else besides.

During 2020 when the church was locked down due to the pandemic, the website proved invaluable as the gateway to the many web-streamed services and events that kept the church alive and functioning as a place of worship.

By 2005 the auditors were warning that the scale of operations at St Mary's was expanding so rapidly that more paid help was going to be needed. For the Parish Office, the experiment was first tried of employing graduate students, each for a short term: successively Andrew Allen, Tamsin Omond and Jack Target. But it was clear that something more permanent was required and, under Marjorie Brown, Celyn Cooke became the first paid long-term Parish Administrator. The remit of that post has grown considerably, in proportion to the parish's expanding commitment to social outreach. In addition to being the first point of contact, and providing secretarial assistance to the clergy, it includes the production of many parish documents including the weekly service sheets, managing bookings for the church and St Mary's Centre, making arrangements for concerts and lectures, and supervising the provision and serving of food, bedding and equipment (as well as organising the rota of volunteers) for St Mary's participation in the Cold Weather Shelter.

Governance

The roles of the elected officers are touched on above. In general, matters of governance within the parish are overseen not only by the vicar and churchwardens, but also by the Archdeacon (who conducts periodic Visitations to ensure that all is well and that the inventory is up to date) and the Auditor who must sign off the annual accounts before they can be approved by the PCC and forwarded to the Charity Commission.

In addition, the kind of pressures which, in the new Millennium, necessitated a paid secretariat and a professional youth worker brought in their wake new requirements for tighter governance and budgetary control across every aspect of the parish's work. Many important changes were introduced under Robert Atwell, ranging from setting up an annual choir meeting (2001) to committing the PCC to regularly-reviewed Vision and Mission Action Plans, to ensuring that bodies like the Friends of St Mary's and the St Mary's Community Centre Trustees were both constituted and run in accordance with the law and best practice. National legislation additionally required compliance on such matters as disabled-access to the church premises, non-discrimination in appointment and employment practice, and criminal records checks for anyone with a public-facing role, with special emphasis on the safeguarding of children (which, for example, affected the running of the Sunday School and Youthwork).

Social activities

Whilst the clergy have always played an important role in the church's social activities, it is in this sphere that lay empowerment has most strikingly flourished. A few examples are offered below, from a very large field.

Frank Marriott's memorandum of 1951 noted, *inter alia*, that:

> The general decline of the district, the changes in the population and the impact of the war have severely affected the size of the congregation. The electoral roll now numbers only 90, and the average congregations at the Sung Eucharists on Sundays are about 30 at 10 a.m. and 50 at 11.15 a.m. There are about 30 children who attend the former service, and the Catechism on Sunday afternoons, but there is little parochial life outside the worship of the church. On the other hand it can be said that the existing congregation is, though somewhat elderly, loyal and keen and remarkably generous.

George Timms told the PCC he was 'anxious to make the church a centre of social life as well as worship,'[13] and not only he but his successors (Buck and Hollis) held occasional garden parties at the old vicarage in Elsworthy Road. Timms was rather shy of crowds, and it was not unknown for him to observe at least part of a garden party from the window of an upper room.[14] He left much of the social and fund-raising effort to the honed organising skill of the formidable Dame May Curwen.[15] With echoes of similar developments in the past, a church 'Fellowship' began (Oct 1952) to host social events – among which Noel Davey's showing of SPCK's filmstrip of the Coronation (1953) stands out. The Fellowship was dissolved in 1956 and replaced the following year by a 'Parish Social Club'. Among other initiatives a branch of the Church of England Men's Society was established,[16] and the idea was mooted of a Friends of St Mary's (1954), although it would be a further four decades before the latter eventually became a reality!

Organised evening social activities became less popular from Hollis's time onwards, perhaps owing to the proliferation of competing social and cultural opportunities both at home and in the city, although a number of significant plays and concerts were still staged by the church, as is described below.

Music at St Mary's and the Sir Peter Pears Prize (1978-92)

In 1978, Lyndon van der Pump (then a lay member of the congregation and Professor of Singing at the Royal College of Music), building on a series of concerts under this name organised by Ivan Fowler, established a new society called 'Music at St Mary's'. He himself became its Artistic Director, and Sir Peter Pears, and from Pears's death in 1986 Sir Georg Solti, were successively its Patrons. Affiliated to the National Federation of Music Societies, it aimed to provide a channel through which young musicians from four London music colleges – the Royal Academy of Music, the Royal College of Music, the Guildhall School of Music and Drama and Trinity College of Music – could be given the opportunity to further their careers, and in this it was strikingly successful. The audiences, even for these top-flight concerts, tended to be rather small and select, though highly appreciative. A Steinway grand and later a fine Bechstein were secured and reconditioned for St Mary's by Darell Moulton, the principal piano technician at the RCM; a wooden concert platform was built by Stanley Taylor, and the south aisle was carpeted and provided with new chairs to make the concert-going experience more agreeable for performers and audience alike.

Annual subscription seasons, each of six concerts, open to the public as well as to the forty or so subscribing members of the society, continued until 1995. Occasional Gala Performances were also offered by established musicians, including, memorably, Schubert's *Die Winterreise* in 1992 sung by Gerald Finlay, baritone, with Malcolm Martineau, piano. Yonty Solomon, played a Mozart concerto with the Royal Philharmonic Orchestra conducted by Sir Charles Groves. When Sir George Solti was at Covent Garden he brought two of his star singers to St Mary's to sing duets, to a packed house. Also included were concerts by aspiring musicians from the junior music schools. Concerts offered by other young performers were accommodated whenever possible under the society's name, even if they fell outside the regular subscription series. When, in 1995 efforts to secure additional financial support for the series from the music colleges were unsuccessful, the society came to an end, although its musical legacy lives on.

A 'Music at St Mary's Prize' for singers was launched at the same time. For its first competition, held in the church in 1979 with a prize of £500 given by Nick Rocke, a member of the St Mary's choir, entrants had to be students at one of the London conservatories. The first winner was the soprano Patricia Rosario, whose subsequent rise to international fame showed the potential of the competition and set a high benchmark for future entrants. It became customary to offer the winner a concert in the subsequent year's recital series. In 1980, when the church was being redecorated and was thus unable to host the competition, the Royal College of Music stepped in as temporary host. But once the scaffolding came down the competition returned to St Mary's. In 1981 sponsorship was found from Messrs WH Smith, and the competition was widened to include students from the principal music colleges outside London. With his permission and delight it was re-branded the 'Peter Pears Singing Prize', and later the 'Peter Pears Award'. From 1983 until his death in 1986 Sir Peter himself led the judges, and among others the panel also included at various times Sir Lennox Berkeley, Malcolm Williamson, Dame Eva Turner, Joan Chissell and Heather Harper. From 1984 until 1987, on account of the logistical complexities of a competition of growing scale and international prestige, it was hosted in turn by each of the four London colleges, although the Music at St Mary's committee continued to offer a helping hand. WH Smith's sponsorship came to an end in 1986 but a member of the congregation who was a staunch supporter of the Society funded the 1987 Competition which was won by Simon Keenlyside. It then seemed as if the competition might come to an end but, again through the good offices of a member of the St Mary's congregation, BP was persuaded to put up the funding to keep it going for a few more years: no longer at St Mary's itself but on a much more impressive scale as an international competition judged by international stars with its Finals at the Queen Elizabeth Hall with one of the major London orchestras and famous conductors. The competition came to an end in 1992 when BP's support finished and no other sponsors were found.[17]

Friends of St Mary's

In 1999, Peter and Mary Cooper – reviving that idea first discussed in George Timms's time – founded the Friends of St Mary's. The Friends were formally constituted as a registered charity to raise funds for the maintenance and beautification of the building. Although the vicar was formally the Chairman, it was essentially a lay-led enterprise which, while of course linking its members in a common love of St Mary's, was also a highly sociable organisation.

Members of the congregation, but importantly also friends from further afield (at their height numbering around 150), gave subscriptions and donations, and many social events and entertainments were organised, with the profits going to the church. By the end of the first five years (2004), for example, foreign trips had been organised to France, Belgium, Russia and Spain. Others would follow, and they are still fondly remembered by participants. Back home, there was a considerable emphasis on providing entertainment and hilarity to accompany good food and drink, and it was typical that the Friends sponsored a cook book as one of their fund-raisers. Activities ranged from Santa Lucia suppers in December, opening with the procession of a spectacular, candle-bedecked Lucia and her attendants, to a host of musical and other entertainments which memorably included an evening with Donald Sinden, a concert by the London Welsh Male Voice Choir, a Noel Coward evening with Michael Paine and several 'spaghetti operas'. On a more practical level the Friends paid for a new guidebook to the church, sponsored new external notice boards and new entry doors, and made financial contributions to support the St Mary's Centre.

The same spirit of hospitality was echoed in the **Tuesday Teas** organised from 1994 by Mary Cooper, aimed especially at the elderly and isolated, which also included musical entertainments. From 2008 work of that kind was taken up by Christine Brace with a weekly drop-in **Primrose Hill Tea Room**, which with the help of Linda Dean staged each summer a one-day 'Holiday at Home', bringing something of the ambience of seaside entertainment to those unable to travel.

Shortly after the Coopers retired from both the Friends and the Tuesday Teas in 2008, the Friends were mothballed. They were revived and reconstituted in 2012-13 with a wider remit to support the church's social outreach, and became for while the umbrella organisation under which most of the church's fund-raising activities (including for a while the Primrose Hill Lectures)[18] were carried out. Subsequently, in a simplification of governance and accounts, the Friends again went into abeyance, prior to being formally wound-up. Fund-raising is now sponsored directly, either by the parish or the St Mary's Community Centre Trust.

Mission, Fair Trade and Ecology

The concern for the wider world that had led to solid financial support for the mission field even throughout the parish's straitened financial times of the 1930s and 1940s, became focussed in the 1950s in a Missionary Committee of the PCC which, for example, organised two exhibitions for the sale of work by local artists to raise money for USPG.[19]

Right up to the 1980s matters such as Fair Trade and environmental issues had a lower profile at St Mary's than missionary activity (broadly defined). From the 1970s a new Overseas Committee took on the mantle of previous Missionary Committees, seeking to raise funds in support of the work of charities providing overseas aid, although not exclusively with the purpose of mission. Separately, there were parish representatives for the Children's Society and Christian Aid, each of which was the subject of an annual appeal. From the 1980s, Ruth Kitching as Chair expanded the Overseas Committee's remit to promote Fair Trade in the congregation, and in 2005 the committee changed its name to the Justice and Peace Committee. Through donations for the refreshments served after the Sunday Sung Eucharist, the Committee continued to support the work of designated charities including CMS and USPG. For a time the parish also gave one week's cash collection per month to a charity, from a rota drawn up by the Committee. The Committee also began to focus the congregation's minds on greater commitment to issues of international peace and justice. One World Week was marked annually, with special preachers. Regular Traidcraft stalls were held in church, and also at the annual Designer Fairs, to raise awareness, and in 2007 the PCC agreed to declare St Mary's a Fair Trade parish, which committed it to using only fairly-traded supplies. Through ALMA, the Diocese of London's link with Angola and Mozambique, St Mary's came to be twinned with the parish of St Peter's, Cazenga, Luanda, Angola.

On environmental issues – which have recently been the subject of various campaigns and initiatives by the national church and the dioceses – St Mary's efforts have thus far been patchy and sporadic, and have depended very largely on the enthusiasm of individuals. One highlight was the work of Oliver Smith (a lay member of the congregation), and Tamsin Omond (parish administrator) during the vacancy of 1998, to raise awareness of 'Creation in Crisis' through a ten-day festival of talks and services, one of which was addressed by the Bishop of London.[20]

Momentum was not sustained when those two active promoters moved on from the parish, although an environmental audit was conducted in 2005. A decade later, however, the urgency of the need for action on climate change and environmental degradation had become impossible to ignore, and in an effort to reduce its own impact on the planet's resources and to work towards 'carbon neutrality' the PCC in 2018 developed a scheme to mount solar panels on the church's south-facing roof.

This encountered some opposition from the local Council at the planning stage, but was carried forward into the 2022 capital project. Meanwhile in 2019-20 Karen Hoffa, another lay member of the congregation, facilitated fresh thinking on how the church might 'green' itself. This initiative was paused because of the prolonged shutdown occasioned by the coronavirus epidemic.

For examples of other lay-led activities, see also:
St Mary's Brewery (p.260). Music (ch.15). Children (p.281). St Mary's Centre (p.339). Cold Weather Shelter (p.342). Art, music and the spoken word (p.344).

Appendix to Chapter 16

Echo by Tom Copeland
A poem written to celebrate the installation of the church's first sound system.

> To Manning, architect of yore,
> Acoustics were an awful bore;
> Thus he designed our church, I fear,
> So we could see but could not hear.
>
> From barrel roof to polished floor
> The echoes rang three times or more,
> So much that Satan with a sneer
> Cried, "Goody, none of them can hear!"
>
> The priests, who thought out what to say
> From pulpit every Holy Day,
> Knew fully well their words so clear
> Would echo so no one could hear.
>
> Each service could have been in Latin
> For all the people who now sat in
> This church so fine and so austere,
> Because they really didn't hear.
>
> The magic man, working alone,
> With wires and hidden microphone
> Fixed things so well, and not too dear,
> So that at last we all could hear.

Traditionalists, in mighty huff,
Moaned, "Take away this modern stuff!"
But others, with a rousing cheer,
Cried, "We have ears and we can hear."

Parish Magazine, June 1981.

Endnotes

1. Especially the Revised Standard, and later the New Revised Standard versions.
2. The separately funded St Mary's Centre through the SMCCT had secured more stable funding after some years in which there was sufficient income at one moment to sustain a dozen workers but only one at the next.
3. The third minister at the High Mass
4. A letter along the same lines from Violet Tatham to Francis Stephens survives in the Archives.
5. LMA: P81/MRV/145, PCC Minutes May 1953.
6. Archives: Supplement to VH King's Parish Chronicle.
7. PM, May 1984, p.9.
8. LMA: P81/MRV/97.
9. The building's fabric constantly needs maintenance, which can be very expensive, often at short notice.
10. PM, Mar 1994.
11. Paula Greenley, PM, Jun, Oct 1993.
12. *The London Churchman,* Apr 1960, p.12. I am grateful to Janet Cowen for this reference.
13. LMA: P81/MRV/145, Jul 1952.
14. When the garden wall had been rebuilt, with its gate on to Primrose Hill, the guests were sometimes allowed to spread out on to the Hill.
15. She had retired in 1949 as National General Secretary of the YWCA and had become among other things vice-chairman of the British Council for Aid to Refugees.
16. Recalled by John Ashby.
17. Prospectuses for most seasons of Music at St Mary's and programmes for many of the Singing Competitions survive in the Archives.
18. PM, Oct-Nov 2013.
19. Information from Andrew St John.
20. PM, Apr-May 2008 and brochure in Archives.

Chapter 17

Serving the community

Understanding the parish and its needs

Getting to know the community served by the church is one of the most fundamental tasks of a parish priest. It has been carried out at St Mary's in a variety of ways, including literally walking the parish; door-to-door visiting; networking (identifying and using contacts within the church and the wider community); inviting people to church events, or ensuring a church presence at community events; arranging activities and publicity to bring the church to the people, and vice-versa; and simply being there as a source of comfort, advice and practical support in an emergency, as well as keeping the church freely open and available as a place for reflection and prayer. Building up such links on the one hand puts the church in a better place to know and address the community's needs: and on the other hand earns friends when the boot is on the other foot and the church itself needs support, as it has found in the present generation with the work of the St Mary's Centre.

Something of this theme has already been considered in the previous chapters of Part Two, in particular:

- The outreach of the Stewardship Campaigns to a wider constituency than the church (ch. 16)
- The pioneering work in the community by Sister Geraldine

under George Timms, and of Sister Judith under Richard Buck (ch. 10)
- The development and extension of the church building to make it better suited to the service of the community, under John Ovenden, Robert Atwell and Marjorie Brown (ch. 11)
- Outreach activities such as the Friends of St Mary's (ch. 16)

The changing physical face of the parish (1950s-80s)

We saw in Part One that when George Timms arrived at St Mary's in 1952 Primrose Hill Court, built on the site of the V1 rocket attack of 1944, had just been officially opened. That was to be only the beginning of a huge wave of new housing development in the parish that would continue over the next two decades. It was not at first clear what the implications of all this might be for the church, and on top of those changes St Mary's found itself having to adjust to the merger of the parish with St Paul's Avenue Road (see ch. 11). By 1963 Timms would tell the Annual Parish Meeting that 'the vast redevelopment plan which over-hung the parish made the future most uncertain and he could not feel that a proper sense of social responsibility was being shown by those who proposed to dispossess people of their homes in favour of blocks of luxury flats'.[1]

At the end of his time as vicar, firm proposals were on the drawing board for five new tower blocks along Adelaide Road, designed by Dennis Lennon as part of the Chalcots redevelopment,[2] (four of 23 storeys each on the north side – Taplow, Burnham, Dorney and Bray; and one of 19 storeys on the south – Blashford), but it would not be until Howard Hollis's time that planning permission was given for these (1965-6) and building proceeded (1967-68). Presumably to avoid the risks of subsidence (which had caused the church itself such trouble in the 1870s), all five blocks were built well clear of the railway line and the Primrose Hill tunnels. The vagaries of parish boundaries meant that whilst Taplow and Burnham were within St Mary's parish, the others were not, including Blashford, the one closest to the church. Even so, Howard Hollis liaised with the local authority in order to be able to offer such pastoral oversight as required to all the new residents.

High-rise development of any kind was wholly new to the area and would significantly change its physical aspect, as indeed would some of the subsequent low-rise developments that replaced the large old houses opposite the church on the north side of King Henry's Road. Some residents from the tower blocks did come to St Mary's. The church's ministry was extended to them on an individual basis, but systematic door-to-door visiting was not the norm in this new environment, where the residents included people of other faiths, and of none. That did not prevent the clergy having feelings of guilt about the situation. At the end of his ministry at St Mary's in 1984, for example, Richard Buck expressed remorse over the 'stubborn testimony of the tower blocks, reminding us that we remain basically a small, middle-class club which has made little or no impact on the vast number of people who live within our parish borders.'[3] That remains the situation today, but it does not engender the same pangs of guilt because much that has happened in our own generation convincingly shows the way in which St Mary's is recognised as a presence at the heart of the local community. Indeed, outreach to that community in ways quite other than door-to-door evangelisation – as a source of prayer, counsel, support and practical help – has driven much of the development at St Mary's in the past half century and more, as the story that follows illustrates.

The steady process of converting many of the large semi-detached houses of King Henry's Road and Elsworthy Road into multiple occupancy as flats or bed-sits, which even Dearmer had recorded, had mostly been completed by the 1950s. As plans then emerged to replace them with low-rise town-houses (Quickswood and the adjacent streets) or, in the case of Elsworthy Road, new premises for St Paul's School, and with the new Meadowbank complex on and behind Primrose Hill Road also looming, Howard Hollis began to share Timms's gloom that much of his parish was being demolished before his eyes. He could only sit tight, await completion of all the rebuilding[4] and prepare to encourage a new generation of residents to regard St Mary's as their spiritual home. A stark reminder of the emptiness of the area as demolitions took place is a 1966 photograph showing the north side of the church across a vacant building lot in King Henry's Road.[5]

Other crises (1970s-80s)

The early 1970s were challenging for other reasons. Andrew St John (curate 1973-75) recalls, for example, the IRA bombing campaign, which included several local attacks on his first Christmas Eve in 1973:

> The booms were too close for comfort. I remember walking to Midnight Mass in the freezing cold with the sounds of sirens wailing. The church was packed and the atmosphere electric. Somehow the message of Peace on Earth and Goodwill among Men sounded more relevant than ever.

As if that were not bad enough, there then followed the 1974 oil crisis and the three-day week, when heating in both church and vicarage was turned down to 55F.[6]

Jeff Heskins offers a useful reminder of chilling events in the wider world in his time, as curate, in the following decade (1981-85):

> The spirit of a social gospel and practical care was still there in a wider social climate that was to see the likes of the miners' strike and the Falklands conflict. The latter had a personal poignancy for older members of the congregation as the first Harrier pilot to be shot down and killed in that engagement [Nicholas Taylor] had formerly been a chorister in St Mary's choir – a young lad whom many of them still remembered.

* * *

It is not possible to describe every outreach activity in the church's recent history, but the following snapshots seem appropriate:

Visiting and outreach[7]

It must be admitted that most visiting throughout this period, other than that to the care homes in the parish, has been focussed on members of the congregation or those people from the wider community whose needs have been particularly commended to the clergy. Having assistant curates enabled both George Timms and Howard Hollis to visit parishioners on a scale that had not been practicable for decades. Martin Draper recalls for example that, under Hollis, in a week after a major festival there might be as many as 40 home communions. The curates' duties, as well as liturgical and pastoral, at that time included a hand in the youth work, and some teaching at St Paul's School. But their remit also extended beyond the immediate congregation to, for example The Hall school (for a while) and to the growing number of retirement homes in the parish; and they served as chaplains to the Central School of Speech and Drama, the Marie Curie hospice at Eden Hall (until its temporary closure for redevelopment), and even to a local hotel.

A serious effort was also made in Howard Hollis's time, some of it lay-led, to address the needs of new residents of the parish who had arrived as a result of the housing development. A parish day conference held at the Royal Foundation of St Katharine, Stepney, in 1971, led to a ferment of ideas too great for all to be implemented at once, but among them were proposals to set up meetings with the tenants' associations of the new blocks; to make particularly the 9.45 service more relaxed and friendly so as to attract first-time worshippers (crèche, more popular music, intercessions led by lay people, communion received standing up, periods of silence …); and to start a parish office.[8] Little, however, seems to have come of these plans in the immediate future.

John Ovenden quickly made friends and allies in the local community and the church school, and encouraged even non church-goers and those of other faiths to regard St Mary's as their parish church, and when appropriate to seek its pastoral care (for example in the case of the parish's retirement homes which have no particular religious affiliation). 'We set forth together on an exciting journey,' he writes, 'in a spirit of outreach and adventure ... and in faith in the community at large.'

Listening Post (1980s-90s)
In the wake of the report *Faith in the City* (1987) the Bishop asked all churches to undertake a 'parish audit' and become more aware of neediness both within congregations and in the communities around them.[9] This was taken up in a parish day conference that year,[10] and in a sense also by the establishment of The Listening Post, a new project of Lyndon van der Pump[11] after his ordination, which aimed to have trained volunteer counsellors on hand in the church, and at the same time help to keep the building open. It continued, albeit scaled down, for some eight years, and was then for a short spell replaced by one-to-one discussions with those who doubted or challenged the faith, but in both cases the take-up was disappointing, essentially owing to the lack of passers-by calling in at the church and becoming aware of this service.[12]

Pastoral networking (1990s-present)
In 1993, as part of a wider push for evangelisation, the Bishop of London issued an Agenda for Action. The PCC, through its Mission sub Committee, conducted a survey of the networks of visiting and contact by members of the congregation, and tentatively began to coordinate pastoral visiting. This was later developed (under Pauline Collett and others) into a **Pastoral Network** involving both clergy and laity. From 2009, on the initiative of Ronnie Fuller, the indefatigable and long-serving churchwarden, the work became for a time more formalised in a **Befrienders**' Group which kept a pastoral eye on elderly and isolated members of the congregation. That highly structured approach has since been modified with several new initiatives. A **Thursday tearoom**, open to all, but aimed particularly at the elderly and those who live alone, is followed by a eucharist with **healing ministry**. Periodic **Death Cafés** have been held to raise awareness of and readiness for death. And in

2017-18 the parish collaborated with Citizens UK and the University of Middlesex in a research project to raise awareness of **mental health issues**.

Relations with St Paul's school (1950s-present)

St Mary's has always taken seriously its connection with St Paul's school. Successive vicars (and many of the curates too) have played a major role there, ranging from assisting with religious instruction to matters of school governance. Four vicars in a row in this period had direct school or teaching connections. George Timms had been a diocesan inspector of schools. Howard Hollis and Richard Buck had both been school chaplains in their previous ministry, and John Ovenden a former teacher. St Mary's has always been directly represented on the governing body of St Paul's. Robert Atwell became chair of its governors, and Marjorie Brown remains on the governing body.

From the school's arrival in Elsworthy Road in the 1970s the church has always welcomed into the worshipping community young families whose children attend or hope to attend the school. Both John Ovenden and Robert Atwell made it part of their mission to shape school worship in such a way that the children were at ease with, and could find their way around, the pattern of the eucharistic liturgy. Under Robert Atwell in particular, school services were arranged more frequently in the church, a tradition that continues today.

St Mary's Centre: Youth work (2000s-present)[13] [Plate 7]

When Robert Atwell arrived as vicar he was given a specific brief by the PCC to build stronger relations with the local community.

The most pressing priority lay in the field of youth work, where concern extended well beyond the congregation's own children. Deep cuts to national and local government youth services in the 2000s had caused the closure of hundreds of youth clubs across London. It quickly became clear that any action on a scale proportionate to the challenges was going to require both significant extra annual funding and an altogether more professional approach to personnel and plant. The story is intimately interwoven with the Blueprint Appeal and the creation of the St Mary's Centre with its Community Trust (SMCCT, a charity set up to obtain external grants as well as receive donations from the parish and friends), to provide premises and a funding-stream to sustain these activities (see p.). The SMCCT's initial funding included generous grants from Camden Council Neighbourhood Regeneration Fund as well as from John Lyons, Henry Smith, the Rank Foundation and other charitable, as well as individual, donors.

Revd Robert Atwell

As a direct result of Blueprint, the church appointed its first paid youth co-ordinator, Paul Perkins, in 2004. He oversaw activities for the limited number of young people from the church itself. But importantly – and here he was at times ahead of both the congregation and the PCC – he also had the vision to look beyond the church and lay the foundations of a more socially aware youth support service, for the marginalised young people in the area. This included a 'Social Inclusion' Project, focussed initially on typical youth-club activities such as sports and games, adventure weekends and outings. But outreach was also rapidly extended through the Eirini Project (2006) under Jason Allen, to give hope and affirmation to those young people in the wider community who were at risk from gang violence and knife crime, or who were socially excluded for whatever reason. A separate Young Women's Project with its own co-ordinators, Anna Goalby and Jo Golding, was also launched. Paul Perkins was succeeded first by Yejide Igwe and then by Jason Allen, whose previous experience in the youth work programme and striking ability to engage with young people in order to understand where further action could be helpful, made him a visionary manager.

Part of Marjorie Brown's remit from the PCC was to encourage the congregation to 'own' this important outreach activity, of which at the time many were still unaware. Much effort was therefore put into demonstrating the good work that was being done, and church members gradually came to understand the range and quality of the youth work service, which at the time of writing is proving more necessary than ever and is now widely known and valued beyond the church. Staff and volunteers are potentially on call at any hour of the day or night, and every day of the year (including Christmas Day), to respond to crises involving street violence and knife crime. At the request of local head teachers, youth workers from the Centre are paid to mentor pupils at risk, and can be available at the school gates to defuse tension. Probation officers seek their help in mentoring young offenders, both in prison and after release.[14] Jason Allen has participated in high level discussions with, among others, the Bishop of London and the police. 'Listen to Jason,' the Metropolitan Police Commissioner Dame Cressida Dick once remarked, 'He knows how to solve youth crime'. In April 2018 St Mary's, working with Citizens UK, hosted[15] a Citizens' Assembly to bring together local politicians, faith leaders and representatives of the police to discuss safety on the streets. This resulted in the establishment of a Camden and Islington Commission on Safety, chaired by the Bishop of Edmonton.

There is another whole side to the youth work: it has helped hundreds of at-risk young people aged between 6 and 18 with mentoring and assistance in accessing work or educational opportunities, providing them with a chance to fulfil their creative and intellectual potential. As Nick Walters put it: 'the presence of SMCCT in St Mary's speaks louder than a hundred sermons.'

At first, youth work was entirely financially self-sufficient, but in recent times the congregation has sometimes been a 'funder of last resort', responding to appeals for financial help. This was never more necessary than in 2013-14 when a number of the initial grants were coming to an end; indeed, funding was so precarious that for a time it even began to seem likely that the Youthwork Manager would have to be made redundant. The congregation's urgent response in that crisis raised enough money to ensure the programme's continuance for the short-term but that kind of hand-to-mouth existence was clearly unsatisfactory. Alongside the parish's direct help, fund-raising efforts continued, and attracted generous support both from individuals and charitable foundations including the Ex-Pat Trust. Meanwhile, Xandra Bingley came forward as a local champion, tirelessly and successfully building up local support and funding. Articles in the local and national press drew attention to the Centre's work and attracted both funding and practical support. By 2017, SMCCT had several years' guaranteed funding, a revivified Board of Trustees, and a new Patron, the broadcaster and local resident, Andrew Marr. The way in which the urgency of the challenge has struck home is reflected in the number of local people not otherwise connected with the church who have come forward as volunteers to help with the Centre and its running. Jason Allen, the Youthwork Manager, was awarded the British Empire Medal in the New Year Honours 2021. Since January 2021 the SMCCT has become the legal employer and overseer for the youth and community work. Led by Mary-Jane Fishwick as (*pro bono*) CEO, it is semi-independent of the church. There is a new SMC Management Team, made up primarily of local volunteers, replacing the earlier Youthwork Committee. Liaison with the congregation continues, with regular reports from Jason Allen and others. As this book was going to press news was received of a magnificent £200,000 grant from the National Lottery to secure funding for the next three years.

Supporting the homeless: The Cold Weather Shelter (2005-present)

The Camden Christian Churches Cold Weather Shelter (C4WS)[16] took in its first guests in January 2005. At that time St Mary's lacked the facilities to participate in the scheme, but the additional space provided by the St Mary's Centre, together with new WC and shower facilities, finally made this possible. From 2011[17] St Mary's has taken its place in a rota of local churches, each opening on one night a week during the winter months, to provide (in St Mary's case) up to 15 homeless people with a hot dinner, company, a hot shower, a bed for the night in a warm environment, and breakfast. This service to the community is lay-led. A large part of the organisation of food and volunteers falls to the Parish Administrator (Celyn Cooke), but to make the scheme a success a small army of volunteers is required: to greet and mix with the guests; prepare and serve the food at dinner and breakfast; and in a few cases to sleep overnight in the church and be on hand in case of any emergency (which, thankfully, has been very infrequent).

Responding to crises today

The Church is clearly not the only, and often not the first, agency that can or should address the crises that befall our communities. But, either on its own or in conjunction with central and local government and the voluntary sector, it can have an important role to play, which may begin simply by standing alongside those in need and expressing support and solidarity, and when possible intervening on their behalf.

Three recent examples illustrate St Mary's response to societal needs. In 2013, after the Archbishop of Canterbury, Justin Welby, had publicly condemned the practice of **pay-day loans** at ruinous rates of interest, representatives of the parish joined London Citizens in promoting Credit Unions as an alternative, community-based solution.[18] Secondly, following the Grenfell Tower fire of 2017 in North Kensington, in which over 70 people lost their lives, when the **tower blocks** in Adelaide Road were also found to have suspect (though different) cladding and Camden Council required the residents to leave at short notice for their own safety, St Mary's for a while became a point of refuge and counselling. Thirdly, during the **coronavirus pandemic** of 2020-21, at least for those periods when government regulations allowed it, the church remained open for private prayer and support.

Art, music and the spoken word (1950s-present)

St Mary's as a venue

Art, music and the spoken word have been regularly harnessed, on the one hand to bring people into St Mary's, and on the other to put the church space at the service of the community. Since the principal doors of St Mary's are on two quiet suburban streets, with comparatively few passers-by, the number of people casually dropping in outside service times, or noticing forthcoming events advertised there, has always been quite limited. When it comes to events in the church aimed at a wider public, such as art exhibitions, concerts or lectures, organisers have had to work hard on publicity to attract an audience from outside the congregation. To some extent these constraints have been eased in recent years as the church has been put more surely on the map as a venue, through crowd-pulling events such as the Designer Fairs and the Primrose Hill Lectures. These have shown that people will turn out, and even travel appreciable distances, if they are sufficiently attracted by a name or a topic. Even so, it can be hard – especially in a city as culturally rich as London – to attract an audience for performers whose names are not yet in the public eye, even if their talent is second to none.

It is therefore only right to recall in passing the many musical and other performances that have been given in St Mary's to discriminating and highly appreciative audiences. The Camden Choir and the Camden Chamber Choir have both given many memorable performances. Fundraising concerts in John Ovenden's time included one conducted before a packed house by Sir Georg Solti (who lived in Elsworthy Road), where every seat was priced at no more than £5 at Solti's insistence.[19] Among other events were concerts with, respectively, Sir Charles Groves and Dennis O'Neill tenor; a memorial concert for Solti conducted by Sir

Charles Mackerras, and a performance of *Messiah* with Anthony Rolfe Johnston as soloist and conductor.[20]

Two recent concerts deserve special mention. In 2014 Charlotte Way presented a piano recital in memory of her great-grandfather, TR Way, the lithographer in whose memory the Rood is dedicated, while some of his images of London in the late 1800s based on prints by JM Whistler were shown. In 2016 the Medici Quartet gave a recital in memory of Malcolm Craddock, churchwarden 2010-14, who died in 2015.

Music at St Mary's, see ch. 16

Drama

Drama and the spoken word, which had played such an important part in the social and cultural life of St Mary's in the early decades of the twentieth century, had become a casualty of the Second World War. The Primrose Hill Players put on what looked like being their last performance in 1944, although there were occasional performances from visiting thespians, such as the New Pilgrim Players' *The Holy Family* in 1955.

In 1962, however, a re-christened 'Drama Group' was revived by Helen Lowry (family name Stutfield), a member of the congregation who after a short stage career had become a professional stage manager, and a teacher at the Webber Douglas Academy. She had been largely drawn into the theatre as an admirer of the work of E Martin Browne who was also a member of the St Mary's congregation. During the last years of the Church Room's existence in the early 1960s, rehearsals and performances sometimes had to be transferred to the church itself for want of available booking times for the Room. After its closure there was for a time little alternative to mounting plays as well as rehearsals in the church itself. At that time however, unlike the position today, these activities were subject to national and diocesan regulations. At least in principle – it is not recorded whether this happened at St Mary's – the script of every play to be performed in a church in the London diocese had to be approved by the Bishop and/or his advisers which for a period from 1959 included the Religious Drama Society. In the case of plays for which an entry charge was made or for which advertisements were issued to attract a public wider than the congregation, not only were play-scripts subject to the same kind of licensing by the Lord Chamberlain as in theatres, but the church itself had to be licensed as a venue approved for such events. Only if performances were simply for the congregation and a few invited guests could they be passed off as 'private' and therefore not subject to the regulations. Vicars and producers understandably had to tread rather carefully to avoid breaking the law.[21] Howard Hollis sought to maintain due reverence in church by blessing the beginning of each rehearsal, although the opening of St Paul's school in Elsworthy Road in 1972 meant that plays of a more secular nature, as well as pantomime offerings at Epiphany, could be performed in the school hall.

The first production by Lowry's revived Drama Group was a one-act play, *The Camp*, the story of the Nativity set in a camp for displaced persons. It was produced by one of the curates, John Crane. In 1963 (and again a decade later) she famously directed Christopher Fry's *The Boy with the Cart*, the legend of St Cuthman. Over the next two decades she would go on to organise and direct many other productions, including Philip Turner's *Christ in the Concrete City* (1968), Dorothy Sayers's *Zeal of Thy House* (1972), and JB Priestley's *When we are married* (1973). Perhaps the most ambitious production was Menotti's one-act opera *Amahl and the Night Visitors* (Epiphany 1974).[22] For the Group's rendering of *Peer Gynt* (1978), the title role was taken by the curate, Martin Draper, whose 'athletic performance,' if Geoffrey Dearmer's sympathetic review may be taken at face value, had 'more than a welcome touch of the ballet'.[23]

Helen Lowry persuaded Martin Browne himself to direct several of the Group's plays. Among his early offerings were *The Green Wood*, *The House by the Stable*, and *Grab and Grace*. As part of the parish celebrations for Dearmer's centenary in 1967 Browne brought to St Mary's a professional production of *Three Music Dramas* which had first been performed under his direction at the York Festival the previous year and would later move on to Winchester and St Paul's cathedrals. These were religious plays with Latin words set to music in the Middle Ages: *Planctus Mariae* (Mary's Lament), *Visitatio Sepulchri* (The Visit to the Tomb) and *Peregrinus* (The Pilgrim). They were performed not by the resident drama group but by an ad hoc professional group under the direction of Roy Jesson. To encourage understanding and broaden the appeal of this distinctly esoteric enterprise, Browne gave an introductory talk to the congregation a week before the performance, but Geoffrey Dearmer (Percy's son) was surely not alone in relying heavily on the English translation provided! He wrote afterwards that he could imagine no greater tribute to the memory of his father, and of Martin and Geoffrey Shaw, who were being commemorated at the same event. Another commentator said that 'every movement was considered with a poet's economy and the grouping reminded one of medieval pictures in the National Gallery.' When Martin Browne's wife, the actress Henzie Raeburn, died in 1973, guests at the memorial service held in St Mary's included Judi Dench, who read a John Donne poem, and (in a wheelchair) Dame Sybil Thorndike.

Although an amateur drama group's performances could never approach the professional standards to which Helen Lowry aspired, its worthy efforts attracted encouraging and good-natured reviews in the parish magazine from the likes of Martin Browne and Geoffrey Dearmer. In addition to full-length plays the group often gave shorter presentations at the Patronal Festival and on other festive occasions, as well as at the traditional Epiphany party. Their productions, together with play-readings such as TS Eliot's *Murder in the Cathedral*, attracted a core of regular as well as many *ad hoc* participants of all ages from the congregation, not to mention a large team of volunteers for stage-management, lighting, costumes, front-of-house duties and publicity. Lowry never missed an opportunity to size-up a talented newcomer to the congregation (even professional actors like Peter Symonds) with an eye to a future dramatic or supporting role. She was particularly gifted at involving and coaching children, but undeniably had a certain way with adults too. One member of the Group later recalled that 'Helen took everyone regardless of experience and drew out skills we did not know we had.'[24]

Scenery and props were made in-house, designed by Francis Stephens (and some by the theatre designer Michael Heard), and built by Stanley Taylor with ingenious improvisation, as when a barrel was used as a substitute for a bath in *The Caucasian Chalk Circle*. Participants included in their turn most of the curates, pretty well as part of their job description, particularly when it came to pantomimes. All enjoyed the diversion and camaraderie. Overall it can be said that the Drama Group was unquestionably a force for good not only among its members but in the parish at large.

The annual half-hour pantomime at the Epiphany Party continued to draw in not only the Group's regular members but almost all the clergy, as well as press-ganged members of the congregation, and few were deemed exempt. A 'script' of sorts would be provided by Lowry and/or one of the curates, but as there was rarely more than one rehearsal the audience delighted in cheering-on players who ad-libbed, fluffed their lines, or (as in the case of Francis Stephens) had them pencilled on the back of their shirt cuffs. Martin Draper remembers particularly:

> the cast of *very* senior ladies who happily donned short skirts and tights to play the robins who covered up the kidnapped children with leaves in *Babes in St John's Wood*, and the fact that it was the cheap brass censer, rather than the beautiful silver one that turned out to be the miraculous one in *Aladdin and the Magic Thurible*.

By 1980 many of the Drama Group's stalwarts had become distinctly long in the tooth and, albeit with sadness, the decision was taken to wind it up.[25]

Regular drama thus came to an end at St Mary's, although the Epiphany party continued for some years, metamorphosing into something more like a 'smoking' concert. In John Ovenden's time Julia Smith arranged a number of Jane Austen readings. More recently, Judy Greengrass revived the pantomime tradition, and again involved many members of the congregation, with *Heaven Has a Humour* (2012) and

The Three Kings in Camden (an alternative take on the Journey of the Magi) (2016). On a more sombre level, in 1999 Peter Symonds brought to St Mary's a professional production of Stephen Macdonald's play *Not about Heroes* (about the friendship of Wilfred Owen and Siegfried Sassoon). In 2014 and again in 2018, to mark the centenary respectively of the beginning and end of the First World War, he devised and presented two different editions of *The Poetry and the Pity* drawing on the works of the war poets. In a lighter vein laughter, as well as eyebrows, have been raised by productions of two skits devised by Lyndon van der Pump on the theme of women priests and the opposition to them, in *The Bishado* (2003)[26] and *The Witches of Widdershire*.

Art

Part One made many references to the work of rated artists and craftsmen, commissioned or purchased for the adornment of St Mary's. Not a few artists have lived and/or had workshops locally. Some, like Clement Skilbeck and Violet Blaiklock in the 1920s, or more recently the book illustrator Dorothy Ralphs (d.2006), were long-standing members of the congregation. So it is perhaps not surprising that from time to time art exhibitions have been organised in the church, to promote the work of local artists and at the same time raise funds for church objectives. An art exhibition was held in June 1982, in aid of the deprived children of an African township at Elsie's River, Cape Town. An Arts and Community festival in 1986 ("Midsummer at St Mary's") included an art exhibition with works by, among others, the eminent photographer David Bailey, Hans Feibusch, David Gentleman, Paul Hogarth RA and Philippa Jacobs. The idea was reprised by popular demand in 1990, and a one-man show of David Bailey's work was also held about the same time. Another art exhibition was staged in 2004 in connection with the Blueprint Appeal, and in 2010 Patrice Moor, a member of the congregation, displayed an arresting series of studies in oil of a skull, as a Passiontide exhibition entitled 'Stations of the Cross'.[27] A further exhibition was held in 2021 as part of the 'Grow the Wonder' appeal for the church's 150th anniversary.

Primrose Hill Lectures

The Primrose Hill Lectures, launched by Robert Atwell in 2006, continue to this day, highlighting the Church's engagement with the big issues of the day and putting St Mary's at the heart of a community much larger than the worshipping congregation.

The series was conceived as a means of drawing out a Christian perspective of 'the hope that is in us' and a sense of vision for the future; and whilst the Lectures have never shirked these and other great moral issues, their scope has been gradually widened in order to continue their appeal to an ever growing and diverse audience. No mere list of the topics covered can do full justice to the way in which they have raised awareness and stimulated discussion on the great (and shifting) spectrum of issues and concerns in our national and community life. But, after more than fifteen years of these annual summer events it is worth pausing to consider the broad range of topics covered. They have included: truth and justice; liberty and democracy; poverty and the plight of refugees; fair trade and the equitable use of money and resources; human rights and women's rights; care for the environment; national and international politics and history; war, peace and reconciliation; religion, faith and doubt; the family, medicine, ageing and dementia; broadcasting and the arts; literature and music; science and philosophy; and even – on the lighter side – food and drink.

Distinguished authors and speakers have addressed these topics in front of large audiences. From the beginning, income from ticket sales, refreshments and the sale of books (in partnership with Primrose Hill Books) has helped the parish's support for the work of St Mary's Centre, and with this charitable objective in mind, speakers and interviewers have given their services *gratis*.

The series has gone from strength to strength, and has attracted a devoted following including many non-church-goers. The original format (formal lecture followed by questions from the audience), has sometimes been varied to allow for interviews and unscripted presentations. Audio recordings had been made available since 2015, but when the pandemic of 2020 caused the live lecture series to be abandoned, the organisers embarked on a whole new approach through on-line streaming.

Although this meant that the valuable social interaction of the live talks (where attendees could bring guests, meet the speaker and discuss the lecture informally over refreshments afterwards) had to be forgone, the new approach made the lectures available to a wider audience.

Endnotes

1. LMA: P81/MRV/97.
2. Camden History Society, *Streets of Belsize* (2009), p.32.
3. PM, Oct 1984.
4. For a more detailed account of the building developments see *VCH Middlesex* (available at British History Online).
5. Historic England File 3007 no 142 (Camden Churches, St Mary the Virgin). There have, of course, been many further building developments since the 1970s, but nothing on the scale of the 1960s and 70s, and on the whole their impact on the parish has been much less than the changes just described.
6. This context would not be evident to someone studying only the parish archives or magazine.
7. The work of Sister Judith under Richard Buck is separately described in ch 10.
8. LMA: P81/MRV/98, PCC Minutes 22 June 1971.
9. Periodic reports and analysis were given in PM, eg Jun 1987.
10. Report in PM, Jan 1988.
11. See PM, Nov 1996.
12. After his retirement from St Mary's Lyndon van der Pump continued his ministry as a spiritual director in the City and privately.
13. See Roger Carter in PM, Feb-Mar 2013, Simon James in PM Oct-Nov 2017, and annual reports to the APCM.
14. For further detail see, for example, Xandra Bingley, 'Keep St Mary's Youth Club open', in *On the Hill*, April 2018, pp.8-9; Andrew Marr in the *Spectator*, 3 March 2018.
15. Through the good offices of St Mary's curate, Revd Nick Walters.
16. Website: www.c4wshomelessproject.org
17. Until the coronavirus pandemic intervened in 2020-21. See, for example, Celyn Cooke, 'Shelter from the storm', in PM, Feb-Apr 2018, pp 10-11.
18. A debt counselling service was also tentatively set up, but proved to be short-lived.
19. Information from John Ovenden.
20. Information from John Ovenden.
21. I am grateful to Janet Cowen for sharing her research on these regulations.
22. Andrew St John recalls: 'I was a singing, dancing shepherd alongside Francis Stephens and other parishioners. What fun we had.'
23. PM, Jul/Aug.
24. PM, Mar 1999.
25. Among its keen members had been Stanley and Sylvia Taylor, and Nicholas Kitchener (churchwarden from 1978 until his tragic death in 1981). Helen Lowry moved soon afterwards to Overstrand near Cromer where she died in 1999. For tributes to Helen Lowry, see PM, Feb-Mar 1999.
26. For a review by Peter Cooper, see PM, Apr 2003, pp.9-10
27. See 'Primrose Hill people. Hands and skulls – painting in Primrose Hill', in *On the Hill*, May 2017, pp. 4-5. The exhibit also toured to St John's College Cambridge and Worcester cathedral.

Envoi

From the building, and its angels:

> DOMINE DILEXI HABITATIONEM DOMUS TUAE
> *Lord, I have loved the habitation of thy house* (Psalm 26 verse 8).
> Inscribed in one of the memorial windows to Thomas Hill in the south aisle.

> GLORIA TIBI DOMINE/ QUI NATUS EST DE VIRGINE/ CUM PATRI ET SANCTO SPIRITU/ IN SEMPITERNA GLORIA
> *Glory to You, O Lord/ Born of a Virgin/ With the Father and the Holy Spirit/ For all ages.*
> On the scrolls carried by angels in the upper lights of the west windows.

From the people and their angel – comments from the congregation:

- St Mary's is a living witness, not just an institution.
- What St Mary's has given to me is incalculable. It is part of the framework of my life, woven into every day.
- I count myself fortunate to have lived in company with the church of St Mary the Virgin, Primrose Hill. A journey with an ever evolving and alive parish, that believes Christianity lives in the world as well as in church.
- The liberal theology of St Mary's made it not only a place where I felt comfortable, but somewhere that it would be possible to learn and exchange ideas.
- The sense of St Mary's as an exciting place to be, with a real sense of purpose and mission, has palpably increased. I believe the greater involvement and encouragement of the laity is in large part responsible for this.

From Percy Dearmer:

The fellowship of St Mary's will endure, and heaven and earth will always be met together within its walls.

Appendix

Episcopal oversight of the parish

Bishops of London

To 1885	John Jackson, previously Bp Lincoln
1885-1896	Frederick Temple, previously Bp Exeter, later Abp Canterbury
1897-1901	Mandell Creighton, previously Bp Peterborough. d. in office
1901-1939	Arthur Winnington-Ingram, previously Bp Stepney
1939-1945	Geoffrey Fisher, previously Bp Chester, later Abp Canterbury
1945-1955	William Wand, previously Bp Bath and Wells
1956-1961	Henry Montgomery-Campbell, previously Bp Guildford
1961-1973	Robert Stopford, previously Bp Peterborough
1973-1981	Gerald Ellison, previously Bp Chester
1981-1991	Graham Leonard, previously Bp Truro
1991-1995	David Hope, previously Bp Wakefield, later Abp York
1995-2017	Richard Chartres, previously Bp Stepney
2018-	Sarah Mullally, previously Bp Crediton

Suffragan bishops with oversight of St Mary's

The Deanery of Hampstead (later North Camden) was successively within the sees of Willesden (created 1911) and Edmonton (created 1970).

1888-[1900]	Alfred Earle, Bishop of Marlborough, an assistant bishop in the diocese of London (later Dean of Exeter)
1898-[1911]	Charles Turner, Bishop of Islington, with responsibility for North London
1911-1929	William Perrin, Bishop of Willesden
1929-1934	William Perrin, retired, but continued as an assistant bishop in London diocese, retained responsibility for Deanery of Hampstead
[1934]-1940	Guy Smith, Bishop of Willesden
1940-1942	Henry Montgomery-Campbell, Bishop of Willesden
1942-1950	Michael Gresford Jones, Bishop of Willesden
1950-1955	Gerald Ellison, Bishop of Willesden
1955-1964	George Ingle, Bishop of Willesden
1964-[1970]	Graham Leonard (Bishop of Willesden until 1973 but the new see of Edmonton was created in 1970)
1970-1974	Alan Rogers, Bishop of Edmonton
1975-1984	Bill Westwood (became first Area Bishop of Edmonton, 1979)
1985-1998	Brian Masters, Bishop of Edmonton
1997-1998	Episcopal oversight of St Mary's briefly transferred to Graham Dow, Bishop of Willesden
1999-2014	Peter Wheatley, Bishop of Edmonton
2015-	Rob Wickham, Bishop of Edmonton

Bibliography

Archival sources
[Individual references are cited in the footnotes].

Archives: The parish archives of St Mary the Virgin Primrose Hill are mostly deposited for safe keeping in London Metropolitan Archives under the reference P81/MRV. References simply to 'Archives' without an LMA citation were at the time of writing retained in the church. These include a chronicle of the parish begun by VH King and continued by JH Arnold.

BL: British Library: Martin Shaw archive [Music Library]. British Newspaper Archive.

Camden Local Studies and Archives Centre, Holborn Library: original material concerning St Mary's, St Paul's Avenue Road and the Boys' Home.

CERC: Church of England Record Centre: Files of the Ecclesiastical Commissioners and of the Central Council for the Care of Churches, consulted before their recent transfer to the new Lambeth Palace Library. The reference numbers cited may therefore be subject to change.

Islington Local History Library: Tender Books, 1869-77, of Messrs Dove Bros.

LMA: London Metropolitan Archives: Archives of the Diocese of London and its Registry, including Faculty Papers, diocesan files concerning St Mary's, and the parish's deposited archives. Papers of the Greater London Council.

LPL: Lambeth Palace Library, including Church Association archives; Fulham Papers: Jackson, Temple; Papers of Percy Dearmer; Incorporated Church Building Society files.

LSE: London School of Economics. Papers of the Booth survey of London poverty [online].

V&A: Victoria & Albert Museum: RIBA Architecture Archive: papers of Dove Bros.

* * *

Websites consulted are individually cited in the footnotes, but more specific information in their respective spheres may be available from:

St Mary's church: www.stmarysprimrosehill.com
Cold Weather Shelter: www.c4wshomelessproject.org

* * *

A selection of the published works consulted
[Limited to those works cited in the text or otherwise relevant to this study, and excluding many other works that have provided useful background]

Abbreviations used
BL   British Library
CT   *Church Times*
PM   St Mary's parish magazine [title varies with date]

Bibliography

Aitken, WF, *Frederick Temple, Archbishop of Canterbury* (1901).

Alcuin Club publications.

Allen, Hugh, *New Llanthony Abbey: Father Ignatius's Monastery at Capel-y-ffin* (2016).

Amsden, John, 'Eton College and the manor of Chalcots', in PM, Aug-Sep 2008, pp.18-20 and Dec-Jan 2008-09, pp.5-7.

Anson, Peter:
A Roving Recluse (1946).
Fashions in Church Furnishings 1840-1940 (1960).

Arnold, John, 'St Mary's – a focus on childhood', in PM, Jun-Jul 2005, p.15.

Arnold, JH, *Plainsong Accompaniment* (1927).

Ashby, John, 'Up-steps, down-steps', in PM, Jun-Jul 2009, p.20.

Atwell, Robert, 'The devil doesn't have all the best tunes…' in PM, Jun-Jul 2006, pp.5-6.

Beck, Gladys:
'A service bright and brief: the story of the Boys' Home, Regent's Park Road', in *Camden History Review*, 2, pp.4-6 (1974).
'Looking back', a series of articles on parish history in PM (late 1950s).

Best, Geoffrey, *Temporal Pillars* [online: Internet Archive].

Bingley, Xandra, 'Keep St Mary's youth club open', in *On the Hill*, Apr 2018, pp.8-9.

[Boy's Home, Euston Road]:
First Annual Report of the Committee of Management of the Boys' Home for the training and maintenance by their own labour of destitute boys not convicted of crime. [BL]
The Budget [Boys' Home paper. Only a single issue survives, in Camden Local Studies Library, for 28 Feb 1890]
www.childrenshomes.org.uk EustonBoysIS/?LMCL=ceHrB9.

Braithwaite, David, *Building in the Blood: the story of Dove Brothers of Islington 1781-1981* (1981).

The Builder, 1 Aug 1919. [Photograph of the rood and chancel].

Bumpus, TF, *London Churches Ancient and Modern* (n.d. c. 1903).

Burgess, JF, 'Plainchant champion' [on Francis Burgess], in PM, Dec 2019-Feb 2020, pp. 40-44.

Burns, Arthur, 'A national church tells its story: The English Church Pageant of 1909': [An address to the Church of England Record Society, July 2017].

Camden History Society:
Camden History Review.
From Primrose Hill to Euston Road (1995).
Streets of Belsize (2nd edn, 2009).

Campanella, Giuseppe Maria, *An Italian on Primrose Hill* (1875).

Carpenter, Edward, *Cantuar: the Archbishops in their Office* (1971).

Carpenter, SC, *Duncan-Jones of Chichester* (1956).

Carter, Roger, 'St Mary's youthwork', in PM, Feb-Mar 2013.

[Catechism]: *The Method of S.Sulpice for the organising of Catechisms* (translated into English 1896).
see also Jones

Chapple, Nick, 'Peter Anson, Pilgrim Artist', in *Ecclesiology Today*, 52 (Summer 2015) pp. 61-68.

Cheshire, Jim, *Stained Glass and the Victorian Gothic Revival* (Manchester 2004).

Cobbe, Hugh (ed), *Letters of Ralph Vaughan Williams 1895-1958* (Oxford [2008]).

Connock, Stephen and Montgomery-Campbell, Isobel (eds), *'The Greater Light' – A compendium of the life and works of Martin Shaw* (Albion Music, 2018).

Cooke, Celyn, 'Shelter from the storm', in PM, Feb-Apr 2018, pp 10-11.

Cox, Jeffrey, *The English Churches in a Secular Society: Lambeth 1870-1930* (1982).

Creighton, Louise (ed.): *Life and Letters of Mandell Creighton* (2 vols, 1904).

[Creighton, Mandell], *The Church and the Nation: charges and addresses* (1901).

Crockford's Clerical Directory [various dates, as cited].

Day, E Hermitage, *Some London Churches* (1911).

Dearmer, Geoffrey, 'Some memories', in PM, Oct 1970, and 'St Mary's Long Ago', in PM, Mar 1980 pp.12-14.

Dearmer, Mabel, *The Difficult Way* [c. 1905].

Dearmer, Nan, *The Life of Percy Dearmer* (1941).

Dearmer, Percy: *The Parson's Handbook* (1899 and subsequent editions). [Many other works are cited individually in the text and notes of ch. 4.]

Draper, Martin P, 'Percy Dearmer and the English Hymnal', in *Alcuin*: The Occasional Journal of the Alcuin Club (1980).

Duncan-Jones, AS:
Archbishop Laud (1927).
Church Music (1920).
Ordered Liberty, or An Englishman's belief in his Church (1917).
'The Art of Movement', in A Clutton Brock et al, *The Necessity of Art* (1924).

Duncan-Jones, AS, and Arnold, JH (ed), *A Liturgical Service for Good Friday*. [SPCK Church Music no 47] (nd, c. 1927).

Duncan-Jones, AS; Stephen Gaselee and EGP Wyatt, *A Directory of Anglican Ceremonial* (Alcuin Club XIII, 1921).

Dunlop, Colin:
Processions: a dissertation together with practical suggestions (Alcuin Club Tracts 20, 1932).
What is the English Use? (Alcuin Club pamphlet 11, 1923).

Dunlop, Francis [posthumous publication], *From London to Lincoln via Baghdad. The life of Bishop Colin Dunlop 1897-1968* (2019).

English Church Pageant 1909 handbook (1910). [online, Internet Archive].

English Heritage: *Victorian and Edwardian Stained Glass: the work of five London studios 1855-1910* (1987). [The first essay is on Clayton and Bell.]

Floud, Cynthia (ed), *A Dysfunctional Hampstead Childhood 1886-1911: the memoir of Phyllis Allen Floud, neé Ford* (Camden History Society 2018).

Floud, R. 'Pricing the past', in *History Today* 69/3 (March 2019).

Foster, Paul (ed), *Chichester Deans: Continuity, Commitment and Change at Chichester Cathedral 1902-2006* (University of Chichester: Otter Memorial Papers no 22, 2007).

Gear, Gillian, 'The Boys' Home Industrial School…' *Camden History Review* 18 (1994), pp. 1-5.

Gedge, David:
A Country Cathedral Organist looks back (Darlington 2005).
More from a Country Cathedral Organist (Llandysul, 2008).

Gray, Donald, *Percy Dearmer: A Parson's Pilgrimage* (2000).

Greengrass, Barry, 'The Friends of St Mary the Virgin Church Primrose Hill', in PM, Apr-May 2013.

Groves, R., *Conrad Noel and the Thaxted movement: an adventure in Christian Socialism* (1967).

Hall, M., *George Frederick Bodley and the later Gothic Revival in Britain and America* (2014).

Harrison, Martin, *Victorian Stained Glass* (1980).

Hawes, John:
'Rubrics and riddel-posts', in *CT,* 3 Sep 1999.
'The tower and bells of St Mary's', in PM, Oct-Nov 2007, pp.6-7.

Herrick, Christopher, 'Three years at St Mary's', in PM, Apr-May 2013, pp. 8-9.

Hinchliff, Peter, *Frederick Temple, Archbishop of Canterbury: a life* (Oxford 1998).

Hope, W StJ and Atchley, EGCF, *English Liturgical Colours* (SPCK, 1918).

Howse, Christopher, 'Sacred Mysteries:

The man who rewrote Bunyan' (*Daily Telegraph*, 10 Feb 2017).

Hughes, Dom Anselm, *The Rivers of the Flood* (1961).

Hunt, W H (comp), *Churchmanship and Labour. Sermons on social subjects.* (1906). [Sermons preached at St Stephen Walbrook 1906 including Dearmer and Noel].

Jagger, PJ. *The Alcuin Club and its publications, an annotated bibliography 1897-1974* (Alcuin Club, 1975, and 2nd edn, 1986, by G Cumming and GB Timms.

James, Colin and Taylor, Cyril, 'Beauty for all': script for a radio broadcast about Percy Dearmer, 12 Feb. 1967 [BBC Sound Archives/BL National Sound Archive].

James, Simon:

'St Mary's Youthwork: a special report,' in PM, Oct-Nov 2017, pp 9-13.

'What do St Mary's youthworkers actually do?' in PM, Nov 2017-Jan 2018, pp. 6-7.

Jasper, RCD. *The Development of the Anglican Liturgy 1662-1980* (1989).

Jones, Spencer, *The Clergy and Catechism, being an attempt to adapt the 'méthode de St Sulpice', as expounded by Mgr Dupanloup, to the ways and wants of the English church* (1896).

Kennedy, Michael. *The works of Ralph Vaughan Williams* (1964).

Kitching, Christopher, 'Not a place for the Archers,' in PM, Dec 2019-Feb 2020, pp. 19-22.

Larkworthy, Peter, *Clayton and Bell, Stained Glass artists and decorators* (Ecclesiol. Soc. 1984).

The London Churchman [periodical].

London Parish Map: a map of the ecclesiastical divisions within the County of London, 1903 (Stanford, reproduced by London Topographical Society 1999).

Mackenzie, C. *The Parson's Progress* (1923).

Maltz, Diana, 'Mabel Dearmer', in *The Yellow Nineties online,* ed Dennis Denisoff and Lorraine Janzen Kooistra.

Mill, Christine, 'Henry Holiday – an eminent Hampstead Victorian', in *Camden History Review*, 6 (1978).

Mitchell, Anthony and Olive, *Thomas Earp: Eminent Victorian Sculptor.* (Buckingham, 2002).

Mulvagh, Jane, *Madresfield, the Real Brideshead* (2008).

Murdoch, Tessa and Vigne, Randolph, *The French Hospital in England: its Huguenot history and collections* (Cambridge, 2009).

Noel, Conrad:

Conrad Noel, an autobiography (1945).

Ought Christians to be Socialists? (New Age Press, 1909).

Oxford Dictionary of National Biography [online].

Oman, CC, *Medieval Brass Lecterns in England,* in *Archaeological Journal*, 87/1, (1930) pp.117-149.

Paflin, Glyn:

'History for the people' [the English Church Pageant 1909], in *CT,* 8 May 2009.

'Eight Englishmen and the wonders that were done', *CT,* centenary review of the English Hymnal, 20 Jan 2006.

Pepper, Leonard, *Conrad Noel* (Oxford Prophets 16, Church Literature Assn 1983).

Purchas, John. *Directorium Anglicanum* (1858 and subsequent editions).

Reed, John Shelton, *Glorious Battle: The cultural politics of Victorian Anglo-Catholicism* (Nashville, 1996).

Rowell, Geoffrey *The Vision Glorious: themes and personalities of the Catholic revival in Anglicanism* (1983).

Royal Commission on Ecclesiastical Discipline: Minutes of Evidence Vol I (1906).

Saint, Andrew, 'On Victorian church building in London: a second bite of the cherry', in *Ecclesiology Today* 40 (July 2008), pp.48-52.

S Mary the Virgin Primrose Hill after fifty years: A Record and a Retrospect (1920).

Sandford, EG, *Frederick Temple: an appreciation* (1907).

Saunders, Matthew, 'Appreciating Victorian Arts and Crafts stained glass. A battle half won', in *Ecclesiology Today* 40 (July 2008), pp. 83-91.

Shaw, Martin, *Up to now* (1929).

Sheffrin, Jill, *Dearmerest Mrs Dearmer* (Toronto, 1999).

Sheppard, Martin, *Primrose Hill: A History* (Lancaster 2013).

Sherlock, F, *Frederick Temple, Archbishop of Canterbury* (Biographies of Eminent Churchmen) 1910.

Skilbeck, Clement O, 'Percy Dearmer'. A memoir reprinted in PM, 1937 from *The English Catholic*.

Smith, Ian, *Tin Tabernacles. Corrugated iron mission halls, churches and chapels of Britain* (2004).

Spowart, Norah B, 'Entertainers and entertainment in Hampstead', *Camden History Review*, 12 (1984).

Thistlethwaite, Nicholas:
The Making of the Victorian Organ (CUP 1990).
'Hill, Norman and Beard: [a] Beginnings to 1855, and [b] The heyday of the Hills (1855-1916)', in *Organists' Review*, Feb and May 1999.

Thompson, FML, *Hampstead: Building a Borough 1650-1964* (1974).

Timms, GB, 'The many-sided influence of Percy Dearmer', in PM, Apr-May 1967, reprinted from *CT*, 24 Feb 1967.

Van der Meulen, Marcus, *The Brass Eagle Lecterns of England* (Stroud, 2017).

Vaughan Williams, Ursula, *R.V.W: A Biography of Ralph Vaughan Williams* (1964).

Vaughan Williams, Ursula and Holst, Imogen (eds), *Heirs and Rebels. Letters written to each other and occasional writings on music by Ralph Vaughan Williams and Gustav Holst* (1959).

Victoria History of the County of Middlesex [VCH, online], Vol. VIII.

Walford, Edward, 'The Boys' Home', in *Old and New London*, V, pp. 297-8.

Wilton, Frances, 'A few memories of Fr Hardcastle', in PM, Jul-Aug 1984.

Woodifield, Robert, 'Conrad Noel, 1869-1942, Catholic Crusader', in Reckitt, MB (ed), *For Christ and the People. Studies of four Socialist Priests and Prophets of the Church of England between 1870 and 1930* (1968). [See also a shorter memoir in PM, Jul-Aug 1969].

Yates, Nigel, *Anglican Ritualism in Victorian Britain* (Oxford, 1999).

Yelton, Michael, *Anglican Papalism: an illustrated history 1900-1960* (2005).

Indexes

General notes

To avoid unwieldy citations, for major themes such as Music and Liturgy the reader is referred to the Contents, Chapter and section headings. Only a few particular points are picked up in the indexes.

+ next to a page number indicates that the reference continues on one or more subsequent pages

Index 1

St Mary's Church and Parish

Note: For Hampstead and other parishes see Index 4

St Mary the Virgin Primrose Hill:

fabric:
corbels and capitals 37, 59, 63
roof 13, 35-6, 56, 59, 103, 141, 147, 169, 186, 191, 196-7, 199, 200, 236, 252, 254, 257-9, 330
war memorials 141+, 168, 206, 260
whitening 83, 93+, 99, 100, 103, 141, 191, 207, 230, 244, 252+, 255, 259, 290
windows, stained glass 20, 51, 56+, 196+, 203, 206+, 21, 259, 352

fittings, ornaments etc:
banner of Our Lady 15, 28, 31; by CM Gere 96
bell 30, 152, 269+, 302
bishop's chairs 51, 146, 264
choir stalls 59+
Dearmer screen 256, 267, 290, 322
eagle lectern 51+, 184, 265; lectern Bibles 51, 184, 295
high altar 15, 23, 52, 59+, 64, 83, 87, 94+, 98, 145+, 150, 152, 175, 194, 230, 264+, 267+, 287, 289+, 295, 312; (gradines) 28, 60, 83-4, 94; (reredos) 59+, 78, 83, 94, 98, 102+, 144, 146, 207, 223, 253, 268+
icons 146, 182, 208, 261, 265, 291
Lenten Array 98+, 151+, 269, 295
Paschal candle 268
pulpit 29, 31, 59, 104
return stalls 61, 252
rood 101+, 151, 186, 209, 251, 266+, 269
sanctuary lamps 95, 194, 263-4, 267, 295
thuribles (censers) 31, 146, 169, 184, 202, 291, 348
trendle 97, 104, 185
vestments 23, 27, 29, 31, 64, 78, 82, 87-9, 97-8, 118, 146-7, 149, 169, 185, 193, 264-5, 267-70, 292, 295

damage and loss 266, 268; (fire) 147, 169, 267; (theft) 147, 208+, 264, 266+, 308; (weather) 59, 143, 200, 261n; (war damage) 195+, 206-7, 308

other subjects:
art exhibitions 258, 329, 344, 349
Bible study 272, 275, 277
brewery 260+, 277, 297
children in church 20, 51, 92, 128, 134, 157, 168, 181, 202, 204, 223, 226, 238, 246+, 253, 281+, 287, 294, 324, 325. *See also guilds; liturgy: Catechism; schools; youthwork*
Church Room 66, 73+, 77, 100-1, 136-142, 152, 168-9, 175, 180, 182, 187, 190-1, 193, 199, 204, 207, 248-9, 257, 279, 282, 345
clergy, see Index 2
Cold Weather Shelter (C4WS) 238, 259, 281, 283, 342
coronavirus pandemic 284, 291+, 308, 317, 323, 343, 350
death cafés 338
drama 21-2, 52, 65+, 74, 125-6, 135+, 150, 168+, 171, 189+, 251, 277, 296, 305, 345+
ecumenism with other traditions: 170; Baptist 203, 281; Jews 233, 281; Methodist 281, Orthodox 122-3, 128,

182-3, 187, 280; Roman Catholic 42, 170, 231, 280-1, 287; Salvation Army 202, 280

environmental issues 329+; *see also* garden

Fair Trade 329+, 350

finance, fund-raising etc 7, 11, 13, 17+, 22, 52+, 60, 74+, 77, 85, 115, 125, 139, 140+, 155, 167, 186+, 191, 204, 206, 224, 233, 251, 257+, 310, 313, 315+, 319+, 329, 342
- Blueprint appeal 236, 258+, 309, 320, 340, 349
- stewardship campaigns 224, 313, 317, 319+, 333

Friends 237, 258, 277, 324-5, 328+, 334

garden 85, 105, 193, 259-60, 297

guilds 18, 21, 42, 51, 71, 86, 121, 134+, 137-8, 149

jubilees: (*1920*): 31, 42, 133, 143+, 157; (*1927*): 154; (*1930*): 174+; (*1935*): 181+, 184+, 187, 191; (*1972*): 210, 227, 278, 302

Listening Post 338

liturgy *passim*, but including:
- Catechism 71, 93, 116+, 119, 134, 149, 163, 187, 282, 315, 325
- Christingle 233, 292, 294; Plate 6
- contemplative prayer 233, 292, 315
- *Exultet* 188-9, 197, 211
- fasting before Communion 18, 42, 72, 86, 152, 177, 181
- healing ministry 120, 239, 294, 338
- hymnals: *A&M* 20, 94, 108; *EH* 108+, 139, 155, 158, 174, 288, 303, 306+; *NEH* 225
- incense 23, 26-8, 31, 69, 85-6, 125, 134, 169, 184, 243, 295
- Litany 7, 19, 20, 139, 194-5
- observances:
  - Assumption, feast of 26, 181, 234
  - Corpus Christi 152, 169
  - Good Friday 98, 113, 152-3, 287-8, 295
  - Maundy Thursday 105, 287, 289, 293, 294
  - Penance, sacrament of 272, 276
  - Tenebrae 26-7, 87, 106, 152, 188
- prayer books: (*BCP*), 18, 20+, 24+, 29, 64, 68, 72, 76+, 82, 87+, 107, 117, 128, 153+, 272, 288+, 292; (*1928*) 142, 149, 152+, 169, 288; (*ASB*) 230, 288; (*CW*) 272, 295, 298 n.17
- processions 15, 27-8, 38, 69, 139, 151, 176, 184, 195, 203, 279+; (Rogationtide) 121, 152, 181, 182, 279, 287, 294; (Palm Sunday) 151, 279; Plate 6
- ritual and ritualism chs1 -2; 65, 67+, 82, 86+, 122, 162, 173, 195, 314
  - Royal Commission on Ecclesiastical Discipline 87, 122
  - Royal Commission on Ritual 24
- Taizé 233, 257, 276-7, 281, 291-2, 315

Missionary Committees 76, 137, 187, 199, 329

missions, parish 7, 11, 16, 72, 134, 241, 277+, 302

music *passim* (See chapter and section headings). For organists and choirmasters see introductory note to Index 2. For organ builders see Index 4
- Choral Society 66, 73, 75, 106
- Music at St Mary's 326+
- Peter Pears prize 326+
- plainsong 15, 20, 65-6, 84, 88, 105-8, 110-1, 113-5, 153, 155-9, 172, 174, 188-9, 200, 212-3, 222, 226, 279, 295, 299, 300, 303-5
- recordings of choir 189, 306-7

Needlework Society 64, 146, 266, 269, 270; kneelers 185, 266, 270

Overseas Committee 329

overseas links (partner parishes) 239, 247, 330+

parish office 256, 321+, 337

Parochial Church Council 139+; *passim* thereafter

pastoral networking 338+

pay-day loans initiative 343

pilgrimages 235, 275, 276, 280

Primrose Hill Lectures 236, 239, 277, 316, 329, 344, 350+

Primrose Hill Tea Room 338

retreats 241, 272, 276, 317

St Mary's Community Centre Trust 340+

schools ch1;17+, 21+, 40; (Sunday School) 40, 73+, 237, 281+, 315, 324; (Hall School) 229, 337; (St Paul's School) 227, 236, 249+, 278+, 289+, 335+, 339+, 345

television broadcasts 288, 292, 307

Trustees of St Mary's 11, 20, 25, 47, 49, 58, 67, 81, 87, 131, 150, 161+, 166+, 171, 178+, 190, 225+, 229+, 232, 235, 238, 250, 263, 318
Tuesday Tea 328
vicarage 84-5, 141, 144, 167-8, 195, 244, 249, 252, 253+, 273, 279, 284, 296, 318, 322, 325, 336
website 323
women's ministry ch 10, and *see Geraldine, Joanna, Judith in Index 4*
youthwork 73, 134+, 187, 235+, 254, 259, 261, 282+, 292, 312, 315+, 324, 337, 339+; Plate 7. *See also children*

streets, buildings etc in and near the parish
   Adamson Road 226, 282
   Adelaide Road 4, 43, 73, 84, 166, 242, 334, 343; Adelaide Neighbours 244
   Ainger Road 4, 6, 17, 64
   Ainger Terrace 17
   Cab rank 76+
   Chalcot Gardens 84
   Chalcots estate 3, 334
   Chesterford Gardens 147
   England's Lane 84, 265
   Elsworthy Rise 228
   Elsworthy Road 4, 54, 63, 73, 77, 85, 134, 139, 144, 162, 192, 195, 203, 205, 227, 249, 251-3, 255, 260, 322, 325, 335, 339, 344, 346
   Erskine Mews 63-4
   Eton Avenue, Blind School 66
   Eton Road 3
   Eyre Arms Assembly Rooms, St John's Wood 22
   Harley Road 63
   King Henry's Road 1, 4, 8, 11, 17, 24, 34, 73, 91, 97, 146-7, 203-4, 253-4, 335-6
   Meadowbank 335
   Merton Road 43
   Oppidans Mews 64, 73-4, 166, 248, 302
   Oppidans Road 4, 196, 203-4, 248
   Quickswood 335
   Pavilion restaurant, Primrose Hill 16, 22
   Primrose Hill Court 204, 334
   Primrose Hill Road 4, 8, 41, 43, 49, 63, 66, 77, 194-5, 203, 334
   Princess Road 40
   Regent's Park Road 1, 2, 4, 17, 40, 43, 73, 101; Boys' Home ch 1; 17, 40, 47
   St George's Road 17
   St Peter's Lecture Hall (Belsize Sq) 65
   Winchester Road 249-50, 282

social matters
domestic servants xiv, 17, 20, 64
housing xv, 3-4, 63+, 80 n.26, 93, 142, 168, 192, 196, 203+, 227, 248, 335
poverty xiv, 1+, 10, 17+, 40, 42, 63+, 73, 75, 116, 118, 123, 222, 242, 290, 314, 350;
Provident fund, 18, 40; Working Men's Provident Club 64, 86

Index 2

Persons

(Other than artists and craftworkers covered by Index 3)

Notes:

Bishops of London and their suffragans (listed on pp.353-4) appear under letter B

*Organists, Choirmaster and Directors of Music at St Mary's

Abbott, Very Revd Eric, trustee 226, 229-30
Adderley, Revd James 105, 122
Addison, Revd Bruce, curate 225
Alexander: Andrew 306; Marie 246
Allen:
    Andrew, administrator 323
    Jason, youthwork manager 340-2
*Almond, Bryan 306, 309
André:
    James Peter 11, 17; **(Mary) Emily [Fuller]**, his daughter, founder of the church 11-12, 17-18, 20, 21-2, 41-2
Andrews, FV 26
Anson:
    Revd Harold 137
    Peter 61, 88, 91
Armstrong [Mrs] 146
Arnold:
    *JH (Jack) 135, 146, 149-59, 153, 156+, 169-178, 185, 189-191, 205, 208, 212-3, 262-4, 267, 270, 287, 301, 306; Olive, his wife 191; John, their son 190-1
Atwell, Revd Robert 235-8, 246, 255, 258, 269, 275-6, 283, 293, 307, 309, 315-6, 322-4, 334, 339-40, 350

Avarne family: 92; Augustus 55
Banks, CJ 32-3
Barbirolli, Lady Evelyn 309
Bate, Jennifer 309-10
Batterbury, Miss E 96
Bax, Arnold 114
Beauchamp, William Lygon, 7th Earl Beauchamp 85, 93, 100, 104, 120, 138, 143, 159, 214; Lettice, his wife [Countess] 85, 104, 138, 146, 164n, 173, 208, 214
Beck, Kathleen (Gladys) xvii, 187, 212, 241, 243, 279
Beer, William 278
Bell:
    George, publisher 1
    George William ch1; 16 24; his wife 7
    Rt Revd George, Bishop of Chichester, 150, 182, 192
Benthall, FB 198
Berke, Roberta 315-6
Berkeley, Sir Lennox 327
Bingley, Xandra 342
Birkbeck, WJ 110
Bishops of Edmonton *in date order:*
    Rogers 279; Masters 234-6; Wheatley 238, 246; Wickham 217, 261, 341

Bishops of London *in date order*
    Jackson 23-5, 28-31, 33, 37-8, 47, 56; Temple 38-41, 47-9, 54, 67-8; Creighton 67-9, 75, 85-6, 106; Winnington-Ingram 150; Wand 287; Montgomery-Campbell 288, 302; Stopford 278; Ellison 290; Hope 328; Chartres 236, 238, 246, 259, 330; Mullally 217, 294

Bishop of Marlborough
    Earle, Alfred 49, 56, 62, 69, 74

Bishops of Willesden *in date order*
    Perrin 123, 148, 167, 180; Ellison 210; Ingle 319; Dow, 234

Bolton, John GV 209

Blaiklock family 92, 162+; Frank 77, 116, 162; Elsie, his dtr, 77, 116, 134, 162; Violet, *his dtr, see Index 3*

Bloxam, Bloxham:
    GW 21
    [? John Francis], *ceremonarius* and choirmaster 41

Bodkin, Sir Archibald 139

Bradbury, PH 137, 163, 175, 198-9

Bradford, Elizabeth 51

Bridge, Dr Frederick 67

Brown, Revd Preb. Marjorie, vicar 217, 238+, 269, 275-6, 284, 293, 315-6, 323, 334, 339, 341

Browne, Dr E Martin, trustee 150, 190, 213, 228-30, 252, 345-6; Henzie (Raeburn), his first wife 252, 347; Audrey, his second wife 264

Brough, Evelyn 253

Buck, Revd Richard, vicar 229+, 243-4, 252, 254-5, 257, 272-3, 275-6, 283, 289, 306, 312, 317, 321-2, 324-5, 334-5

Bucknell, Councillor 204

*Burgess, Francis 105-6, 115, 146, 151

Bury, Rt Revd Herbert 144

Caesar, Revd Anthony 225

Campbell, Dr Sidney 309

Cancellor, Francis, churchwarden 40-1; his wife 73

*Capel, A 21

Cardon, Revd James 26

Carpenter, Revd SC and his wife 134, 144

Chadwick, Revd JW 8, 11, 15

Cherill, Revd and Mrs 73

Child, JL 53

Chissell, Joan 327

Christian, Ewan 36

Chrystal, Revd Susan 235, 245-6

Clabon, John Moxon 6

*Clarke, Arthur 189, 200, 306

Cobb, Sir Cyril 139, 151

Cockson, Revd Harry, curate 64, 75

Collett, Pauline 321-2, 328

Cooke:
    Dr Evelyn 146, 265
    WL 263

Cooper, Peter 328; Mary, his wife 328

Copeland, Tom 322, 331

Corbett, AJ 41

Craddock, Malcolm, churchwarden 260

Craig, Gordon 109; Rosie, his dtr 126

Crane, Revd John, curate 346

Creser, Dr W 67

Crickmay family 96-7

Crouch, Revd Sidney, curate 177

Curwen, Dame May 325

Dampier, Mrs 77

Davey, Revd Noel 188+, 199, 211, 225, 325

Day, Revd E Hermitage, trustee 57, 89, 94, 98, 171

Dean, Revd Linda 237, 239, 245-6, 328

Dearmer, Revd **Percy**, vicar 18, 23, 42;ch4;131, 136, 141, 144, 146+, 160, 162, 167, 170, 175, 180+, 184, 186, 201, 208, 214, 241, 256, 267, 273, 286, 291-7; **Mabel**, his first wife 81, 84, 86, 114, 122, 124+, 134, 136, 146, 184, 214, 296-7; **Nan**, his second wife 84, 125, 133, 182; **Anthony**, son of Percy and Nan 133; **Christopher**, son of Percy and Mabel 126-7, 134; **Geoffrey**, son of Percy and Mabel v, 50, 77, 84, 92-3, 126-7; Revd **Juliet**, dtr of Geoffrey 292, 296

Denissov, Ivan 183

Dent, DH, PCC member 170

Denzil, Sister, DssCSA 278

Dick, Bernard (JBG), churchwarden 146, 157, 163, 173, 263-4; Mary, his wife 157, 163, 270; Godfrey, their son 163

Dick, Dame Cressida 341

Dickinson, CH 22

Donaldson family 95, 126

Draper, Revd Martin, curate 108, 225, 231, 306, 337, 346, 348

Duncan-Jones, Revd A, vicar 18, 82, 116;

ch5; 166, 169, 172, 174, 180, 182, 184, 187, 190, 201, 213, 253, 263-4, 312
Dunlop, Rt Revd Colin, curate 128, 134, 135, 137, 148+, 151, 153, 160-1, 163, 168, 178+, 182, 187, 190, 201, 213-4, 287-8, 295-6, 312
Dunn, Brian 250; Caroline, his wife, trustee 232, 250
Eeles, Francis Carolus 89, 90, 96, 107, 116, 127-8, 138, 151+, 181, 184-5, 194, 196, 200, 210. *His mother, see Index 3*
Eggleton [Mr], donor 151
Eiloart family 92, 133; F 73
Elgood, George 44n
Eliot, TS 190, 213, 347,
Ellerton [Mr], choirmaster and cornet player 31, 44n
Ellison, Randall 322
Elvin, Elizabeth 266
Erica, Constance, drama producer 65
Evans, Revd Emrys, curate 240n.
Eyre, Revd HS 48
Fake, Robert [Bob], verger 175, 192, 199, 204, 207, 212, 241, 252, 300, 315
Fay, WG 126
Finlay, Gerald 326
Fishwick, Mary-Jean 342
*Fleming, Michael 225, 305
Ford, Phyllis Allen 117
*Fowler, Ivan 304+, 326
Frampton, Sir George 101
*Francis, Miss 9
Frere, Revd W 88, 154
Fulford, Revd RM 76
Fuller:
    Revd **Charles James**, vicar chs1, 2; 47, 49, 56, 60, 62, 69-70, 73, 78, 162
    Ronnie, churchwarden 314, 338
Fyfe, Revd Arthur 225
*Gedge, David 300+
Geraldine, Sister (DssCSA) 228, 242, 270, 333
Gerrard, Revd David, curate 240n, 285n.
Giles, Revd JH, curate 75
Gillam, Lawrence, trustee 230
Gilmour, Kimberly 247, 275, 284, 294
Goalby, Anna 340
Godfrey, Arthur E, choirmaster 66, 105
Golding, Jo 340
*Goldsmith, Edmund W 106+, 110-1, 188

Gore, Rt Revd Charles 154
Gray:
    Alan, organist 67
    Philip 270
Greengrass, Judy 348
*Greening, Anthony 279, 302+, 309
Greenley, Paula 322
Groves, Sir Charles 309, 326, 344
Gwynne, Stephen 125
Hallam, Violet 146
Hamilton, J Baillie 62, 67
Harcourt, Revd Hubert, vicar ch6; 180, 318; Charlotte Mary, his wife 176
Hardcastle, Revd JAL, vicar ch7; 252, 280, 287; Ruth (Seth-Smith), his wife 192, 198, 204, 210-1
Harper, Heather 327
Harvey:
    *Patrick 175
    Rupert and Katherine his wife 137-8, 187, 190
Hawes, John 270, 292, 294, 297, 306
Heard, Michael 348
Heathfield, Peter 209, 211
Henderson:
    LC 170
    William 198
*Henwood, Tony 307, 309
Herklots, Revd Gerard A 38-9; *see also Index 1: St Saviour's*
Herrick, Christopher, organist 296, 303+, 307, 310
Heskins, Revd Jeffrey [Jeff], curate 232-3, 273, 283, 290, 336
Higham, Charles 103
Hill:
    Keith 310; Christine (Macsween), his wife 283
    *Malcolm, organist 304, 309
    William, organ builder 20; **Thomas**, his son, trustee 11, 18, 20, 49, 56, 58, 62, 66+, 314, 352; **Arthur**, son of Thomas, trustee 21-2, 40, 66, 87, 89, 94, 115, 119, 171; **Walter**, son of Thomas 27
Hirsch, JF 22
Hoare, Edward Brodie, MP 54-56
Hoffa, Karen 330
Holeyman, Mary Ann 17
Holiday, Sir Frederick 138, 142, 175

Hollis, Revd Howard, vicar 114, 117, 212, 226+, 231, 242, 252, 266, 275, 277, 279-84, 288-9, 296, 303-5, 312, 319, 325, 334-5, 337, 339, 346; Margaret, his wife 227, 304
Holst, Gustav 114, 182
Hope, W St John 122
Horder, Dr John 310
Horton, Arthur Babson 140
Housman, Lawrence 108, 124-6, 169
Huddleston, Fr Trevor, CR 274
Humphries, Margaret 268
Hunt:
    Revd Hubert de Jersey 269
    Revd JB 116
Hutton-Mills, Clement 315
Igwe, Yejide, youthwork manager 341
Inman, John 320
Ireland, John 114, 133
Iremonger, Revd FA 144
Jack, Revd Paul, curate 240n
Jackson, Dr Francis 303
Janssen, Mary 146
Jelley, Revd Jim 282
Jeoffroy, May S 135, 170, 263; Cecilia and Edith, her sisters 263
Jermyn:
    Revd Peter, curate 240n
    Miss 270
Joanna, Sister, DssCSA 224, 228, 241-2, 244
Johnson:
    *H, organist 21
    Revd Michael, curate 231-2, 283
Jones:
    Alice xi, 6
    Revd David 235, 276, 283
    the Misses 146, 151
Joseph, Jane 182
Joslin, Walter 321
Judith, Sister, OHP 230, 244, 254, 290, 334
Keenlyside, Simon 327
Kensit, John 67
King:
    Revd HA, curate 116
    Vivian H, Parish Clerk 135, 138, 143, 148, 151+, 174, 180, 201, 212
Kirk, Revd Kenneth 154
Kitching, Christopher, trustee 269; Ruth, his wife 269, 329
*Knight, Cyril 175, 187, 189

Knowles, Mr 97; Mrs 125; *Nan, their daughter (later Mrs Nan Dearmer): See Dearmer*
Kolltveit, Revd Emily, curate 240
Lampard, [Revd] Ruth 245
Lane, Revd Charlton 3, 11 25
Lang, Revd Peter, curate 240n
Langrish, Roger 166, 203
Lansdowne:
    Margaret 271
    Family 271
Lascelles, Frank 121-2
Learner, F 170
Lee, Lt-Col 167, 319
Leonard, Rt Revd Graham 240n
Lias, Francis James 193, 263
Lloyd, Anthony [Lord Lloyd], trustee 230
Lovell, Arthur George, trustee 11
Lowry (Stutfield), Helen, churchwarden 138, 345+
Lyne, Joseph Leycester [Bro Ignatius] 78
Mackerras, Sir Charles 345
Magrath [McGrath], Revd W, curate 55, 78
McIntosh, A 282
McKay, Revd John, curate 232, 240n, 243
Macsween [Hill], Christine 283
Malet, Revd Leycester, vicar of St Paul's 249
Malleson family 270
Manning, MP, architect 8, 12-3, 50, 52, 54, 83, 255-6, 331
Marriott, Frank J, churchwarden 141, 174, 184, 198, 210, 215n, 263-4, 286, 299, 314, 317+, 325
Marsh [Mr], organ blower 65
Marshall, Revd Walter 121
Martineau, Malcolm 326
Martley, Mrs 97
Masters, Revd Stephen, curate 235
Mathew, Dorothy 263
Maurice, Revd FD 1
May Cecilia, Sister, Society of St Margaret 278
Mensbrugghe, Fr Alexis van der 182
Michaels, David 291
Miller, Revd Timothy, curate 240, 273
Mills, Heath 21
Milns, Revd WR 76
Monk, Dr EG, organist 67
Monroe, Roddy, churchwarden 261, 316
Moore, Revd JC 179

Morris, [Revd] William 237
Morse, Thomas 24-5
Mulholland, Emily 84
Ndungane, [Most] Revd Winston [Njongonkulu] 232
Newland Smith, Revd N, curate 116-7, 151, 265
Newton Smith, Revd Joseph, curate 27
Nicholson, Revd Paul, curate 239,
Noel, Revd Conrad, curate 88, 110, 116, 119+, 188, 273
*Northcutt, Mr 21
Okorji, Tanya 268
O'Malley, Mary (later Mrs Colin Dunlop) 179, 182
Omond, Tamsin 323
O'Neill, Dennis 344
Oppong, Casey 260, 317
Oswald, Beryl 265
Ovenden, Revd John, vicar 232+, 245-6, 256-7, 268, 274, 280-1, 283, 292, 315, 320, 334, 337, 339, 344, 348
Paget, Sir James 41
Paine:
   Michael 328
   Revd WH 116
*Palmer, GH 104+, 306
Parker, Louis Napoleon 121
Pennell, George, trustee 7, 11
Perkins:
   Fr FWB, OGS 278
   Perkins, Paul 284, 340-1
Piercey, [Revd] Liz 245
Plouviez, Charles, churchwarden 252; Margaret (Maggie), his wife, trustee 230
Pollard, Arthur 104
Potorjinsky, Theodore 183
Pritchard, Mary Jean 257
Pulling, Grace E 170, 297n
Rachel Margaret, Sister, Society of St Margaret 278
Ramsay, Revd Andrew C 57
Rayment, Ebenezer and his wife 1, 11
Reynolds, Steve, churchwarden 261
Riddell, Sir WRB, trustee 171
Ridout, Alan 306, 309
Ridpath, Thomas A 11
Rinsler, [Revd] Miriam 247, 269, 315
Robinson, Harold 209
Rocke, Nick 327

Rolfe Johnson, Anthony 345
Roose-Evans, Revd James 232
Rosario, Patricia 327
Rosselli, Clement 170
Rutter, John 302, 307
St John, Revd Andrew, curate 240n.280, 336
Sara, [Rt] Revd EW, curate 166-7, 185
Satterthwaite, Revd John 225
Scott, Judith 263, 302
Selwyn, Revd EG 144
Seth-Smith, David 187, 192; *Ruth, his dtr, see Hardcastle*
Sharp, Cecil 109; Evelyn, his sister 124
Sharpe, Bowdler 22
Shaw:
   ***Geoffrey**, brother of Martin 135-7, 143-4, 146, 148-9, 155-9, 163, 172+, 178, 182, 201, 209, 299, 306, 347; Mary, his wife 209, 263; James, their son 201; Peter, their son 174; Sebastian, their son 252
   ***Martin** 109, 111+, 126, 131-3, 136, 138, 148, 150, 154-8, 182, 190, 213, 289, 299, 305; Joan, his wife 114, 156, 170, 172, 178, 187; Jules, his brother 126
Shaw, Miss, drama producer (1890s) 65
Shewell Cooper, Judge F 138; his wife 138
Shipham, FPB 170
Shirley, Leonore [Leo] 243, 321
Sinden, Donald 328
Skilbeck, [Mr] 22; *Clement O, see Index 3*
Slater, Eric 302
Smith:
   Julia 322
   Oliver 275, 330
Smythe, Lyster 158, 198
Snow, Harry, churchwarden 18, 21
Solomon, Yonty 326
Sokolova, Lydia 190
Solti, Sir Georg 326, 344; Lady [Valerie], his wife 309
Spencer, Revd **Albert**, vicar 18, 42; ch3; 83+.92, 95, 100-2, 104, 116, 146, 162, 186, 312, 317; Ellen, his wife 48-50, 73, 75+104; Katherine, his mother 57
Spiers, WL, architect 36
Spowart, Norah 91
Starnes, Nellie 117
Stedman, Philip 121

Stegall, Dr Charles, organist 67
Stephens, Revd Francis 225, 227-8, 231, 234, 242-3, 252, 256-7, 266-9, 279, 288, 296, 323, 348
Street, Revd John 47
Stuart, Revd Charles 25
Stutfield, Bernard 278; *Helen (Lowry), his dtr, see Index 3*
Sudbury, Graham 300
Swain, Miss 265; Jessie, her sister 265
Symonds, Peter, churchwarden 320, 347, 349
Syrett, Netta 125-6
Tabernacle, Peter 278
Target, Jack 323
Tavener, John 302
Taylor:
    Anthony (Tony), chorister 301
    Nicholas, chorister 301; d. in Falklands War 336,
    Stanley 231, 250, 252, 256, 266, 267-71, 282, 296, 322, 326, 348, 351n
    Sylvia, his wife 266, 351n
Temple, Revd William 154
Thackray, Revd Peter, curate 240n
Thorne:
    May 209, 263; Bishop Thorne of Masasi, her nephew 209
    P, scoutmaster 282
Timms, Revd Preb. GB, vicar 224+, 230, 232, 241, 248, 250-1, 253-4, 262-3, 265, 274-5, 280-1, 284, 286-8, 295-6, 299-300, 309, 311-2, 315, 319-20, 323, 325, 328, 334-5, 337, 339,
Tompson, Revd EJ 58
Trotter [Mrs] 185
Turner:
    *Bradbury, organist 9, 15, 20-131, 65
    Dame Eva 327
Underhill, [Very] Revd Francis 171, 178, 180,
Van der Pump, Revd Lyndon 234, 239, 245, 305, 326+, 337, 349
Vaughan-Lee, Charles 319
Vaughan Williams, Ralph 109, 156, 158, 263, 288, 303
Vidler, Revd Dr Alec 279
Vine, Revd Michael 229
Virvos, [Greek Orthodox] Archimandrite James 182-3
Wainwright, Revd John, curate 227
Wakefield, Revd Mark 237, 239
Walford:
    Revd Edward 4-5
    Miss 5
Walker:
    Revd EJ 55
    Revd J 85
Walters:
    Mr & Mrs GS 96
    Revd Nick, curate 240, 341
Ward
    Frank, churchwarden 250, 266; Mary, his wife 250
    *John C, organist 55, 65+; Clementine, his dtr 66
*Warrell, EH, organist 300, 304
Watson, Mrs, donor 263
Webb, Elizabeth 252
Webber, Miss, donor 263
Webster, Revd Sally, 234-5, 237, 243, 245, 253, 268 283
West:
    Alfred 110
    Marion 270
Whiteley,Eric, churchwarden 252, 266; Mary, his wife 266
Willacy, Revd TR 72
*Willford, Michael, organist 231, 306, 309
Williamson, Malcolm 327
Wilton, Frances 197
Wood, Sir Henry 139; Avril, his dtr, 134
Wright, Revd TW, curate 116
Yates, [Revd] Joanna 234, 243, 245, 292

Index 3

Artists and Craftworkers associated with the church

Art Workers' Guild 96
Ashbee, CR 96
Aumonier, [William] 103
Bailey, David 349
Bayes, Gilbert 101, 103, 186; Plate 4
Bettridge, Winifred 270
Blacking, Randall 262-3
Blaiklock, Violet 77, 89, 98, 116, 132, 144, 162-3
Bodley, GF (and Bodley & Garner) 57, 59-61, 83, 94, 98, 103-4, 144, 223, 259
Bridgeman, Robert 60
Burgess, Miss 97-9, 104-5, 146, 151, 175
Clarke, HC 95
Clayton & Bell 51, 57
Cleverly: CFM 60, [FC?] 96
Cogswell, Gerald 142
Comper, N (Bucknell and Comper) 58, 90, 262; Plate 1
Dorling, Revd EE 105, 122, 146
Dunlop, Sybil 149
Dykes Bower, Stephen 271
Earp, Thomas 37; (and Hobbs) 63; Plate 2
Eeles, Mrs (mother of FC) 146
Ellis, Cyril 98
Ellwood, GM 57, 98
Falconer, Thomas, 96
Feibusch, Hans 349
Fry, Samuel 55; Plate 2
Gentleman, David 349
Geraldine, Sister, DssCSA 270
Gere, CM 96; Plate 3
Gill, Eric 101, 264
Greenwood, F Smythe 97, 146, 174
Guild of Handicrafts 86, 96

Hales, Irene 270
Hardcastle, WE 146
Hems, Harry 52
Hewitt, Graily 96
Hogarth, Paul, RA 349
Holiday, Henry 147+; Plate 4
Howard, FE 262
Jacobs, Philippa 349
Jones, Grace 146
Kempe, CE 58, 259; Plate 1
King, HC 97, 99
Knight, Frank of Wellingborough, goldsmith 209, 263-4
Knight, Frank W, architect 181, 208-8
Kruger [-Gray], George E 90, 97, 295; Plate 3
Lucas, EJ 207
Malleson, Montague (and family) 270-1
Martin, Thomas 60-1
Martyn, Ethel 57
Marus, A 143
Mathews, Leonard 207
Milner, H Victor 58; Plate 1
Moor, Patrice 349
Moore:
    Dorothy 266, 270
    Temple 97, 99-100
Pegram, Henry 139
Pietzsch, Siegfried 266; Plate 5
Powell:
    Alfred H 97
    WO 60
Ralphs, Dorothy 243, 349; Plate 7
Rathbone & Stabler 60-1
    See also Stabler

Rattee & Kett 60-1
Rope, [Miss Dorothy AA?] 164n
St Dunstan's Society 89, 122, 265
Sanderson, Cobden 97
Skelton, John 264
Skilbeck, Clement O: 89-90, 96-7, 121-2, 126, 142-4, 151
Skipworth, AH 96
Stabler, Harold 97; *see also Rathbone*

Stephens, Francis, see Index 2
Taylor, Stanley, see Index 2
Warham Guild 89, 97, 169, 174, 263
Way:
    TR (and family) 100-1, 104, 144, 345
    Barnard, his son 101
Wells, Randall 97, 103-4

Index 4

General Index

Churches brings together references to churches other than St Mary's Primrose Hill.
Organ builders lists those connected with St Mary's organ
Societies and Associations: national organisations, some having local branches

Burford Priory 235
Cambridge, Trinity College 67, 144, 234
Camden Chamber Choir 344
Camden Choir 344
[Central] Council for the Care of Churches 196, 263, 302
Christian Socialism 1, 5, 10, 111, 117+, 120, 123, 127
Church Commissioners 253-4, 318 *See also Ecclesiastical Commissioners*
Churches
   All Saints Finchley Road (St John's Wood) 48, 227
   All Saints Margaret Street 66, 67, 164, 229, 244
   All Souls Loudoun Road 49, 227
   Berkeley chapel 122
   Chalk Farm Baptist Church 203
   Ely cathedral 232
   Emmanuel West Hampstead 111
   John Keble Mill Hill 189, 208, 213, 229, 235
   St Alphege Southwark 270
   St Bartholomew's, Reading 224
   St Dominic's Priory Kentish Town 280-1
   St Francis, Sandycroft, Hawarden 180, 188
   St Francis of Assisi, Isleworth 42
   St James's Bethnal Green 104
   St John's Red Lion Square 179, 262, 267
   St John the Divine, Kennington 180
   St Mark's Marylebone Road 90, 106, 265
   St Mark's Regent's Park 2, 4, 5, 11, 43121, 152, 182, 195, 209, 276, 279-80, 294
   St Mary's Charterhouse 62
   St Mary's, Humbledon, Sunderland 202
   St Mary's Kilburn 24
   St Mary's Paddington Green 119
   St Matthew's Upper Clapton 238
   St Nicolas, Guildford (Surr) 144
   St Paul's Avenue Road 43, 144, 195, 303; union of parish with St Mary's 224, 225-7, 249+, 263, 266-7, 282, 308, 316, 334. *St Paul's school see Index 1*
   St Paul's cathedral 75, 148-9, 209, 239, 303, 347
   St Paul's Vicarage Gate 189
   St Peter's, Chalvey [Slough] 177
   St Saviour's Eton Road 3+, 24, 38, 43, 199, 237, 276
   St Sidwell's, Exeter 47+, 52, 78
   St Stephen the Martyr Avenue Rd 13n
   St Stephen's Gloucester Road 226
   St Thomas's Bethnal Green 104
   St Thomas's Clapton Common 238
   Southwark cathedral 300,
   Truro cathedral 229
Citizens UK 339

Community Service Industries 253
coronations: (1902) 120; (1911) 120; (1953) 227-8, 325
Dove Brothers, Messrs, builders 12+, 36
Ecclesiastical Commissioners 8, 35+, 85, 167, 199; *See also Church Commissioners*
English Church Pageant (1909) 89, 97, 105, 121+
Eton College 3+, 5, 7, 8, 11, 13, 35, 38, 53, 56, 74, 84, 97, 167, 186, 228-30, 248+, 255, 318-9
Goddard and Sons of Farnham, builders 54
Hampstead:
    parish/vicar of xiii, 3+, 11, 25, 28, 32, 39, 87, 97, 111,118, 120, 135, 147-8, 153, 229; Cemetery 67; Church Music Trust 307; Conservatoire 66, 108; Deanery (Synod) 122, 224, 227, 243, 313, 354; Mayor of 204; Synagogue 281; Town Hall 108; West Hampstead Town Hall 65-6; Workhouse 65
Highgate cemetery 101
IRA bombing campaign 336
Kensal Green Cemetery 25
Kentish Town: Weedington Road 64
Kilburn Town Hall 22
King's Cross Theatre 21
Lambeth Conferences: *(1920)* 145; *(1948)* 209; *(1958)* 287; *(2007)* 259
Langham Hall 22
London Welsh Male Voice Choir 328
Medici Quartet 345
Organ builders:
    Harrison & Harrison 309,312
    Hill, Norman & Beard 159, 205, 308
        See also Index 3: Hill
    Mander, NP 308
    Rushworth & Dreaper 267, 309
    Smith & Foskett 205
    Walker, Messrs 187
pageants 121; *see also English Church Pageant*
Poplar mission 81, 122

railways 1, 3, 6, 16, 34+, 43, 73, 166, 334
ritualism, see Index 1
Sadlers Wells Ballet School 204, 249
Societies and Associations
    Alcuin Club 82, 111, 122, 149, 151, 160, 213
    Anglican and Eastern Churches [Union] 122, 128, 182
    Band of Hope 64, 86,
    Boy Scouts 121, 135, 137, 141, 282
    Brownies 135, 168
    Christian Social Union 84, 117, 128, 137
    Church Association 23, 26, 32, 38, 87
    Church Lads' Brigade 74
    Church League for Women's Suffrage 118
    Church of England Temperance Society 86
    Church of England (Working) Men's Society 18, 32, 137, 277, 325
    Confraternity of the Blessed Sacrament 18, 21
    Cubs 168, 282
    English Church Union 69, 86, 87, 181
    Girl Guides 135, 137, 168
    Girls' Friendly Society 64, 86, 137, 146
    Guild of Health 120, 128
    Incorporated Church Building Society 25, 53, 206
    Missionary Union 137
    Morality Play Society 114, 126
    Mothers Union 168, 277
    National Protestant Church Union 86
    Russian Church Aid Fund 182
    Summer School of Church Music 115, 131, 156
suffrage 118, 147
wars: (Boer) 65; (First World) 122, 127, 132+, 139, 297, 349; (Second World) 191+, 222, 318; (Falklands) 336; *war damage* and *war memorials, see Index 1*
Watts, Messrs 183

For exclusive discounts on Matador titles,
sign up to our occasional newsletter at
troubador.co.uk/bookshop